EVERYDAY HANDBOOK SERIES

Barnes & Noble, Inc., 105 Fifth Ave., New York 3, N. Y.

Books in the Everyday Handbook Series summarize popular subjects for students and laymen. They provide a source of quick information and a convenient method of self-instruction. (Prices range from $.75 to $1.50.)

BUSINESS

BOOKKEEPING Made Easy
JOB, YOUR: Selecting, Securing
LAW GUIDE FOR ALL
SHORTHAND FOR ALL
TYPEWRITING, Touch, For All

CULTURAL STUDIES

ECONOMISTS, Teachings of Great
PHILOSOPHERS, Teachings of Great
PSYCHOLOGISTS, Teachings of Great
RELIGIONS of the World
WORLD HISTORY at a Glance

ETIQUETTE, GUIDANCE

CHILDREN ASK
MANNERS FOR MILLIONS
SUCCESSFUL LIVING

HANDICRAFTS, HOBBIES

CERAMICS FOR ALL
CONCRETE AND MASONRY
COOKBOOK, Short-Cut
DRAW AND PAINT, How to
ELECTRICITY: Repairs and Projects
HOME REPAIRS and Improvements
WOODWORKING: Home Craftsman

LANGUAGE, LITERATURE

ENGLISH, Common Errors in
FRENCH for Home Study
GRAMMAR, Rhetoric and Composition
LETTERS For All Occasions
NOVELS, Plot Outlines of 100 Famous
PLAYS, Plot Outlines of 100 Famous
PUNCTUATION
SPEECH: Everyday

MATHEMATICS, SCIENCE

FORMULAS, Money-Saving
MATHEMATICS For Everyday Use
NATURE For All
PHYSIOLOGY, Fundamentals of
SLIDE RULE

RECREATION, SPORTS

BALLROOM Dances for All
BRIDGE: First Book of
CHESS: First Book of
FISHING: Sportsman's Digest
FOLK DANCES For All
HUNTING: Sportsman's Digest
PARTY GAMES For All

(For complete list of College Outlines, see back of this volume.)

FRENCH

FOR HOME STUDY

ABOUT THE AUTHOR

Charles Duff has had wide experience in the practical use of French. After serving with the French Army as an interpreter, he was employed for many years as Press Officer by the British Foreign Office. Thereafter, he devoted his time to teaching, writing, and translating. He has lectured at London University.

Among the many books Mr. Duff has written are *How to Learn a Language* and *France and the French*. He pioneered the modern method of teaching a foreign language, using it in classroom instruction, and basing his books on it. He has translated such masterpieces of French literature as *Nana* and *Sage of Canudos*. Mr. Duff's articles have appeared in many English and American magazines. He is also a contributor to the *Encyclopedia Britannica*.

EVERYDAY HANDBOOK SERIES

FRENCH
FOR HOME STUDY

by CHARLES DUFF

BARNES & NOBLE, INC. New York

PUBLISHERS • BOOKSELLERS • SINCE 1874

©
Copyright, 1955
by
BARNES & NOBLE, Inc.

L. C. Catalogue card number: 55-7809

This revised American edition published by special arrangement with Charles Duff and English Universities Press, Ltd. The original edition entitled **French for Adults** was copyrighted in 1952 in Great Britain by Charles Duff.

Printed in the United States of America

INTRODUCING THE COURSE

THIS is a comprehensive " all-purposes " course in French. It has been prepared on modern principles, evolved from long experience, and so arranged that it can be used by various categories of adult learners; and it can be used in more ways than one. It is *not* intended for children or juveniles.

The most important categories of adults who wish to learn French come under four broad headings :

(1) Absolute beginners.

(2) Those who have " picked up " some French either from travel or desultory dabbling in the language and desire to improve or perfect their knowledge.

(3) The incalculable number of people who "learned French at school " but find that in practice they cannot use the language with any ease, competence, or confidence.

(4) Those who have become conscious of the French contribution to western civilization and culture, and who desire to be able to *read French with ease* in order to have the advantages and joys of firsthand acquaintance with a great literature.

These are the people who have been kept constantly in mind as the course was being prepared. The course begins at the beginning and, by gradual stages, presenting a carefully chosen vocabulary and essential grammar, leads the student as gently as possible toward a standard of knowledge which should enable him to deal with all but exceptional situations. A perusal of the Table of Contents will show that, on reaching a certain stage —when the learner has been made acquainted with essential grammar and a highly practical vocabulary—he is provided with material and instructed how to deal with *actual situations*. He is assumed to be in France and faced with those everyday problems we all have to solve : from merely getting about and getting one's hair cut (or waved, for women are not forgotten in this book!) to ordering a meal or reading the news. Amusements, sport and vacationing are included. And, little by little, with generous help in the form of translation and notes, an acquaintance is made not only with French classical literature but with such mundane things as movie and theater notices, road signs, newspaper advertisements, and what not. It is not possible, within the covers of one book, to provide for the whole gamut of human requirements. Nor is it necessary. But a solid and modern foundation, yes. And here it is.

Such are the general aims of the course, to which it may be added that much care has been devoted to simplification and attractiveness in presentation; in the latter typography plays an important part. The adult learner who may have forgotten English grammar (or never been quite sure of it) receives consideration. In learning French, grammar cannot be avoided; but it can be reduced to essentials. It is as great a mistake to attach too much importance to the apparatus of grammar as it is to imagine that an inflected language such as French can be learned without it. Most French people speak grammatically and are conscious of their language. They expect something more than " pidgin French " from the foreigner. The one who speaks with reasonably good grammar wins their respect and esteem. The learner's difficulties are dealt with as they arise, and care has been taken not to overwhelm or bewilder him with a multitude of grammatical rules. Grammar, so to speak, is " kept in its place."

The course can be used in more ways than one. It can be used either for self-tuition or for private tuition or for class work. In other words, it can be used with or without a teacher, but those who wish to be able to speak French should have a teacher. A good French pronunciation is difficult to achieve without the help of a teacher, who, for preference, should be a native of France or have been educated in France. But even the absolute beginner can use this course without a teacher.

When a teacher is available, everything becomes much easier for the learner. Nothing can replace a good teacher. He is available to correct errors and to solve problems. The rest depends on the learner; and on the text of the lessons and planning of the material from which he learns. If a learner can see his way to have a teacher for even the first five lessons, and so solve the most difficult of pronunciation problems, his subsequent progress will be smoother and the results more satisfactory.

The course consists of twenty-six lessons, each divided into five sections. Each section is intended for a minimum of half an hour of class tuition, a period which can with great advantage be extended to one hour. The self-taught make their own pace. In testing the course, it was found that when a group of learners had progressed well into it, they could be left to absorb a section by their own efforts. The teacher uses his discretion about this and many other things in the course. The abundance of well-explained reading matter can relieve the hard-pressed teacher of effort which, he may consider, could be used to better purpose otherwise.

As for the spoken language, so for the written; the course provides a great variety of reading matter embracing not only literary French but that of the newspapers and periodicals : advertising matter as well as the perfect prose of Daudet, Voltaire, Flaubert, and Maupassant. *This is adult reading.* The student who works through it conscientiously and follows the advice given will be well launched on the way toward achieving a high standard in French.

So many friends, English and French, teachers, learners and absolute beginners, have been consulted and have helped me in the preparation of this course, that I can only thank them collectively, laying emphasis on my gratitude to some of my own former students at the Institute of Education, London University. Those students were all teachers, and all of them were and are interested in the problems of teaching and learning a language. Hence the great value of their replies to my queries. I particularly wish to thank that brilliant woman, the late Marie-Louise Berneri, for the weeks of careful work she devoted to a minute scrutiny and scholarly improvement of the manuscript. Without all this help and collaboration the course would not be what it is. The collaboration explains why I have often used the first person plural, instead of the singular.

Grateful acknowledgments are also due to writers and publishers for excerpts from modern sources used to enliven and vary the reading matter. Wherever possible, the name to whom acknowledgment is due is given in the text, but, in some cases, either the publication no longer exists or the authorship is anonymous. We hope that in such circumstances this collective acknowledgment will be accepted. For the excerpt (p. 318) from *La France*, which is published in London, our thanks are due to Messrs. Evans Brothers Ltd., the proprietors.

Finally, may I thank those friends who so kindly read the proofs, and especially W. H. Stevenson, F. S. Flint and André Laurens. If any errors survive, the responsibility for them is entirely mine.

CHARLES DUFF

TABLE OF CONTENTS

xi

PART II : The Framework of the Language

PART III : The Spirit of the Language

WHY WE LEARN FRENCH

Because :

It is one of the great cultural languages of the world.

A knowledge of French is an essential in the education of every person who wishes to have direct access to the culture and literature of this great people.

It is spoken by over 100,000,000 people, of whom there are some 40,000,000 in France.

It is spoken in Belgium, Luxemburg, and Switzerland.

It is the administrative language of over 130,000,000 people.

It shares with English the honor of being the language of diplomacy.

It is, next to English, the most useful travel or " hotel " language : the language of hotel and restaurant menus.

It helps English-speaking people toward a better appreciation and understanding of their own language, being one of the main sources from which English is drawn.

It is worth learning for itself alone, being one of the least ambiguous, most exact, and beautiful languages of western civilization.

PART I
FIRST PRINCIPLES

LESSON I

§ 1. *Alphabet—Accents—Vowels—Nasals*

THE French alphabet is the same as the English but, for reasons of pronunciation and to distinguish between certain words similarly spelled, French uses "diacritical signs"—often called "accents," though strictly they are not all accents, as these are used only on vowels.

The three French accents are: (´) the acute; (`) the grave; and (^) the circumflex. Below, you will learn their importance in pronunciation.

The other diacritical signs are: (,) the cedilla, which is used under *c* to indicate when this letter sounds like *ss* and not like *k* or hard *c* before the vowels *a, o* or *u*, and (¨) the diaeresis which is used to indicate separate vowel-sounds when two vowels follow one another, thus making a distinction from what might be a diphthong or two vowels making one sound: (**Noël**, *Christmas*).

The apostrophe (') is much used to indicate that a vowel has been eliminated: **j'ai** is written and not **je ai.**

VOWELS: You may have noticed that English people do not pronounce their vowels "pure" or very clearly. A fundamental rule of French pronunciation is that all vowel sounds are "pure"—they are clearly pronounced and slightly shorter and sharper than our English vowels. The only exception to this rule is the letter *e*, which, at the end of words, is silent. Note well the following equivalent sounds:

French **a**	=	English	*a* in **father,** but sharper.
,, **e**	=	,,	*e* in **silent, quiet.**
,, **é**	=	,,	*ay* in **hay,** but it is curt.
,, **è** and **ê**	=	,,	*e* in **get, set.**
,, **i** and **y**	=	,,	*i* in **machine.**

23

French **o** = English *o* in **go,** but sharper.

" **u** has no equivalent in English. It is not pronounced like the English **u**. Round your lips as for whistling and say *ee,* holding the lips in the whistling position as you say it. This is the French **u**.

French **y** never has a circumflex or other accent. A circumflex accent indicates a long, deep pronunciation, in contrast to the shorter, sharper sound of the unaccented vowel. French **â** is a deep **ah**-sound; **ô** is a deep **oh**; **û** is a long French **u**-sound, etc.

One French vowel may cause a little trouble: *e.* Normally it resembles English *u* in **fur,** or English *e* in **quiet,** but at the end of words it is silent, and is then called *e*-mute. This *e*-mute sometimes occurs in the middle of a word; *e*-mute always sharpens the sound of the consonant which precedes it.

NASALS: There are no exact equivalents in English for the French nasals, which occur when a vowel comes before *n* or *m* not followed by *e*-mute. The nasalized pronunciation is identical whether the vowel comes before *n* or *m*. Thus, in the word *Grandcamp* (a little town in Normandy) there is no difference between the *an* of the first syllable and the *am* of the second.

TO PRONOUNCE A FRENCH " NASAL ," SAY THE VOWEL AND ALLOW YOUR BREATH TO PASS INTO THE NOSE. This will produce a " nasalized vowel," which is what you want. There are only four nasal sounds in French, and they are all to be found in the simple sentence: **Un bon vin blanc,** *a good white wine,* giving the four vowels concerned: *u—o—i—a.* You must remember this sentence and go back to it, repeating it again and again, after you have studied the following approximate equivalents for the nasals:

an, am⎱ Pronounce like the **aun**-sound in the English
en, em⎰ word **aunt**—as pronounced in Great Britain—
with the breath going into the nose.

in, im⎱ Similar to the **an**-sound in **sang, tang,** but with-
yn, ym⎰   out the g-sound.

on, om = on-sound in **song,** but without the g-sound.

un, um = not unlike the **er**-sound in **fern,** but nasalized.

When other vowels come before these nasals (**ain, aim, oin,
uin,** etc.), the pronunciation of the nasal is unchanged, the one
exception being when **-ien** comes at the end of a syllable. Then
-ien is pronounced as if it were written *i-in.*

When **n** or **m** are doubled, there is no nasal sound.

§ 2. *Diphthongs—Consonants—Stress*

DIPHTHONGS : When two vowels coming together make one
sound, this is a diphthong. One sometimes meets triphthongs,
three vowels making one sound. Note the following :

ay, ai⎱ English *ay* in **say** pronounced purely.
ey, ei⎰

au, eau =   „   *oh* in **mote, note.**

eu, œu =   „   *u* in **turn, burn,** but longer.

   oi =   „   *wa* in **water,** or **o'ah** as one sound.

   ou =   „   *oo* in **moor.**

   ui =   „   French *u* quickly followed by *i.*

  oui =   „   *wee* pronounced curtly.

CONSONANTS : Excepting those noted below, French consonants
and combinations of consonants are pronounced as in English,
but the general rule is that a consonant at the end of a French
word is silent—excepting *c, f, l, r.*

Note the following equivalents :

c before e, i, y = English *ss.*

c   „   a, o, u =   „   *c* in **cat.**

ç   „   a, o, u =   „   *ss.*

ch is always like English *sh* in **shirt.**

-er, -ez at the end of words = **é** or English *ay.*

est and **et** are pronounced like *ay.*

j = English *s, z* in **measure, azure** (a *zh*-sound).

g before **e** and **i** = French *j*, otherwise like *g* in **go.**

gn = our *-ni-* in **onion** or *-gn-* in **mignonette.**

gu always like *g* in **go**

h is **always silent,** though sometimes called *h-aspirate,* otherwise *h-mute.*

-il, -ill have in French a " liquid " sound like our *y* in **yes.** This is called " liquid *l*."

-ail, eil at the ends of words have **ahee, ayee** sounds. The *l* is silent.

qu = English *k.*   **qü** = English *qu* (kw) in **quick.**

r in French is never like our indistinct, half-sounded *r*, but resembles the Scotch rolled or vibrated *r*. It is always strongly pronounced in French.

s between vowels = English *z.* Also in " liaison "—see below.

th = English *t.*

-tion is pronounced as if written *-cion* [**seeon(g)**].

-stion = *stion.*

-ent when it is the third person plural of verbs is always silent.

-isme = *issme.*

STRESS : There is an almost equal stress—not a very strong one—on every French syllable, with a somewhat heavier stress on the *last* syllable of each word.   This greatly simplifies French pronunciation, as there are no exceptions to this general rule.

§ 3. " Liaison "—*Advice to Beginners*

LIAISON OR LINKING OF WORDS : When a consonant at the end of a word—even a silent consonant—is followed by a word beginning with a vowel or *h*-mute, that consonant is pronounced and the words run together (are " linked ") as if they were one. In such *liaisons*, French **s** and **x** are pronounced *z*; **d** = *t*; **f** = *v*; and **g** almost like *k*.   The **p** of the word **trop** (meaning *too much*) is always linked to a vowel following.   In quick, familiar speech there are more *liaisons* than in slow.   **Link**

sparingly until you are well accustomed to the language, and when in doubt do not link. *Liaison* is largely a matter of taste, and whether to link words or not often creates heated controversy among the best French speakers. Faulty usage in *liaison* rarely affects meaning, though it may indicate inadequate training in the finer points of the language.

ADVICE TO SELF-TAUGHT BEGINNERS: A correct pronunciation of French can be acquired in only one way: *constant listening to native speakers, imitation of their pronunciation, and correction of faults by a native.* Speech is learned from speech—not from a book.* We should greatly deceive you by stating the problem otherwise. But, a *practical working pronunciation* can be achieved from the above outline, one that should enable you to make yourself understood and to understand, when you have mastered French, at the movies, on records, and on the radio. You have been provided with a statement of equivalents and essentials. *You must refer to them again and again until you know them.* Do not allow them to worry you greatly to begin with. To make mistakes—especially at this stage—is no crime. Never miss an opportunity of speaking with French people; or with friends who know French and can help you. Practice will bring fluency, when you know the material to be presented in the pages which follow. We shall provide hints on how to overcome difficulties, and you will never be burdened with having to learn anything not likely to be of practical use. Hasten slowly must be your motto, especially in at least the first five lessons. After that, you should progress more rapidly. Millions of people have learned the French language: so why not you?

IMPORTANT NOTE

There is no need for you to attempt to master at this stage all the details in these first three sections of Lesson I. *But try*

* The HMV record, "French Speech Sounds," (#B4148)', might be helpful for self-taught beginners. It is available by mail from Goldsmith's Music Shop, 401 W. 42 Street, New York City.

to get the general principles into your mind : the pronunciation of the vowels and nasals, of those consonants which differ in pronunciation from their equivalent English consonants, silent letters at the end of words, stress and *liaison.*

In the next two sections of this first lesson, take each French word and try to work out the pronunciation in accordance with the equivalents given in §§ 1, 2, 3.   If there is an irregularity in pronunciation, your attention will be drawn to it.

IN THE FIRST FIVE LESSONS YOU WILL HAVE TO REFER AGAIN AND AGAIN TO THESE FIRST THREE SECTIONS OF LESSON I. YOU MUST BE PREPARED TO DO THIS. DO YOUR BEST, BUT DO NOT ALLOW PRONUNCIATION TO HOLD YOU UP AT THIS STAGE. SOON YOU WILL BE ABLE TO LISTEN TO FRENCH, TO UNDERSTAND MUCH, AND THEN YOUR PRONUNCIATION WILL STEADILY IMPROVE.

§ 4. *Gender—Articles—Nouns*

IN English we talk of a ship as *she*, and our poets often refer to the sun as *he* and the moon as *she*.   Otherwise we have no difficulties about " gender ":   our masculine, feminine and neuter are very simple.   Not so in French, in which everything is either a HE or a SHE.   All nouns (names of things) are either of masculine or feminine gender.   This characteristic of French is highly important, so you must learn the gender of French nouns *as you meet them*, and this is made much easier if you learn an article with each noun as it occurs.   The definite article *the* in the singular is expressed in French by :

> **le** before a masculine noun ; **la** before a feminine : **l'** before either masculine or feminine nouns beginning with a vowel or **h**-mute.

Thus : **le livre,** *the book*—**la plume,** *the pen*—**l'avion,** *the airplane.*

Male persons are masculine, female are feminine—as in English :

> **le père,** the father—**la mère,** the mother

In order to be sure of learning the right gender of words

beginning with a vowel or *h*-mute, we use the indefinite article *a* before them: **un** = *a* (masculine) and **une** = *a* (feminine). Thus:

un avion (*masculine*)   **un élève,** pupil (*male*)
une élève, pupil (*female*)

IMPORTANT RULE

ALWAYS LEARN THE ARTICLE—DEFINITE OR INDEFINITE—
WITH EVERY FRENCH NOUN YOU MEET

Vocabulary :

le père, the father	**la mère,** the mother
le frère, brother	**la sœur,** sister
un homme, (a) man	**la femme,** woman, wife *
un avion, airplane	**un aviateur,** pilot
le crayon, the pencil	**la plume,** the pen

You will now learn something which will give you heart. *Thousands* of French words are almost like their English equivalents. Above, you see **aviateur,** which is almost the same as our "aviator," though we generally speak of a "pilot" and not of an "aviator."

Consider these French words:

un acteur	une fureur	un prédécesseur
un constructeur	un honneur	un professeur
un directeur	un inférieur	un successeur
un empereur	un intérieur	un supérieur
un extérieur	un inventeur	une terreur
une faveur	un opérateur	une vapeur
une ferveur	une odeur	

You do not require much help to tell you the meaning of any of these words, but a hint or so will be useful. **Constructeur** is of course "constructor," but a special kind of constructor: a builder. **La construction** in French means "building." **Odeur** is "odor," but our commoner word is "smell." And **vapeur**

* *e* in **femme** is pronounced as if written *a* : pronunciation *la famme*.

is "vapor," but of the kind we know best: "steam." You will have to look out for such little subtleties when you meet French words that appear exactly like English. But, at this point, we have introduced to you twenty of those dozens of French words ending in **-eur** (equivalent to English -or, -er, -our) merely to inform you of a vast French vocabulary which will give you little trouble to memorize or recognize. Little by little, you will be introduced to these linguistic similarities.

Learn: **et,** and   **est,** is

    (*Note.*—These words are pronounced *ay.*)

       où, where   **ou,** or

    (Pronounced the same; the accent distinguishes the meaning.)

       ici, here   **là,** there

PRACTICE

It would be quite easy to provide you with a long "Exercise" made up with the French words and grammar you have learned up to now. But, it is *you* who will make up the "Exercise"— and this is the best practice of all. With the material you have learned, try to make up simple sentences in French, such as those given below as samples. Make all the combinations you can think of. For example:

Où est le père? Le père est ici. Et la mère? La mère est là. Le père est ici et la mère est là. Où est le frère? Le frère est ici. Où est la sœur? La sœur est là. Et l'aviateur?

Write down the sentences as you make them up. Try to think of them in French only and not as the equivalent of something in English.

One piece of advice is necessary. Do not worry if you find that you cannot at this stage remember all the words given you in the lesson. Just do your best. Words will recur again and again, and this will help to drive them home.

§ 5. *Plural of Nouns—Greetings*

To form the plural of French nouns add **-s**. That is the general rule of the language.

There is one plural form **LES** (pr. *lay*) for the definite articles **le, la, l'**.

Thus we can state the plurals:

les pères   les mères   les frères   les soeurs

Remember that the final **-s** of all these words is silent.

Remember also that when the final **-s** of **les** comes before a vowel or *h*-mute, there is liaison, the **s** is pronounced *z* and article and noun are pronounced as if they were one word: **les avions,** pronounce as if written *lézavion* in French.

Exceptions to the general rule of adding **s** to form the plural:

Nouns ending in
- **-s, x, z**—do not change in the plural
- **-u**   —add **x**
- **-ail, al** —change these letters to **-aux**

le fils, son (pronounce *le fiss*)—plural **les fils.**

l'hôpital, hospital—plural **les hôpitaux** (pr. *lézôpitô*)

Two further exceptions must be learned:

le ciel, sky—**les cieux,** the heavens
l'œil, eye—**les yeux,** eyes (pr. *lézyieu*)

And now meet our very common friends to be:

MONSIEUR (pr. *mesyeu*) = Mr., Sir, gentleman.
MESSIEURS (pr. *mésyeu*) = Messrs, Sirs, gentlemen.
MADAME, plural **MESDAMES** (pr. *médame*) = Mrs., Madame.
MADEMOISELLE, MESDEMOISELLES (pr. *mad'moisel, médmoisel*) = Miss, Misses.
MONSIEUR is abbreviated to **M. MME = MADAME.**
MLLE = MADEMOISELLE. Notice that the abbreviation **M.** ends with a period, but **MME** and **MLLE** do not.

The French usage of these words differs from our use of Mr., Mrs., and Miss. When two Americans meet, they usually say simply *Good morning* or *Good evening*. So do two French people who meet, but they nearly always add **Monsieur, Madame,** or **Mademoiselle,** as the case may be. If they wish to be formal, they add the person's surname; if informal, and if they are intimate friends, just the given name without the **Monsieur,** etc. Learn these greetings, and then we shall see how it works out:

Bonjour = Good morning, good day, good afternoon, *and* is always followed by **Monsieur, Madame, Mademoiselle** (or the given name of a friend).

Bonsoir = Good evening (*after sundown*). **Bonsoir, Monsieur.**

Bonne nuit = Good night, *when parting or just going to bed.*

Thus : **Bonjour, Monsieur Dupont—Bonsoir, Madame Fragonard—Bonne nuit, Mademoiselle Brachet.**

Among friends : **Bonjour, Charles—Bonsoir, Jean— Bonne nuit, Jeanne.**

The French do not say " *Good afternoon* " They say **bonsoir,** if it is late ; otherwise, **bonjour.**

Phrases and Vocabulary :

vous avez, you have
vous voulez, you wish, want

avez-vous, have you ?
voulez-vous ? do you wish, want ?

je, j' = I   **j'ai** = I have
ou = or (*without accent, to distinguish from* **où** = where)

oui = yes   **non** = no

le cheval, horse
les chevaux, horses
le chapeau, les chapeaux,
    hat, hats
un enfant, child
l'oncle, uncle

la tante, aunt
le pain, bread
le lait, milk
le thé, tea
le café, coffee
l'eau, water (*fem.*)

PRACTICE

As before, try using your own ingenuity to make sentences with the words and phrases you have learned. You now have over fifty common words and phrases, and you will be quite surprised how much you can express with them. *Do not translate*, but try to think in French as much as possible. Thus, when **le cheval** is in your head, do not think of the English word " horse," but imagine a horse before you. Here are some examples to help you :

Bonjour, Monsieur. Voulez-vous le café? J'ai le café. Avez-vous le chapeau? Non, Monsieur. Avez-vous le pain? Oui, Monsieur. Voulez-vous le thé ou le café? J'ai le thé et le café ici. Où est Jean? L'enfant est là. Où est l'acteur? L'acteur est ici.

Again you are advised not to worry greatly if you find that you have not memorized all the material given. But do not proceed with the next lesson until you feel confident that you have *understood* everything so far. If you have not understood, review. Constant review will enable you to memorize.

It may interest you to know that this first lesson is not only one of the most important, but it is also perhaps the most difficult lesson in the whole course. Hence, it would be strange if you did *not* find it difficult! It is worth going over several times ; and this also applies to the next four lessons. The first stage is troublesome in every language. One thing you must never do : pass by anything which you do not *understand*.

LESSON II

§ 1. *Prepositions* **de** *and* **à**—*How to Say* "*Some*"

A PREPOSITION is a word which marks the relation between a noun (name of a thing) or pronoun (word replacing a noun) and another word. Thus, I am *in* the room; he is *at* the window; she is asleep *on* the bed: *in*, *at*, *on* are prepositions. You will learn more about these words later, but meantime you must make the acquaintance of two of the commonest and most frequently recurring.

These two important prepositions are **à** = *to* and **de** = *of*. When they are used with the definite article, certain contractions take place:

à le is contracted to **AU,** but **à l'** is used before a vowel or *h*-mute.

de le becomes **DU,** but **de l'** is used before a vowel or *h*-mute.

à les becomes **AUX** and **de les** becomes **DES.**

à la and **de la** are used before feminine nouns in the singular beginning with a consonant. The **à l'** and **de l'** are used before both masculine and feminine nouns singular beginning with a vowel or *h*-mute. **AUX** and **DES** before *all* plural nouns.

Turn back to Lesson I, § 4, Vocabulary, and go over the nouns in it and in § 5, using the articles and prepositions **à** and **de** and with the definite article.

Thus: **au père—à la mère—aux frères—aux sœurs** =
      to the father, mother, brothers, sisters

      à l'acteur—aux acteurs—du professeur—des professeurs

and so on, practicing (and memorizing) all those words with these two prepositions and the article.

34

Du, de l', de la, des are used in French to express our English word *some*. Thus: *some bread* = **du pain; de l'eau** = *some water*.

When we say *John's hand*, John's is possessive case. In English, the possessive case is represented by *'s*. But in French we must say *the hand* or *John*—**La main de Jean. Le frère du professeur** = *the professor's brother*. And so on. There is no exception to this rule. We can make up innumerable new phrases in this way: **Le père de l'acteur, la femme de l'aviateur,** and so forth. By going over all the nouns already met, using this grammatical device, you can drive home both the nouns and the device. This is admirable for practice. It explains why you were advised not to worry very much about memorizing all those words. They come up again and again.

There are certain usages of the article in French which differ from English and are very common. Most important to know is that the indefinite article is omitted in French when stating a rank, profession, or nationality. To understand this, first learn the following words:

> **anglais,** English—**français,** French—**américain,** American *
>
> **médecin,** doctor—**capitaine,** captain—**officier,** officer

Learn also: **Je suis** = *I am*—**il est** = *he is*—**il a** = *he has*
Thus:

> **Je suis anglais,** I am an Englishman
> **Je suis capitaine,** I am a captain
> **Il est médecin,** he is a doctor

A very useful general rule to know is that the feminine of many nouns can be formed by adding **-e** to the masculine. Thus:

> **Je suis anglaise,** I am an Englishwoman
> **Je suis américaine,** I am an American (woman)

—but **la médecine** is " medicine," and not a female doctor.

* Note the small letters-instead of our capitals.

Now proceed as before, making up your own little phrases, and, as you have learned the nationalities, you may also learn the countries:

l'Angleterre, England	la France, France
l'Allemagne, Germany	l'Espagne, Spain
l'Irlande, Ireland	l'Ecosse, Scotland
la Grande Bretagne, Great Britain	les États Unis, the United States

Examples to help in practice: **Le frère du médecin est ici. L'américain est officier. L'anglais est médecin. Le français est directeur**—directeur de théâtre. **Voulez-vous du café? J'ai du thé.** Le professeur est le frère de **Mlle Jeanne. Bonjour, Monsieur le capitaine** = Good morning, captain. **Avez-vous le chapeau? Oui, j'ai le chapeau. Le fils du constructeur est ici. Où est le frère de Madame Dupont? Il est là. Paris est la capitale de la France et Londres est la capitale de l'Angleterre. La capitale de l'Ecosse est Edimbourg.**

Continue making up such sentences until you feel that you are familiar with the words and rules.

Note that in the above examples we have put in a few words not given in the lists. **La capitale, le théâtre,** for example. But they are words almost the same as in English. In future, we shall often put in such words without giving the English equivalent. This, you will find, helps to accustom you to these similar words; and it is not really necessary to explain the obvious.

§ 2. *Adjectives—their Place and " Agreement "*

An adjective is a word added to the noun, to qualify or describe that noun. Thus: the good man—" good " is an adjective.

In French, the adjective is usually placed *after* the noun. Thus: **le crayon bleu,** *the blue pencil.*

It is a rule to which there are no exceptions that in French the adjective agrees in gender and number with its noun. Thus :

les crayons bleus, the blue pencils.

la femme polie, the polite woman

l'homme poli, the polite man

les femmes polies, the polite women

les hommes polis, the polite men

Adjectives make the feminine form by adding **e**—as you have seen in the above examples. Adjectives which end in **-s, -l, -n, -t** form the feminine by doubling the last letter and adding **e**-mute. Thus: **exprès,** *express,* feminine **expresse; bon,** *good,* feminine **bonne.**

Adjectives ending in **-eau** change these letters to **-elle** in the feminine : **beau,** *beautiful,* **belle** in the feminine. And adjectives ending in **-f** change to **-ve,** while those ending in **-x** do not change in the masculine plural, but change to **euse** in the feminine singular and to **-euses** in the feminine plural. Thus :

vif, *living, lively,* feminine **vive.**

heureux, *happy,* feminine **heureuse,** feminine plural **heureuses.**

l'homme heureux, the happy man

les hommes heureux, happy men

la femme heureuse, happy woman

les femmes heureuses, happy women

You will learn later that there are some exceptions and irregularities, but the above few rules cover the majority of French adjectives.

Vocabulary :

chaud, warm
froid, cold
mauvais, bad
dur, hard

nouveau (nouvelle), new
agréable, pleasant
aimable, amiable

Merci, thanks, thank you, *and also* no thank you.
Voici, here is, here are.
Voilà, there (over there) is, there are.
Regardez, see, look at.
Regardez le nouveau chapeau, Look at (see) the new hat.
Voici le frère et voilà la sœur, Here is the brother and there is the sister, over there.

Qui est? Who is?	**Qui a?** Who has?
il a, he has	**elle a,** she has
ils ont, they have	**elles ont,** they have (*feminine*)

ils sont, elles sont, they are

une automobile, automobile	**le bateau,** the boat, ship
les bagages, luggage	**un aérodrome,** airport
un autobus, bus	**un avocat,** lawyer
brun, brown	**brave,** brave
capable (de), capable (of), able to	**certain,** certain, sure
	commun, common

PRACTICE

You are now equipped with some very practical material in words, phrases, and grammar. You can make all sorts of useful sentences :

> **Bonjour, Charles, où sont les bagages?**
> **Ah bonjour, Jean—les bagages sont là.**
> **Et l'auto** (short for automobile) ? **Elle est là.**
> **J'ai l'auto ici.**
> **Voulez-vous du café? Ou du thé?**
> **Où est l'autobus? Il est ici.**
> **Regardez le mauvais enfant—il a le crayon de ma sœur.**
> **Qui est l'aviateur? C'est un officier américain et son frère est professeur à l'université** (at the university).

Proceed yourself in this manner, and you will be quite surprised to find the wide range of subjects it is possible to deal with very simply with the material you have learned.

REVIEW: These two sections of Lesson II are important, and may be found a little difficult. But remember that you are not expected to have memorized everything in a section or lesson before going ahead with the next. Whatever you do, you must not strain or weary yourself: learning French should be something of a game of ingenuity in which you have to use your wits and concentrate to make sense of it all. Never be dismayed because you don't happen to remember a word or phrase. Have patience, turn back and hunt it down.

What is most important at this stage is that you should begin to see how the language works, and this is far more important than just memorizing undigested material.

It is better to know how to use a dozen words correctly and with ease than to know fifty which are just so many pieces of material which you cannot put together in the way necessary to comprehension. Hasten slowly. This will produce the best results.

§ 3. *Some General Practice—Visualization*

Read the following words aloud and at the same time try *visualize* the person or thing:

le père—la mère—le frère—la sœur—un enfant—un élève—une élève—un avion—un aviateur—les pères—les mères—les sœurs—les frères—les enfants—le ciel—les cieux—un œil—les yeux—le fils —les fils—le cheval—les chevaux—le chapeau—les chapeaux—un oncle—la tante—le pain—du pain —le lait—du lait—de l'eau—du thé—du café—au père—à la mère—aux enfants—des chevaux—des avions—des fils—des anglais—un français—un médecin—le capitaine—un officier—un officier américain —un capitaine anglais—le frère du médecin—la femme de Jean.

It is important at this early stage to get into the habit of thinking of persons and things in French rather than in English. It will still be impossible for you to avoid translating into French or from French into English: for example, when the idea of "brother" comes to mind, of first thinking of the word "brother" and then thinking of the French **le frère,** or, when you see **le frère,** of translating it into "*brother*." But what you must do is to *see in imagination* a brother and at the same time think intensely of the words **le frère.**

If you give the matter a little thought, you will appreciate that, by doing this every time you come across a noun, whether it be one you know already or a new one, you will be training your mind in the elementary stage of what must one day become a *habit*, almost second nature, namely—*thinking in French*. It may be a little odd and difficult at first. But if you persist at this stage you will reap the benefits later. The harvest will come more quickly and be much richer than if you pursue the old method of learning by translation. We can assure you that this practice is well worth while. And there is *no limit to it*, as you will discover as you go along.

Never miss an opportunity of VISUALIZATION. From time to time, turn back and go over the ground already covered, bringing the French into your mind and, as far as possible, eliminating the English.

§ 4. *Numbers—Days of the Week—Months*

un	deux	trois	quatre	cinq
1	2	3	4	5
six	sept	huit	neuf	dix
6	7	8	9	10

cinq is pronounced as if written *cinc*.

six, pronounce as if written *siss* and **dix** as *diss*.

sept = *sett*.

et = *and*, pronounce *ay* and note that the **t** of **et** is *never* pronounced in "liaison"—see Lesson I, § 3.

First go over the numbers a few times until you can say them straight off from 1 to 10. Then try to do a little addition *in French*, thus:

un et un (pause) **deux,** (*one and one, two*)

un et deux, trois	**un et trois, quatre**
deux et trois, cinq	**deux et deux, quatre**
trois et trois, six	**trois et quatre, sept**

and so on.

You will, of course, realize that this is merely carrying one stage farther what we taught you to do in § 3, and it is part and parcel of what we wish you to be able to do with ease as quickly as possible: *think in French*.

DAYS OF THE WEEK: **lundi, mardi, mercredi, jeudi, vendredi, samedi, dimanche.** *Monday*, *Tuesday*, etc., and note that in French they are not written with capital letters. Similarly:

MONTHS OF THE YEAR: **janvier, février, mars** (pr. *marss*), **avril, mai, juin, juillet, août** (pr. *ou*), **septembre, octobre, novembre, décembre.**

le jour, the day	**la semaine,** week
quel, what	**sont,** are

Quels sont les jours de la semaine? What are the days of the week?

Les jours de la semaine sont, The days of the week are . . .

nous sommes, we are—**sommes-nous,** are we?

Quel jour sommes-nous? What day are we? (What day is today?)

Nous sommes vendredi, We are Friday. (This is Friday.)

hier, yesterday	**aujourd'hui,** today
demain, tomorrow	

Note that the days of the week and the months are all masculine: **le lundi, le décembre.**

le mois, the month   **une année,** a year

Combien? How many?   **il y a,** there is *or* there are

  y a-t-il? is there, are there?

Combien y a-t-il de jours dans une semaine? How many days are there in a week?

Il y a sept jours dans une semaine. There are seven days in a week.

Combien y a-t-il de mois dans l'année? How many months are there in a year?

Il y a douze (12) mois dans l'année. There are 12 months in a year.

onze	douze	treize	quatorze	quinze
11	12	13	14	15
seize	**dix-sept**	**dix-huit**	**dix-neuf**	**vingt ***
16	17	18	19	20

PRACTICE

Read aloud the following in French: 1, 2, 3, 4, 5, 6, 7, 8, 9, 10, 11, 12, 13, 14, 15, 16, 17, 18, 19, 20. You must not think of these numbers in English.

When you can do this perfectly, try to say the French for the numbers which follow, at first slowly, visualizing the number and holding it in your mind while repeating the French a few times, and gradually increase the speed until you can read off the French without hesitation:

12	19	11	2	7	9	13	15	17	14	20	1
6	9	12	15	18	2	4	3	5	7	9	10
16	8	3	2	5	12	15	20	1	2

Now, if you feel like it, try addition as before:

  12 et 3, 15   7 et 8, 15

and so on.

Be warned again not to weary yourself. Remember that these numbers are *highly important* and that without them you cannot hope to get very far in French life.

* Pronounce *vin*.

§ 5. *Adjectives—Comparison*

You have already become acquainted with adjectives in Lesson II, § 2 (their simple usage). Next you must learn the " Degrees of Comparison." In English we have a general working rule—we add -*er* and -*est* to the simple form to express the comparative and superlative degrees. Thus, *fat, fatter, fattest*; or, *free, freer, freest*. But, in reverse, we say *less fat, least fat, less free, least free*. In French they say *more fat, most fat, more free, most free* as well as *less fat, least fat, less free, least free*. Thus:

Superiority .	1	2	3
	PLUS (more)	—	**QUE** (than)
	plus	gros	que
	more	fat	than
	plus	libre	que
	more	free	than

Inferiority .	1	2	3
	MOINS (less)	—	**QUE** (than)
	moins	gros	que
	less	fat	than
	moins	libre	que
	less	free	than

Equality .	1	2	3
	AUSSI (as)	—	**QUE** (as)
	aussi	gros	que
	as	fat	as
	aussi	libre	que
	as	free	as

THE SUPERLATIVE : **le plus,** *the most,* and **le moins,** *the least* —these words serve generally for the superlative :

le plus gros, the fattest—**le moins gros,** the least fat

One must not forget that every noun in French is a " he " or a " she "—masculine or feminine—and then **le plus** becomes **la plus** and **le moins, la moins,** to agree with the noun :

> **Mon père est gros, plus gros que ma mère, mais ma sœur est la plus grosse.**
>
> *My father is fat, fatter than my mother, but my sister is the fattest.*

You will note that in the feminine **gros** becomes **grosse,** and that **mon** is " *my* " in the masculine and **ma,** feminine.

> **LES PLUS GROS,** the fattest (*plural masculine*)
> **LES PLUS GROSSES,** the fattest (*plural feminine*)

The above few simple rules and words enable you to express the degrees of comparison in French, but note carefully the following irregularities :

bon, good	**meilleur,** better	**le meilleur,** the best
mauvais, bad	**pire,** worse	**le pire,** the worst
petit, small	**moindre,** smaller	**le moindre,** the smallest

though the last is not so common as :

> **petit**   **plus petit**   **le plus petit**

In addition to these words, you should know the following :

> **très,** very (**très bon,** very good ; **très mauvais,** very bad).
>
> **assez,** enough (**assez bon,** good enough ; **assez mauvais**).
>
> **trop,** too much (**trop petit,** too small ; **trop grand,** too big).
>
> **peu,** little (**le livre est peu intéressant,** the book is not very (little) interesting.
>
> **beaucoup,** much

Note the following :

> **MON,** *my,* before a masculine noun : **mon chapeau,** *my hat.*

MA, *my*, before a feminine noun : **ma sœur,** *my sister*.

MES, *my*, before a plural noun of either gender :

mes chapeaux, mes sœurs.

SON, SA, SES, *his* or *hers*.

Thus : **son chapeau, sa sœur—ses chapeaux, ses sœurs.**

Practice

L'Asie est plus grande que l'Europe.   M. Dupont est un homme très gros, mais il est bon.   Sa femme est plus petite que sa soeur (his sister). **La femme du médecin est assez grande** (big, tall)**, beaucoup plus grande que le médecin.   Charles est meilleur que Jean.   Il est aussi bon que Jacques** (James).

Now try to make up some sentences without help, going back over the words you have learned. There is really very little grammar to be learned in this section, but it is important that you should know all the *words* for " comparison," as the need for them constantly recurs.

LESSON III

§ 1. *Pronouns—Personal*

A PRONOUN is a word used instead of a noun to indicate a person or thing already mentioned or known. As you will learn in this section and in what follows, there are various kinds of pronouns called for convenience: personal, relative, possessive, interrogative, demonstrative, and indefinite pronouns.

PERSONAL PRONOUNS: *I, thou, he, she, it, we, you, they.* For purposes of reference, though also to simplify the process of learning, we shall tabulate the personal pronouns in French. But first you must get clearly into your head that the personal pronouns, in French as in English, vary in form to indicate subject, direct object, and indirect object.

The subject is the person who talks or acts.

The direct object is the direct recipient of the action.

The indirect object is the indirect recipient of the action.

Thus, in the sentence *I give IT to HIM*, *I* is the subject personal pronoun, *IT* is the direct object, and *HIM* the indirect.

Do not proceed further until you have this perfectly in mind. Because of the nature of French, it is highly important to be clear about it. Otherwise you are liable to make silly mistakes. It is impossible to read even elementary French or carry on the simplest conversation without these personal pronouns; and they must be used correctly. Now for the Table:

1	2	3
Subject	*Direct Object*	*Indirect Object*
je, I	**me,** me	**me,** to me
tu, thou *	**te,** thee	**te,** to thee
il, elle, he, she	**le, la,** him, her, it	**lui,** to him, to her

* **Tu,** *thou,* is given in this table, though you will not require it for some time. The French use **tu** only when speaking to intimates or old friends; it is essentially a " familiar " form. The word universally used is **vous,** *you.*

1	2	3
Subject	*Direct Object*	*Indirect Object*
nous, we	**nous,** us	**nous,** to us
vous, you	**vous,** you	**vous,** to you
ils, elles, they, they	**les,** them	**leur,** to them

Before a vowel or *h*-mute, **je, te, me, le** become **j', t', m', l'.**
The word **EN** * often replaces **de lui** etc. and it is used for
persons and things. The word **Y** often replaces **à lui** etc.
but is used for things only. **SE** = (to) himself, herself, itself,
themselves.

ORDER OF PRONOUNS WITH VERB :

$$\left.\begin{array}{l} \textbf{me} \\ \textbf{te} \\ \textbf{se} \\ \textbf{nous} \\ \textbf{vous} \end{array}\right\} \left.\begin{array}{l} \textbf{le} \\ \textbf{la} \\ \textbf{les} \end{array}\right\} \left.\begin{array}{l} \textbf{lui} \\ \textbf{leur} \end{array}\right\} \textbf{y} \} \textbf{en} \} \text{Verb}$$

You see that in French the pronouns come *before the verb* and
in a definite order, which must be learned. Also, you will observe
that they are placed in the order of persons and, if both are in
the same person, the *direct object comes first :* **je le lui donne.**

You cannot make much use of these pronouns without verbs,
so let us take a common example : **DONNER,** *to give.*

Je donne, I give
tu donnes, thou givest
il, elle donne, he, she gives
nous donnons, we give
vous donnez, you give
ils, elles donnent, they give (the **ent** is silent).

Thus :
je le lui donne, I give it to him
je vous donne, I give you
je vous le donne, I give it to you
nous vous les donnons, we give them to you

* *Pronoun* meaning *of it, of him, her, them.* **Y,** *Pronoun*—to it, them.

It will be sufficient for the moment if you memorize all these words and get a general idea of how the pronouns work. Your practice this time consists in going over a few times what has been given above. There is still more to be learned about these pronouns.

§ 2. *Pronouns apart from the Verb*

The personal pronouns given in the preceding section are used with the verb, but there are others which are used apart from the verb, or for emphasis, or with a preposition. These are :

MOI, I, myself, me	**à moi,** to me
TOI, thou, thyself, thee	**à toi,** to thee
LUI, ELLE, he, she	
LUI, ELLE, SOI, him, her	**à lui, à elle, à soi,** to him, her, it
NOUS, we, us	**à nous,** to us
VOUS, you	**à vous,** to you
EUX, ELLES, they, them	**à eux, à elles, à soi,** to them

SOI, *him, her, itself, themselves*, is used after certain words : **on,** *one, they, people ;* **chacun,** *each ;* **aucun,** *none ;* **celui qui,** *he who.*   Thus : **Chacun pour soi,** *every one (or each) for himself.*

Même, *self*, can be added to all the words in the above list :

moi-même, myself	**lui-même** ⎱ himself,
elle-même, herself	**soi-même** ⎰ herself etc.
nous-mêmes, ourselves	**vous-mêmes,** yourselves
eux-mêmes, elles-mêmes, themselves *(masc. and fem.)*	

PRONOUNS AND THE IMPERATIVE : In the imperative, that is, when an order is given—as in, say, " *Give me* ," the pronouns are placed after the verb. Thus: **Donnez-moi,** *give me.* **Donnez-le-moi,** *give it to me.* Observe that the direct object

comes first. The following table shows the order of pronouns
after the imperative:

$$\text{VERB} \left\{ \begin{array}{l} \text{le} \\ \text{la} \\ \text{les} \end{array} \right. \left\{ \begin{array}{l} \text{moi} \\ \text{toi} \\ \text{lui} \\ \text{nous} \\ \text{vous} \\ \text{leur} \end{array} \right. \left\{ \text{y} \right. \left\{ \text{en} \right.$$

Thus :

donnez-le-lui, give it to him

donnez-les-nous, give them to us

There is still more to be learned about these pronouns, but
what has been given should carry you a long way.   For practice
in their use, it will be necessary to learn some more verbs, so,
for a beginning, let us take three which follow exactly the model
given for **DONNER** in § 1 of this lesson.

PARLER, to speak   **PENSER,** to think

JOUER, to play   **penser à,** to think of

je parle, I speak

tu parles, thou speakest

il, elle parle, he, she speaks

nous parlons, we speak

vous parlez, you speak

ils, elles parlent, they speak (**ent** *is silent*)

JOUER and **PENSER** follow the same model : **Je joue, tu
joues, il joue; nous pensons, vous pensez, ils pensent.**
Note that the **-ent** of the third person plural of all verbs is
always silent. Thus **ils parlent** is pronounced as if it were
written **il parle.** There are no exceptions to this rule.

PRACTICE

Je joue avec (*with*) lui. Il joue avec moi.   Moi, je parle
avec lui ; et lui, il parle avec nous.   Je pense à moi-même.
Pensez-vous à moi ?   Non, je pense à eux.   Voulez-vous
jouer avec moi ?   Non, je joue avec mon frère.   Pensez-
vous à votre mère ?   Je pense souvent (*often*) à elle.

**Nous parlons de vous et de votre oncle.   Donnez-le-moi.
Je vous le donne avec plaisir** (*with pleasure*).   **Moi, je suis
anglais et mon ami** (*friend*) **est directeur de théâtre.
Regardez-moi un moment.   Me voilà!   Le voici!   Combien
y a-t-il de personnes ici?   Il y en a trois.   Aujourd'hui
nous parlons français, tous les trois** (*all three*)**, Charles,
Jacques, et moi-même.   Qui est là?   C'est moi.   Qui
parle?   Moi.   Voulez-vous parler avec moi?   Merci,
je parle avec l'américain.   Où sont les bagages?   Je les
donne au capitaine qui est là.**

Now continue to practice by yourself, making up sentences
such as these and using the material learned in Lessons I and II.

Vocabulary :

You will remember that in Lesson I, § 4, we told you that
thousands of French words resemble their English equivalents.
Now consider the following: **un opéra—une brigade—une
salade—un camarade—la limonade—un amiral—un refus**
(refusal)—**une proposition—la répétition** (means " repetition " and also " rehearsal ") **un océan—un vétéran—la
chance** (means " chance " and " luck ")—**une balance—une
élégance—une extravagance—une ignorance—une ré-
pugnance.** Note that all these words ending in **-ce** are
feminine.   There is an exception—that which a woman cannot
keep (so they say): **Le silence.   Une assurance** means
" assurance " and " insurance."   And **la ressemblance** is
"resemblance."   Twenty words easily learned!

§ 3. *Possessive Pronouns—" Basic Vocabulary "*

Masculine	Feminine	Plural	
MON	MA	MES	—my, mine
TON	TA	TES	—thy, thine
SON	SA	SES	—his, hers, its
NOTRE	NOTRE	NOS	—our
VOTRE	VOTRE	VOS	—your
LEUR	LEUR	LEURS	—their

French differs from English in that the possessive pronoun always agrees in gender and number with the noun which follows it. Thus: **mon frère, ma sœur, mes frères, mes sœurs. Ma, ta, sa** become **mon, ton, son** before a vowel or *h*-mute: **mon enfant.**

In some grammars, the above words are called " possessive adjectives," which, strictly, may be more correct, though not so convenient for learning. A pronoun stands instead of a noun, as when we say " This is mine." My what ? My hat, or my brother. The French for " mine," " his," " hers," etc., is given in the list below:

Masculine	*Feminine*
LE MIEN	**LA MIENNE**
LE TIEN	**LA TIENNE**
LE SIEN	**LA SIENNE**
LE NÔTRE	**LA NÔTRE**
LE VÔTRE	**LA VÔTRE**
LE LEUR	**LA LEUR**

Plural

LES MIENS, LES MIENNES
LES TIENS, LES TIENNES
LES SIENS, LES SIENNES
LES NOTRES (both genders)
LES VÔTRES   „
LES LEURS   „

Thus: **Ce chapeau est le mien. Cette table est la mienne. Ces crayons sont les miens. Ces tables sont les miennes.**

" Basic Vocabulary :"

You may perhaps think that up to now you have been given a stiff dose of grammar and that, therefore, grammar is of more importance than vocabulary. This is not so. *WORDS are the raw material of language*, and if you know the words you can make *some* sense of *anything* ! But do not ever forget that in French especially—a much more *exact* language than English— it is the grammar which " sharpens " and clarifies the meaning of the sentence. We therefore continue to provide this instrument, which *you need not completely master at this stage*. But you must : (1) KNOW HOW THE GRAMMAR WORKS and (2) KNOW ALL THE WORDS. Thus, if you know **mon, ma, mes** and **le mien, la mienne, les miens, les miennes,** you will know the meaning of : **mon médecin, ma mère** and **mes chapeaux.** Little by little, you will grow accustomed to saying almost without having to think of it : **mon médecin, ma mère,** and **mes chapeaux,** or **ce chapeau est le mien, cette table est la sienne,** and you will find yourself speaking French that is grammatically correct. That is your ultimate objective. Meanwhile, you must not worry too greatly about memorizing grammar, but never pass any point until you *understand clearly what it means*.

Without words, you get nowhere and can do nothing. That is important to remember. You have already been given a fair number of useful words, but, because of the need to acquire some knowledge of the working of grammar, the words hitherto given have been chosen to illustrate the grammar and to help generally with grammar rather than because of their absolute utility. From now on, the words given will be carefully chosen for their " basic " utility. In each lesson will be given a selection of words without which a general working knowledge of the language would be impossible of achievement. Often you will find a word you have met before, but never mind. We shall also give you from time to time common phrases. Because these words and phrases are " basic ," you must begin to memorize as many as possible even before you get to the reading phase, when you will have ample practice to drive them home. Here is your first list of " basic " words and phrases :

à, to, at
accepter, to accept
un accident, accident
l'acier (*m.*), steel
une action, action
une adresse, address
une addition, addition, bill
un aérodrome, airport
les affaires, business
un agent, agent
un agent de police, policeman
d'ailleurs, besides
aimer, to love

ainsi, thus
l'air (*m.*), air
ajouter, to add
allemand, German
allumer, to light
une allumette, match
l'Allemagne (*f.*), Germany
alors, then
américain, American
l'Amérique, (*f.*) America
l'amour (*m.*), love
un an, une année, year
un animal, animal

Verbs ending in **-er** always follow the model of **DONNER** (Lesson III, § 1).

Note.—In these lists, words found elsewhere are often repeated. Concentrate on words which differ in the two languages.

§ 4. *Demonstrative Pronouns*

CELUI, this (*masculine*)   **CELLE,** this (*feminine*)
CEUX, these (*masc. plural*)   **CELLES,** these (*fem. pl.*)

-ci, abbreviation of **ici,** can be added to any of the above to indicate that the person or persons are nearby; and similarly **-là** (*there*). **Celui-ci est mon frère et celle-là est ma sœur.** *This person* (*here*) *is my brother, and that one* (*there*) *is my sister.*

CE meaning "*this*" is also used with **-ci** and **là** to make the words **ceci, cela** (*this, that*), and there is an all-purposes abridgment, **ça** (*that*), which is very much used. **Je donne ça à l'enfant,** *I give that to the child.* **QUI** = *who, which.* **QUE** = *whom, which.*

Celui qui, celle qui, ceux qui, celles qui are used for *he who, she who, the one who* or *which, anyone who, the man* or *woman who.*   **Ceux qui** and **celles qui** = *the people who.*   **Ceux qui sont ici sont mes frères et celles qui sont là sont mes sœurs.   Voici ceux que je donne au capitaine,** *Here are the ones (that) I give to the captain.*

You will find that these words are among the most useful in the language, in that they are constantly being used with other words to make everyday phrases.

> **À qui est ce chapeau ?**   Whose is (to whom is) this hat ?
>
> **C'est celui de mon père,** It is my father's, (*literally* " It is that of my father ").
>
> **Est-ce là votre bagage ?**   Is that (over there) your baggage ?
>
> **Non, ceci est mon bagage.** No, this (here) is my baggage.
>
> **Sont-ce là vos crayons.**   Are those (there) your pencils ?

You remember from Lesson I, § 5, the phrase **voulez-vous,** " *do you wish* " or " *want* ".   **Voulez-vous du café ?**   From Lesson III, § 1, you will remember that **EN** means " *of it* " and often replaces **de lui** etc., and is used for persons and things.   **Je veux,** *I wish* or *I want.*   Thus :

> **Voulez-vous du café?   J'en veux,** I would like some (*literally,* I of it wish).
>
> **Voulez-vous un crayon?   Je veux celui-ci,** I want this one (here).
>
> **Voici du thé.   En voulez-vous?** Here is some tea. Would you like some ?

Add to your phrases **s'il vous plaît,** *If you please* (literally, *If it you pleases*), and you have the material to make innumerable useful phrases.

PRACTICE

Voici mon crayon et celui de mon frère.   Voilà le bagage de l'aviateur anglais et le mien est ici.   Voulez-vous ceux-ci ou ceux-là?   Je veux ceux-là.   Qui est là?

C'est un monsieur qui désire vous parler. **Qui est celle-ci?** C'est la dame (*lady*) qui me donne le chapeau. **Voulez-vous de la bière** (*beer*)? **Merci** (*NO, thank you*), je veux du thé. Oui, s'il vous plaît. **Où est-ce que nous jouons au football?** (lit. "*Where is it that we play at the football?*"—"*Where do we play football?*") **C'est ici que nous jouons au football. A qui pensez-vous? A mon frère** qui est à Londres (*London*). **Est-ce que vous parlez français? Oui, monsieur, un peu** (*a little*). **Non, monsieur, mais** (*but*) je parle anglais. **En voulez-vous? J'en veux, s'il vous plaît.**

And you can make up many more.

Basic Vocabulary :

une absence, absence	**apporter,** to bring
absolument, absolutely	**après,** after
un acteur, actor	**un après-demain,** day after
une actrice, actress	tomorrow
un âge, age	**un après-midi,** afternoon
une agriculture	**un arbre,** tree
une ambulance	**une arme,** weapon
un âne, ass, donkey	**une armée,** army
un ange, angel	**arracher,** to tear (up)
une annonce, announcement,	**un arrêt,** stopping place
advertisement	**arrêter,** to stop
annoncer, to announce	**une arrivée,** arrival
annonceur (radio)	**arriver,** to arrive
un appareil, apparatus	**un ascenseur,** elevator
appeler, to call	**assez,** enough
appliquer, to apply	**une assiette,** plate

il y a, there is, there are
Qu'est-ce qu'il y a? What is the matter?
il y a is a most useful phrase, and with it you might note:
il y en a, there is *or* there are some.
Y a-t-il du café? Oui, il y en a.

LEARNING WORDS: You will find that you can learn daily, without much effort, at least *ten* and possibly up to *twenty* French words by going over them a few times, not forgetting what you have been told about " visualization ." Some learners memorize as many as thirty, but if you are *sure* of *fifteen*, you are doing quite well. It will be sufficient if you just " make the acquaintance " of the others in the lists at this stage. The constant review and the practice in reading which will come later will drive them home, but it is advisable for you to keep on going back over these lists.

§ 5. *Relative Pronouns*

A relative pronoun is one which "relates" the noun or personal pronoun to which it refers with the part of the sentence which follows. It may be said that the relative pronoun in a sense qualifies the clause following it, like an adjective. Thus: *The gentleman* WHOM *I know, the dog* WHICH *barked, he* WHO *was here.* WHOM, WHICH, WHO are relative pronouns.

QUI (Subject)—*who, which, that*—of persons or things
QUE (Object)—*whom, which, that*   ,,   ,,
DONT   —*of whom, of which*   ,,   ,,
LEQUEL   —*who, which, that* (*of two*) ,,   ,,
DUQUEL   —*of whom, which, that* (*of two*)—of persons or things
AUQUEL   —*to whom, which, that* (*of two*)—of persons or things
DE QUI   —*whose, of whom*—persons only
À QUI   —*to whom, whose*   ,,
QUOI   —*what*   —things only
DE QUOI   —*of what*   ,,
À QUOI   —*to what, which*   ,,

LEQUEL	is masculine singular	And similarly
LESQUELS	,, plural	**DUQUEL,**
LAQUELLE	is feminine singular	**AUQUEL**
LESQUELLES	,, plural	*etc.*

Examples :

Une mère qui aime son enfant, a mother who loves her child.

Le chapeau que je donne à mon frère.

L'homme dont vous parlez, the man of whom you speak.

Voulez-vous le lait dont je parle? Would you like the milk of which I speak ?

Note how precise French can be :

La sœur de Jean qui est riche, the sister of John who is rich. But who is rich? John or the sister? There need be no doubt : **La sœur de Jean, laquelle est riche:** here **laquelle** is the feminine form to agree with sister, and hence one knows immediately that it is the sister.

La dame à qui je donne le livre.

C'est à quoi je pense, It is what I'm thinking of.

A-t-il de quoi écrire? Has he anything to write (with) ?

Le crayon que je donne à mon frère.

The most important words in this list are **QUI** and **QUE,** and one has to remember that, while both apply to persons and to things, **QUI** is always the subject and **QUE** the object :

Le livre que vous me donnez est intéressant.

Le chien (dog) **qui est ici.**

L'enfant que j'aime.

La dame qui me donne du café.

Learn this well and be able to use **QUI** and **QUE** correctly. The remaining words may be treated as vocabulary for the moment.   That is, know their meanings.

PRACTICE this time consists in going over what has been learned in previous sections and making up phrases with the relative pronouns.   For example, turn to the PRACTICE in

Lesson II, § 1, and recast the sentences, introducing **QUI** or **QUE**:

> **Le frère du médecin qui est ici est américain.**
> **Le café que vous voulez est sur la table.**
> **Le chapeau que j'ai est à ma soeur** (is my sister's).
> **Paris, que j'aime, est la capitale de la France.**

and so on with the other sections.   **Voilà l'auto que j'aime.**
L'autobus qui est là est le nôtre.

Vocabulary :

> **affable — compréhensible — noble — vénérable — aimable responsable—correct—direct—exact—intact—acte—un pacte —un dialecte—un insecte—un architecte—un effet—un projet—un sujet—un objet—un fait** *(fact)*—**une conférence —une différence—une expérience—une correspondance— prudent—ancien—un logement—un bombardement—un juge- ment—un gouvernement.**

Study these higher numbers:

> **vingt et un (une), vingt-deux, vingt-trois,** etc.
>   21   22   23
>
> **trente, trente et un, trente-deux, trente-trois,**
> 30   31   32   33
>
>   **trente-quatre,** etc.
>   34
>
> **quarante, cinquante, soixante, soixante-dix**
> 40   50   60   70
>   (pr. *soissante*)
>
> **soixante et onze, soixante-douze, soixante-treize,** etc.
>   71   72   73
>
> **quatre-vingts, quatre-vingt-un, quatre-vingt-deux,** etc.
>   80   81   82

quatre-vingt-dix, quatre-vingt-onze,
90   91

  quatre-vingt-douze, etc.
92

cent, cent un, cent deux, deux cents, trois cents,
100   101   102   200   300

   quatre cents, cinq cents, mille, mil
400   500   1,000

The word **MIL** (=1000) is used in writing dates: *L'an mil neuf cent cinquante trois*—The year nineteen hundred and fifty-three.

LESSON IV

§ 1. *Interrogatives—Reading French*

ALL the relative pronouns except **DONT** can be used as interrogative pronouns—that is, pronouns which ask questions: Who? Which? What? The two most useful interrogatives are **QUI**, *who?* and **QUE**, *what?*

> **Qui est là?** Who is there? **C'est moi.**
>
> **Que donnez-vous?** **Je donne de la bière.** What do you give? I give (some) beer.
>
> **Qui est-ce qui** *is also used for* Who? (*literally*, Who is it that?)
>
> **Qu'est-ce que?** What?

Then there are:

> **De qui? à qui? avec qui?** Whose, to whom, with whom?
>
> **De quoi? à quoi? avec quoi?** Of, to, with what?

Which of two? is translated by **Lequel de, laquelle de;** and **lesquels de, lesquelles de,** asks the question: *Which among many?*

QUEL, QUELLE, QUELS, QUELLES are alternatives (persons and things) for *Which one? which ones?* But **LEQUEL** is more precise, more definite, as it means *Which of two or more?*

> **Quel argent donnez-vous?** Which money do you give?
> **Je donne de l'argent anglais,** I give English money.

à qui, whose (*of things*). **À qui est cet argent?** Whose is this money? **C'est le mien.**

de qui, whose (*of persons*). **De qui est ce chauffeur?** **C'est le chauffeur du médecin.**

60

Practice

Un de vos frères est ici—lequel? C'est Jean qui est ici. Deux de ses soeurs sont ici—lesquelles? Marie et Jeanne. Lequel de vos frères est à Paris? C'est Guillaume (*William*). Qui est là? C'est lui—Charles. Pour qui est ce chapeau? C'est pour ma soeur. De quoi parlez-vous? Je parle du cinéma. A qui est ce crayon? C'est à Charles. Qu'est-ce qu'il y a sur (*on*) la table? Le livre est sur la table. Quel livre? Le livre bleu. Voici des couteaux (*knives*)—lesquels sont à vous? Les deux couteaux qui sont là sont à moi. A qui est le livre qui est sur la table? C'est à moi. Que voulez-vous, Monsieur? Je veux acheter (*to buy*) des crayons et du papier. Lequel de ces deux couteaux est à vous? Celui-là. Est-ce là votre chapeau? Oui, Madame. Voici du pain et du beurre—en voulez-vous?

Continue as before—making your own sentences.

Basic Vocabulary :

aujourd'hui, today
auprès (de), near
autant (que), as much (as)
une automobile, automobile
l'automobilisme, motoring
un automne, autumn
une autorité, authority
autour (de), around
autre, other
avec, with
avril, April
un atelier, workshop
une attaque, attack
en attendant, meanwhile
un auteur, author

autrefois, formerly
aviateur, pilot
l'aviation, flying
un athlète, athlete
avant, before
les bagages, luggage
le bain, bath
bas, low
là-bas, yonder
le bateau, boat
beau (bel, belle), beautiful
beaucoup, much
le besoin, need
le beurre, butter

READING

Mark Twain, grand écrivain américain, nous informe que la bonne éducation consiste à concilier le grand bien que nous pensons de nous-mêmes avec le peu de bien que nous pensons des autres.

Literally : Mark Twain, great American writer, informs us that (the) good education consists in conciliating (*i.e.*, reconciling) the great well (*i.e.*, good) which we think of ourselves with the little (of) good which we think of (the) others.

This is the first piece of " real " reading we have given, and for very good reasons. Your practice up to now has been concerned with acquiring sufficient knowledge of the elementary working of the language to be able to deal with simple things. We have therefore given you French for that specific purpose. But, you are getting on! From now on you will have more and more READING, and this reading will consist not of " made-up " pieces, but of excerpts from French as it is spoken and written in France today.

READING PRACTICE

When you have understood every word and every item of grammar in the above little piece—when you know its WHOLE MEANING—cover up the English and read the French, thinking *only of the French.* This is the royal road to learning.

§ 2. *Indefinite and Miscellaneous Pronouns*

There is a number of words of a pronominal nature which cannot be exactly classified, so we must put them under the heading of " Indefinite and Miscellaneous." These are nearly all very common words which recur again and again, and they must therefore be regarded as important. In this Section we are omitting the usual " Basic Vocabulary," because the list given below is essentially " basic." Here it is :

on, l'on, they, people
chacun, chacune, each
aucun, aucune, none, not one
quelqu'un } someone,
quelqu'une } anybody
quelques-uns } some
quelques-unes }
personne ne, nobody
l'un . . . l'autre, les un(e)s, les autres, the one . . . the other. Some . . . the others
l'un et l'autre, both
l'un ou l'autre, either
ni l'un ni l'autre, neither

tel, tels
telle, telles } such
plusieurs, several
la plupart (des), most (of)
quelconque, any, whatever
quiconque, whoever
tout, tous
toute, toutes } all
quelque chose, something
rien ne, nothing
le, la même, les mêmes, the same
quelque, quelques, a few
certain, certain
tout le monde, everybody (all the world)

ON is very important. You have already met this word, and now you must more closely appreciate its value. **ON** is the French equivalent for our " *One,*" " *They,*" " *People* " in such sentences as " *One stays at home in bad weather,*" " *They say that there will not be war,*" "*People are very strange at times,*" and so on. For all these, the French would use **ON**. **On dit,** *one says,* *they say.* **On dit que Monsieur Dupont est à Paris. On pense à soi-même,** *One thinks of oneself.* **On aime le sien,** *One loves one's own.* **On reste chez soi,** *One remains at home.*

L'on is employed instead of **on** after the words **et,** *and,* **si,** *if,* **ou,** *or,* **où,** *where.* Thus: **Si l'on est chez soi,** *If one is at home.* **On chante et l'on danse,** *One sings and one dances.* **Dans la maison où l'on est,** *In the house where one is.*

The other words in the list may be learned as vocabulary, and from what you have already learned of grammar, there ought not to be any great difficulties about using them. Nevertheless, it may be useful to run over a few of them for practice.

PRACTICE

Où est-ce qu'on joue au football ?   On le joue partout (*everywhere*)—en France, en Angleterre, en Amérique. Est-ce que tout le monde est heureux ?   Ah non, Monsieur !   Chacun à son goût (*taste*).   Qui sont ces deux messieurs ?   Ils sont M. Dupont et M. Boillot—l'un est riche, l'autre est pauvre.   Quelques-uns dansent, les autres parlent.   Avez-vous des crayons ?   J'en ai quelques-uns.   Il y a quelqu'un chez mon père.   Qu'est-ce que vous avez ?   Rien.   Qui est là ?   Personne.   Un certain homme qui parle bien français.   Donnez-moi quelques-uns de vos crayons.   Parlez-vous avec les enfants ?   Oui, je parle avec quelques-uns des enfants.

READING

Il existe à Paris plusieurs journaux de " grande information " et deux ou trois agences télégraphiques. Ces journaux et une grande quantité d'autres ont des services d'information très complets.   L'un de leurs rouages parmi les plus utiles est le " préfecturier."   Ce rédacteur spécial passe son existence dans un petit bureau réservé à la Préfecture de Police, boulevard du Palais.   Ses camarades appellent ce local " la cage." Ses habitants disposent d'une cabine téléphonique et sont informés de tous les événements que M. le Préfet livre à la curiosité publique.

Literally : There exist in Paris several newspapers of " great (wide) information " and two or three telegraphic agencies.   These newspapers and a great quantity of others have very complete reporting (information) services.   One of their most useful wheels (wheels among the most useful) is the " prefecturier " (the man who deals with police headquarters).   This special editor passes (spends) his existence in a little office reserved (for him) at Police Headquarters, boulevard du Palais.   His comrades call that place the " cage."   Its inhabitants have a telephone booth at their disposal and are informed about all the events which the Prefect releases to the curiosity of the public.

Words : **le journal,** newspaper, pl. **journaux.**
   le rouage, from **la roue,** the wheel, means " wheelwork,"
   hence a "part of the machinery."
  La Préfet de police, the commissioner of police.
  La Préfecture de police, headquarters of the (Paris) police.

§ 3. *Negative, Interrogative and Imperative Forms of Verbs*

You have from time to time learned various verbal forms, and
in Lesson III, § 2, you learned the present tense of the verb
PARLER. Turn to that lesson and refresh your memory
about this tense.

That is the direct form. It makes the direct statement " I
speak." There are two other forms to be learned, first the
" negative " and second the " interrogative," respectively :
" I do not speak ; Do I speak?" That little word " do " is very
useful in English, and there is nothing like it in French.

THE NEGATIVE FORM : In English, this is expressed simply
by the word " not," but in French there are *two* negative words :
NE, which is placed *before* the verb, and **PAS,** which is placed
after. Thus :

Je parle, I speak, I am speaking	**Je NE parle PAS,** I do not speak
tu parles, thou speakest	**tu NE parles PAS**
il parle, he speaks	**il NE parle PAS**
nous parlons, we speak	**nous NE parlons PAS**
vous parlez, you speak	**vous NE parlez PAS**
ils parlent, they speak	**ils NE parlent PAS**

THIS APPLIES TO EVERY VERB, AND THERE ARE NO EXCEPTIONS.

Je ne joue pas, I do not play	**Je ne pense pas,** I do not think

There are other negatives besides " not," and the same
principles apply :

NE . . . (Verb) . . .	**PLUS,**	no more, no longer
NE	„	**JAMAIS,** never
NE	„	**POINT,** not (*stronger than* ne . . pas.)

NE . . . (Verb) . . . **PERSONNE,** nobody
NE   „   **RIEN,** nothing
NE   „   **PAS ENCORE,** not yet
NE   „   **QUE,** only

Thus :

Je ne parle plus, I speak no more, I do not speak any more.
Je ne parle jamais, I never speak, I do not ever speak.
Je ne pense rien, I do not think anything (I think nothing).
Je ne joue pas encore, I do not play yet.
Je ne parle avec personne, I do not speak with anyone.

It is convenient at this point to note that "*only*" in French is expressed by **NE** before the verb and **QUE** after :

Je ne parle qu'avec mon frère, I speak only with my brother.
Je ne pense qu'à ma mère, I think only of my mother.

INTERROGATIVE : The interrogative of verbs is expressed in French simply by placing the pronoun after the verb :

Parlez-vous? Do you speak ?

Pensez-vous? Do you think ?

Euphony : For the sake of euphony, the French place a **t** between verb and pronoun when the verb ends with a vowel : **Parle-t-il?** *does he speak?* **Joue-t-il?** **Pense-t-il?**

And when the first person singular ends with *e*-mute (as is always the case in -**ER** verbs) an acute accent (') is placed over the final **e** : **Parlé-je?** *Do I speak?* **Donné-je?** *Do I give?* This form is not very common.

Do not forget that very useful interrogative which you have already learned : **Est-ce que. . . .** *Is it that?*

Est-ce que vous parlez? Do you speak ?
Est-ce que je donne? Do I give ?

NEGATIVE INTERROGATIVE: The order of words is different, and becomes:

Ne . . . (Verb) (Pronoun) **. . . PAS**
Ne donnons-nous pas? Do we not give?
Ne jouons-nous pas? Do we not play?
Ne pensez-vous pas? Do you not think?

THE IMPERATIVE: You need learn to give commands only in the second person, and for this the second person plural form is used: **Parlez!** *Speak!* **Jouez!** *Play!* **Donnez-moi,** *give me.* And in the negative **NE . . .** (Verb) **. . . PAS: Ne parlez pas,** *do not speak.* **Ne donnez pas,** *do not give.*

PRACTICE this time consists in going over previous lessons and turning positive statements into negative. Thus, beginning at Lesson I, § 4: **Le père n'est pas ici. La mère n'est jamais là. Le frère n'est pas encore ici. L'aviateur n'est plus là. La sœur ne parle pas.** And so on.

Basic Vocabulary :

le baiser, the kiss
la bière, beer
le ballon, balloon, football
le bifteck, beefsteak
la balle, bullet, ball
la balle de tennis
la blanchisserie, laundry, washing
le blé, wheat
la barbe, beard
la boîte, box, can
en boîte, canned
le bruit, noise
la bataille, battle

brûler, to burn
la bénéfice, profit
la boisson, drink
le buffet de la gare, restaurant (in railroad station)
la beauté, beauty
bon, bonne, good
le bureau, office
bien, well; **le bien,** the good
la bonne, maid
le bout, end
au bout de, at the end of
bonjour
bonsoir
bonne nuit

§ 4. **C'EST** *and* **IL EST**—*Ordinal Numbers, etc.*

" *It is* " can be stated in two ways in French: **C'EST** and **IL EST** (Pl. **CE SONT, ILS SONT**).

IL EST is used:

(1) For time. *It is one o'clock.* **Il est une heure** (*one hour*). **Il est deux heures** = *It is 2 o'clock*, etc.

(2) When an adjective which follows **EST** is followed by a phrase. **Il est bon que mon frère parle. Il est agréable de manger des bonbons,** *It is pleasant to eat sweets.* **Il est certain que Charles n'est pas chez lui,** *It is certain that Charles is not at (his) home.*

Use **C'EST** in ALL OTHER CASES:

C'est agréable. C'est moi. C'est bon. C'est le boucher *(butcher)*. **Qui est-ce? C'est Charles. Ce sont mes amis.**

Note that when an adjective which follows **EST** is itself followed by **à** or **de**, then **C'EST** is used. **C'est facile de parler,** *It is easy to speak.* **C'est difficile à jouer,** *It is difficult to play.*

ORDINAL NUMBERS, ETC.: It is quite unnecessary to learn all the ordinal numbers at this stage, but the following should be known:

1st, **premier** (f. **première**)	6th, **sixième**
2nd, **deuxième**	7th, **septième**
3rd, **troisième**	8th, **huitième**
4th, **quatrième**	9th, **neuvième**
5th, **cinquième**	10th, **dixième**
20th, **vingtième**	21st, **vingt-et-unième**
100th, **le centième**	

The first of the month is expressed by **le premier**:

le premier janvier, the 1st of January

But: **le deux janvier, le trois mai, le neuf septembre.**

QUEL JOUR DU MOIS SOMMES-NOUS? *What day of the month are we?* (is it?). **NOUS SOMMES LE DIX AVRIL.**

MISCELLANEOUS USEFUL PHRASES: **Une fois, deux fois, trois fois** (one time, two times, three times) = *once, twice, thrice,* etc.

> **LE DOUBLE,** the double
> **LA DOUZAINE,** the dozen
> **UNE PAIRE DE,** a pair of
> **LA MOITIÉ DE,** the half of
> **UNE VINGTAINE,** a score
> **UNE CENTAINE DE,** a hundred of

Time in the past is expressed by **IL Y A : il y a trois jours,** *three days ago.* **Il y a un an,** *a year ago.*

A week is often expressed by **huit jours** as well as by the word **une semaine. Il y a huit jours, il y a une semaine,** *a week ago.*

Cardinal numbers are used for kings, dates, page, chapter and verse—excepting **premier:**

Louis XIV.   Le 3 mars.   Chapitre 10.   Page 21. Edouard premier.

THE HOUR: **QUELLE HEURE EST-IL?** *What hour is it? What time is it?*

IL EST une heure, deux heures, dix heures. 1 o'clock, 2, 10.

A quarter past = **et quart** (*and a quarter*): **Il est une heure et quart.** *Half past* = **et demi** (*and a half*). **Il est une heure et demi.**

A quarter to = **moins quart** (*less a quarter*). **Il est 6 heures moins quart.** *It is a quarter to six.*

For the most part, French people use the form we use when speaking of the time of departure of trains: 5.15, 6.30, 6.45, etc. This form applies throughout to all the twenty-four hours. The French use the 24-hour clock frequently, and always for travel time tables.

Basic Vocabulary :

ce, c', this

le caleçon, drawers, pants

le caleçon de bain, bathing suit

le café

le camarade, comrade

le canard, duck

le canot, rowboat

le canotage, rowing

la carotte, carrot

la capote, soldier's overcoat

la chaise, chair

la chambre, room

le château, castle

le chanteur (*m.*), singer

la chanteuse (*f.*), singer

le chat, cat

chaud, warm, hot

la chausette, sock

la chemise, shirt

le cheval, horse

chez, the house of

la chose, thing

le cigare, cigar

la cigarette, cigarette

le cinéma, movies

cent, 100

certainement, certainly

la chance, luck

le chantier, shipyard

la cause, cause

You will find that in these lists the words are not always in alphabetical order. This does not matter, as we wish you first to concentrate on learning words which differ in the two languages.

§ 5.   *Reading French—Recapitulation*

It has been made clear to you that in this course our *first* aim is to get you quickly to the point at which you can read simple French and make sense of it. Grammar, words, phrases, and practice up to now have been chosen carefully, and are calculated to help you over the main obstacles in the elementary stage. You have already been ˙introduced to some simple reading in §§ 1–2 of this lesson. Now you may try a more difficult piece, a newspaper excerpt. Do not be surprised if you do not immediately or easily grasp the full meaning of the excerpt given below. That could hardly be expected just yet. Take it quietly, read it through once or twice with the aid of the words given beside it before you look at the translation.

CONSTANT REVIEW AND REREADING OF ALL PASSAGES FOR READING MUST BECOME A HABIT. THE OBJECT OF THE READING IS TO GET YOU ACCUSTOMED TO THE LANGUAGE AS IT IS WRITTEN BY FRENCH PEOPLE FOR FRENCH PEOPLE. DO NOT BE SATISFIED UNTIL YOU CAN READ A PASSAGE THROUGH AND UNDERSTAND IT FULLY WITHOUT THINKING OF THE ENGLISH—THIS MEANS THAT YOU WILL BE THINKING IN FRENCH.

The excerpt given below is not " made up " French, but has been taken at random from a 1948 periodical.

AU cours de l'année scolaire 1946–1947, la Correspondance scolaire internationale (C.S.I.) a mis cent mille jeunes Français en relation avec des écoliers et des étudiants étrangers de plus de cinquante nations. Elle a en outre facilité l'établissement de liens amicaux entre la jeunesse de la métropole et celle de l'Union française, entre les Corses et les Français du " continent ", entre les Alsaciens ou les Lorrains et les Français d'autres provinces.

Fondé en 1919, le bureau français de la Correspondance scolaire internationale, avait, en 1939, mis en rapports plus d'un million d'enfants français et étrangers. Interrompue pendant la guerre, son activité a repris sous la double impulsion de M. Barrier et de Mlle Brunot, fille de l'éminent philologue.

La tâche du bureau est compliquée d'éléments psychologiques. Il ne suffit pas en effet qu'il y ait entre les gens désirant correspondre équivalence numérique. Il faut " apparier " des personnes d'âge comparable, tenir compte du degré de culture, des goûts, des mentalités, des usages nationaux.

WORDS

Au cours de = in the course of.
en relation avec = in relation, contact with.
étudiants = students.
en outre = besides, furthermore.
lien = link. **amical, amicaux** = friendly.
les Corses = Corsicans.
les Lorrains = Lorrainers.
mis en rapports = put into communication, established communication.
mis = Past Participle of **mettre,** to put.
philologue = philologist.
la tâche = the task.
Il ne suffit pas = it is not enough.
en effet = in fact.
apparier = to pair, match.
tenir compte de = take into account.
le goût = the taste.

Literal Translation : In the course of the scholastic year 1946–1947, the International School Correspondence (C.S.I.) has put one hundred thousand young French people in contact with foreign scholars and students of more than fifty nations. It has furthermore facilitated the establishment of friendly links among the youth of the metropolis and that of the French Union, between Corsicans and French of the " continent " (mainland), between Alsatians or Lorrainers and the French of other provinces.

Founded in 1919, the French office of the International School Correspondence had, in 1939, put into communication (with one another) more than a million French and foreign children. Interrupted during the war, its activity has resumed under the double impulse (" drive ") of Mr. Barrier and Miss Brunot, daughter of the eminent philologist.

The task of the office is complicated by psychological elements. It is not in fact enough that there should be among people desiring to correspond a numerical equivalence. It is necessary to " match " persons of comparable (corresponding) age, (and) to take into account degree of culture, tastes, mentalities, (and) national usages (customs).

CONTINUOUS READING: Continuous reading of French written for French people is introduced in this course very much earlier than is customary, and we have not done this without a purpose. This purpose is to make you *work at reading*. To assist you in understanding every word, we provide a close, almost literal translation. From now onward, nearly all your " practice " will consist in working through the passages given for reading.

METHOD: First read the French passage, covering the translation. Try your best to understand the French without the assistance of the translation. By reading it through two or three times in this way you may be able to grasp the general sense. Then try it with the translation, noting the words you do not know. Learn these words, and then read the whole passage again—until you can understand it thoroughly. You should satisfy yourself that you can read it while *thinking only of the French*—which you must thoroughly understand—before proceeding. This must be your method from now on and until the end of the course.

NEWSPAPER EXCERPTS: Many of the passages given are excerpts from contemporary French newspapers. Some are well written, others are not; but they are the sort of French you will find in newspapers. The literal translations given are deliberately close, and if the original French in the newspaper excerpts is sometimes vague, the translation will follow it.

PART II

THE FRAMEWORK OF THE LANGUAGE

LESSON V

§ 1. *The Essentials of the Verb*

THE verb is the word of *being* or *doing*. Thus, *to sit, to eat, to walk, to fly,* I *run,* she *sings* : sit, eat, walk, fly, run, sings—all these are verbs.

The French verb is more complex than the English : it has more forms and " inflexions." But it is not necessary to know all the forms and inflexions of the French verb : one can get along well with a mastery of less than half of them. The student must concentrate on these essentials until later in the course, when the less commonly used forms will be given for reference and for those who wish to complete and perfect their knowledge. One MUST KNOW the following parts of every verb :

THE INFINITIVE : The part of the verb which does not name any person or thing. Thus *to speak, to eat.* French verbs have one of the following four endings in the infinitive : **-ER, -IR, -OIR, -RE. PARLER,** *to speak*; **FINIR,** *to finish*; **RECEVOIR,** *to receive*; **VENDRE,** *to sell.* The majority of French verbs end in **-ER.** All new verbs added to the language end in **-ER** : **téléphoner,** *to telephone. All* **-ER** *verbs are regular*, except **ALLER,** *to go*, and **ENVOYER,** *to send*; they will be dealt with in § 5 of this lesson.

PRESENT PARTICIPLE : This corresponds to the English ending -ING : speakING. It has **-ANT** for ending in French : **parlANT.**

PAST PARTICIPLE AND PAST TENSE : *I have spoken—spoken* is the past participle. It is used as in English to form compound tenses, and its commonest usage is to form the ordinary past tense in French : **J'ai parlé,** *I have spoken*—is nearly always used for our *I spoke* or *I have spoken.* This is very important.

PRESENT TENSE : *I speak, I eat, I am speaking, I am eating*—all are represented by only one form in French : **Je parle, je mange,** etc.

FUTURE TENSE: *I shall speak, I shall eat*, etc.: **Je parlerAI, je mangerAI.** The future tense is formed by adding to the "root" of the verb the present tense of **AVOIR,** *to have.* (See next section.)

AUXILIARY VERBS: The two verbs **AVOIR,** *to have,* and **ÊTRE,** *to be,* are called auxiliaries because with them compound tenses of *all* verbs can be made.

Thus, what you have to learn first will consist of selected parts of the verbs **AVOIR, ETRE, PARLER, FINIR, RECEVOIR** and **VENDRE.**

CONTINUOUS READING: In this and the next three lessons we are going to give you some "continuous reading" from Alphonse Daudet's famous and entertaining novel TARTARIN DE TARASCON.

¶ 1. TARTARIN DE TARASCON

Premier épisode—à Tarascon

Ma première visite à Tartarin de Tarascon est restée
My first visit to Tartarin of Tarascon has remained
dans ma vie comme une date inoubliable ; il y a douze ou
in my life as an unforgettable date ; it is twelve or
quinze ans de cela, mais je m'en souviens mieux que
fifteen years since that, but I remember it better than
d'hier. L'intrépide Tartarin habitait alors, à l'entrée de
yesterday. The intrepid Tartarin was living, then, at the entrance of
la ville, la troisième maison à main gauche sur le chemin
the town, the third house to (the) left hand on the Avignon
d'Avignon. Jolie petite villa tarasconnaise avec jardin
road. (A) pretty little Tarasconian villa with garden
devant, balcon derrière, des murs très blancs, des per-
in front, a balcony behind, (some) very white walls, green
siennes vertes, et sur le pas de la porte une nichée de
(Venetian) shutters, and on the doorstep a cluster of little
petits Savoyards jouant à la marelle ou dormant au bon
Savoyards playing hopscotch or sleeping in the good

soleil, la tête sur leurs boîtes à cirage. Du dehors, la
sunshine, the (their) head on their boxes for boot polish. From out-
maison n'avait l'air de rien. Jamais on ne se serait cru
side the house looked nothing. Never would one have believed
devant la demeure d'un héros. Mais quand on entrait,
oneself before the dwelling of a hero. But when one entered,
coquin de sort! . . . De la cave au grenier, tout le bâti-
ye gods! . . . From (the) cellar to (the) garret, all the build-
ment avait l'air héroïque, même le jardin! O le jardin
ing had an heroic look, even the garden! Oh the (that) garden
de Tartarin, il n'y en avait pas deux comme celui-là en
of Tartarin, there were not two like that in
Europe. Pas un arbre du pays, pas une fleur de France;
Europe. Not a local tree, not a flower of France;
rien que des plantes exotiques . . . à se croire en pleine
nothing but exotic plants . . . to (make one) believe oneself right in
Afrique centrale à dix mille lieues de Tarascon.
central Africa (at) ten thousand leagues from Tarascon.

Basic Vocabulary:

causer, to chat
le châtiment, punishment
chaque, each
le charpentier, carpenter
charmant, charming
chausser, to put on one's shoes
chef, chief, head
chef de bureau, head of an office
le chiffre, figure, estimate
le chocolat, chocolate
le chou-fleur, cauliflower
le cirque, circus
cirer, to shine shoes
combien, how much?
comme, as
commencer, begin
commode, convenient, comfortable
la connaissance, knowledge
le cuisinier, cook
le cou, neck
cultiver, cultivate
coûter, to cost
cher, dear
coûter cher, to cost dearly, to be expensive
le crayon, pencil
la couleur, color
le couloir, corridor
le civil, civilian
le citoyen, citizen
la civilisation

§ 2. *The Auxiliary Verb* AVOIR

AVOIR, *to have*, is an irregular verb, and the essential parts *must be memorized*, as they cannot be formed by following certain rules, as with regular verbs.   The following must be known :

Present Tense	*Past Tense*
j'ai, I have	**j'ai eu,** I had *or* I have had
tu as, thou hast	**tu as eu**
il a, elle a, he has, she has	**il a eu, elle a eu**
nous avons, we have	**nous avons eu**
vous avez, you have	**vous avez eu**
ils, elles ont, they have (*m. and f.*)	**ils ont eu, elles ont eu**

Present Participle : **AYANT,** having
Past Participle : **EU,** had (*pronounce* U)

Future Tense

j'aurai, I shall have
tu auras, thou wilt have
il aura, he will have
nous aurons, we shall have
vous aurez, you will have
ils auront, they will have

You will quickly see how useful this verb is going to be, and hence how vitally important it is to know the above parts.   You see above that the past tense is made with the present plus the past participle.   With the future tense plus the past participle you can make the " future anterior "—**j'aurai eu,** *I shall have had.*   And you will see later, when you learn the regular verbs **PARLER, FINIR, RECEVOIR,** and **VENDRE,** that you will be able to make for all verbs all the compound tenses you are likely to require.

IDIOMATIC USE OF **AVOIR :** Instead of using the verb *to be,* the French use **AVOIR** for the following :

AVOIR FROID, to be cold	**AVOIR CHAUD,** to be hot
AVOIR SOIF, to be thirsty	**AVOIR FAIM,** to be hungry

AVOIR TORT, to be wrong **AVOIR RAISON,** to be right
AVOIR PEUR (DE), to be **AVOIR SOMMEIL,** to be
afraid (of) sleepy
AVOIR ENVIE (DE), to feel **AVOIR HONTE (DE),** to be
inclined (to) ashamed (of)

And for age : *I am twenty-five years old*—**j'ai vingt-cinq ans.**
Thus : **J'ai froid—il a peur—elle a soif—vous avez
raison.**

And in French **AVOIR MAL A** (*to have ill at*) means there is
something wrong with the part of the body mentioned : **j'ai mal
à la tête,** *I have a headache.* **Il a mal au pied,** *He has a pain
in his foot,* or, *There's something the matter with his foot.*

¶ 2. TARTARIN DE TARASCON

Tout cela, bien entendu, n'était pas de grandeur natur-
All that, of course, was not of natural (full) size ;
elle ; ainsi les cocotiers n'étaient guère plus gros que des
thus the coconut trees were scarcely bigger than
betteraves, et le baobab (arbre géant) tenait à l'aise dans
beetroots, and the baobab (a giant tree) held (grew) comfortably in
un pot de réséda ; mais c'est égal ! pour Tarascon, c'était
a mignonette pot ; but all the same ! for Tarascon, that was
déjà bien joli, et les personnes de la ville, admises le
already quite pretty, and the people of the town, admitted on
dimanche à l'honneur de contempler le baobab de Tartarin,
Sunday to the honor of contemplating Tartarin's baobab,
s'en retournaient pleines d'admiration.
went away from it full of admiration.

Pensez quelle émotion je dus éprouver ce jour-là en
Think what emotion I must have experienced that day
traversant ce jardin mirifique ! . . . Ce fut bien autre
going through that wonderful garden ! . . . It was quite another
chose quand on m'introduisit dans le cabinet du héros.
matter when I was introduced into the hero's private room.

Ce cabinet, une des curiosités de la ville, était au fond
This sanctum, one of the curiosities of the town, was at the bottom

du jardin, ouvrant de plain-pied sur le baobab par une
of the garden, opening on a level to the baobab by a
porte vitrée.
glass door.

Imaginez-vous une grande salle tapissée de fusils et de
Picture to yourself a big hall (room) adorned with guns and
sabres, depuis en haut jusqu'en bas ; toutes les armes de
sabres, from top to bottom, all the arms of
tous les pays du monde : carabines, rifles, tromblons,
all the countries of the world, carbines, rifles, blunderbusses,
couteaux corses, couteaux catalans.
Corsican and Catalan knives.

Basic Vocabulary :

le climat, climate
le client, customer
climatisé, acclimatized, *also*
    air-conditioned
la colle, paste, glue
le coiffeur, barber, hair-
    dresser
la colline, hill
le commandant, major, com-
    mander
complètement, completely
comme ci comme ça, so-so
le compte, account
le compte en banque, bank
    account
le conseil, council, *also*
    counsel, advice

la constitution
content, satisfied
(au) contraire, (on the) con-
    trary
le coq, cock
la corbeille, basket
la corbeille à papier, waste-
    paper basket
le cordonnier, shoemaker
le côté, side
se coucher, to go to bed
le canif, penknife
la course, race, course
le couteau, knife
le courrier, mail, letters

IMPORTANT NOTE
Translations of Reading Matter

In this lesson you have begun to read Daudet's novel **Tartarin
de Tarascon.** For purposes of " continuous reading " twenty-
two extracts from it are provided—twelve with an interlinear
translation, ten with the translation underneath.

☞ ALL TRANSLATIONS THROUGHOUT THIS COURSE ARE *LITERAL* AND NOT LITERARY.

The object of providing you with close translations is to help you to understand each word of the original French as you meet it in the reading. Once you have grasped the meaning, you may find it an interesting exercise to turn the literal translation into one that is literary—that is, free and idiomatic and in English such as an English-speaking author might write. Here, is a free translation of ¶¶ 1–2 of **Tartarin de Tarascon:**

¶ 1. My first visit to Tartarin of Tarascon has remained as an unforgettable date in my life; it was twelve or fifteen years ago, but I remember it better than yesterday. The dauntless Tartarin was then living in the third house on the left side of the Avignon Road at the entrance to the town. It was a pretty little Tarasconian villa with a garden in front, a balcony behind, very white walls, green Venetian shutters, and a cluster of brats playing hopscotch on the doorstep or sleeping in the broad sunshine with their heads on their boot-polish boxes. The house looked of no account from the outside. You would not have thought yourself before the residence of a hero. But when you went in, ye gods! . . . the whole building had an heroic appearance, even the garden! . . . Oh, that garden of Tartarin, there was no other like it in Europe. Not a local tree, not a French flower —none but exotic plants . . . so that you fancied yourself right in central Africa ten thousand leagues distant from Tarascon.

¶ 2. Of course all this growth was not of natural size. Thus, the tropical palms were hardly bigger than beets, and the giant baobab was easily accommodated in a mignonette pot. But, all the same, for Tarascon it was quite pretty as it was, and the townsfolk, who on Sundays were allowed in to have the honor of beholding Tartarin's baobab, returned from it full of admiration. Think of the emotion I must have experienced that day walking through that wonderful garden. It was quite another matter when I was introduced into the hero's private sanctum. One of the curiosities of the town, this sanctum was at the bottom of the garden and opened through a glass door on a level with the baobab. Imagine a large room bedecked from top to bottom

with guns and sabres : all the arms of all the countries in the
world—carbines, rifles, blunderbusses, Corsican knives, and
Catalan knives. . . .

§ 3. *The Auxiliary Verb* ÊTRE

With **AVOIR,** the auxiliary verb **ÊTRE** is one of the commonest in the language. Present Participle : **étANT.** Past
Participle : **été.**

Present Tense	*Past Tense*
je suis, I am	**j'ai été,** I have been, I was
tu es, thou art	**tu as été,** etc.
il, elle est, he, she, is	
nous sommes, we are	
vous êtes, you are	
ils, elles sont, they are	

Future Tense : **je serAI, tu serAS, il serA, nous serONS,
vous serEZ, ils serONT.**

At this point you should turn back to Lesson IV, § 3, and go
over again the negative and interrogative forms. Your practice
now should consist in applying those principles to **AVOIR** and
ÊTRE :

> **Ai-je? Je n'ai pas. Vous n'avez pas. N'avez-vous
> pas? Avez-vous froid? Non, j'ai chaud. Quel âge
> avez-vous? Je n'ai pas encore 19 ans.**

You have already learned the form **il y a,** *there is* or *there are.*
The infinitive is **Y AVOIR,** *there to be,* and you can use it throughout all the forms of **AVOIR. Il y aura,** *there will be.* **Il y a eu,**
there was. **Il y avait,** means *there was*—in a continuous or
" imperfect " sense.

¶ 3. TARTARIN DE TARASCON

Par là-dessus, un grand soleil féroce qui faisait luire
Over it all (fell) a great fierce sunlight which made shine
l'acier des glaives et les crosses des armes à feu, comme
the steel of the blades and the butts of firearms, as

pour vous donner encore plus la chair de poule. Ce qui
if to give you still more the creeps (chicken flesh). What
rassurait un peu pourtant, c'était le bon air d'ordre et de
reassured a little, however, was the good orderly appearance and
propreté qui régnait sur toute cette yataganerie. Tout y
tidiness which reigned over all that caboodle. Everything there
était rangé, soigné, brossé, étiqueté comme dans une phar-
was set in place, looked after, brushed (and) labelled as in a
macie ; de loin en loin, un petit écriteau bonhomme sur
drugstore; from place to place (i.e., at long intervals) a nice little
lequel on lisait :
placard on which one read :

FLECHES EMPOISONNÉES, N'Y TOUCHEZ PAS !
POISONED ARROWS, DO NOT TOUCH !

Ou :
Or :

ARMES CHARGÉES, MÉFIEZ-VOUS !
LOADED ARMS, BE CAREFUL !

Sans ces écriteaux, jamais je n'aurais osé entrer. Au
But for those tickets, I should never have dared to enter. In the
milieu du cabinet, il y avait un guéridon. Sur le guéridon,
middle of the room, there was a pedestal table. On the table,
un flacon de rhum, une blague turque, les Voyages du
a decanter of rum, a Turkish tobacco pouch, the Voyages of
capitaine Cook, les romans de Cooper, de Gustave Aimard,
Captain Cook, the novels of Cooper, of Gustave Aimard,
des récits de chasse, chasse à l'ours, chasse au faucon,
accounts   of   hunting,   bear hunting,   falcon hunting,
chasse à l'éléphant, etc. . . . Enfin, devant le guéridon,
elephant-hunting, etc. . . . Lastly, in front of the table,
un homme était assis, de quarante à quarante-cinq ans,
a   man   was   seated,   of   forty   to   forty-five   years,
petit, gros, trapu, rougeaud, en bras de chemise, avec des
small, stout, thickset, ruddy, in shirt sleeve(s), with

caleçons de flanelle, une forte barbe courte et des yeux
flannel drawers (pants), a strong, short beard and flaming
flamboyants.
eyes.

Basic Vocabulary:

la cuisine, kitchen, cookery
le coup, blow, stroke
couper, to cut
la coupe de cheveux, haircut
court, short
la croix, cross
le courage, courage
le cousin, cousin
courir, to run
croire, to believe
une cuiller, spoon
cuir, to cook

tout à coup, suddenly
le coup de téléphone, telephone call
le coup de pied, kick
coûter bon marché, to cost
cheap, to be inexpensive
crier, to cry, to yell
la dame, lady
la dactylo, typist
dangereux, dangerous
dans, in
le débit, retail shop
débit de tabac, tobacco shop

§ 4. *Regular Verb* PARLER

From now on, whenever necessary, we shall give you the
principal parts of each verb in the following form:

> *Infinitive:* **PARLER.** *Present Participle:* **PARLANT.**
> *Past Participle:* **PARLÉ.**
> *Present Tense:* **je parle.** *Future Tense:* **je parlerai.**

But we shall state them thus: **Parler, parlant, parlé, je
parle, je parlerai.**

As already noted, the majority of the verbs in the language
end in **-ER.** It is therefore highly important for you to know
the conjugation of **-ER** verbs:

> *Present Tense:* **je parle, tu parles, il parle, nous parlons,
> vous parlez, ils parlent.**

Note: In Lesson III, § 1, we mentioned **tu,** *thou,* and stated
that you would not require it for some time. Nor will you.
But, we have decided to give this form throughout the verbs
because it is very easily learned with the others and it comes into

reading very much. Yet you must not forget that it is a *familiar* form and that you must yourself always use the polite form **vous**. For a long time, it is safer to leave **tu** to be used by the French themselves; but you must know what they are talking or writing about.

PARLER, *Past Tense :* **j'ai parlé, tu as parlé,** etc.
Future : **je parlerai, tu parleras,** etc.

TABLE OF CONJUGATION—*For Reference only :*

Pronoun	Present	Imperfect	Future	Ending of Past Participles
je	-e	-ais	-ai	-ER verbs all end in -É. -IR, -OIR, -RE verbs vary and have past participles in -I, -U, -S, and -T
tu	-es	-ais	-as	
il, elle	-e, -t, -d	-ait	-a	
nous	-ons	-ions	-ons	
vous	-ez	-iez	-ez	
ils, elles	-ent	-aient	-ont	

The future tense regular is formed by adding the above endings to the infinitive : **PARLER, JE PARLERAI.** The imperfect tense is given above for reference, as it is always regular and fairly often used. You should be able to recognize it.

IMPERATIVE : This is the same as the present tense, but without the pronoun : **Parlez !** Speak ! You need know only this second person plural form.

BASIC VOCABULARIES : With each section is given a number of " basic " words. Learn as many as you can, and go back over them all from time to time. But don't let them worry you !

¶ 4. TARTARIN DE TARASCON

D'une main il tenait un livre, de l'autre il brandissait
With one hand he held a book, with the other he brandished
une énorme pipe à couvercle de fer, et, tout en lisant je
an enormous pipe with an iron cap, and, while reading, I do not
ne sais quel formidable récit de chasseurs de chevelures,
know what formidable recital (fearsome account) of hunters of scalps,

il faisait, en avançant sa lèvre inférieure, une moue terri-
he made, in putting out his lower lip, a terrifying pout,
ble, qui donnait à sa brave figure de petit rentier taras-
which gave to his honest face of a Tarasconian man of little
connais ce même caractère de férocité bonasse qui
means that same character of kindly ferocity which
régnait dans toute la maison.
reigned in all the house.

    Cet homme, c'était Tartarin, Tartarin de Tarascon,
    That man was Tartarin, Tartarin of Tarascon,
l'intrépide, le grand, l'incomparable Tartarin de Tarascon.
the intrepid, the great, the incomparable Tartarin of Tarascon.

Basic Vocabulary :

debout, upright, standing up
déjà, already
le petit déjeuner, breakfast
le déjeuner, lunch
demander, to ask (for)
demander à un agent, to ask
  a policeman
le demi, the half
démolir, to demolish
démoli, broken down
la démocratie, democracy
déranger, to disturb
se déranger, to disturb oneself
descendre, to go down
désirer, to want
se déshabiller, to undress

le dessert, dessert
détruire, to destroy
la dette, debt
devenir, to become
Qu'est-il devenu ? What has
  become of him ?
devoir, to have to, to owe
on dit, they say
le diable, devil
le Dieu, God
Mon dieu ! Good gracious !
Dieu merci ! Thank
  heavens !
dire, to say
Vous dites ? You say ?
le directeur, manager
diriger, to direct, to guide

§ 5. **-ER** *Verbs conjugated unlike* **PARLER**

  ALLER, *to go*: **allant, allé, je vais, j'irai.**

  Present Tense : **je vais, tu vas, il va, nous allons, vous**
  allez, ils vont.

  Future : **j'irai, tu iras, il ira, nous irons, vous irez, ils**
  iront.

Compound tenses of **ALLER** (and of all verbs of motion) are made with **être**. Thus, *I have gone, I went :* **je suis allé.**

ENVOYER is conjugated like **PARLER** excepting the future, which is : **j'enverrai, tu enverras,** etc. There is no other irregularity.

-ER VERBS—PECULIARITIES : There are some **-ER** verbs which have what may be called peculiarities rather than irregularities. These peculiarities apply to other verbs, and are chiefly related to euphony. The following should be noted :

Verbs ending in **-CER** change the **C** to **Ç** before **A** and **O.**

Thus **PLACER,** *to place :* **Je place, tu places, il place, nous plaçons, vous placez, ils placent.**

Verbs in **-GER,** add **e** before **a** and **o** : **MANGER,** *to eat,* **nous mangeons.**

And note that, similarly for euphony, in verbs such as **SEMER,** *to sow,* when a part of the verb ends in *e*-mute or a silent syllable, the *e* preceding the consonant changes to **è.** Thus : **il sème,** *he sows,* **ils sèment.** Note also : **POSSÉDER, je possède,** etc. Verbs in **-OYER, -UYER,** change the **y** to **i** before *e*-mute : **PLOYER,** *to bend,* **je ploie.** With **-AYER** verbs this is optional, so that one writes either **je payerai** or **je paierai.**

APART FROM THE ABOVE IRREGULARITIES AND PECULIARITIES, ALL VERBS ENDING IN **-ER** ARE REGULAR AND FOLLOW THE MODEL OF **PARLER.**

AGREEMENT OF PAST PARTICIPLE : The French past participle agrees in gender and number with a *direct* object which has preceded it in a sentence. Thus, in the sentence *I have bought an apple,* apple is the direct object coming after the verb, and there is no change in the past participle : **j'ai acheté une pomme.** But in the sentence *There is the apple (which) I have bought,* this direct object precedes, and therefore there is agreement of the past participle : **Voilà la pomme que j'ai achetée.** And : **Combien de pommes avez-vous achetées ?** *How many apples have you bought?* The same rule applies to compound tenses : **Les pommes que j'ai vues acheter,** *The apples I have seen bought.*

¶ 5. TARTARIN DE TARASCON

Au temps dont je vous parle, Tartarin de Tarascon
At the time of which I speak to you, Tartarin of Tarascon
n'était pas encore le Tartarin qu'il est aujourd'hui, le
was not yet the Tartarin (which) he is today, the
grand Tartarin de Tarascon, si populaire dans tout le midi
great Tartarin of Tarascon, so popular in all the South
de la France. Pourtant—même à cette époque—c'était
of France. However—even at that time—he was
déjà le roi de Tarascon.
already (the) king of Tarascon.

Disons d'où lui venait cette royauté.
Let us tell whence came to him this royalty (royal rank).

Vous saurez d'abord que là-bas tout le monde est chas-
You shall know to begin with that thereabouts everybody is (a)
seur, depuis le plus grand jusqu'au plus petit. La chasse
hunter, from the biggest down to the smallest. Hunting is the
est la passion des Tarasconnais, et cela depuis les temps
passion of the Tarasconians, and that (has been so) since mythological
mythologiques où la Tarasque faisait les cent coups dans
times when the Tarasconian dragon wrought havoc in the
les marais de la ville et où les Tarasconnais d'alors organi-
marshes of the town (and) where the then Tarasconians organized
saient des battues contre elle. Il y a beau jour, comme
beats (hunts) against it. It is a long time ago, as
vous voyez.
you see.

Donc, tous les dimanches matin, Tarascon prend les
So, every Sunday morning, Tarascon takes up arms
armes et sort de ses murs, le sac au dos, le fusil sur l'épaule,
and goes out from its walls, gamebag on back, gun on shoulder,
avec un tremblement de chiens, de furets, de trompes, de
with a hurly-burly of dogs, ferrets, trumpets,
cors de chasse. C'est superbe à voir. . . . Par malheur,
hunting horns. It is wonderful to see. . . . By bad luck (unhappily),
le gibier manque, il manque absolument.
game is lacking, lacking absolutely.

Si bêtes que soient les bêtes, vous pensez bien qu'à la
However stupid the beasts may be, you (can) well think that in the
longue elles ont fini par se méfier.
long run they finished by taking care (distrusting).

Basic Vocabulary :

distributeur automatique, slot machine.

la dizaine, ten of

le docteur, doctor

c'est dommage, it's a pity

je voudrais bien, I should much like to

donner, to give

dormir, to sleep

sans doute, doubtless

je n'en doute pas, I don't doubt it

droit, right (*also* **le droit,** the law)

à droite, to the right

tout droit, straight on, ahead

dur, hard

dû, had to (*Past Part. of* **devoir**)

Nous aurions dû voir, We ought to have seen

échapper, to escape

l'écoute, listening (in)

un écran, screen (movies)

un écrivain, writer

Eh bien ! Well ? And so ?

une église, church

électrique, electric

élever, to bring up, to educate

embarquer, to embark

s'embarquer, to take a ship, boat

un emploi, a job, employment

un employé, employee, clerk

enchanté, delighted

encore, yet, still

pas encore, not yet

LESSON VI

§ 1. *Verbs ending in* -IR, -OIR *and* -RE : **LA RADIO**

I. *Principal Parts :* **FINIR**, to finish, **finiSSANT**, **fini**, **je finiS**, **je finirAi**.

It will be noted that this differs from **PARLER** chiefly by the introduction of the **-SS-**.

> *Present Tense :* **je finis, tu finis, il finiT, nous finiSSons, vous finiSSez, ils finiSSent.**
> *Past Tense :* **j'ai fini, tu as fini,** etc.

HAÏR, *to hate*, is regular excepting in a few forms, the most important of which is the Present Indicative *singular* : **je hais, tu hais, il hait.** But : **nous haïssons, vous haïssez, ils haïssent.**

II. *Principal Parts :* **RECEVOIR**, to receive, **recevant, reçu, je reçois, je recevrai.**
> *Present Tense :* **je reçois, tu reçois, il reçoit, nous recevons, vous recevez, ils reçoivent.**

III. *Principal Parts :* **VENDRE**, to sell, **vendant, vendu, je vends, je vendrai.**
> *Present Tense :* **je vends, tu vends, il vend, nous vendons, vous vendez, ils vendent.**
> *Future Tense :* **je vendrai, tu vendras,** etc.

You have now had models of the four regular conjugations and, with the rules given for the formation of compound tenses, you should be able to form the various parts of regular verbs, which are the majority in the language. There are a number of irregular verbs ending in **-IR, -OIR** and **-RE,** and later you will be given a list of those which you must regard as essential.

LISTENING TO THE RADIO AND TO SPOKEN FRENCH: Although there is still much that you have to learn of essential grammar and "basic" vocabulary, what you have already been given should justify you at this stage in making some effort to listen to radio broadcasts in French. As you listen, make every possible effort to catch words. If you can catch a word here or there, this is encouraging. If not, try again. Gradually, your ear will become accustomed to the French sounds, and in time you will find yourself able to get the gist of what is spoken.

At the back of this book you will find a list of stations throughout the United States which carry programs in French. Look up your city in this list to see if any of its stations have such programs. Or, you may be able to pick up a French short-wave broadcast. If you live near the Canadian border in the northeastern part of the country, you might be able to tune in on a Canadian station which broadcasts in the French language. Whenever you get the chance to do so, listen to some of these broadcasts. Some of the programs which you may hear are:

Bulletins d'information—"The News"
Commentaires des Nouvelles—News Commentaries
Revues de Presse—Press Summaries

Although listening to the radio is an excellent way to get practice in listening to French, it is not the only way. Joining a club or engaging in a group activity in which you will hear people speak French, and get a chance to talk in French yourself, is a very good way to become fluent in the language. In the United States, there are branches of the Alliance Francaise throughout the country. This French organization brings together people who share an interest in French culture and the French language. It also gives its members a chance to speak and to hear conversational French.

¶ 6. TARTARIN DE TARASCON

A cinq lieues autour de Tarascon, les terriers sont vides,
For five leagues around Tarascon, the burrows are empty,
les nids abandonnés. Pas un merle, pas une caille, pas
the nests abandoned. Not a blackbird, not a quail, not
le moindre lapereau, pas le plus petit cul-blanc.
the smallest young rabbit, not the smallest wheat-ear (bird).

Elles sont cependant bien tentantes, ces jolies collinettes
They are, however, very tempting, those pretty Tarasconian
tarasconnaises, toutes parfumées de myrte, de lavande, de
hillocks,   all   perfumed   with   myrtle,   lavender,
romarin ; et ces beaux raisins muscats gonflés de sucre,
rosemary ; and those fine muscatel grapes blown out (full) of sugar,
qui s'échelonnent au bord du Rhône, sont diablement ap-
which, spaced along the bank of the Rhône, are devilishly ap-
pétissants aussi. . . . Oui, mais il y a Tarascon derrière,
petising also. . . . Yes, but there is Tarascon behind (all this)
et dans le petit monde du poil et de la plume, Tarascon
and in the little world of fur and feather, Tarascon
est très mal noté. Les oiseaux de passage eux-mêmes
is   very   ill-noted.   The   very   birds   of   passage
l'ont marqué d'une grande croix sur leurs feuilles de
have marked it with a big cross on their itineraries,
route, et quand les canards sauvages, descendant vers la
and when the wild ducks going down toward the
Camargue en longs triangles, aperçoivent de loin les
Camargue   in   long   triangles,   see   from   afar   the
clochers de la ville, celui qui est en tête se met à crier bien
steeples of the town, the one which is leading (at the head) begins to
fort : " Voilà Tarascon ! . . . voilà Tarascon ! " et toute
cry loudly : " There is Tarascon ! . . . there is Tarascon ! " and
la bande fait un crochet.
the whole band makes a swerve (goes in a roundabout way).

Basic Vocabulary :

encore mieux, still better	**entendu,** understood
un ennemi, enemy	**bien entendu,** of course
une encre, ink	**un enthousiasme,** enthusiasm
faire enregistrer, to register	**entier,** entire, full
s'engager, to enlist	**entre,** between
enlever, to take away	**un entr'acte,** intermission
ensemble, together	**j'ai envie de,** I would like to
ensuite, next, following	**une équipe,** team
entrer, to enter, go in	**l'Espagne,** (*f.*) Spain
une entrée, way in, entry	**espagnol,** Spanish

espérer, to hope
est-ce que, is it that?
environ, about
aux environs (de), near, round about
un étage, floor, story (of a house)

et caetera
un état, state
les États-Unis, *(m.)* United States
éteindre, to put out a light or fire
un été, summer

§ 2. *Reflexive Verbs*

When we say in English *to wash oneself*, or *I wash myself*, the action is both performed and suffered by the subject. A verb of this nature is called a " reflexive verb." There are many such verbs in French, **SE LAVER,** *to wash oneself*, being a good example. They may be called reflexive verbs *proper*.

But French differs from English in that it has what may conveniently be called reflexive verbs *by nature*. Thus, in English the verb *to rejoice, to be very pleased*, has nothing reflexive in its nature, but the French equivalent is **SE RÉJOUIR** (conjugated like **FINIR**).

Present Tense	*Future Tense*
je me réjouis, I rejoice	**je me réjouirai,** etc.
tu te réjouis	
il, elle se réjouit	
nous nous réjouissons	
vous vous réjouissez	
ils, elles se réjouissent	

COMPOUND TENSES OF REFLEXIVE VERBS ARE MADE WITH **ÊTRE** and not **AVOIR**. There is no exception to this rule. Thus :

> **je me suis réjoui,** I have rejoiced
> **tu t'es réjoui, il s'est réjoui,** etc.

NEGATIVE : **je ne me réjouis pas, tu ne te réjouis pas,** etc.

INTERROGATIVE : The only part you need learn at this stage is the second person plural : **Vous réjouissez-vous ?** *Do you rejoice?*

PRACTICE : Take the reflexive verb **SE LAVER,** *to wash oneself*, and make up the various forms as given above for **SE**

RÉJOUIR. Work out the French for the following : *Do you wash yourself? I have not washed myself. I shall wash myself. Did he wash himself? Who washed himself?*

LISTENING TO SPOKEN FRENCH: Have you tried to listen to French radio programs or to French records? You can help yourself learn to pick up words by jotting down the ones you recognize as you listen. Even if at this stage you can catch very few words, you can note the pronunciation of certain difficult sounds such as nasals, **u** and **-tion** *seeon(g)* at the end of words. If you do this you are not wasting time, and you will be somewhat surprised to find that this can get you into the habit of pronouncing sounds correctly. LISTEN AND IMITATE, even when you do not fully understand. You will recognize simple expressions even now. You will also hear the *rhythm* of French speech, and, highly important, the *intonation.*

¶ 7. TARTARIN DE TARASCON

Bref, en fait de gibier, il ne reste plus dans le pays qu'un
In short, in the matter of game, there remains in the (that) country
vieux coquin de lièvre, échappé comme par miracle aux
only an old rogue of (a) hare, escaped as by (a) miracle from the
septembrisades tarasconnaises et qui s'entête à vivre là !
Tarasconian (September) massacres and who is determined to live
A Tarascon, ce lièvre est très connu. On lui a donné un
there ! In Tarascon, this hare is well known. They have given him
nom. Il s'appelle le *Rapide*. On sait qu'il a son gîte
a name. He is called Rapid. It is known that he has his resting-
dans la terre de M. Bompard,—ce qui, par parenthèse, a
place in M. Bompard's land —which, by the way, has
doublé et même triplé le prix de cette terre,—mais on n'a
doubled even tripled the price of that land —but they have
pas encore pu l'atteindre. A l'heure qu'il est même, il
not yet been able to get at him. At this very time, there
n'y a plus que deux ou trois enragés qui s'acharnent après
are not more than two or three fanatics who persist after him. The
lui. Les autres en ont fait leur deuil, et le *Rapide* est
others have made their mourning for him (given him up) and Rapid

passé depuis longtemps à l'état de superstition locale, bien
has long since passed into the state (realm) of local superstition,
que le Tarasconnais soit très peu superstitieux de sa nature
although the Tarasconian is very little superstitious by (his) nature
et qu'il mange les hirondelles en salmis, quand il en
and   eats   swallow   stew   when   he   can   find
trouve.
any.

  —Ah çà! me direz-vous, puisque le gibier est si rare à
  " Now then !" you will say to me, "since game is so rare in
Tarascon, qu'est-ce que les chasseurs tarasconnais font
Tarascon,   what   do   the   Tarasconian   huntsmen   do   then
donc tous les dimanches ?
all the (every) Sunday(s) ?"

Basic Vocabulary :

être, to be	**la faiblesse,** weakness
un étudiant, student	**la faim,** hunger
étudier, to study	**faire,** to make, to do
s'excuser, to excuse oneself	**faire mal à,** to do bad to
excusez-moi, excuse me	**faire laver son linge,** to get
exactement, exactly	one's laundry done
exister, to exist	**un fait,** a fact
l'Europe, (*f.*) Europe	**falloir,** to be necessary
la face, face, front	**il faut,** it is necessary
en face de, in front of	**il fallait,** it was necessary
la façon, the making, manner	**il faudra,** it will be necessary
de façon à, so as to	**il a fallu que,** it was necessary
facilement, easily	that . . .
facile, easy	**fatigué,** tired
le facteur, postman	**la femme,** woman, wife
faible, weak	**la fenêtre,** window

§ 3. *The Passive—Impersonal Verbs*

When we say *I am given, I am praised, I am spoken to,* this is
called the " passive " form of the verb. It is a form much
more used in English than in French, but because you will meet
it in reading and speech, we must mention it briefly. The

passive form is made with the auxiliary verb **être** and the past participle of the principal verb. Thus **être donné,** *to be given*; **être loué,** *to be praised*.

Present Tense : **je suis loué,** I am praised, **tu es loué.**

English *by* with the passive, as in *I am praised by* . . . is expressed in French by **DE** if it is a question of a feeling or a mental act and by **PAR** if it is a physical act : **je suis loué de tout le monde,** *I am praised by everybody.* **Paris a été pris par les allemands,** *Paris has been (was) taken by the Germans.*

The negative and interrogative forms are quite regular : **je ne suis pas loué. Ne suis-je pas loué ?**

If the subject is feminine, the past participle is in the feminine. Thus, a female person would write : **je suis louée.**

However, this form is little used, and in speaking or writing you can avoid it altogether by using **ON** (*one, they, people*) with **AVOIR.** Thus, instead of saying *I was praised, I was told,* you can say *One told me, People praised me :* **On m'a dit ; on m'a loué.** This is the form most used in everyday speech. **On dit que Madame Dupont n'est plus chez elle,** *It is said that Mme Dupont is no more at home.*

IMPERSONAL VERBS : Certain verbs are called " impersonal " when they express an action which has no reference to a subject or object. Thus : *it rains, it is necessary, it seems.* These verbs are impersonal. You should know the following : **Il pleut,** *it rains, it is raining.* **Il a plu,** *it has rained.* **Il pleuvra,** *it will rain.* **PLEUVOIR** is *to rain,* and one can say : **il va pleuvoir,** instead of **il pleuvra,** for *It is going to rain.* You should also know **FALLOIR,** *to be necessary.* **Il faut,** *it is necessary.* **Il a fallu,** *it was necessary.* **Il faudra,** *it will be necessary.*

Note also : **NEIGER,** *to snow*; **il neige,** *it snows.* **GELER,** *to freeze*; **il gèle,** *it freezes.* And : **il suffit,** *it suffices*—**il semble,** *it seems*—**il arrive,** *it happens*—**il s'agit,** *it is a matter of*—**il vaut,** *it is worth*—**il reste,** *there remains.* **Il y a, il y aura, il y a eu.**

¶ 8. TARTARIN DE TARASCON

Ce qu'ils font ? Eh mon Dieu ! ils s'en vont en pleine
What do they do ?   Good Heavens ! they go out in the full (open)
campagne, à deux ou trois lieues de la ville. Ils se réunis-
country two or three leagues from the town.   They gather
sent par petits groupes de cinq ou six, s'allongent tranquille-
together in small groups of five or six, spread themselves out peace-
ment à l'ombre d'un puits, d'un vieux mur, d'un olivier,
fully in the shadow of a well, of an old wall, of an olive tree,
tirent de leurs carniers un bon morceau de boeuf en daube,
draw from their gamebags a good piece of braised beef,
des oignons crus, un saucissot, quelques anchois, et com-
raw onions, a sausage (long, dry), some anchovies, and begin
mencent un déjeuner interminable, arrosé d'un de ces
an interminable luncheon, washed down with one of those
jolis vins du Rhône qui font rire et qui font chanter. Après
nice Rhône wines which incite (to) laughter and singing.   After
quoi, quand on est bien lesté, on se lève, on siffle les chiens,
which, when they are well fed, they get up, whistle (for) the
on arme les fusils, et on se met en chasse. C'est-à-dire
dogs, load the guns, and set about the hunt.   That is to say that
que chacun de ces messieurs prend sa casquette, la jette
each one of those gentlemen takes (off) his cap, throws it
en l'air de toutes ses forces et la tire au vol avec du 5, du
in the air with all his strength and fires at it in flight with No. 5,
6 ou du 2,—selon les conventions.
6 or 2 shot—according to the conventions.

Celui qui met le plus souvent dans sa casquette est
He who puts (a shot) most often into the cap is
proclamé roi de la chasse, et rentre le soir en triomphateur
proclaimed king of the hunt, and returns (in) the evening as victor
à Tarascon, la casquette criblée au bout du fusil, au milieu
(triumphantly) to Tarascon, his riddled cap on the end of his gun, amid
des aboiements et des fanfares.
barkings and fanfares.

Basic Vocabulary:

la ferme, farm	**fou (folle),** mad
fermer, to shut	**la maison de fous,** insane
fiancé (*m.*), engaged man	asylum
finir, to finish	**frais, fraîche,** fresh
la fièvre, fever	**français,** French
le filet, net	**le franc,** franc
le film, film	**La France,** France
la fleur, flower	**le frère,** brother
le fils, son	**froid,** cold
la fille, daughter	**le fromage,** cheese
la fin, end	**le fruit,** fruit
le fond, bottom	**frit,** fried
la force, strength	**le feu,** fire
fort, strong	**avoir froid,** to be cold
former, to form	**la friction,** scalp massage
formidable	

§ 4. *Irregular Verbs*

You now come to what has been regarded by students as the bugbear of French : the irregular verbs. A full list gives about 400 of them!* There is one great comfort which a careful scrutiny of that list soon provides : many of them are hardly ever used. A list of the very commonest in everyday usage is what you need, and this, with the simplification of the verb already given, means that there is nothing in the least formidable in store for you so far as these verbs are concerned. A warning is, however, necessary. Some of the irregular verbs are among the commonest in general usage, *basic* in every sense. They are indicated in large type in what follows. Only the principal parts are given.

IRREGULAR VERBS IN **-ER** (see Lesson V, § 5): **ALLER** and **ENVOYER.**

IRREGULAR VERBS IN **-IR** :

COURIR, to run   **courant, couru, je courS, je courrAI**
DORMIR, to sleep   **dormant, dormi, je dorS, je dormirai**

* Bellows' Dictionary (see p. 158) has a good list, which you will one day need.

MENTIR, to tell lies   **mentant, menti, je menS, je mentirai**

Partir, to depart, set out   is conjugated like **MENTIR : je pars,** etc.

Sentir, to feel   like **MENTIR. Je sens,** etc.

Servir, to serve   like **MENTIR. Je sers,** etc.

MOURIR, to die   **mourant, mort, je meurs, tu meurs, il meurt, nous mourons, vous mourez, ils meurent**

OUVRIR, to open   **ouvrant, ouvert, j'ouvre, j'ouvrirai**

Couvrir, to cover   like **OUVRIR. je couvre,** etc.

Offrir, to offer   like **OUVRIR. j'offre,** etc., **j'ai offert**

Souffrir, to suffer   like **OUVRIR**

SORTIR, to go out   **sortant, sorti, je sors, tu sors, il sort, nous sortons, vous sortez, ils sortent**

Do not forget that ALL VERBS OF MOTION ARE CONJUGATED WITH **ÊTRE** and not **AVOIR.** Thus :

     je suis parti, I set out, departed

     je suis sorti, I have gone out

VENIR, to come   **venant, venu, je viens, tu viens, il vient, nous venons, vous venez, ils viennent**

     Future : **je viendrai.** And note : **je suis venu.**

Tenir, to hold   like **VENIR. je tiens,** etc.

VÊTIR, to clothe   All you need know is the past participle : **vêtu,** a useful word. **Je suis vêtu de noir.**

This is your first list and, sooner or later, the various forms must be memorized. But take them gently. You will find that certain principles run through even the irregular verbs, and that, all in all, they are not nearly so difficult as they first seem to be.

§ 5. *Irregular Verbs*—contd.

IRREGULAR VERBS IN **-OIR :**

DEVOIR, to owe, to have to   **devant, dû, je dois, tu dois, il doit, nous devons, vous devez, ils doivent**

     Future : **je devrai**

FALLOIR, to be necessary

Past Participle: **fallu. Il faut,** it is necessary

Future: **il faudra** (*Impersonal*)

PLEUVOIR

pleuvant, plu, il pleut, il pleuvra (*Impersonal*)

POUVOIR, to be able (physically)

pouvant, pu, je puis, tu puis, il peut, nous pouvons, vous pouvez, ils peuvent

Note that in the negative present it is usual to say and write : **je ne peux pas,** etc., but **je ne puis.**

Future: **je pourrai**

SAVOIR, to know

sachant, su, je sais, tu sais, il sait, nous savons, vous savez, ils savent

Future: **je saurai**

VALOIR, to be worth

valant, valu, je vaux, tu vaux, il vaut, nous valons, vous valez, ils valent

Future: **je vaudrai**

Not much used except in the forms : **il vaut,** it is worth, **il vaudra,** it will be worth, **il a valu,** it was worth

VOIR, to see

voyant, vu, je vois, tu vois, il voit, nous voyons, vous voyez, ils voient

Future: **je verrai**

VOULOIR, to be willing

voulant, voulu, je veux, tu veux, il veut, nous voulons, vous voulez, ils veulent

Future: **je voudrai**

A useful verb in this category is reflexive : **S'ASSEOIR,** *to sit down, to be seated.*

Present Participle: **s'asseyant.**

Past Participle: (**s'être) assis.**

Present Tense: **je m'assieds, tu t'assieds, il s'assied, nous nous asseyons, vous vous asseyez, ils s'asseyent.**

Future: **je m'assiérai.**

Imperative: **asseyons-nous,** let us sit down.

asseyez-vous, be seated, sit down.

CONTINUOUS READING: You will notice that, as you become acquainted with these irregular verbs—and from your knowledge of the regular verbs—the reading becomes steadily easier. But don't expect it to be very easy just yet. This continuous reading is important, as it serves to drive home all that you have learned. It must, for a time, be your *main practice* in the language. It is important, however, that you continue to listen to records and, when possible, to radio programs, and that you go to French movies. This book will teach you written French, but never forget that printed matter is not spoken matter. You must *hear* French in order to learn to speak it, and these are the best substitutes for actual conversation with French people.

¶ 9. TARTARIN DE TARASCON

Inutile de vous dire qu'il se fait dans la ville un grand
Needless to tell you that in the town is done a great
commerce de casquettes de chasse. Il y a même des
business in (of) hunting caps. There are even
chapeliers qui vendent des casquettes trouées et déchirées
hatters who sell caps with holes and torn in
d'avance à l'usage des maladroits ; mais on ne connaît
advance for the use of the unskillful ones; but one hardly knows
guère que Bézuquet, le pharmacien, qui leur en achète.
anybody but Bézuquet the druggist who buys them.
C'est déshonorant !
That is dishonorable!

Comme chasseur de casquettes, Tartarin de Tarascon
As a hunter (marksman) of caps, Tartarin de Tarascon
n'avait pas son pareil. Tous les dimanches matin, il
had not his equal. Every Sunday morning, he
partait avec une casquette neuve ; tous les dimanches soir,
went out with a new cap ; every Sunday evening,
il revenait avec une loque. Dans la petite maison du
he returned with a rag. In the little house of the
baobab, les greniers étaient pleins de ces glorieux trophées.
baobab, the attics were full of those glorious trophies.

Aussi, tous les Tarasconnais le reconnaissaient-ils pour
Also,　all　the　Tarasconians　recognized　him　as
leur maître, et comme Tartarin savait à fond le code du
their master, and as Tartarin knew profoundly the hunts-
chasseur, qu'il avait lu tous les traités, tous les manuels
man's code, as he had read all the treatises, all the manuals
de toutes les chasses possibles, depuis la chasse à la
of　all　(kinds　of)　hunts　possible,　from　hunting　the
casquette jusqu'à la chasse au tigre birman, ces messieurs
cap　to　hunting　the　Burmese　tiger,　those　gentlemen
en avaient fait leur grand justicier et le prenaient pour
had　made　him　their　great　judge　and　took　him　for
arbitre dans toutes leurs discussions.
arbitrator in all their arguments.

Tous les jours, de trois à quatre, chez l'armurier Coste-
Every　day,　from　three　to　four,　at　Costecalde　the
calde, on voyait un gros homme, grave et la pipe aux
gunsmith's, was seen a stout man, stern and with a pipe between
dents, assis sur un fauteuil de cuir vert, au milieu de la
his teeth, seated on an armchair of green leather, in the
boutique pleine de chasseurs de casquettes, tous debout et
middle of the shop full of cap-marksmen, all standing and
se chamaillant. C'était Tartarin de Tarascon qui rendait
wrangling.　It　was　Tartarin　of　Tarascon　who　delivered
la justice, Nemrod doublé de Salomon.
justice, Nimrod doubled by Solomon.

Basic Vocabulary :

faire noir, to get dark
s'en faire, to worry
Que faire ? What's to be
done ?
Qu'est-ce que cela fait ?
What does it matter ?
cela ne fait rien, it does not
matter
faire attention, to pay attention

faire partir, to send away
　(also, to fire, discharge)
gagner, to win, gain
gai, gay
garçon, boy, waiter
garçon de bureau, office boy
gaieté, joy
garer, to park a car
le garage, garage
la gare, railway station

le chef de gare, stationmaster
le gâteau, cake
gauche, left, awkward
à gauche, to the left
gentil, nice
gentiment, nicely
geler, to freeze
la géographie, geography

le golf, golf
le grade, grade, rank
général (-ale, -aux), general
le général, general
en général, in general
grand, great, big, tall
pas grand'chose, nothing much

LESSON VII

§ 1. *Irregular Verbs in* -RE

The irregular verbs in this group are very important, many of them being "basic" words by almost any test. You are not expected to learn all these lists of irregularities at this stage. But you should be able to recognize any of these forms in reading, so as at least to be able to get an idea of the meaning. Let memorizing be a gradual process.

Irregular Verbs in -RE :

BOIRE, to drink — **buvant, bu, je bois, je boirai (bu** is used for " drunk ")

CONNAÎTRE, to be acquainted with — **connaissant, connu, je connais, je connaîtrai**

CONDUIRE, to lead — **conduisant, conduit, je conduis, je conduirai**

CRAINDRE, to fear — **craignant, craint, je crains, tu crains, il craint, nous craignons, vous craignez, ils craignent**

Future : **je craindrai**

CROIRE, to believe — **croyant, cru, je crois, je croirai**

CUIRE, to cook — like **CONDUIRE.** cooked = **cuit**

DIRE, to say, tell — **disant, dit, je dis, tu dis, il dit, nous disons, vous dîtes, ils disent**

Future : **je dirai**

ECRIRE, to write — **écrivant, écrit, j'écris, j'écrirai**

FAIRE, to make, to do, to cause to — **faisant, fait, je fais, tu fais, il fait, nous faisons, vous faites, ils font**

Future : **je ferai**

LIRE, to read — **lisant, lu, je lis, je lirai**

METTRE, to put — **mettant, mis, je mets, je mettrai**

PARAÎTRE, to appear — like **connaître**

PLAIRE — **plaisant, plu, je plais, tu plais, il plait, nous plaisons, vous plaisez, ils plaisent**

Future : **je plairai**

PRENDRE, to take — **prenant, pris, je prends, tu prends, il prends, nous prenons, vous prenez, ils prennent**

Future : **je prendrai,**

COMPRENDRE, *to understand,* is like **PRENDRE**

RIRE, to laugh — **riant, ri, je ris, tu ris, il rit, nous rions, vous riez, ils rient.**

Future : **je rirai**

ROMPRE, to break — This is regular except : **il, elle rompt,** he, she, breaks

SUFFIRE, to suffice — **suffisant, suffi, je suffis, tu suffis, il suffit, nous suffisons, vous suffisez, ils suffisent**

Future : **je suffirai**

SE TAIRE, to be silent — like **PLAIRE. Taisez-vous !** Shut up! Hold your tongue !

VIVRE, to live — **vivant, vécu, je vis, tu vis, il vit, nous vivons, vous vivez, ils vivent.**

Future : **je vivrai**

This concludes the fourth and last group of essential irregular verbs and, as already made clear, *all* these verbs and their irregularities will have to be known sooner or later. There is no need to disguise the fact that this part of the course relating to the verb is not easy : French people often make mistakes in the verbal forms. But you must make your best effort to master the *general principles*, and can be assured that, if you do this, you will find yourself steadily becoming familiar with the irregularities through meeting them in reading.

¶ 10. TARTARIN DE TARASCON

A la passion de la chasse, la forte race tarasconnaise
To the passion for hunting, the strong Tarasconian race
joint une autre passion : celle des romances. Ce qui se
joins (adds) another passion : that for ballads. What is
consomme de romances dans ce petit pays, c'est à n'y pas
consumed (practiced, sung) in ballads in that little locality is not

croire.   Toutes les vieilleries sentimentales qui jaunissent
to be believed.   All the old sentimental stuff(s) which grow(s) yellow
dans les plus vieux cartons, on les retrouve à Tarascon
in the oldest portfolios, are (is) to be found in Tarascon
en pleine jeunesse, en plein éclat.   Elles y sont toutes,
in (their) full youth, in full burst (blast).   They are all there,
toutes.   Chaque famille a la sienne, et dans la ville cela
all (of them).   Each family has its own, and in the town that
se sait.   On sait, par example, que celle du pharmacien
is known.   It is known, for instance, that that of the pharmacist
Bézuquet, c'est :
Bezuquet is :

> **Toi, blanche étoile que j'adore**
> *Thou, white star that I adore*

> **Celle de l'armurier Costecalde :**
> *That of Costecalde the gunsmith :*
> **Veux-tu venir au pays des cabanes?**
> *Wouldst thou come to the land of cabins?*

> **Celle du receveur de l'enregistrement :**
> *That of the official registrar :*
> **Si j'étais-t-invisible, personne n'me verrait.**
> *If I was invisible, nobody would see me.*
>
> > **(Chansonnette comique)**
> > *(Comic Song)*

Et ainsi de suite pour tout Tarascon.   Deux ou trois fois
And so on for the whole of Tarascon.   Two or three times
par semaine, on se réunit les uns chez les autres et on se
per week, there was a gathering of some in each others' houses and
les chante.   Ce qu'il y a de singulier, c'est que ce sont
they were sung.   What is singular (about it) is that they are
toujours les mêmes, et que, depuis si longtemps qu'ils se
always the same ones, and that for however long that they
les chantent, ces braves Tarasconnais n'ont jamais envie
sing them together, those worthy Tarasconians never wish to
d'en changer.
change them.

§ 2. *Adverbs*

Just as the adjective is a word which qualifies a noun, so an adverb is a word which qualifies or modifies a verb.

First Rule: The majority of French adverbs are formed by adding **-MENT** to the feminine of the adjective. Thus: **doux**, feminine **douce** ("*sweet*"). Adverb: **doucement. Heureux, heureusement. Courageux, courageusement.** The **-MENT** in French corresponds to *-ly* in English: *sweet, sweetly. Happy, happily. Courageous, -ly.*

Second Rule: If an adjective ends in a vowel, simply add **-MENT : facile, facilement ; vrai, vraiment.**

Third Rule: If an adjective ends in **-ANT**, or **-ENT**, the adverb is formed by cutting off the **-ANT** or **-ENT** and adding **-AMMENT, -EMMENT : constant, constamment ; prudent, prudemment.**

Certain adjectives, for euphony, take an **é** before the **-MENT.** The following are the most useful: **commun, communément ; précis, precisément ; énorme, énormément.**

Comparatives and superlatives are formed as in adjectives (see Lesson II, § 5):

| **facilement** | **plus facilement** | **le plus facilement** |

But the following are irregular:

bien, well	**mieux,** better	**le mieux,** the best
mal, badly	**pis,** worse	**le pis,** the worst
peu, little	**moins,** less	**le moins,** the least
beaucoup, much	**plus,** more	**le plus,** the most

And note:

> **tant pis,** so much the worse; **tant mieux,** so much the better

A few adjectives are not changed when they become adverbs: **vite,** *quick;* **fort,** *strong;* **haut,** *high, loud;* **bas,** *low;* **soudain,** *sudden;* **exprès,** *expressly, purposely;* and, most important, **DROIT,** *straight*—as in **tout droit,** *straight ahead ;* **droit devant vous,** *straight before you.*

In this brief statement you have the essentials relating to the formation of the adverb. One other thing must, however, be known: its position 'in the sentence. This is quite simple. It comes *after* a simple verb or the auxiliary: **Il a bien parlé. Vous ne le faites pas souvent. Vous le trouvez facilement. Cet homme a beaucoup parlé.**

Bien and **trop** precede an infinitive, but all other adverbs follow it: **Il a peur de trop oublier,** *He is afraid to forget too much.* **On lui a demandé de bien écrire,** *He has been asked to write well.*

¶ 11. TARTARIN DE TARASCON

On se les lègue dans les familles, de père en fils, et
They are willed down in families, from father to son, and
personne n'y touche ; c'est sacré. Jamais même on ne
nobody touches (alters) them ; it is (all) sacred. Never does
s'en emprunte. Jamais il ne viendrait à l'idée des Coste-
one even borrow (from) one. Never would it come into the Coste-
calde de chanter celle des Bézuquet, ni aux Bézuquet de
caldes' thoughts to sing the Bézuquets', nor into the Bézuquets'
chanter celle des Costecalde. Et pourtant vous pensez
to sing the Costecaldes'. And however you think (would think)
s'ils doivent les connaître depuis quarante ans qu'ils se
that they must know them after forty years that they are
les chantent. Mais non ! chacun garde la sienne et tout
singing them. Not at all ! Each one keeps his own and
le monde est content. Pour les romances comme pour
everybody is satisfied. For ballads as in regard to
les casquettes, le premier de la ville était encore Tartarin.
caps, the first (foremost) of the town was still Tartarin.
Sa supériorité sur ses concitoyens consistait en ceci :
His superiority over his fellow citizens consisted in this :
Tartarin de Tarascon n'avait pas la sienne. Il les avait
Tartarin of Tarascon had not (one of) his own. He had them
toutes. Toutes !
all. All !

Seulement c'était le diable pour les lui faire chanter.
Only it was the (very) devil to make him sing them.

Revenu de bonne heure des succès de salon, le héros
Returning early from drawing-room successes, the hero
tarasconnais aimait bien mieux se plonger dans ses livres
of Tarascon liked very much better to dive into his books
de chasse ou passer sa soirée au cercle que de faire le joli
about hunting or pass his evening at the club than to
cœur devant un piano de Nîmes, entre deux bougies de
play the ladies' man before a Nîmes piano, between two Tarascon
Tarascon.
candles.

Basic Vocabulary:

gris, grey
la grève, strike
la guerre, war
gratter, to scrape
le gratte-ciel, skyscraper
un habit, dress, costume
habiter, to dwell, live
les habits, clothes
habituer, to accustom
habitué, accustomed
un haricot, a bean, a stew
les haricots verts, French beans
haut, high
en haut, above, upstairs
au haut de, at the top of

tout haut, aloud
heureux, happy
heureusement, happily
un hiver, winter
un homme, man
un honneur, honor
hors d'œuvres, side dishes
humide, damp
une horloge, a (big) clock
une idée, idea
une image, picture
immédiatement, immediately
un incendie, fire
une infirmière, nurse
une indépendence, independence

§ 3. *Reference List of Essential Adverbs*

As already explained in the previous section, the majority of French adverbs can be formed from adjectives. But there is a list of very common adverbs to which this does not apply. These words are given in the " Basic Vocabulary," and you will have learned or will learn them there and in the reading. Nevertheless, because they are so common, and so very useful, a list is given here to which you can refer and quickly refresh your memory.

Relating to Place:

où, where — d'où, whence — ici, here—d'ici, hence
là there — là-bas, yonder — près d'ici, near here
y, there — par ici, this way — par là, that way
ailleurs, elsewhere — dessous, underneath — dessus, above
en haut, above, up-stairs — en bas, downstairs, below — dedans, inside
dehors, outside — derrière, behind — par derrière, from behind
devant, before — près, auprès (de), near (to) — proche, close to, close by
quelque part, some-where — nulle part, nowhere — loin, far off
ensemble, together.

Relating to Time:

quand, when — combien de temps, how long — aussitôt, as soon as
aujourd'hui, today — hier, yesterday — avant-hier, day before yesterday
demain, tomorrow — après-demain, day after tomorrow — bientôt, soon
trop tôt, too soon — tard, late — d'abord, at first
depuis, since — à present, maint-enant, now, at present — quelquefois, some-times
— — en train de, in the course of
autrefois, formerly — alors, then — puis, then
après, after(wards) — enfin, at last — de bonne heure, early
tôt, soon — plus tôt, sooner — souvent, often
longtemps, for a long time — toujours, always — déjà, already
jamais, ever, never — encore, still, yet — pas encore, not yet
— ne . . . jamais, never — à jamais, for ever

Affirmation and Negation:

oui, yes (si, after a negative) — non, no — peut-être, perhaps
certainement, cer-tainly — presque jamais, hardly ever — ne . . . pas, not
— ne . . . plus, no . . . more — non plus, neither, either
ne . . . point, a stronger form of ne . . . pas — pas du tout, not at all — point du tout, strong-er than pas du tout.
— ne . . . rien, nothing —

GENERAL :

comment ? how ?	combien ? how much	beaucoup, much
trop, too much	tant, so much, many	peu, little
bien, well, *also* very	très, very	plus, more
moins, less	tout, quite, wholly	tout à fait, quite
presque, almost	environ, about	à peu près, almost
si, so	ainsi, thus	aussi, also
autant, as much	plutôt, rather	surtout, above all
au plus, at most	seulement, only	même, even
pas même, not even	pas seulement, not only	ne . . . que, only
à peine, scarcely	en effet, really	peu à peu, little by little
à la fois, at a time	en même temps, at the same time	sans doute, without doubt
à droite, to the right	à gauche, to the left	tout droit, straight ahead

¶ 12.   TARTARIN DE TARASCON

Ces parades musicales lui semblaient au-dessous de
Those   musical   parades   seemed   to   him   beneath
lui. . . . Quelquefois cependant, quand il y avait de la
him. . . . Sometimes,   however,   when   they   were   having
musique à la pharmacie Bézuquet, il entrait comme par
music at Bézuquet the druggist's shop, he went in as if by
hasard, et après s'être bien fait prier, consentait à dire le
chance, and after having had himself well besought, consented to say
grand duo de Robert le Diable, avec madame Bézuquet
(do) the grand duet Robert the Devil with Madame Bézuquet,
la mère. . . . Qui n'a pas entendu cela n'a jamais rien
the mother. . . . Who (ever) has not heard that has never heard
entendu. . . . Pour moi, quand je vivrais cent ans, je
anything. . . . For myself, if I should live 100 years, I
verrais toute ma vie le grand Tartarin s'approchant du
should see all my life the great Tartarin going to the
piano d'un pas solennel, s'accoudant, faisant sa moue, et
piano with solemn step, leaning (on it), making his pout, and
sous le reflet vert des bocaux de la devanture, essayant
under the green reflection of the display bottles in the window
de donner à sa bonne face l'expression satanique et
trying to give to his face the satanic and fierce mien (expres-

farouche de *Robert le Diable*.   A peine avait-il pris posi-
sion) of Robert the Devil.   *Hardly had he taken his posi-*
tion, tout de suite le salon frémissait ;   on sentait qu'il
tion (than) immediately the room (audience) quivered ;   one
allait se passer quelque chose de grand. . . . Alors, après
felt that something great was going to happen. . . . Then, after
un silence, madame Bézuquet la mère commençait en
a silence, Madame Bézuquet the mother began in (while) accompanying
s'accompagnant :
herself :

> **Robert, toi que j'aime**
> *Robert, thou whom I love*
> **Et qui reçus ma foi,**
> *And who receivedst my faith (troth),*
> **Tu vois mon effroi (bis),**
> *Thou seest my fright (twice)*
> **Grâce pour toi-même**
> *Mercy for thyself*
> **Et grâce pour moi.**
> *And mercy for me.*

Basic Vocabulary :

une indication, sign (road)
une influence, influence
inspirer, to inspire
un instant, instant
intelligent, intelligent
interdit, prohibited
intéresser, to interest
intéressant, interesting
inutile, useless
jeune, young
une jeune fille, girl
joli, pretty
le jour, day
les jumelles, twins (girls),
 also binoculars
le jus, juice

jusque, until, as far as
jusqu'ici, until here, now
jusque là, until there, then
le kilo, le kilogramme
le kilomètre
là, there
là-bas, yonder
là-haut, up there
laisser, to let, allow
le lait, milk
le lac, lake
laid, ugly
la langue, tongue, language
large, broad
la larme, tear
laver, to wash

§ 4. *Prepositions*

A preposition is a word which helps to express the relations which certain words have to one another (see Lesson II, § 1). For example : *He is at the door. She is in the room. At* and *in* are prepositions. These words are invariable—that is, they have none but the one form. If a preposition relates to more than one word, it must be repeated before each word in French : *I have traveled by land and sea*: **j'ai voyagé par terre et par mer.**

LIST OF USEFUL PREPOSITIONS (for reference):

à, at	**après,** after	**avant,** before (of time)
contre, against	{**dans,** in (precise) / **en,** in (vague)	**de,** of, from
		derrière, behind
devant, before (place)	**pendant,** during	**depuis,** since
entre, between	**envers,** towards	**jusque,** until, as far as
vers, toward	**avec,** with	**chez,** at the house of
parmi, among	**sous,** under	**sur,** on
voici, here is, are	**voilà,** there is, are	**à côté de,** beside, next to
au-dessous de, under	**au-dessus de,** over	**au lieu de,** instead of
en face de, opposite	**loin de,** far from	**près de,** near
excepté, excepting	**malgré,** in spite of	**par,** by
sans, without	**selon,** according to	**pour,** for
à travers, through		

You will notice that some of these words have already been given with the adverbs—the reason is that some words can be both prepositions and adverbs.

You will also have noticed that you have made the acquaintance of many of these words in the lessons. They also come into

your " Basic Vocabularies." You were informed in the first
lesson that certain words would recur again and again; here
you see it working out. This provides you with a means for the
repetition necessary to memorize the material given and, in the
reading, you see it all in practice. We have for this very reason
deliberately refrained from giving you more than an absolute
minimum of those " made-up exercises." In this course we
have tried to get you to deal with *real French* from the earliest
possible moment, and that is why you now have some real
French to read with each section of each lesson. This is far
the best of all " exercises," the best possible practice in the
language. By the way, it is assumed that you are making every
effort to listen to some French daily. If you have been doing
this, you ought soon to be able to catch more than isolated
sounds or isolated words. Your aim, of course, must be to
catch whole sentences.

¶ 13. TARTARIN DE TARASCON

A voix basse, elle ajoutait : " A vous, Tartarin," et Tartarin
de Tarascon, le bras tendu, le poing fermé, la narine frémissante,
disait par trois fois d'une voix formidable, qui roulait comme un
coup de tonnerre dans les entrailles du piano : " Non ! . . .
non ! . . . non ! . . ." ce qu'en bon Méridional il prononçait,
" Nan ! . . . nan ! . . . nan ! " Sur quoi madame Bézuquet la
mère reprenait encore une fois :

> *Grâce pour toi-même*
> *Et grâce pour moi.*

" Nan ! . . . nan ! . . . nan ! . . ." hurlait Tartarin de plus
belle, et la chose en restait là. . . . Ce n'était pas long, comme
vous voyez : mais c'était si bien jeté, si bien mimé, si diabolique,
qu'un frisson de terreur courait dans la pharmacie, et qu'on lui
faisait recommencer ses : " Nan ! . . . nan ! . . . nan ! " quatre
et cinq fois de suite.

Là-dessus Tartarin s'épongeait le front, souriait aux dames,
clignait de l'œil aux hommes, et, se retirant sur son triomphe,

s'en allait dire au cercle d'un petit air négligent : " Je viens de
chez les Bézuquet chanter le duo de *Robert le Diable !* "

Et le plus fort, c'est qu'il le croyait !

TRANSLATION : *In a low voice she added : " Your turn, Tartarin,"
and Tartarin of Tarascon, arm(s) outstretched, fist closed, nostril
quivering, said three or four times in a powerful voice which rolled like
a thunderclap in the bowels of the piano: "No! . . . No! . . .
No !" which in good southern speech he pronounced " Naw ! . . .
Naw ! . . . Naw !" On which Madame Bézuquet the mother
repeated once again :*

> Mercy for thyself
> And mercy for me.

*" Naw ! . . . Naw ! . . . Naw !" roared Tartarin still louder,
and there the matter ended. . . . It was not long, as you see ; but
it was so well thrown (done), so well mimed, so diabolical, that a
shudder of terror ran through the druggist's shop, and they made him
begin again his : " Naw ! . . . Naw ! . . . Naw !" four or five
times running.*

*Thereupon Tartarin sponged his brow, smiled at the ladies, winked
his eye at the men and, withdrawing on his triumph, went out to
tell the club with a slightly offhand air : " I have just sung at the
Bézuquets' the* Robert the Devil *duet."*

And what is strongest (the joke is) is that he believed it !

Basic Vocabulary :

le légume, vegetable
les légumes, vegetables, greens
lent, slow
lentement, slowly
la lettre, letter
une lettre par avion, air mail letter
libre, free
lieutenant, lieutenant
le linge, laundry, clothes
le lion, lion
la limite, limit
le lit, bed
le livre, book
la livre, pound

loin (de), far (from)
long, longue, long
la location, rental
lorsque, at the time that, when
le loup, wolf
Lyon, Lyons
Madame
Mademoiselle
Monsieur
la machine
le magasin, store, shop
mais, but
la maison, house
maintenant, now
le maître, master
la maîtresse, schoolmistress

§ 5. *Conjunctions—Interjections*

Conjunctions are words used to connect other words or sentences. Thus: *you and I.* "And" is a conjunction. *He came but I did not see him*—"but" is a conjunction. These are also invariable words, and their usage is generally straightforward, as it is in English. But they are so common that you must *now* memorize this list:

et, and	**et . . . et,** both . . . and	**aussi,** also
car, for	**comme,** as	**donc,** then
mais, but	**ni,** neither	**ou,** either
quand, when	**que,** that	**si,** if
puisque, since	**quoique, bien que,** although	**aussitôt que,** as soon as
de manière que, so that	**lorsque,** when	**parce que,** because
	pourtant, yet, however	**puis,** then
ainsi, thus		**savoir,** namely

At this point we are able to give you some cheerful information. In the material already presented in these seven lessons you have an outline of the absolute essentials of French grammar. We would almost be ready to claim that, if you knew this amount of grammar *perfectly*—that is to say, if you could use it spontaneously without having to puzzle it out in your head each time you tried to make a sentence—you would possess a very useful working instrument, one which would carry you a long way. But, of course, we do not expect anything like that at this stage. You still require much practice in reading to drive it all home thoroughly. No doubt you have by now appreciated the importance of the reading, which—presented as it is here, with a careful, literal translation—should now be a pleasure rather than a task. It is, alas, unfortunately true that a foreign language cannot be learned without this preliminary stage of hard work and concentration. We would offer one hint. If you are not in a great hurry to get on—and we have advised you to "hasten slowly"—you would gain much at this point by devoting a week entirely to review of grammar. You will probably be able to pick up the time later.

INTERJECTIONS: These are common words used as exclamations in conversation. For example: **Attention!** *Look out! Pay attention there!* **Bon! Très bien! Bien!** *Good! Very good! That's good! Fine! O.K.!* **Assez!** *Enough of that!* **Pas possible!** *Not possible! You don't say so!* **Comment!** *How is that!* **Allons donc!** *Now then* (tell that to the marines!) **Vraiment?** *Really?* And the French often say **"Mon Dieu!"** when we would say "*Good gracious!*" Never translate it by *My God!*

¶ 14. TARTARIN DE TARASCON

C'est à ces différents talents que Tartarin de Tarascon devait sa haute situation dans la ville.   Du reste, c'est une chose positive que ce diable d'homme avait su prendre tout le monde.   A Tarascon, l'armée était pour Tartarin.   Le brave commandant Bravida, capitaine d'habillement en retraite, disait de lui: " C'est un lapin ! " et vous pensez que le commandant s'y connaissait en lapins, après en avoir tant habillé.

La magistrature était pour Tartarin.   Deux ou trois fois, en plein tribunal, le vieux président Ladevèze avait dit, parlant de lui : " C'est un caractère ! "

Enfin le peuple était pour Tartarin.   Sa carrure, sa démarche, son air, un air de bon cheval de trompette qui ne craignait pas le bruit, cette réputation de héros qui lui venait on ne sait d'où, quelques distributions de gros sous et de taloches aux petits décrotteurs étalés devant sa porte, en avaient fait le lord de l'endroit, le Roi des halles tarasconnaises.

TRANSLATION : *It was (due) to those different talents that Tartarin of Tarascon owed his high position in the town.   Moreover, it is a positive thing that this devil of a man had known how to take (in) everybody.   In Tarascon the army was for Tartarin.   The worthy commandant Bravida, Clothing Department captain in retirement, said of him : " He's a lad ! " (rabbit) and you think (know) that the commandant knew about lads (rabbits) after having clothed so many of them.*

The magistrature was on Tartarin's side.   Two or three times in open court the old chairman Ladevèze had said, speaking of him : " He's a character ! "

Lastly, the people were for Tartarin. His broad shoulders, his walk, his air, an air of a good trumpet-horse which does not fear noise, that reputation of a hero which came to him nobody knows whence, some distributions of pennies and clouts to ragamuffins stretched (basking) before his door, had made him lord of the place, king of the Tarasconian markets.

Basic Vocabulary :

malade, sick, ill
le malade, invalid
la maladie, sickness
malheureusement, unhappily
la malle, trunk
la mallette, suitcase
manger, to eat
la manière, manner, way
de toutes les manières, in every way
la manufacture, factory
la marche, march, hike
le mari, husband
se marier, to marry
marié, married

le marin, sailor
la marine, navy
Marseille, Marseilles
le match, game, match
le matelot, sailor
mauvais, bad
mécanique, mechanical
meilleur, better
le membre, limb
même, same
de même, the same
tout de même, all the same
moi de même, the same applies to me
mener, to lead, take
le menu, bill of fare

LESSON VIII

§ 1. *Word Building—Enlarging the Vocabulary*

By the time this course is finished, you will have in the " Basic Vocabulary " and reading all the words you are ever likely to require for making sentences to express yourself. But, it is not enough to possess in your memory merely this limited vocabulary. You must have, in addition to these words " on the tip of your tongue," what might be called a " background " vocabulary; that is, a vocabulary of words which you can *recognize* at sight or when they are heard. Whereas, the first or " active " vocabulary is something over 1,000 words, the second or " background " vocabulary must be much larger. In Lesson I, § 4, we began to introduce you to that large group of words which so greatly resemble each other in French and English that when you see the French word you know almost immediately what it means. In listening to spoken French, you must accustom yourself to recognize these words when they are heard. For example, *opérateur* as pronounced in French is very different from " operator " in English. There are at least 6,000 of these French words which are almost the same as in English; and they are useful to know. We cannot give you all of them— there is no need—but from time to time we shall give you indications of the nature of these similar words. This is one way of helping you to enlarge your vocabulary.

There are others, and perhaps the most important is by " word-building." It is possible from the " Basic Vocabulary " to make many other words. We shall in this lesson give you some general principles and indications as to how you can make words from those which you already know.

The first and simplest way of making new words is by using the same form of the word in different parts of speech. For example, **BOIRE** means *to drink*, but **LE BOIRE** means *the drinking*. **Vif** is an Adjective meaning *living*, *lively*, but it can be made a Noun—**LE VIF**—and then it means what you would expect it to mean: *the living flesh, the quick.* **Malheureux** means *unhappy*; **le malheureux,** *the unhappy man*; **la malheureuse,** *the unhappy woman.* So already you know that from the infinitive of verbs and from adjectives you can make nouns. So you have: **le parler,** *the speaking*; **sage,** *wise*; **le sage,** *the wise man*; **gros,** *fat*; **le gros,** *the fat man.*

In this way, your vocabulary can be increased by *hundreds* of words.

¶ 15. TARTARIN DE TARASCON

Sur les quais, le dimanche soir, quand Tartarin revenait de la chasse, la casquette au bout du canon, bien sanglé dans sa veste de futaine, les portefaix du Rhône s'inclinaient pleins de respect, et se montrant du coin de l'œil les biceps gigantesques qui roulaient sur ses bras, ils se disaient tout bas les uns aux autres avec admiration: " C'est celui-là qui est fort! . . . Il a DOUBLES MUSCLES! " DOUBLES MUSCLES! Il n'y a qu'à Tarascon qu'on entend de ces choses-là!

Et pourtant, en dépit de tout, avec ses nombreux talents, ses doubles muscles, la faveur populaire et l'estime si précieuse du brave commandant Bravida, ancien capitaine d'habillement, Tartarin n'était pas heureux; cette vie de petite ville lui pesait, l'étouffait. Le grand homme de Tarascon s'ennuyait à Tarascon.

TRANSLATION: *On the quays on Sunday evening, when Tartarin returned from the hunt, cap on the end of his gun, well girthed in his corduroy jacket, the Rhône dock hands bowed, full of respect, and noting from the corner of their eye(s) the huge biceps which rolled on his arms, said to themselves (some to the others) with admiration: " It's that fellow who is strong! . . . He has DOUBLE MUSCLES!" DOUBLE MUSCLES! It is only in Tarascon that such things as those are heard!*

Nevertheless, in spite of everything, with his numerous talents, his double muscles, popular favor and the so precious esteem of the worthy commandant Bravida, former captain of clothing, Tartarin was not happy; this small town life weighed upon him, stifled him. The great man of Tarascon was bored in Tarascon.

Basic Vocabulary:

la mer, sea	**la mère,** mother
merci, thanks, *also* no thanks	**le Métro,** subway (in Paris)
mercredi, Wednesday	

le mètre, meter
mettre, to put
les meubles, furniture
un mille, 1,000*
un million, million
le milliard, one thousand million (francs, etc.)
mieux, better
tant mieux, so much the better
de mieux en mieux, better and better
se mettre à, to start, set about
aimer mieux, prefer
le ministre, minister

la mite, moth
la mitrailleuse, machine gun
moins, less
le monde, the world, people
tout le monde, everybody
monter, to climb
monter dans une auto, dans le train, to get into a car, the train
la montre, watch
le mouvement, movement
montrer, to show
le mouton, sheep, mutton
la motocyclette, motorcycle
la musique, music

§ 2. *Word Building*—contd.

COMPOUND WORDS: As in English, it is possible to make compound words in French, though in this respect French is not as flexible as English. **PORTER** means *to carry*, and **LE MANTEAU** means *the cloak*. So, we have **LE PORTEMANTEAU**, which is the same in English, and means literally *that which carries the cloak*. **CONTRE** means *against*, and **LE VENT** means *the wind*. So we have **LE CONTREVENT,** *the against the wind*—in other words, *the shutter*. You have already made the acquaintance of **Monsieur, Madame, Mademoiselle,** and you know that the plurals are: **Messieurs, Mesdames, Mesdemoiselles.** We mention this in order to explain that there are two kinds of compound nouns in French: (1) Those, like **le portemanteau** and **le contrevent,** which have plurals formed in the normal way (**les portemanteaux, les contrevents**); and (2) those, like **Monsieur,** which form the plural by changing each constituent of the word into the plural. **Bon,** *good*; **un homme,** *a man*; **un bonhomme,** *a good (natured) man*; plural, **les bonshommes.** Similarly, **gentilhomme,** *nobleman* (not *gentleman,* which is **monsieur**); plural, **gentilshommes.** **Coffre,** *chest, bin*; **le coffre-fort,** *the safe*; plural, **les coffres-forts.** It will be noted that these compound nouns

* *See* p. 59.

are made of nouns. But compound nouns can be made of other words, and here is a brief list of some of the commonest to be found in everyday reading :

> **Une basse-cour,** *a farmyard* (**bas** + **cour**); plural, **les basses-cours.**
>
> **Un grand'père,** *grandfather*; **les grand'pères.**
>
> **Une grand'mère,** *grandmother*; **les grand'mères.**
>
> **Les grands-parents,** *grandparents*.
>
> **Un chou-fleur,** *a cauliflower*; **les choux-fleurs.**
>
> **Un arc-en-ciel,** *a rainbow*; **les arcs-en-ciel.**
>
> **Un chef d'œuvre,** *a masterpiece*; **les chefs-d'œuvres.**
>
> **Un tête-à-tête,** *private conversation*. N.B. Plural, **Les tête-à-tête.**
>
> **Un pied-à-terre,** a temporary lodging or *footing*, which is **les pied-à-terre** in the plural. **L'après-midi,** *afternoon*, and **un hors-d'œuvre** are likewise the same in the plural. And also **le passe-partout,** *the master key*, skeleton key.

These are all fairly common compound words which you should know. You will see from the examples given the general principles involved, and this will help you to make sense of others which you may meet in reading.

¶ 16. TARTARIN DE TARASCON

Le fait est que pour une nature héroïque comme la sienne, pour une âme aventureuse et folle qui ne rêvait que batailles, courses dans les pampas, grandes chasses, sables du désert, ouragans et typhons, faire tous les dimanches une battue à la casquette et le reste du temps rendre la justice chez l'armurier Costecalde, ce n'était guère. . . . Pauvre cher grand homme ! A la longue, il y aurait eu de quoi le faire mourir de consomption.

En vain, pour agrandir ses horizons, pour oublier un peu le cercle et la place du Marché, en vain s'entourait-il de baobabs et autres végétations africaines ; en vain entassait-il armes sur armes, krish malais sur krish malais ; en vain se bourrait-il de lectures romanesques, cherchant comme l'immortel don Quichotte, à s'arracher par la vigueur de son rêve aux griffes de l'impitoyable réalité. . . . Hélas ! tout ce qu'il faisait pour apaiser sa soif d'aventures ne servait qu'à l'augmenter. La vue de toutes ses armes l'entretenait dans un état perpétuel de colère et d'excitation.

TRANSLATION: *The fact is that for a heroic nature like his, for an adventurous and wild soul which dreamed only of battles, races across pampas, great hunts, desert sands, hurricanes, and typhoons, to take part every Sunday in a cap-shoot, and the rest of the time to dispense justice in Costecalde the gunsmith's, was hardly. . . . Poor dear great man! In the long run there would be in it (enough, the wherewithal) to cause him to die of consumption.*

In vain, to widen his horizons, to forget somewhat the club and the Market Square, in vain did he surround himself with baobabs and other African vegetation(s) ; in vain did he heap up arms upon arms, Malay kris on Malay kris; in vain did he cram himself with romantic reading, seeking like the immortal Don Quixote to tear himself by the vigor of his dream from the talons of unpitying reality. . . . Alas ! all that he did to appease his thirst for adventures only served to increase it. The sight of all his arms kept him in a perpetual state of anger and (nervous) excitement.

Basic Vocabulary :

la natation, swimming	**la nuit,** night
la nature, nature	**le numéro,** number
naturel, natural	**un objet,** object
naturellement, naturally	**on,** people, they
né, born	**un oncle,** uncle
la neige, snow	**un opéra,** opera
ne . . . pas, not	**un orchestre**
ne . . . que, only	**où,** where
nettoyer, to clean	**ou,** or
le nettoyeur, cleaner	**oublier,** to forget
noir, black, dark	**un ouvrier,** workman
nouveau, new	**un outil,** tool
neuf (neuve), new	**la page,** page
moi, I, me; **moi non plus,**	**le pain,** bread
nor I either	**la paire,** pair

§ 3. *Word Building*—contd.

There are two other big groups of words in French, which are made from the simple or " basic " words by adding: (1) a prefix; or (2) a suffix. These prefixes and suffixes bear a certain resemblance, sometimes a complete resemblance, to their English equivalents :

PREFIXES ; **im-, il-, ir-.** These correspond to the same prefixes in English. Thus : **possible, impossible,** same as English ; **lisible,** *readable, legible* ; **illisible,** *illegible*.

RE- means to do a thing again, and is prefixed chiefly to verbs. Thus : **venir,** *to come* ; **revenir,** *to come again, return* ; **lire,** *to read* ; **relire,** *to read again.* This is a very important prefix.

CONTRE-, equivalent to English *counter*, as **une contre-attaque,** *a counterattack.*

Ex-, ess-, e-, generally means *out of.* **La patrie,** *the mother country;* **expatrier,** *to expatriate, to send out of the mother country.*

MI-, DEMI-, meaning *mid, half.* **Mi-août,** *mid-August* ; **un demi-litre,** *half a litre* ; **la demi-lune,** *the half-moon* ; **le demi-monde,** *the half-world,* meaning *outskirts of society* ; **demi-mort,** *half-dead.* **Pension** = *board, boardinghouse;* **la demi-pension,** *half-board* ; **le demi-pensionnaire,** *a person taking partial board,* also a *day boarder in a school* ; **la demi-sœur,** *the half-sister, stepsister.*

SUR-, meaning *over.* **Voler,** *to fly* ; **survoler,** *to fly over* ; **monter,** *to climb up, mount* ; **surmonter,** *to surmount.*

SOU-, SUB-, meaning *under.* **Mettre,** *to put* ; **soumettre,** *submit* ; **lever,** *to lift* ; **soulever,** *to raise with effort, to lift up* (*a weight*) ; **soulever une objection,** *to raise an objection.*

IDIOMS : An idiom is a form of expression peculiar to a language. This means that very often literal translation does not help you to find the meaning of an idiom. Take, for example, the phrase : **Il n'y a pas de quoi.** Translated literally, this would be : *There is not of what*—which has little sense and does not even correspond to our ideas of good English. The phrase means *It does not matter,* or it might be *Don't mention it.* You go into a shop and, having bought something, say to the assistant " **Merci, Monsieur** " (or **Madame** or **Mademoiselle;** never forget this), and the assistant replies : **Il n'y a pas de quoi, Monsieur.** French is rich in these idiomatic forms, and there is only one way of dealing with them. THEY HAVE TO BE MEMORIZED. From time to time we shall introduce idioms, those most in use.

¶ 17. Tartarin de Tarascon

Ses rifles, ses flèches, ses lazos lui criaient: " Bataille ! bataille ! " Dans les branches de son baobab, le vent des grands voyages soufflait et lui donnait de mauvais conseils. Pour l'achever, Gustave Aimard et Fenimore Cooper. . . .

Oh ! par les lourdes après-midi d'été quand il était seul à lire au milieu de ses glaives, que de fois Tartarin s'est levé en rugissant ; que de fois il a jeté son livre et s'est précipité sur le mur pour décrocher une panoplie !

Le pauvre homme oubliait qu'il était chez lui à Tarascon, avec un foulard de tête et des caleçons, il mettait ses lectures en actions, et, s'exaltant au son de sa propre voix, criait en brandissant une hache ou un tomahawk :

" Qu'ils y viennent maintenant ! "

Ils ?   Qui, *Ils ?*

Tartarin ne le savait pas bien lui-même. . . . *Ils !* c'était tout ce qui attaque, tout ce qui combat, tout ce qui mord, tout ce qui griffe, tout ce qui scalpe, tout ce qui hurle, tout ce qui rugit . . . *Ils !* c'était l'Indien Sioux dansant autour du poteau de guerre où le malheureux blanc est attaché.

TRANSLATION : *His rifles, his arrows, his lassoes shouted to him : " Battle ! battle ! "   In the branches of his baobab, the wind of great voyages blew and gave him bad advice(s).   To finish him, Gustave Aimard and Fenimore Cooper. . . .*
.Oh !   On heavy (sultry) summer afternoons when he was alone reading in the midst of his blades, how many times did he get up shouting ;   how often has he thrown (away, aside) his book and rushed to the wall to unhook a suit of armour !
The poor man forgot that he was at home in Tarascon, with a kerchief on his head and in his drawers, and (would) put his readings into action and, exalting himself with the sound of his own voice, would cry brandishing a hatchet or a tomahawk :
" Let them come now ! "
Them ?   Who (were) they ?
Tartarin did not know this well himself. . . . They ?   They were everything that attacks, fights, bites, claws, scalps, howls, roars. . . .
They !—the Sioux Indian dancing round the war-stake where the unfortunate white is tied up.

Basic Vocabulary:

le parc, park
par, by
par une nuit noire, on a dark night
le parachute
par-dessus, over, above
le pardessus, overcoat
le parent, relation
pardon, pardon, excuse me
le parlement, parliament
parler, to speak
particulier, special, private
la part, share, part
pour ma part, for my part, as for me
quelque part, somewhere
la partie, game

partir, to go away, leave
pas, not
pas mal, not bad, quite a few, a fair number
passer, to pass, go past
payer, to pay
le patinage, skating
la patrie, native land
pauvre, poor
le paysan, peasant
la pêche, fishing, *also* peach
le peintre, painter
pendant, during
penser, to think
penser à, to think of
le père, father

§ 4. *Word Building*—contd.

We now come to the last of the principal ways of making new words. This is by adding suffixes. We do this in English as, for example, in words ending in *-able*, *-er*, etc. (*debate*, *debatable*; *farm*, *farmer*). You must be able to recognize these endings when you see them in reading or hear them in speech.

SUFFIXES USED IN WORD BUILDING: **-ET**, **-ETTE** are diminutives (masculine and feminine). **Le garçon**, *the boy*; **le garçonnet**, *the little boy*; **la fille**, *the girl*; **la fillette**, *the little girl*.

-ABLE has two meanings: (1) to make an adjective of a noun or other word as we do in *debatable*—an adjective which shows the possibility of something; and (2) it can represent an agent or the person doing something. Examples of (1): **comparer**, *to compare*; **comparable**, *comparable*. The ending varies, the commonest variation being **-IBLE**. **comprendre**, *to understand*; **compréhension** = *understanding*; **compréhensible**, *understandable*, *comprehensible*. Example of (2): **compter**, *to count*; **le comptable**, *the accountant*.

-AGE represents action. **Laver,** *to wash*; **le lavage,** *washing* (the *act* of washing).

-EUR corresponds to English *-er*, and indicates the doer or agent. This is a very common suffix, almost as common as *-er* in English. **Le voyage,** *journey, trip*; **le voyageur,** *the traveller.*

-TION, -aison. Usually indicates some form of action related to the original word. **Administrer,** *to administer*; **une administration,** *administration.*

-ÉE indicates fullness. **La bouche,** *mouth*; **la bouchée,** *the mouthful.*

-IER also corresponds to our *-er* and indicates profession. **La ferme,** *the farm*; **le fermier,** *the farmer.* It is also used in a limited number of words to indicate the holder or container of something. **Le sucre,** *sugar*; **le sucrier,** *the sugar bowl;* **le poivre,** *pepper*; **le poivrier,** *the pepper shaker.*

ADJECTIVAL SUFFIXES: The following endings indicate an adjective that has been made from a noun: **-IBLE, -ABLE, -OIS, -AIS, -ISTE.** Examples: **paix, paisible ; durer, durable ; France, français ; Hongrie, Hongrois,** *Hungary, Hungarian*; **social, socialiste.**

VERBS: The suffix **-ER** can be added to new words in the language to make verbs. **Le téléphone, téléphoner ; la télégraphie, télégraphier ; le téléscope, téléscoper.**

Suffixes enlarge your vocabulary by thousands of new words.

¶ 18. TARTARIN DE TARASCON

C'était l'ours gris des montagnes Rocheuses qui se dandine, et qui se lèche avec une langue pleine de sang. C'était encore le Touareg du désert, le pirate malais, le bandit des Abruzzes. . . . *Ils*, enfin, c'etait *ils !* . . . c'est-à-dire la guerre, les voyages, l'aventure, la gloire.

Mais, hélas ! l'intrépide Tarasconnais avait beau *les* appeler, *les* défier . . . *ils* ne venaient jamais . . . Pécaïre ! qu'est-ce qu'*ils* seraient venus faire à Tarascon !

Tartarin cependant *les* attendait toujours ; surtout le soir en allant au cercle.

TRANSLATION: They (*were*) *the grizzly bear of the Rocky Mountains who walks with a roll and licks himself with a tongue full of blood.* They *were, too, the desert Tuareg, the Malay pirate, the bandit of the Abruzzi.* . . . They, *in short*, they *were* (*all*) they . . . *that is to say, war, voyages, adventure, glory.*

But, alas! the intrepid Tarasconian in vain called for them, *defied* them . . . they *never came.* . . . *Alackaday! What should* they *come to do in Tarascon!*

Tartarin nevertheless always expected (*awaited*) them—*especially by evening as he went to the club.*

DO NOT NEGLECT TO LISTEN TO SPOKEN FRENCH!

Basic Vocabulary:

permettre, to permit
personne (ne), nobody
perdre, to lose
la personne, person
peser, to weigh
petit, small, little
un peu, a little
à peu près, almost
la pharmacie, drugstore
le pétrole, petroleum *
le pied, foot
aller à pied, to go on foot
la permission, leave
le peuple, people
la peur, fear

avoir peur, to be afraid
faire peur à, to frighten
le piano
le plaisir, pleasure
la plaisanterie, joke
la plage, beach
placer, to place, invest
s'il vous plaît, if you please
plein (de), full (of)
il pleut, it is raining
faire le plein, to fill up
pleurer, to cry, weep
plusieurs, several
plonger, to dive
plus, more

§ 5. *Recapitulation and Hints*

With this lesson, you shall have completed what most learners of French regard as the most difficult part of the language. You now have, so to speak, the bones of the language, the framework. From this point onwards your task will be—with our help—to put flesh on those bones and finally to clothe them. You are beginning to see all these forms appearing in the reading; and, the more observant you are, the more you will notice. In the preparation of this course an experiment, a very necessary one,

---

* The word **essence** (f.) is perhaps more common for "gasoline."

was made.   An absolute beginner in French was faced with the material given up to this point and then asked for comments and criticisms.   The first criticism was that there was " too much grammar " and it was presented in " too concentrated a form." Next he said that he did not think it was any longer necessary to provide a word-for-word translation of the reading, that he could " make good sense of it without much difficulty " and that the provision of a translation tended to make him take things a little too easily.

The mere fact that, from a start representing zero, this student was now able *to make good sense of the reading*, and felt that, he could *do without the translation*, proved one thing : that he had absorbed a great part of the grammar and vocabulary and general principles of the language so far presented.

Although this learner was not above average intelligence, there was no reason to abandon just yet the provision of word-for-word translation.   Some students learn more quickly than others, and the slow ones must be remembered—the fact being that some people who are slow about learning a language often turn out in the end to be the best linguists !   This is because they hesitate to forge ahead unless they know *every word* presented to them in lessons.

It has been made quite clear that the student need not stop to learn every word, to memorize thoroughly every item of grammar. His first aim is to get a *good general idea* of the mechanics of the language and a sufficient vocabulary for reading.   And, by reading constantly and carefully, with the help here given, he is enabled to *absorb the language as it works*.

Here are three important hints : (1) make a habit of going back over all that you are not sure of; (2) go over the *Reading* without the aid of the translation until you find yourself thinking in French with the text—*until it becomes easy*; (3) learn as many *words* as you possibly can.

¶ 19. TARTARIN DE TARASCON

Le chevalier du Temple se disposant à faire une sortie contre l'infidèle qui l'assiège, le *tigre* chinois s'équipant pour la bataille, le guerrier comanche entrant sur le sentier de la guerre, tout cela n'est rien auprès de Tartarin de Tarascon s'armant de pied en cap pour aller au cercle, à neuf heures du soir, une heure après les clairons de la retraite.

Branle-bas de combat! comme disent les matelots.

A la main gauche, Tartarin prenait un coup-de-poing à pointes de fer, à la main droite une canne à épée ; dans la poche gauche, un casse-tête ; dans la poche droite, un revolver. Sur la poitrine, entre drap et flanelle, un krish malais. Par exemple, jamais de flèche empoisonée ; ce sont des armes trop déloyales ! ...

Avant de partir, dans le silence et l'ombre de son cabinet, il s'exerçait un moment, se fendait, tirait au mur, faisait jouer ses muscles ; puis, il prenait son passe-partout, et traversait le jardin, gravement, sans se presser.—A l'anglaise, messieurs, à l'anglaise ! c'est le vrai courage.

TRANSLATION : *The Templar knight preparing to make a sally against the infidel who besieges him, the Chinese tiger equipping himself for battle, the Comanche warrior going on the warpath, all that is nothing compared with Tartarin de Tarascon arming himself from foot to head to go to the club, at nine o'clock in the evening, one hour after the bugles of the tattoo.*

Pipe to action stations ! as the sailors say.

In his left hand, Tartarin took an iron-pointed brass knuckle, in his right hand a sword cane; in the left pocket a tomahawk; in his right pocket, a revolver. On his chest, between cloth and flannel (clothes and underclothes), a Malay kris. Never, by any chance, a poisoned arrow; those weapons are too disloyal (unfair)! ...

Before leaving, in the silence and shadow of his private room, he did exercise(s) for a moment, guarded himself, lunged at the wall, gave play to his muscles ; then, he took his master key and gravely crossed the garden without hastening—English fashion, gentlemen, English fashion ! That's true courage.

Basic Vocabulary :

plutôt, rather	**poli**, polite, polished
plutôt que, rather than	**la politesse**, politeness
la poire, pear	**la pomme**, apple
le pois, pea	**la pomme de terre**, potato
les petits pois, green peas	**la porte**, door, gate
le poisson, fish	**le port**, port

le porc, pork, pig

se porter, to be (as regards health)

se porter mal, to be ill

se porter bien, to be well

pour, for

pour que, in order that

le pourboire, tip, gratuity

le poulet, chicken

pourquoi, why

la poule, the hen

pouvoir, to be able

premier, first

prendre, to take

présenter, to present, introduce

prier, to ask, beg

le prisonnier, prisoner

la promenade, walk

LESSON IX

§ 1. *The Subjunctive*

IN the general treatment of verbs, that part known as the subjunctive has been deliberately omitted. We hardly use this " mood " in English now; and it is possible to speak and write excellent French without it. Nevertheless, French writers use it; and one hears it in speech. Although you need seldom *use* it—it is not easy and it can be done without—it is advisable for you to be able to *recognize* it when you see it. Even so, all you need know something about are two tenses of the French subjunctive: the present and the past. The endings of **-ER** verbs in the present subjunctive are:

> **-e, -es, -e, -*i*ons, -*i*ez, -ent**
> **(que) je parle, tu parles, il parle, nous parlions, vous parliez, ils parlent.**

You will see that the only differences from the present of the indicative (the ordinary present) are in the first and second persons plural.

The past subjunctive has the following endings:

> **-se, -ses, -t, -sions, -siez, -sent**
> **(que) je parlasse, tu parlasses, il parlât, nous parlassions, vous parlassiez, ils parlassent.**

The present subjunctive is translated *that I may . . .*; the past, *that I might. . . . that I may speak, that I might speak.*

In **-IR, -OIR,** and **-RE** verbs, the subjunctive is mostly formed in the same way, and you will nearly always recognize it by looking for the endings given above.

USE OF THE SUBJUNCTIVE: The subjunctive is used in French: (1) after certain conjunctions; (2) after verbs of EMOTION (joy, sorrow, etc.), WISH, COMMAND, APPROVAL, and DISAPPROVAL; (3) after verbs of SAYING and THINKING; (4) after the word *whatever*; (5) after impersonal verbs; (6) after a negative or interrogative principal clause. All you need do now is make a mental note of these uses, of the endings which indicate the subjunctive, and of the following conjunctions, which are followed by the subjunctive :

avant que, before	**de peur que,** for fear that
en attendant que, until	**à moins que,** unless
pas que, not that	**en cas que,** in case that
pour que, afin que, in order that	**pourvu que,** provided that
quoi que, whatever	**qui que,** whoever
bien que, although	**où que,** wherever
	quoique, although

These brief indications are sufficient for practical purposes.

¶ 20. Tartarin de Tarascon

Au bout du jardin, il ouvrait la lourde porte de fer. Il l'ouvrait brusquement, violemment, de façon à ce qu'elle allât battre en dehors contre la muraille. . . . *S'ils* avaient été derrière, vous pensez quelle marmelade ! . . . Malheureusement, *ils* n'étaient pas derrière.

La porte ouverte, Tartarin sortait, jetait vite un coup d'œil de droite et de gauche, fermait la porte à double tour et vivement. Puis en route. Sur le chemin d'Avignon, pas un chat. Portes closes, fenêtres éteintes. Tout était noir. De loin en loin un réverbère, clignotant dans le brouillard du Rhône. . . . Superbe et calme. Tartarin de Tarascon s'en allait ainsi dans la nuit, faisant sonner ses talons en mesure, et du bout ferré de sa canne arrachant des étincelles aux pavés. . . . Boulevards, grandes rues ou ruelles, il avait soin de tenir toujours le milieu de la chaussée, excellente mesure de précaution qui vous permet de voir venir le danger, et surtout d'éviter ce qui, le soir, dans les rues de Tarascon, tombe quelquefois des fenêtres.

TRANSLATION : *At the end of the garden he opened the heavy iron door. He opened it sharply, violently, so that it should beat (slam) outside against the wall. . . . If they had been behind (it), just think what a marmalade (squash) ! . . . Unhappily they were not behind it. The door open, Tartarin went out, threw a glance right and left, shut the door (locking it) doubly and smartly. Then off he set. On the Avignon Road, not a cat. Doors closed, windows extinguished (no lights). All was black. Spaced widely (from far to far) a*

*street lamp, blinking in the fog from the Rhône. . . . Superb (arrogant)
and calm, Tartarin de Tarascon went out thus into the night, making
his heels ring (sound) in measure, and from the iron end of his cane
tearing sparks from the cobbles. Boulevards, main streets or lanes,
he was careful to keep always (to the) middle of the road, (an) excellent
measure of precaution which permits you to see danger coming, and
above all to avoid what (in the) evening in the streets of Tarascon falls
sometimes from the windows.*

Basic Vocabulary :

propre, proper, *also* own,
   clean, *or* neat
puis, then
le puits, the well
se promener, to take a walk
le professeur, teacher, professor
produire, produce
profond, deep
à propos, by the way
à propos de, with regard to
proche, near
prochain, next
le quai, quay, *also* station
   platform
la qualité, quality
quand, when

la quantité, quantity
le quart, quarter
quelque, some
quelquefois, sometimes
quelqu'un, somebody
que, that, etc.
la question, question
qui, who
la quinzaine, fifteen, fortnight
quitter, to leave
quoi, what
la radio, radio
la radiodiffusion, broadcasting
quel, which
radiodiffuser, to broadcast

§ 2. *Hints on the Gender of Nouns*

In Lesson I, § 4, we gave you the only really safe method of
mastering the French genders : learn the article— definite or
indefinite—with each noun as you meet it.

But, it would be unwise to suppose from this that there is
" neither rhyme nor reason " about the French genders, for this
is not so. Here are some general hints which will help you, but
they are intended merely as general helps, and must not be taken
as covering everything, nor that you need now abandon the old,
safe rule about learning an article with each noun. That rule
must never be abandoned.

MASCULINE ARE: days of the week, months, seasons, North, South, East, West, trees, shrubs, colors, metals, and decimal weights and measures.   Also words with the following endings: -age, -ège, -ier, -ent, -ment.   Exceptions: **la cage, la nage** (*swimming*), **la page, la plage** (*beach, shore*), **la peau**, *skin*, **la dent**, *tooth*.   Important: other parts of speech used as nouns are always masculine.   **Le boire**, *drinking*; **le parler**, *speaking*.

FEMININE ARE: nouns with the following endings:

-ance, -ence, -anse, -ense, -aison, -sion, -tion, -xion.
-ffe, -lle, -mme, -nne, -ppe, -rre, -tte, -sse, -ade, -ude.
-é, -ée, -ie, -ue, -té, -tié

Names of moral qualities, sciences, and arts are usually feminine.

COUNTRIES: Some are masculine, some are feminine.   Learn the following: **le Canada, le Portugal, le Japon, le Mexique.**

As a general rule, names of countries which end in *e*-mute are feminine.   They *always* take the article.   **La France; l'Angleterre.**

DOUBLE GENDERS: A few nouns have double gender, with a different meaning for masculine and feminine.   The following should be known:

un aide, a helper	**le livre,** book
une aide, a help	**la livre,** the pound (*weight* or
un tour, a turn	*sterling*)
une tour, a tower	**un vapeur,** a steamer
	une vapeur, steam

As already indicated, do not rely too strongly on the hints for gender.   You may have noticed something which is rather difficult to explain, and it is that in French there is usually *something* about a noun, whether in origin, meaning, or ending, which *can* indicate the gender.   In time, when you have become thoroughly familiar with the language, this matter of genders seems perfectly natural.

¶ 21. TARTARIN DE TARASCON

A lui voir tant de prudence, n'allez pas croire au moins que Tartarin eût peur. . . . Non! seulement il se gardait.   La meilleure preuve que Tartarin n'avait pas peur, c'est qu'au lieu d'aller au cercle par le cours, il y allait par la ville, c'est-à-dire par le plus long, par le plus noir, par un tas de vilaines petites rues au bout desquelles on voit le Rhône luire sinistrement.   Le pauvre homme espérait toujours qu'au détour d'un de ces coupe-gorge *ils* allaient s'élancer de l'ombre et lui tomber sur le dos. *Ils* auraient été bien reçus, je vous en réponds. . . . Mais, hélas! par une dérision du destin, jamais, au grand jamais, Tartarin de Tarascon n'eut la chance de faire une mauvaise rencontre.   Pas même un chien, pas même un ivrogne.   Rien!

Parfois cependant une fausse alerte.   Un bruit de pas, des voix étouffées. . . . "Attention!" se disait Tartarin, et il restait planté sur place, scrutant l'ombre, prenant le vent, appuyant son oreille contre terre à la mode indienne. . . . Les pas approchaient.   Les voix devenaient distinctes. . . . Plus de doutes!   *Ils* arrivaient. . . . *Ils* étaient là.

TRANSLATION : *On seeing in him so much prudence, you must not (don't go to) believe in the least that Tartarin was afraid. . . . No! Only he protected himself.   The best proof that Tartarin was not afraid is that instead of going to the club (circle) by the course (short-cut), he went by the town; that is to say, by the longest, by the blackest, by a heap (mass) of ugly little streets at the end of which one sees the Rhône shine ominously.   The poor man hoped always that on the turn of one of these cutthroat (places) they were going to launch themselves from the shadow and fall on his back.   They would have been well received, I reply (to that). . . . But, alas!   By a derision of destiny (mockery of Fate), never, emphatically never, had Tartarin the chance of making a bad (evil) meeting.   Not even a dog, not even a drunk man.   Nothing!*

At times nevertheless a false alarm.   A noise of steps, of stifled voices. . . . "Look out!" Tartarin said to himself, and he remained planted on the spot scrutinizing the shadow, taking (sniffing) the wind, pressing his ear against the ground Indian-fashion. . . . The steps approached. . . . The voices became distinct. . . . No more doubts! They were coming. . . . They were there.

Basic Vocabulary:

la raison, reason, rightness	**raisonnable,** reasonable
avoir raison, to be right	**ralentir,** to slow down
avoir tort, to be wrong	**raser,** to shave
le raisin, grape	**se raser,** to shave oneself

le rasoir, razor
la raquette, tennis racket
reconnaître, to recognize
recharger, recharge
la recherche, research, quest
reculer, to step back, withdraw
réfléchir, to reflect
regarder, to look at
regretter, to regret
relire, to reread
remettre, to put again, to deliver

remplacer, to replace
repasser, to iron
rentrer, to go in again
réparer, to repair
le réservoir, tank
ressembler à, to look like
le restaurant
le retard, delay
être en retard, to be late
le revenu, income
revoir, to see again

§ 3. *Useful Feminine Forms*

A general rule in French is that if you wish to form the feminine of a noun, you add *e*-mute.   For example : **un ouvrier,** *a workman*, **une ouvrière,** *a workwoman*.

Exceptions are : Nouns in **-eur** change to **-euse**

	-teur	,,	-trice
	-x	,,	-se
	-f	,,	-ve

And nouns in **-et, -en, -ot,** double the last consonant and add *e*-mute.

Examples : **fumeur,** *smoker,* **fumeuse ; acteur, actrice ;** le **veuf,** *widower,* **la veuve,** *widow*; **le poulet,** *chicken,* **la poulette,** *young hen, pullet*; **un chien, une chienne.**

With these general rules, you will generally recognize the feminine forms, but most of the following deviate from the rules and, as they are all in fairly common usage, they should be known :

un ambassadeur	une ambassadrice (*fem.*) wife of an ambassador
un empereur	une impératrice, empress
le gouverneur	la gouvernante (in the feminine means *a governess,* and often *a housekeeper*)
le compagnon	la compagne
le héros	l'héroïne

le neveu, nephew	la nièce, niece
le paysan, peasant	la paysanne
le vieillard, old man	la vieille, old woman
le dieu, god	la déesse, goddess
le comte, count	la comtesse, countess
le duc	la duchesse
le marquis	la marquise
le nègre	la négresse
le lion, lion	la lionne, lioness
le loup, wolf	la louve, she-wolf
le mulet, mule	la mule
le tigre	la tigresse
le bélier, ram	la brebis, ewe
le bouc, male goat	la chèvre, nanny goat
le cheval, horse	la jument, mare

FEMININES OF ADJECTIVES TO NOTE: As you know, the general rule to form the feminine is add e-mute. But, note the following :

bas, basse, low	frais, fraîche, fresh
épais, épaisse, thick	grec, grecque, Greek
faux, fausse, false	public, publique, public
gras, grasse, fat	turc, turque, Turk
gros, grosse, fat, big	gentil, gentille, nice
las, lasse, weary, tired	nul, nulle, no one
doux, douce, sweet	favori, favorite, favorite,
blanc, blanche, white	favored one
franc, franche, frank	malin, maligne, wicked

Again, you will notice that, in most cases, certain principles prevail. But, it is best to memorize all these words.

¶ 22. TARTARIN DE TARASCON

Déjà Tartarin, l'œil en feu, la poitrine haletante, se ramassait sur lui-même comme un jaguar, et se préparait à bondir en poussant son cri de guerre . . . quand tout à coup, du sein de l'ombre, il entendait de bonnes voix tarasconnaises l'appeler bien tranquillement:

"Té ! vé ! . . . c'est Tartarin. . . . Et adieu, Tartarin ! "

Malédiction ! c'était le pharmacien Bézuquet avec sa famille qui venait de chanter *la sienne* chez les Costecalde.   " Bonsoir ! bonsoir ! " grommelait Tartarin, furieux de sa méprise ; et, farouche, la canne haute, il s'enfonçait dans la nuit.

Arrivé dans la rue du cercle, l'intrépide Tarasconnais attendait encore un moment en se promenant de long en large devant la porte avant d'entrer. . . . A la fin, las de *les* attendre et certain qu'*ils* ne se montreraient pas, il jetait un dernier regard de défi dans l'ombre, et murmurait avec colère : " Rien ! . . . rien ! . . . jamais rien ! "

Là-dessus le brave homme entrait faire son bésigue avec le commandant.

TRANSLATION : *Already Tartarin (with) eye afire, chest heaving, gathered himself like a jaguar and prepared to bound (leap) while uttering his war cry . . . when suddenly from the depth (bosom) of the shadow he heard good Tarasconian voices call him quietly :*
" *Hi ! . . . What ! . . . It's Tartarin. . . . Cheerio, Tartarin !* "
Curse ! It was the druggist Bézuquet with his family who had just been singing his (*favorite song*) *at the Costecalde's.*   '" *Good evening, good evening," growled Tartarin, furious at his error ; and, fierce, (his) cane on high, he plunged into the night.*
Arrived (arriving) in the street of the club, the intrepid Tarasconian waited yet a moment walking back and forth in front of the door before going in. . . . In the end, weary of awaiting them *and certain that* they *would not show themselves, he threw a last glance of defiance into the shadow, and murmured with anger :   " Nothing ! . . . Nothing ! . . . Never anything ! "*
Thereupon the worthy man went in to play his bezique with the commandant (major).

Basic Vocabulary :

la revue, review, magazine	**les États-Unis,** the United States
riche, rich	
la robe, woman's dress	**la rue,** street
rien, nothing	**la Russie,** Russia
rire, to laugh	**le rosbif,** roast beef
le rire, laughter	**sale,** dirty
le roi, king	**la salade,** salad
rouge, red	**la salle,** hall
la route, road, route	**la salle d'attente,** waiting room

la salle à manger, dining-room

la salle de bain, bathroom

sans, without

sans doute, without doubt, doubtless

savoir, to know

le savon, soap

le sang, blood

sec (sèche), dry

la seconde, second

le sel, salt

sentir, to feel

le sergent, sergeant

le senateur, senator

§ 4. *How to Write a Letter*

Letter-writing in French is more formal and, at the same time, a little warmer and more cordial than in English. You may not have noticed it, but, generally speaking, when you receive a letter in English from a complete stranger, it is probably polite, but it is somewhat cold and distant, and deals perhaps a little abruptly with the matter in hand. If you receive a letter in French, even though it be an ordinary business letter, it will be polite as a matter of course—perhaps a little more polite than an English letter—but you will generally find that there is cordiality about it, as though the writer really wished to regard you as a friend. The French are clever correspondents! It is therefore only mere politeness to treat your French correspondents on the same basis. The French carry politeness farther than we do, and it behooves you to remember this, not only in letter-writing but in everything.

Certain formalities have to be observed, the first of which is that, for the first of the month—and the first only—the date is written thus: **le 1ᵉʳ janvier 1949.** *All* other dates are written: **le 2 janvier 1948, le 3 février 1950, le 4 mars 1951, le 5 avril 1952,** etc.

For a formal opening to a letter, corresponding to our *Dear Sir, Dear Madam*, etc., in French you use simply the word **Monsieur, Madame, Mademoiselle,** as the case may be. Only if you know the person fairly well is it advisable to write: **Cher Monsieur, Chère Madame, Chère Mademoiselle.** When you know the person really well, you may write **Mon cher M. Dupont, Ma chère Mme Dupont, Ma chère Mlle Dupont.**

Experience will teach you how important it is to follow this advice.

If you should ever have to write to an official or a person occupying some position, you must use his title. Thus, if you have to write to a stationmaster, you write to him as *Mr. Stationmaster*, and open your letter thus : **Monsieur le chef de gare.** If you have to write to the Prefect of Police or to the Mayor of a town, you begin your letter : **Monsieur le Préfet, Monsieur le maire ;** and so on.

Similarly, your envelope should be addressed : **Monsieur Charles Dupont,** or **M. Charles Dupont ; Madame,** or **Mme Dupont ; Mademoiselle** or **Mlle Dupont.** But, remember that you are hardly ever committing a fault if your letters open with simple **Monsieur, Madame,** or **Mademoiselle.**

Une Lettre de Victor Hugo a Paul Meurice

dimanche, le 24 juillet, 1859

Mon cher ami,

C'est encore moi, voici la chose : ce que je vais vous demander est excessif, mais, cher doux ami, refusez-moi tout net si le temps vous manque. Pouvez-vous passer deux heures pour moi dans les bibliothèques, lire dans quelque dictionnaire de conversation ou encyclopédie les articles biographiques sur *Torquemada*, faire copier (à mes frais, bien entendu) le mieux fait, le plus détaillé, et me l'envoyer ?

Votre dévoué,

V. H.

TRANSLATION :

Sunday, 24th July 1859

My dear friend,
It is still I, (and) this is the thing (what it is about) : what I am going to ask you is excessive (too much), dear sweet friend, (and) refuse me sharply if you have not the time (if time is lacking to you). Can you pass (spend) two hours for me in the libraries, to read in some conversation dictionary or encyclopædia the biographical articles on Torquemada, *have copied—at my expense, of course—the best made (written), the most detailed, and send it to me ?*

Your devoted (Yours ever),
V. H.

How ARE YOU ? There are several ways of asking this question. You should know the following three :

> *Very formal :* **Comment vous portez-vous ?** (Literally : *How do you carry yourself?*)
> *General :* **Comment allez-vous ?** (Literally : *How go you?*)
> *Familiar :* **Comment ça va ?** *How goes it?* Or, simply : **Ça va ?**

The usual answer is : **Très bien, merci. Et vous ?** And do not forget the **Monsieur, Madame,** or **Mademoiselle.**

Basic Vocabulary :

serrer, to shut, lock
la semaine, week
la sentinelle, sentry
le service, service
la serveuse, waitress
la serviette, towel
la serviette de table, table napkin
seul, alone, only
si, if (*also* " yes " after a negative)
le shampooing, shampoo
le ski, skiing
faire du ski, to ski
la sœur, sister
la soif, thirst
avoir soif, to be thirsty
le soir, evening

le soldat, soldier
le soleil, sun, sunshine
la sortie, way out, exit
la sortie d'incendie, fire escape
le soulier, shoe
la soucoupe, saucer
soûl (pronounce " **sou** "), drunk
le sous-marin, submarine
se souvenir (de), to remember
suffire, to suffice
ça suffit, that's enough
sur, on
sûr, sure
bien sûr, quite sure.
la surprise, surprise

§ 5. *How to Write a Letter*—contd.

If you have to be careful about the opening of letters, you must be still more so about the ending. Endings of letters may for convenience be classified under three heads : (1) formal ; (2) moderately familiar—that is, when you know the person slightly ; and (3) familiar—when you know the person well.

If you are to make a mistake, let it always be on the side of the less familiar and more formal.

(1) *The formal ending:* **Veuillez agréer, Monsieur (Madame, or Mademoiselle), l'expression de mes sentiments distingués** (or **de mes sentiments les plus sincères**). Literally: *Please accept the expression of my (most) distinguished sentiments,* or *of my most sincere feelings.*

(2) *The moderately familiar ending:* **Croyez en l'expression de mes sentiments distingués** (*Believe in the expression of my distinguished feelings*).

(3) *The familiar ending:* **Recevez mes meilleurs souvenirs.** Or, **Tout à vous,** which means *Yours ever,* but this is for *very* familiar use only.

If, however, you are writing to an official or a person of position, let your ending be, say, in a letter to a Prefect: **Veuillez agréer, Monsieur le Préfet, l'expression de la haute considération de votre très humble et très obéissant serviteur.**

This last ending (for a letter addressed to an official) is becoming somewhat old-fashioned, especially in Paris and the big cities; far less so in the smaller country towns. Writing as a foreigner, you would be well advised to use it everywhere, and to everybody in " a position," whether it be a postmaster, a stationmaster, the manager of a movie, theater, or firm. If a woman is writing, naturally she observes all the rules of gender. So: **Toute à vous. Très obéissante servante.**

Another little point. The phrase **j'ai l'honneur de,** *I have the honor to,* is very useful for opening your letters, especially in matters of business:

> **Monsieur le Directeur,**
> **J'ai l'honneur de vous informer que.** . . .

What you have been given in this and § 4 applies to letter-writing in general. Observe these rules, and you will not go far wrong. *The main body of your letter is in straightforward French.* A few special considerations apply to commercial letter-writing. These will be dealt with in the next lesson.

Basic Vocabulary:

le tabac, tobacco
la table, table
le temps, weather (*also* time)
de temps en temps, from time to time
terrible, terrible
la tente, tent
la tige, stalk, stem
timide, timid
le titre, title
la toilette, toilet
faire la toilette, to wash and dress
les toilettes, toilet place
la tomate, tomato
T.S.F. = télégraphie sans fils, wireless
faire chaud, to be hot (weather)
faire beau temps, to be bright, clear (weather)

tomber, to fall
toujours, always
le tournant, turn, curve (in a road)
tout, all
tout le monde, everybody
tout droit, straight on
tout près, quite near
tout savoir, to know all
tout à fait, quite
tout à coup, suddenly
tout de suite, now, at once
toute une partie, a whole part
le train, train
le travail, work
travailler, to work
travailleur, worker, toiler
faire froid, to be cold
faire mauvais temps, to be bad (weather)

LESSON X

§ 1. *Commercial Correspondence*

COMMERCIAL correspondence in French follows the same traditions and rules as general correspondence in that it is a little more cordial, polite, and less matter-of-fact than in English. It is certainly more polite. Your author wrote to a Paris bookseller asking if an illustrated edition of Gabriel Chevalier's famous novel *Clochemerle* was available, and here is the actual reply:

> **Monsieur,**
>
> **En réponse à votre carte du 6 courant, nous avons le regret de vous informer que toutes les éditions illustrées de *Clochemerle* sont épuisées.**
>
> **Avec tous nos regrets de ne pouvoir vous satisfaire, nous vous prions d'agréer, Monsieur, l'expression de notre considération distinguée.**
>
> (signature)

An English-speaking bookseller would probably send a post-card with the title of the book asked for and the words "Out of print;" or, at most, he might write:

> With reference to your request, we regret that the book for which you ask is out of print.

This is a perfect little example of the difference between French and English commercial correspondence. Supposing the French bookseller had been able to send the book asked for, one might have been tempted to ask for a second copy to give as a present to a friend. In such case, no offence would be taken by the bookseller if you simply sent the money and asked for the book. But if a Frenchman made such a request, he would probably write a punctilious letter, somewhat as follows:

> **Monsieur,**
>
> **J'ai bien reçu le *Clochemerle*, dont je vous remercie infiniment. Votre extrême obligeance**

m'enhardit à m'adresser à vous pour obtenir un autre exemplaire. Je vous envoie ci-inclus la somme de Fcs. 500.

En vous remerciant, je vous prie d'agréer, Monsieur, mes salutations empressées.

(signature)

remercier, to thank
enhardir, to embolden
salutations empressées,
    eager salutations

infiniment, infinitely
le comptant, the amount, cost
obligeance, kindness
la somme, sum

All this may seem like carrying things a little too far. In French it is not so, and even if the case cited may seem a little extreme, you will be well advised to overdo politeness rather than omit to observe it.

NEWSPAPER EXCERPTS:

(1)

M. Edouard Herriot chez le négus

M. Edouard Herriot est infatigable. Il va profiter des vacances de Pâques pour se rendre à Addis Abeba, où il inaugurera le lycée français. Le Président Herriot s'y rendra par la voie des airs et fera une courte escale à Alexandrie. Il sera accompagné pendant son déplacement par le directeur de son cabinet, M. Friol.

(2)

M. Vincent Auriol à St-Jean

M. Vincent Auriol se rend sur la Côte d'Azur à Saint Jean-Cap Ferrat. Il y séjournera dans une confortable petite villa, située au bord de la baie de Beaulieu avec une magnifique vue sur les Etats voisins ; la principauté de Monaco et la république italienne. A ses pieds un minuscule et coquet rocher, dont la villa tire son nom " le Scoblietto," qui signifie l'écueil, le rocher. Cette belle demeure appartient à une vieille famille niçoise représentée par MM. Jacques et Claude Bounin.

(3)

Le continent antarctique est généralement considéré comme découvert depuis 127 ans et plusieurs milliers de marins, pêcheurs et explorateurs l'ont déjà visité. Mais, nous dit *Collier's*, jusqu'ici aucune femme ne s'y est encore risquée.

Pourquoi ?

Notez que la superficie de ce continent est évaluée à 10 millions de kilomètres carrés, soit à peu près celle de l'Europe. Dernier détail ; quoi qu'on en ait dit, et écrit, il ne semble pas, d'après toutes les dernières recherches, qu'il y ait le moindre grain d'uranium dans cet Antarctique.

TRANSLATION :

(1)

M. Edouard Herriot at the Negus's

M. Edouard Herriot is indefatigable. He is going to profit by the Easter holidays to go to Addis Ababa, where he will inaugurate the French (secondary) school. President Herriot will go there by air route and make a short stop at Alexandria. He will be accompanied during his absence by the director (head) of his Secretariat, M. Friol.

(2)

M. Vincent Auriol at St. Jean

M. Vincent Auriol is going to the Côte d'Azur (Blue Coast)* to St. Jean-Cap Ferrat. He will stay there in a comfortable little villa, situated beside the Bay of Beaulieu with a magnificent view on the neighbouring States : the principality of Monaco and the Italian Republic. At his feet a minute and coquettish (dainty) rock from which the villa draws its name "The Scoblietto," which means the reef, rock. This beautiful dwelling belongs to an old Nice family represented by Messieurs Jacques and Claude Bounin.

(3)

The Antarctic continent is generally considered as discovered 127 years, and several (a good many) thousand sailors, fishermen, and explorers have already visited it. But Collier's (magazine) tells us, until now no woman has ever risked herself there.

Why ?

Note that the surface of this continent is estimated at 10 million square kilometres, that is about that of Europe. Last detail : whatever one may have said and written, it does not seem, after all the latest researches, that there is the least grain of uranium in this Antarctic.

Note: The above are excerpts from a French newspaper.

* The Riviera.

Basic Vocabulary :

trop, too much, too many
le tramway, streetcar
trouver, to find
uni, united
un uniforme, uniform
une usine, factory
vacciner, to vaccinate
les valeurs, securities
le vendeur, salesman
la vendeuse, saleswoman
venir, to come
venir de, to have just
je viens de parler, I have just
  spoken
le vent, wind
la vente, sale

la viande, meat
vieux (vieille), old
le vieux, the old man
mon vieux, "old chap," old
  fellow
la victoire, victory
la vie, life
le vin, wine
le violon, violin
le visage, face
le vocabulaire, vocabulary
la voie, track, way
la voiture, carriage
en voiture ! "Take your
  seats ! "
le voisin, neighbour
vouloir, to wish

§ 2. *Common Idioms and Useful Phrases*

You will remember that, in Lesson VIII, § 3, you made a nodding acquaintance with " Idioms ", those expressions peculiar to the language in which a literal translation does not always give you a key to the meaning. Meanwhile, the time has come when you must begin to master certain idioms. We do not propose to burden you unduly, but as these idioms are of everyday recurrence, the sooner the commonest of them are known the better. Some you will have already met. Here is a first list :

VOULOIR DIRE (literally *to wish to say*), *to mean.* Thus : **Que voulez-vous dire ?** *What do you mean?* **Je veux dire que mon ami n'est pas ici.** *I mean that my friend is not here.* **Qu'est-ce que ça veut dire ?** *What does that mean?*

AVOIR BESOIN DE, *to require, have need of.* You use this for a physical or material requirement. For instance, when you go into a shop, the assistant will say : **Que désirez-vous Monsieur ?** or simply : **Vous désirez ?** *What do you wish, or* *desire?* And unless it was merely to ask him a question that you went into the shop, you will say in reply : **J'ai besoin d'un kilo de café, d'une boîte d'allumettes, de cigarettes.** *I want a kilo of coffee, a box of matches, some cigarettes.*

VEUILLEZ, first person plural of the imperative of **VOULOIR,** *to wish,* when used with the infinitive of a verb means *please.* Thus : **Je ne vous comprends pas. Veuillez répéter.** *I do not understand you. Please repeat.* **Veuillez vous asseoir,** *please sit down.*

Qu'est-qu'il y a ? *What is the matter?*

Q'est-ce qu'il a ? (literally : *What has he?*) *What is the matter with him?*

N'est-ce pas ? *Is it not (so)?* French people tend to use this phrase very much. If you ask a person the way to the Town Hall, you say, **Où se trouve la mairie ?** *Where does the Town Hall find itself?* and in reply the person will often use **N'est-ce pas ?** after each instruction he gives you. Thus : **Vous allez tout droit, n'est-ce pas ? Et puis vous tournez à gauche, n'est-ce pas ?** *You go straight on, is it not so? And then you turn to the left, is it not so?* The **N'est-ce pas** here really means *Do you understand? Do you follow?*

Il y a un mois que je suis ici. (Literally : *There is a month that I am here.*) *For a month I've been here.* **Il y a un an qu'elle est à Paris.**

In Lesson IX, § 5, you learned that **FAIRE** is used for *to be* in regard to the weather. **Il fait chaud, froid,** etc. Similarly, to ask what the weather is, you say : **Quel temps fait-il aujourd'hui ?**

Text :

Un souvenir

Juin 1940. Les Allemands entrent dans une petite ville de Saône-et-Loire. Un sous-officier et deux soldats pénètrent chez le dépositaire Hachette. Sur la banque, journaux et publications sont étalés, et, parmi eux, le dernier numéro de *Aux Ecoutes.*

Le sous-officier bondit, se saisit de l'exemplaire, hurle des paroles de menace, et veut l'emporter. Aussi vif, le dépositaire, un vieux et vrai Français, qui souffre atrocement de " les " voir

là, l'arrête et crie à son tour : " Pour l'emporter, il faut d'abord
le payer." L'autre refusant de payer, il lui arracha le journal
des mains.

Les trois Allemands sortent, au comble de la colère . . . mais
reviennent une demi-heure après, avec soldats en armes, et
arrêtent le dépositaire et sa fille, mère de deux petits enfants, et
dont le mari est mobilisé. Ils sont emmenés à la kommandantur
où on parle tout de suite, ni plus, ni moins, de les fusiller ! Le
maire, brave homme, multiplie les interventions auprès du
commandant de la place pour les faire libérer.

Ils sont finalement emmenés dans une petite bourgade, à vingt
kilomètres de là, et passés en conseil de guerre, après trois jours
d'angoisse, trois jours où on les laisse avoir faim.

Heureusement la sinistre comédie se termine par une libération.
Mais le dépositaire, déjà vieux et malade, mourra avant de " les "
voir repartir. . . .

TRANSLATION :

A Souvenir

*June 1940. The Germans enter a little town of Saône-et-Loire.
A noncommissioned officer and two soldiers go into the Hachette
newsagent's (shop). On the counter newspapers and publications are
displayed, and among them the last issue of* Aux Ecoutes.

*The noncommissioned officer jumps and seizes the copy, bawls
threatening words, and wishes to take it away. As quick, the newsagent, an old and true Frenchman who suffers terribly to see " them "
there, stops him and shouts in his turn: " To take that, it is necessary
first to pay for it." The other refusing to pay, he tears the newspaper
from his hands.*

*The three Germans go out in the greatest anger . . . but come back
half an hour later with armed soldiers and arrest the newsagent and
his daughter, mother of two little children (and) of whom the husband
is mobilized. They are brought to the* kommandantur, *where they
immediately talk, neither more nor less, of shooting them ! The
mayor, worthy man, multiplies (redoubles) his interventions with the
officer in command to have them liberated.*

*They are finally taken to a little town twenty kilometers from
there and court-martialed after three days of agony, three days
during which they are left in hunger.*

*Happily the sinister (baleful) comedy ends with a release. But the
newsagent, already old and ill, will die before seeing " them " depart.*

Basic Vocabulary :

le voyage, voyage, journey, trip

voyager, to travel

le voyageur, traveler

vraiment, truly

la vue, the sight, view

vouloir dire, to mean

le wagon, railway coach, car

le wagon-lit, sleeper

le wagon-restaurant, diner

y avoir, there to be

il n'y a pas de quoi, don't mention it

NOTE : This ends the first stage of " Basic Vocabulary," which equips you with a most useful all-purposes word list. With the grammar given, this list should enable you to express most of the ideas continually recurring in everyday life. From this point on, it is a question of expanding your vocabulary for both speaking and writing, but especially for understanding and reading. Many new words will be found in the reading.

§ 3. *Common Idioms and Useful Phrases*—contd.

In Lesson IX, § 5, you learned that the verb **FAIRE,** *to do* or *make*, is used for the weather. **Il fait chaud, il fait froid,** etc. To ask what the weather is, you say : **Quel temps fait-il aujourd'hui ?** Answer : **il neige, il fait un temps superbe.**

But note well that **COMBIEN DE TEMPS** means *How long?* Thus : **Combien de temps faut-il pour aller de Paris à Marseille ?** Answer : **Il faut six heures.**

And **COMBIEN DE FOIS** means *How many times?* *How often?* Thus : **Combien de fois par mois allez-vous à Paris ?** *How many times a month do you go to Paris?*

LE COMBIEN SOMMES-NOUS ? *The how many are we?* In other words, *What is the date?* And **COMBIEN VENDEZ-VOUS CELUI-CI ?** *How do you sell this?* Or, *How much is this?*

IL ME FAUT (literally *It is necessary to me*), *I want, I have need of.* Almost the equivalent of **j'ai besoin de,** for which it is often used. Thus, in a **tabac** (*tobacconist's*), when asked what are your requirements, you can either say **j'ai besoin de cigarettes** or **il me faut des cigarettes.** There is a slight difference between the two, though it need hardly worry you. Your sense will guide you. **Avoir besoin de,** means what it says, *I have need of*, whereas **il me faut** means *It is necessary for me to have.*

FAIRE, followed by the infinitive of a verb, means *to cause to.* Thus : **faire voir,** *to cause to see, to show.* **Voulez-vous me faire voir des cravates, s'il vous plaît ?** *Will you please show me some neckties?*

(NOTE: s.v.p. is much used as an abbreviation for **s'il vous plaît.**)

If you wish to say : *How do you say " nice " in French?* you can express it either **Comment dîtes-vous** " *nice* " **en français ?** or, better, **Comment dit-on** " *nice* " **en français ?** Answer : **On dit " gentil."**

CETTE NUIT means *last night*, not *this night*, which would usually be **ce soir. Avez-vous bien dormi cette nuit ?** *Did you sleep well last night?*

There are two verbs in French for *to know* : **SAVOIR,** which means *to know intellectually*, and **CONNAÎTRE,** which means *to be acquainted with.* Thus : *Do you know Mr. Brown?* **Connaissez-vous M. Brown ?** *Do you know French?* **Savez-vous le français ? Connaissez-vous ce français ?** *Do you know that Frenchman?*

PAYER means both *to pay* and *to pay for.* Thus: **Je vais vous payer une bouteille de bière,** *I'm going to pay for a bottle of beer for you.*

TEXT :

Les raisons du déficit de la Radio

La Radiodiffusion française annonce pour cette année un déficit de 800 millions ! Elle prétend que la hausse des salaires, des prix du matériel et surtout de l'électricité, est responsable de ce déséquilibre budgétaire.

Possible. Mais personne ne nous fera croire que des économies massives ne puissent être réalisées.

Ainsi, la Radio compte-t-elle 3,000 personnes employées au mois. Sur ce chiffre, plus d'un tiers, c'est-à-dire plus de 1,000 sont affectées à la perception de la taxe radiophonique. 1,000 fonctionaires pour envoyer les formules aux détenteurs de postes et encaisser les mandats. On imagine volontiers le volume de papier que ces employées doivent remuer.

Est-ce que cette taxe, qui vient d'être portée à 750 francs par an, ne pourrait être perçue par les contributions directes ? Cela ferait une économie de temps et de papier et surtout d'argent. Si l'on pense, en effet, que le moindre de ces percepteurs touche 12,000 francs par mois, la somme dépensée par an pour payer les seuls salaires de ces employés est de 144 millions !

Il existe en France, a estimé l'autre jour Paul Rivet, lors d'une conférence de presse, près de 2 millions de postes clandestins ; ce qui représente, au nouveau taux (de la taxe) 1 milliard 500 millions !

Est-ce que tout cela n'appelle pas une réforme radicale ?

TRANSLATION :

Reasons for the Radio deficit

The French broadcasting (system) announces for this year a deficit of 800 millions ! It claims that the increase in salaries, the price of material, and above all of electricity is responsible for this budgetary disequilibrium (lack of balance).

Possible. But nobody will make us believe that massive economies cannot be realized (effected).

Thus, the Radio counts 3,000 people employed on a monthly basis. Of this number more than a third, that is to say more than 1,000, are dealing with the collection of the radio tax. 1,000 officials to send (out) the forms to owners of receivers and collect the money orders. One willingly (easily) imagines the volume of paper which these employees must turn over.

Cannot this tax, which has just been increased to 750 francs per year, be collected by direct contributions (payments)? That would make an economy of time and paper and above all of money. If one thinks, in fact, that the least of these collectors touches (earns) 12,000 francs a month, the sum expended over a year to pay the salaries only of these employees is 144 millions !

There exist in France, it was estimated the other day by Paul Rivet at a press conference, nearly 2 million clandestine receivers ; which represents at the new rate (of the tax) 1 milliard * 500 millions !

Does not all that call for a radical reform ?

WORDS SIMILAR IN BOTH LANGUAGES : In Lesson I, § 4, and elsewhere, we have drawn your attention to the important factor of resemblance between French and English words. We

* **un milliard** = 1,000,000,000.

have also given you some lists of examples, and shall continue
to do so, though we shall not attempt to exhaust the subject.
Now we wish to point out that, when a French and English word
are the same or almost the same, you must be careful when giving
the English equivalent—the best equivalent may not be the exactly
similar word. Thus **compréhensible**, *comprehensible*, but there
is also *understandable*. **Croyable**, *credible*, also *believable*. The
French word has both a similar and a dissimilar equivalent in
English, and more often than not the dissimilar one makes the
best English. Look out for this in the READING.

§ 4. *Radio*

If you are lucky enough to have a powerful short-wave radio,
perhaps you have been tuning in on overseas French-language
broadcasts, as a means of hearing spoken French. Perhaps you are now catching the gist of such items as the *news*
(**les nouvelles**) and *weather reports* (**les bulletins météor-
ologiques**). Until you begin to feel confident of your ability
to follow the *announcer* (whom the French call, curiously
enough, **Le speaker!**), you should be satisfied with the news
bulletins. Or you might venture on an occasional *Talk* (**une
causerie**). You will have become accustomed to the announcer's:
Allo! Allo! Ici radio . . . (name of station), or **Ici le poste de
radiodiffusion de** (name of station), or **Ici le poste de** (name
of station). As you know, there are:

> **l'onde courte,** the short wave
> **l'onde moyenne,** the medium wave
> **la grande onde,** the long wave

And the following terms are useful :

> **la station de radiodiffusion,** broadcasting station
> **l'émission,** transmission (also **la transmission**)
> **la réception,** reception
> **le haut-parleur,** the loudspeaker
> **l'antenne,** the aerial

You yourself are **l'auditeur**, *the listener*; and **accorder la
réception** is to *tune in*. *To listen* is **se mettre à l'écoute**.

Un poste is a *radio set*. **Une lampe** is *a tube*. *A two-tube set*, **un poste à deux lampes**. *A five-tube set*, **un poste à cinq lampes**. **Capter des postes étrangers**, *to catch foreign stations*.

It will be a happy day when you feel you can listen to **les numéros en vedette**. **La vedette** means literally a *sentry* or important person, but it is used for our word *star* in reference to a theater or film star (**une vedette de théâtre, une vedette de l'écran** *(screen)*). Hence, **un numéro en vedette** means a *"star-turn,"* which, on the radio, means a skit or an act in which one or more stars take part. This is something to look forward to, as these items may be a little difficult for you just yet. **La station a terminé l'émission de ce soir**, *the station is closing down for this evening (tonight)*. **Bon soir, chers auditeurs, bon soir.**

TEXT:

Squatters au Waldorf

Richard Cox, ex-G.I. sans logement depuis deux ans, lit dans son journal la description de l'appartement qu'occupe au Waldorf Astoria le roi Michel de Roumanie. Il jette sa femme et ses deux enfants dans un taxi, se présente à la réception de l'hôtel, demande une belle chambre dont il accepte le prix (3,600 fr. par jour). Il monte immédiatement donner un vrai bain à ses boys, et téléphone au directeur de l'hôtel : " Cette chambre me plaît, je la garde. Je vous donnerai 8,000 francs par mois ! Pour le reste, addressez-vous au maire de New-York City."

M. O'Dwyer a répondu que ses services allaient, conformément à la loi, chercher un logement pour ce vétéran. En attendant, les garçons du Waldorf ont offert de payer la différence et même de servir à leurs frais le breakfast quotidien des squatters. Mais la clientèle chic de l'étage s'est plainte de "vulgaires odeurs de cuisine," car les Cox, pour éviter les frais de restaurant, déjeunent dans leur chambre.

*

A Pittsburg, un certain Nathaniel Evans demande le divorce parce que, chaque fois qu'elle le surprend au café avec des amis,

sa femme lui brise sur la tête un moulage de la statue de la
Liberté ! ! !

Mrs. Evans est une humoriste.

TRANSLATION :

Squatters at the Waldorf

*Richard Cox, ex-G.I., without a lodging (home) for two years,
reads in his newspaper the description of the apartment (suite) at the
Waldorf-Astoria occupied by King Michael of Roumania. He
throws his wife and his two children into a taxi, presents himself at
the reception (desk) of the hotel (and) asks for a beautiful room, for
which he accepts (agrees to) the price (3,600 fcs. a day). He goes up
(to it) immediately to give a real bath to his boys, and telephones to
the manager of the hotel : " This room pleases me, I am keeping·it.
I shall give you 8,000 francs a month ! For the rest, apply to the
mayor of New York City."*

*Mr. O'Dwyer has replied that his services (department) would, in
accordance with the law, look for a dwelling for this veteran. Meanwhile, the waiters at the Waldorf have offered to pay the difference and
even to serve at their expense the daily breakfast of the squatters. But
the smart clientèle of the floor has complained of the " vulgar smells
of cooking," for the Coxes, to avoid restaurant costs, lunch in their
room.*

*

*At Pittsburg, a certain Nathaniel Evans asks for divorce because,
each time that she surprises him at the café with his friends, his wife
breaks on his head a (plaster) casting of the Statue of Liberty !*
Mrs. Evans is a humorist (has a sense of humour).

SIMILAR WORDS: To illustrate what we said in § 3 of this
lesson, there is a group of about 350 adjectives which resemble
each other in the two languages and have the following endings :
-ABLE, -IBLE, -OBLE, and **-UBLE.** Thus :

affable   capable   éligible   noble   soluble

Among them we meet the French word **sensible,** and the
unwary student might immediately think that the English
equivalent is *sensible*. Not at all. The English for **sensible** is
sensitive or *susceptible*. What, then, is the French for the English
word ´sensible? Answer : **sensé.** This should serve as a warning that you must take care, when you meet a French word
(especially an adjective) like an English one, to scrutinize the
equivalent and see that it is one. Look out for this in the
Reading.

§ 5. *Spoken French:*

Since it may not be possible for you to hear French-language radio programs, you may choose to get practice in listening to French by hearing French records. If such records are not available in your city, they can be bought by mail from: Period Music Company, 884 Tenth Ave., New York City; and Goldsmith's Music Shop, 401 West 42 St., New York City. Both these companies offer recordings by well-known French writers and actors, including the actors of the Comedie Française, reading famous plays, poems, and speeches. You can hear Charles Boyer reading Lafayette's ideas on a Declaration of the Rights of Man, or Gide, Camus, and Cocteau reading their own works.

IMITATION OF PRONUNCIATION: The *first* object of listening to spoken French—as we have already explained—is to accustom your ears to the sounds of French. When your ears are accustomed to these sounds, *and* you know what you have been taught, you will understand what is being said. Remember that those two conditions are absolutely necessary for success. If you cannot understand, it may be due to one of two reasons —or both : (1) either you have not caught the sounds; or (2) you do not know or recognize the words spoken. THIS IN-DICATES A NEED EITHER FOR CAREFUL REVIEW OF WHAT YOU HAVE LEARNED, OR IT MEANS THAT YOU MUST START AGAIN AT THE POINT INDICATED IN LESSON VI, § 1—AND PRACTICE IN THE MANNER INDICATED FOR A WEEK OR TWO. Do not be impatient or get worried because you cannot yet do all you wish. It is merely a matter of patience and practice; and success will come if you persist. NEVER MISS AN OPPORTUNITY OF REPEATING AFTER THE SPEAKER—IMITATING HIM EXACTLY—EITHER A NEW WORD OR PHRASE.

Once again, we repeat the basis of the method in this course :

(1) We provide you with the essential " mechanics " of the language—grammar.

(2) We provide you with the " basic vocabulary ."

(3) We provide you with a generous measure of " assisted reading "—that is actual French as used by French people, plus a complete translation.

With this material you have—the language.

But to understand it *spoken* and *to speak it*, you must listen to it spoken and imitate the speaker.   There is *no* other way!
From now on, we shall leave the question of listening in your hands. Concentrate for all you are worth on the reading and learn as much of the "basic vocabulary" as you possibly can.

A useful acquisition at this stage would be a good small dictionary.   Although this course can be worked through without the aid of a dictionary, the sooner the learner gets into the habit of looking up words, the better it is.   Admirable dictionaries for the pocket are those of Bellows (published by Longmans Green) and Kettridge's *French-English, English-French* Dictionary. These are in French and English. The *Nouveau Petit Larousse Illustré,* an all-French dictionary, is strongly recommended, since in using it the learner will accustom himself to thinking in French.

Text :

Les Ruinés

Depuis vingt ans—autant dire depuis toujours !—les directeurs de théâtre se plaignent: " Ruinés ! Nous sommes ruinés ! "
Ecrasés par les taxes, ils se posent, avec angoisse, la question de savoir s'ils peuvent encore s'offrir ce luxe : une belle pièce dont les recettes soient mauvaises ? " Nous voilà contraints de négliger le génie, de tourner le dos au talent, et de nous mettre au régime du . . . succès perpétuel ! Que voulez-vous, il faut joindre les deux bouts ! "

Quant à leurs confrères, ceux qui président aux destinées des music-halls, ils vont encore plus loin : " Nous sommes morts ! " s'exclament-ils.

Et pour bien le prouver, savez-vous ce qu'ils ont fait ? Ils viennent de se réunir à—et avec les vedettes de—l'A.B.C. Ils se sont constitués en " Comité de Défense ."   Ils ont frappé du poing sur la table : " Ça ne doit plus durer comme ça ! "

Un journaliste, dans les couloirs, souriait :
" Ils sont inouïs, ces directeurs ! " disait-il, " tous se plaignent. . . . Aucun d'eux, que je sache, n'a encore fait faillite ! "

TRANSLATION :

The Ruined

*For twenty years—as well say always—theater directors complain :
" Ruined ! We are ruined ! "   Crushed by taxes they put to themselves with agony the question of knowing if they can yet offer themselves this luxury : a fine piece (play) of which the takings might be bad ?   " There we are, compelled to neglect genius, to turn our back on talent, and to put ourselves on the regimen of . . . perpetual success !   What would you, it is necessary to make ends meet ! "*

As regards their colleagues who preside over the destinies of the music-halls, they go still further : " We are dead ! " they exclaim.

And to prove it well, do you know what they have done?   They have just met at—and with the stars of—the A.B.C.   They have constituted themselves into a " Committee of Defense."   They have struck their fist on the table : " That must not continue like that ! "

A journalist in the corridors smiled :

" They are unheard of (unparalleled, outrageous), those directors ! " he said.   " All complain. . . . Not one of them that I know has yet gone bankrupt."

NOTE : *The translation is literal—it could be made much more idiomatic—to enable you to follow the French word for word.*

SIMILAR WORDS—ENDING -ION : There are more than 2,000 words ending in -ION which resemble each other in French and English.   The ending -ion is the same throughout, but the letters which precede it vary.   Thus : -cion, -gion, -nion, -sion, -ssion, and, perhaps commonest of all, -tion (pronounced as if written -ssion).   They are *all* feminine except le bastion, ·bastion.   But even these words need attention. Note, for example, the following :

les munitions, ammunition
la condamnation, conviction
la crucifixion *or* le crucifiement, crucifixion
la transpiration, perspiration

la reprise, resumption
la sujétion *or* l'assujétissement, subjection
l'instruction *or* l'enseignement, tuition, teaching

LESSON XI

§ 1. *Vocabulary for Speaking and Reading*

At this point, please turn back to Lesson III, § 3, and reread the note on " Basic Vocabulary." When you have done so, but not before, you should continue to read below.

From Lesson III to Lesson X, you have been provided with :

(1) Nearly 1,000 of the " basic " words of French.

(2) A number of hints as to how to make the best of this vocabulary, how to increase it by " word-building," and how to assimilate thousands of words " similar " in both languages.

Although it may seem much to you, the amount of grammar we have asked you to study has not been great—but it is sufficient to enable you, if you know the words given, to read normal, standard French.

From this point onward, we wish you to concentrate most of your effort on the *Reading*.

From now on, each section will have a "Reading Vocabulary" of words carefully chosen and set out, the most important in large type, to enable you to memorize them as you go along. You have now had enough experience in the readings, and have been given enough hints, so that you should be able to guess the gender of each noun you come to in the "Reading Vocabulary." If you wish to look up the gender of these nouns, however, you will find a glossary at the back of the book where all nouns from the "Reading Vocabulary" are listed with the article indicating gender.

Many words from the "Basic Vocabulary" already given are repeated in the "Reading Vocabulary." When you know both these vocabularies, you will be equipped with the 2,500 MOST USEFUL WORDS IN THE LANGUAGE, plus many others hardly less useful which have come up in the course of the reading matter : in all, well over 3,000 words. This, with grammatical inflections, word-building, and "similar words" provides a total vocabulary of remarkable range.

READING: You will now begin to read the famous work of Voltaire known as **Candide.** You have already sampled a pleasant modern style in **Tartarin de Tarascon.** Now you will enjoy the brilliance of one of the greatest writers of all time. Voltaire's style is simple and straightforward, lucid and sparkling; and you may find yourself comparing it with that of George Bernard Shaw. As before, we shall first help you with a complete translation; and then with notes to explain difficulties. First make out the sense with the aid of the translation; then read the French by itself. GO OVER EACH EXCERPT SEVERAL TIMES UNTIL YOU CAN READ AND UNDERSTAND IT WITH EASE. In this way, you will *absorb* the language.

¶ 1. CANDIDE OU L'OPTIMISME
Par Voltaire
CHAPITRE PREMIER
Comment Candide fut élevé dans un beau château, et comment il fut chassé d'ici

Il y avait en Westphalie, dans le château de M. le baron de Thunder-ten-tronckh, un jeune garçon à qui la nature avait donné les mœurs les plus douces. Sa physionomie annonçait son âme. Il avait le jugement assez droit, avec l'esprit le plus simple; c'est, je crois, pour cette raison qu'on le nommait Candide. Les anciens domestiques de la maison soupçonnaient qu'il était fils de la sœur de monsieur le baron et d'un bon et honnête gentilhomme du voisinage, que cette demoiselle ne voulait jamais épouser, parce qu'il n'avait pu prouver que soixante et onze quartiers, et que le reste de son arbre généalogique avait été perdu par l'injure du temps.

TRANSLATION:
CANDIDE or OPTIMISM
By Voltaire
CHAPTER I
How Candide was brought up in a beautiful castle and how he was chased (expelled) from it

There was in Westphalia, in the castle of Baron Thunder-ten-tronckh, a young boy to whom nature had given the most gentle manners (character). His physiognomy (face) expressed his soul.

His judgment was quite upright (and) with it the simplest mind ; it is, I believe, for this reason that he was called Candide. The old servants of the house suspected that he was (the) son of the Baron's sister and a good and honest gentleman of the neighborhood whom this young lady never wished to marry, because he could prove only seventy-one quarterings (heraldic signs), and (that) the rest of his genealogical tree had been lost by the injury of time.

Reading Vocabulary—1–2

ABAISSER, *to lower*
ABANDONNER, *to abandon*
abattre, *to cast down, overthrow*
abbé, *abbot*
aborder, *to address, approach*
aboutir, *to end in, to come to*
ABRI, *shelter*
absence, *absence*
absorber, *to absorb, engross*
accent, *accent, tone*
ACCEPTER, *to accept*

accuser, *to accuse*
ACHETER, *to buy*
achever, *to finish*
acquérir, *to acquire*
ACTE, *act*
ACTION, *action*
ADIEU, *farewell*
ADMETTRE, *to admit*
administration, *administration*
ADMIRATION, *admiration*
admirer, *to admire*

ACCIDENT, *accident*
ACCOMPAGNER, *accompany*
accomplir, *to accomplish*
ACCORD, *agreement, understanding*
accorder, *to grant, agree*
accourir, *to turn or hasten to*
accrocher, *to hook*
accroître, *to increase, grow*
accueillir, *to greet*

adopter, *to adopt*
ADRESSE, *skill, address*
adresser, *to apply, to address*
adversaire, *adversary*
LES AFFAIRES, *business, affairs*
affecter, *to affect, to feign*
affection, *affection*
affirmer, *to affirm, to assure*
âge, *age*

§ 2. *Use of Certain Tenses—The Imperfect*

In Lesson V, § 1, we dealt with the " Essentials of the Verb," and in subsequent lessons you have been given sufficient knowledge to enable you to *use* the simple forms of the verbs for the ordinary purposes of life. But in reading and listening to radio you will come upon other forms which you need not *use* until your knowledge of the language is much farther advanced, but which you must be able to *recognize* when you see or hear them. Of these, the most important is the imperfect tense, of which the regular endings are :

(je) **-AIS**	(nous) **-IONS**
(tu) **-AIS**	(vous) **-IEZ**
(il) **-AIT**	(ils) **-AIENT**

These endings for the imperfect are easily recognizable, and the general signification of the imperfect corresponds to the English " continuous " past tense expressed by I WAS -ING, as in *I was speaking*, *I was giving*, *I was finishing* : **je donnais, je parlais, je finiSSais.** It is important to remember this simple, " basic " meaning of the French imperfect. But the French imperfect has a more subtle meaning which you will meet again and again in reading. The Grammar of the French Academy explains it thus :

> " The imperfect records a past event in relation to the moment at which one speaks, but which *still continued* at a determined moment of the past."

That may seem a little complex, but it is not. It merely means that you have to notice two kinds of past, one which is *continuous* and goes on parallel with another kind which is *sharply defined*. The example given by that final grammatical authority is :

Les cloches sonnaient quand le cortège arriva sur la place.

The bells *were ringing* when the procession *arrived* in the square.

The word **arriva** is past definite tense, which will be dealt with in the next section.

The imperfect tense is always used to indicate a constantly recurring event or action. Thus : **Tous les hivers il séjournait un mois en Italie,** *Every winter he resided (used to reside) one month in Italy*.

Text:

L'Union Douanière

Au moment où la question de l'union douanière européenne est à l'ordre du jour, il est intéressant de rappeler que la première union douanière de quelque importance est apparue en 1882 avec le *Zollverein* allemand organisé entre la Prusse et certains petits Etats de la Confédération germanique.   Mais des droits de douane intérieurs ont néanmoins subsisté pendant de nombreuses années à l'intérieur de ce *Zollverein*.   Et celui-ci n'a été achevé qu'en 1888 par l'adhésion de Brême et de Hambourg.

On peut encore citer comme exemple l'union douanière entre l'Allemagne et le Luxembourg de 1842, entre le Liechtenstein et l'Autriche en 1852, entre la France et Monaco en 1865, entre la Belgique et le Luxembourg en 1921, entre le Liechtenstein et la Suisse en 1924, entre l'Allemagne et la Bohême-Moravie en 1940.   Dans la plupart des cas il s'agissait soit d'un prélude à une fusion politique, soit de l'abdication par un petit Etat de toute initiative commerciale au profit d'un voisin plus puissant, soit d'une fusion imposée par la force.   C'est pourquoi l'union hollando-belgo-luxembourgeoise, réalisée récemment et connue sous le nom de *Benelux*, n'entre dans aucune de ces catégories et constitue une expérience des plus intéressantes.

Translation:

The Customs Union

At the moment when the question of European customs union is the order of the day, it is interesting to recall that the first customs union of some importance appeared in 1882 with the German Zollverein *organized between Prussia and certain little States of the Germanic Confederation.   But interior customs duties have nevertheless existed for many years inside this* Zollverein. *And the latter was only achieved in 1888 by the adhesion (joining) of Bremen and of Hamburg.*

One can still (also) cite as (an) example the customs union between Germany and Luxemburg of 1842, between Liechtenstein and Austria in 1852, between France and Monaco in 1865, between Belgium and Luxemburg in 1921, between Liechtenstein and Switzerland in 1924, between Germany and Bohemia-Moravia in 1940.   In most cases it was a matter (let it be) either of a prelude to a political fusion or abdication by a smaller State of all commercial initiative to the benefit of a more powerful neighbor, or a fusion imposed by force.   That is why the Holland–Belgium–Luxembourg union achieved recently and known under the name of Benelux, *does not enter into any of these categories and constitutes a most interesting experiment.*

Reading Vocabulary—3

AGENT, *agent*

S'AGIR DE, *to be a question of*

agiter, *to agitate*

AIDE, *aid*

AIDER, *to help*

aile, *wing*

AIMER, *to like, love*

AIR, *air*

aise, *ease*

AJOUTER, *to add*

allée, *passage, path*

allumer, *to light*

allure, *pace, gait, bearing*

ambition, *ambition*

âme, *soul*

AMENER, *to bring, lead*

AMI, *friend*

AMITIÉ, *friendship*

AMOUR, *love*

amuser, *to amuse*

§ 3. *Use of Certain Tenses—the Past Definite*

A less frequently recurring tense which you will meet in reading but hardly ever in speaking is the past definite, which is what its name indicates : a *definite* past.

In **-ER** verbs, its endings are: **-ai, -as, -a, -âmes, -âtes, -èrent.**

In **-IR** and **-RE verbs** the regular endings are : **-is, -is, -it, -îmes, -îtes, -irent.**

In **-OIR** verbs, the endings are : **-us, -us, -ut, -ûmes, -ûtes, -urent.**

Thus :

je donnai, je finis.   Nous donnâmes, ils finirent.
je reçus, ils reçurent.

The simple usage of the past definite is that it records something which happened strictly within a past period, and has either begun or ended—there is no question of *duration* as there is with the imperfect—and is not related to the present. It is used for narrative and for past events happening in succession. It is sometimes called the " historical past," being much used in historical statements.

Thus : **la première guerre mondiale dura quatre ans.**

There will be no need for you to know much more about this tense, but from what has been said above you will appreciate why French writers of narrative find it very useful. Note also its precision. You will meet it in reading newspapers, novels, and most branches of literature; but only pedantic speakers would use it in conversation. *You* will *never* use it to express the past, but it is important that you should be able to recognize it when you see it.

PREPOSITIONS **à** AND **de:** You have already learned the simple meanings of these two common prepositions : **à** = *to*, **de** = *of*. Now note the following :

> **à** is used to express *locality* : **à Paris, à Londres, à Rome.** *In* Paris, *in* London, *in* Rome. **Il est à Paris,** etc.
>
> **à** is used to express a *purpose* : **une bouteille à vin,** *a bottle for wine, a wine bottle.* **La salle à manger,** *the hall* (*or room*) *for dining, the dining room.* **Une tasse à thé,** *teacup.*
>
> **à** can express a distinguishing feature or way of doing things : **à l'anglaise, à la française,** *in English, French fashion.*
>
> **de** expresses *ownership* : **le chien du capitaine,** *the captain's dog. Instrument* : **un coup de fusil,** *a gunshot. Contents* : **une bouteille de vin,** *a bottle of wine.* Nature, or *substance* of which made : **un encrier de verre,** *a glass inkpot.*

It is important to know these usages, as they are continually recurring.

¶ 2. CANDIDE

M. le baron était un des plus puissants seigneurs de la Westphalie, car son château avait une porte et des fenêtres. Sa grande salle même était ornée d'une tapisserie. Tous les chiens de ses basses-cours composaient une meute dans le besoin ; ses palefreniers étaient ses piqueurs ; le vicaire du village était son grand aumônier. Ils l'appelaient tous monseigneur, et ils riaient quand il faisait des contes.

Madame la baronne, qui pesait environ trois cent cinquante livres, s'attirait par là une très grande considération, et faisait les honneurs de la maison avec une dignité qui la rendait encore plus respectable. Sa fille Cunégonde, âgée de dix-sept ans, était haute en couleur, fraîche, grasse, appétissante. Le fils du baron paraissait en tout digne de son père. Le précepteur Pangloss était l'oracle de la maison, et le petit Candide écoutait ses leçons avec toute la bonne foi de son âge et de son caractère.

TRANSLATION : *The Baron was one of the most powerful lords of Westphalia, for his castle had a door and windows. His great hall was even adorned with a tapestry. All the dogs of his stable yards made up a (hunting) pack in case of need ; his grooms were his huntsmen ; the village curate was his (head) chaplain. They all called him " My Lord," and they laughed when he told tales.*

The Baroness, who weighed about three hundred and fifty pounds, was on this account greatly respected and did the honors of the house with a dignity which rendered her still more respectable. Her daughter Cunégonde, aged seventeen years, was high in colour (rosy), fresh, plump and tempting. The Baron's son seemed in every way worthy of his father. Pangloss the tutor was the oracle of the house-(hold), and little Candide listened to his lessons with all the good faith of his age and disposition.

Reading Vocabulary—4

an, *year*

angoisse, *agony*

ANIMAL, *animal*

animer, *to animate*

ANNÉE, *year*

annoncer, *to announce*

AOÛT, *August*

apaiser, *to pacify, to appease*

apercevoir, *to perceive*

APPARAÎTRE, *to appear*

appareil, *apparatus*

apparence, *appearance*

APPARTEMENT, *apartment, flat*

appartenir, *to belong*

appel, *roll call, call*

APPELER, *to call*

applaudir, *to applaud*

appliquer, *to apply*

APPORTER, *to bring*

apprécier, *to appreciate*

§ 4. *Verbs Followed by* à *and* de

When a verb is followed by an infinitive—for example, **il doit faire cela,** *he must do that*—in French it may either be : (*a*) followed by **à** or (*b*) followed by **de** or (*c*) without a preposition ·following. There was no preposition following **il doit** in the sentence just quoted. But : **il a cessé de faire ça,** *he has ceased from doing that.* And : **Il aime à parler,** *he likes to speak.*

To explain *why* a French verb is not followed by a preposition, or why it should sometimes be followed by **à** or by **de,** would be far outside the scope of these lessons—if it could be explained satisfactorily!—and you would probably end by being more puzzled than when you began. As in the case of the gender of nouns—we advised you to learn the article with each noun as the safest solution of the problem—the safest way to deal with this problem of the preposition after the verb is by memorizing. Below, you will find three lists of essential verbs classified into : (*a*) those which are not followed by a preposition; (*b*) those followed by **à**; and (*c*) those followed by **de**. You need not learn (*b*) and (*c*) now, but you should make sure to memorize (*a*).

(*a*) *Verbs followed by an infinitive* WITHOUT *preposition* :

ALLER, to go
DÉSIRER, to desire, wish
DEVOIR, ought, must
ENTENDRE, hear
ENVOYER, send
ESPÉRER, to hope
FAIRE, to make, do
FALLOIR, to be necessary

LAISSER, to let, allow
POUVOIR, to be able
SAVOIR, to know how to
SEMBLER, to seem
VENIR, to come from *
VOIR, to see
VOULOIR, to wish

Thus : **je vais faire mon devoir.   Je vois tomber la pluie.**

(*b*) *Verbs followed by* **à** *and an infinitive* :

AIDER, to help
AIMER, to like, love
APPRENDRE, to learn
AVOIR, to have
CHERCHER, to seek
COMMENCER, to begin

INVITER, to invite
SE METTRE, to begin
RÉUSSIR, to succeed
ÊTRE PRÊT, to be ready
VENIR À, to happen

Thus : **il aime à parler français.**

(*c*) *Verbs followed by* **de** *and an infinitive* :

cesser, to cease
se contenter, to be satisfied
craindre, to fear
décider, to decide to
défendre, to forbid
demander, to ask
dire, to tell
empêcher, to prevent
essayer, to try
éviter, to avoid
être obligé de, to be obliged
  to (compelled)

oublier, to forget
persuader, to persuade
prendre soin de, to take care to
prier, to beg, pray
promettre, to promise
proposer, to propose
refuser, to refuse
regretter, to regret
se souvenir, to remember
venir de, to have just

* **Venir de** *also means* to have just . . .

Thus : **je viens de lui donner une cigarette**, *I have just given him a cigarette*. **DÉFENSE DE FUMER**, SMOKING FORBIDDEN.

TEXT :

EXPOSITION DU TOURISME PÉDESTRE

Aux Galeries Lafayette se tient actuellement une grande exposition organisée par le Touring-Club de France et consacrée au Tourisme pédestre et les Sentiers.   Donnant une rétrospective des sentiers de promenades créés dans notre pays par les associations de tourisme et les syndicats d'initiative, l'exposition du " Tourisme Pédestre " présentera en outre les réalisations de grande envergure qui se rencontrent à l'étranger où de véritables routes du marcheur ont vu le jour sur des parcours considérables. La Commission des sentiers du T.C.F. a mis à l'étude des projets analogues dont les principaux tracés retiendront à coup sûr l'attention des fervents de la randonnée et seront peut-être une révélation pour ceux qui en ignorent jusqu'ici les joies.

Nos lecteurs trouveront dans notre prochain numéro une étude complète sur cette question touristique de première importance, car il ne faut pas oublier que, quel que soit le mode de transport qui amène au but du voyage, la seule façon de pénétrer au cœur d'une région et d'amasser des souvenirs durables, c'est encore la longue promenade ou la randonnée sac au dos.

TRANSLATION :

TOURING ON FOOT EXHIBITION

At the Galeries Lafayette there is being held at this moment a big exhibition organized by the Touring Club of France and devoted to Touring on Foot and the (country) footpaths.   Giving a retrospect of the footpaths for walking created in our country by the tourist associations and the " initiative associations " (for encouraging touring), the exhibition of " Touring on Foot " will besides present the far-reaching achievements to be found abroad where veritable routes for the walker have seen the day (appeared) on (over) considerable distances.   The Commission of Footpaths of the T.C.F. has put under study similar projects of which the principal sketches will certainly hold the attention of the fervents (enthusiasts) of the outing and will perhaps be a revelation for those who hitherto are unaware of its joys.

Our readers will find in the next issue a complete study on this subject of touring, one of first importance, for one must not forget that, whatever may be the mode of transport which leads to the objective of the trip, the only way to penetrate to the heart of a region and to amass (collect) lasting remembrances is still the long walk or the hike with a bag on one's back.

Reading Vocabulary—5

APPRENDRE, *to learn*
approcher, *to approach*
approuver, *to approve*
appuyer, *to support, to lean*
APRÈS-MIDI, *afternoon*
ARBRE, *tree*
ardeur, *ardor, fervor*
argent, *money*
arme, *weapon, arm*
ARMÉE, *army*
armer, *to arm*

arracher, *to pluck out, to tear out*
  or *away*; also *tear up* or *off*
arranger, *to arrange*
ARRÊTER, *to stop*
arrivée, *arrival*
ARRIVER, *to arrive*
art, *art*
article, *article*
artiste, *artist*
aspect, *aspect*

§ 5. *Use of* **DANS, EN**—*and more about* à

You will have noticed in the last two sections that what you are now being taught is an extension of the *basic* knowledge provided in previous lessons.   In Lessons I to X was given the rough framework of the language.   Now you are learning its *refinements*, and French is notable for its refinements, for they are what makes it so delicate and subtle.   It need not in the least discourage you to know that they are vast in scope and sometimes capable of causing heated controversy among the best speakers and writers of French!   The " refinements " which you will be taught in this course are in *everyday usage*, and not to use them correctly does not necessarily mean that you would not be understood, but it would mean that you might be offending the ears of French people, most of whom are very conscious of their language.   Never forget that.   The more correctly you speak French, the more the average French person will admire you and go out of his or her way to please you.   Thus, you would be making a great mistake not to pay careful attention to what we say about seemingly unimportant " refinements ."

You know that in French there are two words for the English *in*—**DANS** and **EN**.   If you think it out, you will find that the

English word *in*, when it relates to time, has two meanings : it can mean *at the end of* or it can mean *during* or *in the space of*. In French **DANS** means *at the end of* and **EN** means *in the space of*. Thus : **je vais revenir DANS dix minutes** means *I am going to return at the end of ten minutes* and **je l'ai fait en cinq minutes** means *I have done it in the space of five minutes*. It is really quite simple.

As regards locality, the English word *in* becomes in French **EN** before the names of *countries* and **à** before the names of *towns*. Thus : **en France, en Angleterre.** But : **à Paris, à Londres.** Exceptions : **au Canada, au Japon, aux Etats-Unis.**

NOTE THE FOLLOWING : **à la campagne,** *in the country*. **au printemps,** *in spring*. **à mon avis,** *in my opinion*. **en même temps,** *at the same time*. **chez mon frère,** *at my brother's house*.

EN never takes an article before the noun it governs, except in the phrase **en l'air,** *in the air*. **En été,** *in (the) summer*.

¶ 3. CANDIDE

Pangloss enseignait la métaphysico-théologo-cosmolo-nigologie. Il prouvait admirablement qu'il n'y a point d'effet sans cause, et que, dans ce meilleur des mondes possibles, le château de monseigneur le baron était le plus beau des châteaux, et madame la meilleure des baronnes possible.

" Il est démontré," disait-il, " que les choses ne peuvent être autrement ; car tout étant fait pour une fin, tout est nécessairement pour la meilleure fin. Remarquez bien que les nez ont été faits pour porter des lunettes, aussi avons-nous des lunettes ; les jambes sont visiblement instituées pour être chaussées, et nous avons des chausses ; les pierres ont été formées pour être taillées et pour en faire des châteaux, aussi monseigneur a un très beau château ; le plus grand baron de la province doit être le mieux logé ; et les cochons étant faits pour être mangés, nous mangeons du porc toute l'année : par conséquent ceux qui ont avancé que tout est bien, ont dit une sottise ; il fallait dire que tout est au mieux."

TRANSLATION; *Pangloss taught metaphysico-theologo-cosmolo-nigology. He proved admirably that there is no effect without cause and that in this best of possible worlds the castle of My Lord the Baron was the most beautiful of castles, and Madame the best baroness possible.*

" It is demonstrated," said he, " that things cannot be otherwise ; for all being made for an end, all is necessarily for the best end.   Note well that noses have been made for wearing spectacles ; and so we have spectacles ; legs are visibly instituted to be breeched, and we have breeches; stones have been formed to be cut and for having castles made of them, and so My Lord has a very beautiful castle ; the greatest Baron of the province must be the best lodged ; and pigs being made to be eaten, we eat pork all the year ; consequently those who have advanced (submitted) that all is well have said a silly thing ; it was necessary to say that all is for the best."

Reading Vocabulary—6

S'ASSEOIR, *to sit down*

assister, *to be present at*

associer, *to associate*

assurer, *to assure*

attacher, *to attach*

attaque, *attack*

attaquer, *to attack*

ATTEINDRE, *to reach, to obtain*

ATTENDRE, *to wait for*

ATTENTION, *attention, care*

attirer, *to attract, entice*

attitude, *attitude, position*

augmenter, *to increase*

AUJOURD'HUI, *today*

auteur, *author*

autoriser, *to authorize*

autorité, *authority*

avance, *start, advance*

AVANCER, *to advance*

avantage, *advantage*

LESSON XII

§ 1. *More about* EN—*also* Y

EN as well as being a preposition is also a pronoun meaning *of* something or some person. It is the equivalent of DE plus a noun. It is used for persons and things, and it is both masculine and feminine and singular and plural—a useful word! Thus:

Avez-vous du lait? Avez-vous de l'encre? Avez-vous des plumes?

The answer in every case can be: **j'en ai,** *I have of it, of them.*

When you say **En avez-vous?** it embraces *Have you some of it?*, *Have you (of) them?*—irrespective of gender.

When you speak of number or use a word of quantity in French, the word EN is used where its equivalent would be omitted in English. Thus, in French you do not say *How many have you?* but *How many (of it, them) have you?* and the answer in French would be *I have six (of it, of them)*, and not just *I have six.*

Combien en avez-vous? How many have you?

J'en ai une douzaine, I have a dozen.

In § 4 of the last lesson you were given a list of verbs followed by **de** and the infinitive. EN is used with those verbs where we would say *it*. Thus: **En êtes-vous content? j'en suis content. Je m'en souviens,** *I remember it.*

You will remember the word Y in the verb Y AVOIR, *there to be.*

Y means *there*, and it is used both as a preposition of place and as the object of those verbs (XI, § 4) which take **à**. The chief difference between Y and EN is that Y is seldom used for persons. Use it for things only.

Thus:

j'y vais, I am going (there).

Avez-vous été à la gare? Have you been to the station?

j'y ai été, I have been (there).

And : **Il faut penser aux vacances.   J'y pense.**

Turn back to Lesson III, § 1, dealing with " Order of Pronouns with Verb," and you will see that **Y** and **EN** come last and always in the order **y, en.**   It is seldom that you will meet, and you will probably never have to express, such a sentence as this :

Nous leur y en avons parlé, We spoke to them of it there

—but there it is for you to contemplate and work out!   It is a useful mnemonic for the order of pronouns.

¶ 4. CANDIDE

Candide écoutait attentivement, et croyait innocemment ; car il trouvait mademoiselle Cunégonde extrêmement belle, quoiqu'il ne prît jamais la hardiesse de le lui dire.   Il concluait qu'après le bonheur d'être né baron de Thunder-ten-tronckh, le second degré de bonheur était d'être mademoiselle Cunégonde, le troisième de la voir tous les jours, et le quatrième d'entendre maître Pangloss, le plus grand philosophe de la province, et par conséquent de toute la terre.

Un jour Cunégonde, en se promenant auprès du château, dans le petit bois qu'on appelait parc, vit entre des broussailles le docteur Pangloss qui donnait une leçon de physique expérimentale à la femme de chambre de sa mère, petite brune très jolie et très docile.   Comme mademoiselle Cunégonde avait beaucoup de dispositions pour les sciences, elle observa sans souffler les expériences réitérées dont elle fut témoin.

TRANSLATION ;   *Candide listened attentively and believed innocently ; for he found mademoiselle Cunégonde extremely beautiful, although he never had (took) the boldness to tell her so.   He concluded that after the good luck to be born Baron de Thunder-ten-tronchk, the second degree of good fortune was to be mademoiselle Cunégonde, the third to see her every day, the fourth to hear master Pangloss, the greatest philosopher of the province and as a consequence of the whole earth.*

One day Cunégonde, when walking near the castle in the little wood they called a park, saw among the brushwood Doctor Pangloss giving a lesson in experimental physics to her mother's chambermaid, a very pretty and very docile brunette.   As mademoiselle Cunégonde had many inclinations for the sciences, she observed without breathing the repeated experiments of which she was witness.

Reading Vocabulary—7–8

avenir, *future*

aventure, *adventure*

avertir, *to warn*

AVIS, *opinion*

aviser, *to advise, inform*

avouer, *to confess, admit*

baisser, *to lower*

balancer, *to balance*

banc, *bench*

bande, *band*

bête, *beast*

BIEN, *good* (noun), *well* (adv.)

BILLET, *note, ticket* *

blessé, *wounded man*

BLESSER, *to wound*

blessure, *wound*

BOIRE, *to drink*

BOIS, *wood*

BOÎTE, *box*

bonheur, *good fortune*

bonhomme, *good fellow*

barbe, *beard*

BAS, *bottom*, also *stocking*

bataille, *battle*

BÂTIMENT, *building*

bâtir, *to build*

bâton, *stick*

battre, *to beat*

beauté, *beauty*

besogne, *task*

BESOIN, *need*

BONSOIR, *good night*

BONTÉ, *goodness*

bord, *edge, bank*

borner, *to limit*

BOUCHE, *mouth*

bouger, *to move*

boule, *ball*

bouleverser, *to destroy, to overturn*

bouquet, *bouquet*

§ 2. *Use of the Past Participle*

You have already (Lesson V, § 1) made the acquaintance of
the past participle, and you should have a fair idea of its simple
use to make compound tenses. There are other common usages
which you should be able to recognize.

(*a*) The past participle can be for all practical purposes
an adjective, as in **les lettres reçues hier,** *the letters
received yesterday,* **les plaisirs passés,** *the past pleasures,*
etc. This usage is not only easy to recognize, but you are
always safe in using the past participle of any verb as an
adjective, not forgetting that the adjective agrees in gender
and number with the noun.

(*b*) A few past participles are in common usage for commercial or general purposes and are then invariable : **payé,**

* **un ticket** = a bus ticket; *also* a coupon *or* numbered slip, check.

paid (for bills, accounts), **approuvé**, *approved*, **certifié**, *certified*; and there is **trouvé**, *found*, which one sees in notices. **Trouvé dans la rue Scribe, un carnet**, *Found in the Rue Scribe, a notebook.*

PAST PARTICIPLE WITH ÊTRE : When a past participle is conjugated with **être**, it agrees in gender and number with the *subject* : **Votre lettre est écrite, mes lettres sont écrites. La porte est fermée, les portes sont fermées.**

PAST PARTICIPLE WITH AVOIR : When the past participle is conjugated with **avoir**, it agrees in gender and number with the direct object **when this precedes**. Note well :

J'ai vu la sœur.	**La sœur que j'ai vue.**
J'ai écrit une lettre.	**La lettre que j'ai écrite. Les lettres que j'ai écrites.**

REFLEXIVE VERBS : Reflexive verbs (see Lesson VI, § 2) are *always* conjugated with **être**. As the reflexive pronoun is the preceding direct object, this means that the past participle always agrees with it. Thus **se laver**, *to wash oneself*, a very common reflexive verb, becomes in the past participle **Je me suis lavée**, when the speaker is feminine. Similarly, **Elles se sont lavées** and **Ils se sont lavés.**

If you wish to write correct French, you must know these simple rules, and it is as well to know the reason for such changes when you come across them in the written language.

TEXT :

CETTE SEMAINE

VENDREDI.—Grand gala de la Radio au Théâtre Mogador. Gaby Morlay qui a perfectionné jusqu'à la grâce et même jusqu'au génie, le visage, la voix, les gestes, et ce regard de bonbon au miel de la midinette parisienne, raconte, dans les coulisses, avant d'aller se poster devant le micro où elle va accueillir, tout à l'heure, de solennelles déclarations de Charles Boyer qui, lui, parlera de Hollywood—comblant ainsi douze mille kilomètres d'océan, de ciel, de vagues, de nuit, d'espace—qu'elle a rencontré, dans l'après-midi, un petit garçon de huit ans, fils d'une de ses amies. C'est la première fois qu'il la voit.

C'est la première fois qu'elle peut l'embrasser. Il a été élevé à Cannes, chez ses grands-parents. Il vient d'arriver à Paris. Mais il a vu Gaby Morlay, souvent, au cinéma. Alors, émerveillé par la réalité, il la regarde longuement, la mange des yeux, la détaille depuis le front jusqu'au menton. Pensez donc! Une de ses " idoles " en chair et en os, là, à portée de sa main. . . . Et, sans y prendre garde, il laisse échapper:

" Oh! Madame! Comme c'est drôle. . . . Je croyais que tu étais une image! "

TRANSLATION;

THIS WEEK

FRIDAY.—Great Radio Gala at the Mogador Theatre. Gaby Morlay, who has perfected to grace and even to genius, face, voice, gestures, and that honey-sweet look of the Parisian dressmaker, tells in the corridors, before going to take her stand before the micro(phone) where she is going to receive very soon, solemn declarations from Charles Boyer, who (himself) will speak from Hollywood—thus filling 12,000 kilometers of ocean, sky, waves, night, space—that she met in the afternoon a little boy of eight years, son of one of her friends. It is the first time that he sees her. It is the first time that she can embrace (kiss) him. He has been brought up at Cannes at his grandparents. He has just arrived in Paris. But he has seen Gaby Morlay often at the cinema. Then, marveling at the reality, he looks at her for a long time, eats her with his eyes, goes over the details from forehead to chin. Just think! One of his " idols " in flesh and bone there, within reach of his hand. . . . And without taking care he allows to escape:

" Oh! Madame! How funny it is. . . . I thought that you were a picture! "

*Reading Vocabulary—*9

BOUT, *end, extremity*
BOUTEILLE, *bottle*
branche, *branch*
BRAS, *arm*
briller, *to shine*
briser, *to break open, smash*
BRUIT, *noise*
brûler, *to burn*
bureau, *office*
but, *goal, aim, target*

cabinet, *study, private room;*
  water closet
CACHER, *to hide*
CAFÉ, *coffee*
caisse, *chest, cashbox, till*
calme, *calm*
calmer, *to calm*
camarade, *comrade*
camp, *camp*
campagne, *country*
capitaine, *captain*

Reading Vocabulary—10

capitale, *capital*	cent, *a hundred*
caractère, *character, temper*	centaine, *about a hundred*
caresser, *to caress*	CENTRE, *center*
carrière, *career*	cercle, *circle, club*
CARTE, *map, card*	certitude, *certainty*
cas, *case*	cesse, *ceasing*
casser, *to break*	cesser, *to cease*
cause, *cause*	chagrin, *sorrow, grief*
causer, *to cause* and also *to*	chaise, *chair*
converse	chaleur, *heat*
CÉDER, *to yield*	

§ 3. *Table of Conjugations—for Reference*

This and the next two sections are intended to be chiefly for purposes of reference. It has already been explained in Lesson V, § 1, that, for practical purposes, what you MUST KNOW of each verb are : the infinitive, present participle, past participle, present 'tense and the simple future (also called the future indicative). In Lesson XI, §§ 2–3, it was explained that in reading you often meet the imperfect and past definite tenses, and in Lesson IX you were introduced to the subjunctive. In Lesson V, § 4, we gave you a simple table of conjugation which is now extended to include other tenses as follows :

	Present	Imperfect	Past Definite	Future
JE	-e, -s	-ais	-ai, -s	-rai
TU	-e, -s	-ais	-as, -s	-ras
IL, ELLE	-e, -t, -d	-ait	-a, -t	-ra
NOUS	-ons	-ions	-mes	-rons
VOUS	-ez	-iez	-tes	-rez
ILS, ELLES	-ent (silent)	-aient	-rent	-ront

	Conditional	Present Subjunctive	Imperfect Subjunctive
JE	-rais	-e	-sse
TU	-rais	-es	-sses
IL, ELLE	-rait	-e	-êt
NOUS	-rions	-ions	-ssions
VOUS	-riez	-iez	-ssiez
ILS, ELLES	-raient	-ent [1]	-ssent [2]

Present Participles : -ant
Past Participles : -é, -i, -u, -s, -t

The above table may seem a little formidable but, as you are not expected to memorize it, that need not disturb you. It illustrates one fact which you will gradually learn to appreciate : that the French verb is not built up in a haphazard fashion but follows logical, consistent, and definite lines. Is it not remarkable that a brief table such as that given above should embody the principles which dominate all but a few of the verbs in the whole language ? In the reading, whenever you meet with an unfamiliar ending to a verb, you have only to turn to this table and you will find it.

The conditional tense corresponds to the English *I should, I would* : **Je parlerais,** *I should speak.* **Il donnerait,** *he would give.* The imperfect subjunctive you will rarely meet. See Lesson IX, § 1.

¶ 5. CANDIDE

Elle vit clairement la raison suffisante du docteur, les effets et les causes, et s'en retourna tout agitée, toute pensive, toute remplie du désir d'être savante, songeant qu'elle pourrait bien être la raison suffisante du jeune Candide, qui pouvait aussi être la sienne.

Elle rencontra Candide en revenant au château, et rougit : Candide rougit aussi. Elle lui dit bonjour d'une voix entre-coupée ; et Candide lui parla sans savoir ce qu'il disait. Le lendemain après le dîner, comme on sortait de table, Cunégonde

---

[1], [2] ENT silent.

et Candide se trouvèrent derrière un paravent; Cunégonde laissa tomber son mouchoir, Candide le ramassa; elle lui prit innocemment la main, le jeune homme baisa innocemment la main de la jeune demoiselle avec une vivacité, une sensibilité, une grâce toute particulière.   M. le baron Thunder-ten-tronckh passa auprès du paravent, et, voyant cette cause et cet effet, chassa Candide du château à grands coups de pieds dans le derrière.   Cunégonde s'évanouit: elle fut souffletée par madame la baronne dès qu'elle fut revenue à elle-même; et tout fut consterné dans le plus beau et le plus agréable des châteaux possibles.

TRANSLATION ; *She saw clearly the doctor's sufficient reason and the effects and causes and returned from it much excited, pensive, full of desire to be learned, dreaming that she might be the sufficient reason of the young Candide, who could also be hers.*
She met Candide in returning to the castle and blushed.   Candide blushed also.   She said good day to him in a hesitating voice ; and Candide spoke to her without knowing what he said.   The morrow after dinner as they were going from table, Cunégonde and Candide found themselves behind a screen ; Cunégonde let fall her handkerchief, Candide picked it up ; she took his hand innocently, the young man innocently kissed the young lady's hand with a very special vivacity, tenderness and grace. . . . Baron Thunder-ten-tronckh passed near the screen and, seeing this cause and this effect, chased Candide from the castle with great kicks in the behind.   Cunégonde swooned : she was slapped (had her ears boxed) by the Baroness when (as soon as) she returned to her senses ; and all was consternation in the most beautiful and agreeable of (all) possible castles.

*Reading Vocabulary—*11

CHAMBRE, *room*
CHAMP, *field*
chance, *luck*
changement, *change*
CHANGER, *to change*
chant, *song, poem*
CHANTER, *to sing*
CHAPEAU, *hat*
charge, *expense*
charger (se), *to take charge of*

charme, *charm*
charmer, *to charm*
chasse, *hunting*
chasser, *to hunt*
château, *castle*
CHEF, *chief*
CHEMIN, *road*
cheminée, *chimney, fireplace*
chercher, *to look for*
CHEVAL, *horse*

§ 4. *Conjugation of Verbs—for Reference*

	Avoir.	Être.	Porter.	Finir.
1. *Infinitives*	avoir	être	porter	finir
2. *Present Participle*	ayant	étant	portant	finissant
3. *Past Participle*	eu	été	porté	fini
4. *Present*	j'ai tu as il a nous avons vous avez ils ont	je suis tu es il est nous sommes vous êtes ils sont	je porte tu portes il porte nous portons vous portez ils portent	je finis tu finis il finit nous finissons vous finissez ils finissent
5. *Imperfect*	j'avais tu avais il avait nous avions vous aviez ils avaient	j'étais tu étais il était nous étions vous étiez ils étaient	je portais tu portais il portait nous portions vous portiez ils portaient	je finissais tu finissais il finissait nous finissions vous finissiez ils finissaient
6. *Past Definite*	j'eus tu eus il eut nous eûmes vous eûtes ils eurent	je fus tu fus il fut nous fûmes vous fûtes ils furent	je portai tu portas il porta nous portâmes vous portâtes ils portèrent	je finis tu finis il finit nous finîmes vous finîtes ils finirent
7. *Future*	j'aurai tu auras il aura nous aurons vous aurez ils auront	je serai tu seras il sera nous serons vous serez ils seront	je porterai tu porteras il portera nous porterons vous porterez ils porteront	je finirai tu finiras il finira nous finirons vous finirez ils finiront
8. *Conditional*	j'aurais tu aurais il aurait nous aurions vous auriez ils auraient	je serais tu serais il serait nous serions vous seriez ils seraient	je porterais tu porterais il porterait nous porterions vous porteriez ils porteraient	je finirais tu finirais il finirait nous finirions vous finiriez ils finiraient
9. *Present Subjunctive*	que j'aie que tu aies qu'il ait que nous ayons que vous ayez qu'ils aient	que je sois que tu sois qu'il soit que nous soyons que vous soyez qu'ils soient	que je porte que tu portes qu'il porte que nous portions que vous portiez qu'ils portent	que je finisse que tu finisses qu'il finisse que nous finissions que vous finissiez qu'ils finissent
10. *Imperfect (Past) Subjunctive*	que j'eusse que tu eusses qu'il eût que nous eussions que vous eussiez qu'ils eussent	que je fusse que tu fusses qu'il fût que nous fussions que vous fussiez qu'ils fussent	que je portasse que tu portasses qu'il portât que nous portassions que vous portassiez qu'ils portassent	que je finisse que tu finisses qu'il finît que nous finissions que vous finissiez qu'ils finissent
11. *Imperative*	aie qu'il ait ayons ayez qu'ils aient	sois qu'il soit soyons soyez qu'ils soient	porte qu'il porte portons portez qu'ils portent	finis qu'il finisse finissons finissez qu'ils finissent

Text:

Molière chez les nordiques

En Finlande, la semaine de Pâques voit se dérouler tous les ans des fêtes spéciales en l'honneur de l'art théâtral. Toutes les salles de province sont fermées à cette occasion, et les acteurs, professionnels ou amateurs, se rendent à Helsinki pour assister à ces manifestations placées sous le parrainage d'une haute personnalité de l'art dramatique. Le plus souvent, pour ne pas dire chaque année, c'est sous les auspices de notre grand Molière que se déroule cette semaine théâtrale.

M. Lehtonen, professeur de belles-lettres à l'Université de Helsinki, a pu écrire justement que " Le théâtre et Molière, sont les deux passions du peuple finlandais." Les meilleurs acteurs de ce pays ont connu leurs plus grands succès en jouant *Tartuffe* ou le *Malade Imaginaire*. Il y a là—bien agréable à souligner—une tradition émouvante, qui constitue un hommage au rayonnement culturel de notre pays.

*

On demandait à Bernard Shaw quel serait le personnage mort ou vivant avec lequel il aurait le plus de plaisir à s'entretenir pendant un quart d'heure :

" Je ne tiens à converser avec aucun vivant, ni mort, répondit-il, mais je suis sûr qu'Oscar Wilde aurait plaisir à se rencontrer quelques instants avec moi."

Translation :

Molière among the Nordics

In Finland, Easter week sees the holding every year of special festivals in honor of theatrical art. All the provincial halls are closed on this occasion and the actors, professional or amateur, go to Helsinki to take part in those manifestations placed under the auspices (parrain = godfather) of a high personality of the dramatic art. More often (than not), not to say each year, it is under the auspices of our great Molière that this theatre week unfolds (takes place).

M. Lehtonen, professor of literature at the University of Helsinki, has been able to write justly that " The theatre and Molière are the two passions of the Finnish people." The best actors of this country have known their greatest successes in playing Tartuffe *or the* Malade Imaginaire. *There is in this—it is very pleasant to emphasize (underline)—a moving tradition which constitutes a homage to the cultural expansion of our country.*

*

Bernard Shaw was asked which would be the (great) person, dead or living, with whom he would have the most pleasure to speak for a quarter of an hour.

"I have no wish to speak with anybody living or dead," he replied, "but I am sure that Oscar Wilde would have pleasure in finding himself some instants (moments) with me."

Reading Vocabulary—12–13

LES CHEVEUX, *hair*
chien, *dog*
chiffre, *figure*
CHOISIR, *to choose*
CHOIX, *choice*
CHOSE, *thing*
chrétien, *Christian*
chute, *fall*
CIEL, *sky*
circonstance, *circumstance*

combattre, *to fight*
combler, *to load*
commander, *to order*
COMMENCEMENT,
  beginning
COMMENCER, *to commence*
commerce, *commerce*
commettre, *to commit*
communiquer, *to communicate*
compagnie, *company*
compagnon, *companion*

cité, *city*
citer, *to quote*
civilisation, *civilization*
clarté, *brightness*
CLEF, *key*
CŒUR, *heart*
coin, *corner*
colère, *anger*
colonie, *colony*
combat, *combat*

comparer, *to compare*
compliquer, *to complicate*
composer, *to compose*
COMPRENDRE, *to understand*
compte, *account*
compter, *to account*
comte, *count* (title)
concerner, *to concern*
concevoir, *to conceive*
conclure, *to conclude*

§ 5. *Conjugation of Verbs—for Reference*—contd.

AVOIR

Compound Tenses

Past Indefinite : j'ai eu, tu as eu, il a eu, etc., I have had
Pluperfect : **J'avais eu, tu avais eu, il avait eu,** etc.   I had had
Past Anterior : **J'eus eu,** etc.   I had had
Future Perfect : **J'aurai eu,** I shall have had
Past Conditional : **J'aurais eu,** I should have had

Subjunctive

Present : (Que) **J'aie, tu aies, il ait, nous ayons, vous ayez, ils aient**

Imperfect : **J'eusse, tu eusses, il eût, nous eussions, vous eussiez, ils eussent**

Perfect : **J'aie eu**
Pluperfect : **J'eusse eu** } = the above two tenses + **eu**

ÊTRE

Compound Tenses

Past Indefinite : **J'ai été**
Pluperfect : **J'avais été**
Past Anterior : **J'eus été**
Future Perfect : **J'aurai été**
Past Conditional : **J'aurais été**

Subjunctive

Present : (Que) **je sois, tu sois, il soit, nous soyons, vous soyez, ils soient**

Imperfect : **Je fusse, tu fusses,** etc.

Perfect : **J'aie été**
Pluperfect : **J'eusse été**

PORTER

Compound Tenses

Past Indefinite : **J'ai porté**
Pluperfect : **J'avais porté**
Past Anterior : **J'eus porté**
Future Perfect : **J'aurai porté**
Past Conditional : **J'aurais porté**

Subjunctive

Present : (Que) **je porte : -es, -e, -ions, -iez, -ent**

Imperfect : **Je portasse : -asses, ât, -assions, -assiez, -assent**

Perfect : **J'aie porté**
Pluperfect : **J'eusse porté**

FINIR

Compound Tenses

Past Indefinite : **J'ai fini**
Pluperfect : **J'avais fini**
Past Anterior : **J'eus fini**
Future Perfect : **J'aurai fini**
Past Conditional : **J'aurais fini**

Subjunctive

Present : **(Que) je finisse** : **-isses, -isse, -issions, -issiez, -issent**
Imperfect : **Je finisse, tu finisses, il finît, -issions**, etc.
Perfect : **J'aie fini**
Pluperfect : **J'eusse fini**

NOTE.—Of all these tenses, the only one constantly required is the *past indefinite*, which is the simple past tense used in everyday speech. All the others are likely to be met only in reading. See Lesson V, § 1.

-OIR and **-RE** verbs follow the same principles as **FINIR** without the **-SS-** element.

¶ 6. CANDIDE

CHAPITRE II

Ce que devint Candide parmi les Bulgares

Candide, chassé du paradis terrestre, marcha longtemps sans savoir où, pleurant, levant les yeux au ciel, les tournant souvent vers le plus beau des châteaux, qui renfermait la plus belle des baronnettes ; il se coucha, sans souper, au milieu des champs entre deux sillons. La neige tombait à gros flocons : Candide tout transi se traîna le lendemain vers la ville voisine, qui s'appelle Valdberghoff-trarbk-dikdorff, n'ayant point d'argent, mourant de faim et de lassitude. Il s'arrêta tristement à la porte d'un cabaret. Deux hommes habillés de bleu le remarquèrent : " Camarade," dit l'un, " voilà un jeune homme très bien fait, et qui a la taille requise."

CHAPTER 2

What became (of) Candide among the Bulgarians

Candide, chased from the earthly paradise, walked a long time
without knowing where, weeping, raising his eyes to heaven, turning
them often toward the most beautiful of castles which held the most
beautiful of little baronesses ; he lay down without supping in the
middle of the fields between two furrows. Snow fell in big flakes ;
Candide all numb dragged himself on the morrow towards the neighbouring town, which is called Valdberghoff-trarbk-dikdorff, not
having any money, dying of hunger and weariness. He stopped sadly
at the door of an inn. Two men clad in blue noticed him : " Comrade," said one, " there is a young man very well built and who has
the necessary height."

Reading Vocabulary—14-15

condamner, *to condemn*

condition, *condition*

CONDUIRE, *to conduct*

conduite, *conduct*

confiance, *confidence*

confier, *to entrust, confide*

confondre, *to mix, confound*

CONNAISSANCE, *conscious-
ness, knowledge of*

CONNAÎTRE, *to know*

consacrer, *to devote*

constater, *to ascertain, establish*

constituer, *to constitute*

construire, *to construct*

consulter, *to consult*

contact, *contact*

CONTENIR, *to contain, re-
strain*

contenter, *to satisfy*

CONTINUER, *to continue*

contraire, *contrary*

contribuer, *to contribute*

conscience, *conscience*

CONSEIL, *advice, council*

conseiller, *to advise*

consentir, *to consent*

conséquence, *consequence*

conserver, *to keep, retain*

considération, *consideration*

considérer, *to consider*

consister, *to consist*

consoler, *to console*

convaincre, *to convince*

convenir, *to agree*

CONVERSATION, *conversa-
tion*

conviction, *conviction*

CORPS, *body*

costume, *costume*

côte, *coast*

CÔTÉ, *direction, side*

cou, *neck*

coucher (se), *to go to bed*

LESSON XIII

§ 1. *The Two Kinds of Idioms*

You have already been introduced to idioms (Lesson VIII, § 3, and Lesson X, §§ 2-3), those expressions peculiar to the language in which a literal translation will not always give you a key to the meaning. Because we are about to begin giving you hints and phrases to meet the commonest situations, we wish first to emphasize the importance of idioms and of what are called Gallicisms. You know what an idiom is. A Gallicism is a phrase or turn of phrase which represents a mode of thought that is *essentially French*. For example : **parler français comme une vache espagnole** means *to speak French very badly*. It is a rather vulgar expression, but very French. And : **vivre au jour le jour** means *to live from hand to mouth*. Learned gentlemen often attempt to provide explanations to account for such Gallicisms. **Vache espagnole** is said to be a corruption of **Vasco espagnol,** a *Spanish Basque*—and the Spanish Basques who cross the frontier speak a notoriously bad French. **Vivre au jour le jour** is a sort of telescoped or contracted sentence for a longer one meaning *to live in such a manner that what is earned or obtained in the course of a day is sufficient for that day's sustenance and no more*. From these two examples you will see how *sprightly* the French language can be. Its idioms and Gallicisms greatly contribute to the liveliness combined with grace which is characteristic of French. In the pages which follow, we shall introduce to you some of the commonest idioms and Gallicisms, and you are strongly advised at this point to obtain a notebook with a stout cover for permanency and, from now on, to enter in it every idiom and Gallicism you meet. Do not be frightened when we inform you that there is no known end to such a task. The reason is simple. French, like all spoken languages, is a living organism, and new turns of phrase, new idioms, new Gallicisms are continually being added to it. This means that you must be continually on the **qui-vive**

(another idiom!) for these new creations as well as for those long
established by usage.   Incidentally, **Qui vive?** is the military
sentry's phrase for *Who goes there?*   And **être sur le qui-vive**
means *to be on the alert.*

Il a de quoi vivre, *He has the wherewithal to live* (*He has
enough to live on*).   But in conversation one often says : **Il a de
quoi,** a more " snappy " phrase which may have a touch of irony
in it.   We might translate it : *He's got the cash!*

¶ 7. CANDIDE

Il s'avancèrent vers Candide, et le prièrent à dîner très civile-
ment. " Messieurs," leur dit Candide avec une modestie
charmante, " vous me faites beaucoup d'honneur ; mais je n'ai
pas de quoi payer mon écot."   " Ah, monsieur ! " lui dit un des
bleus, " les personnes de votre figure et de votre mérite ne payent
jamais rien : n'avez-vous pas cinq pieds cinq pouces de haut ? "
" Oui, messieurs, c'est ma taille," dit-il en faisant la révérence.
" Ah, monsieur ! mettez-vous à table ; non seulement nous vous
défrayerons, mais nous ne souffrirons jamais qu'un homme comme
vous manque d'argent ; les hommes ne sont faits que pour se
secourir les uns les autres."   " Vous avez raison," dit Candide ;
" c'est ce que M. Pangloss m'a toujours dit ; et je vois bien que
tout est au mieux."   On le prie d'accepter quelques écus ; il les
prend, et veut faire son billet ; on n'en veut point ; on se met à
table.   " N'aimez-vous pas tendrement . . . ? "   " Oh, oui ! " ré-
pond-il, "j'aime tendrement mademoiselle Cunégonde."   "Non,"
dit l'un de ces messieurs, " nous vous demandons si vous
n'aimez pas tendrement le roi des Bulgares."

TRANSLATION : *They went toward Candide and asked (prayed)
him to dine very civilly. " Gentlemen," said Candide to them with
a charming modesty, " you do me much honor ; but I have no money
to pay my share."   " Ah, Sir ! " said one of the (men in) blue,
" persons of your figure and your merit never pay anything ; are you
not five feet five inches in height ? "   " Yes, gentlemen, that is my
height," said he, bowing (making the bow).   " Ah, Sir ! sit down at
(the) table ; not only will we pay for you, but we shall never allow
(that) a man like you go short of money ; men are made only to help
each other."   " You are right," said Candide ; " that is what Mr.
Pangloss has always told me ; and I see well that everything is for the
best."   They ask him to accept a few crowns ; he takes them and*

wished to make (write) his note (of acceptance) ; they did not want it ; (and) they (all) sat at table. " Do you not love tenderly . . . ? "   " Oh, yes ! " he replied, " I love tenderly Miss Cunégonde."   " No," said one of these gentlemen, " we are asking you if you do not love tenderly the King of the Bulgarians."

Reading Vocabulary—16

LE COUCHER, *going to bed*
couler, *to flow*
COULEUR, *color*
COUP, *blow, shot, stroke*
COUPER, *to cut*
couple, *couple*
COUR, *yard, court*
courage, *courage*
courant, *current*
COURIR, *to run*

cours, *course*
course, *journey, course, race*
cousin, *cousin*
COUTEAU, *knife*
COÛTER, *to cost*
coutume, *custom*
couvert, *cover*
couverture, *blanket*
COUVRIR, *to cover*
CRAINDRE, *to fear*

§ 2. Getting Around—Travel by Railway

le train, train
la voiture }
le wagon } the coach
le compartiment, compartment
le compartiment de première classe, de seconde classe, de troisième classe
le wagon-lit, sleeper
la couchette, berth
la couchette supérieure, upper berth
la couchette inférieure, lower berth
la gare, station
le billet, ticket
le guichet, ticket office
le wagon-restaurant, dining car, diner

le lavabo }
la toilette } lavatory
la place, seat
la place de coin, corner seat
le fumeur, smoker
l'arrivée, arrival
le départ, departure
le quai, platform
la barrière, barrier
le passeport, passport
le contrôle des passeports, passport examination
le visa, visa
le chemin de fer, railway
le bureau de renseignements, information bureau
un aller et retour, return ticket
le rapide, express train

While you should by now be able to make up innumerable sentences to help you along, you will find that almost every situation demands a somewhat specialized vocabulary. Above, for example, is a list of words particularly useful for the first stage of railway travel. The list is not exhaustive, but it contains most of the essentials. We shall now indicate the sort of phrases you will have to make up, with the warning that they are given merely as examples and that we do not wish you to learn them parrot fashion. The same can be said of all the phrases and " conversations " in the pages which follow. You should use them as models, and expand them by making further sentences of your own, until you feel that you are capable of dealing with the situation. Speak French with your fellow students.

Où est le guichet ?   Où se trouve le guichet ?
Le guichet est-il ouvert ?
Quel est le prix du billet ?
J'ai besoin d'un aller (single) pour Londres, troisième classe.
Je voudrais faire retenir une place (reserve a seat) dans un fumeur dans le train de 16 heures du lundi le 23.
Quels trains y a-t-il pour Londres mardi prochain ?
Est-ce que je peux m'arrêter en route ?
Est-ce qu'il y a un wagon-restaurant ?
Je voudrais réserver une couchette inférieure, seconde classe, dans le train pour Bordeaux.
De quel quai part le train pour Dieppe ?
Est-ce que je dois changer pour aller à Marseille ?
J'ai manqué (raté) mon train, I've missed my train.
Je voudrais faire enregistrer mes bagages, I would like to register my luggage.
Vous seriez bien aimable de me dire quand nous serons à Toulouse.

A very useful phrase is je vous en prie (*I beg you to, please do* . . .). Puis-je prendre cette place ? To which the answer would be : Je vous en prie. Or simply : Oui, s'il vous plait !

TEXT:

Négligence généralisée

Les administrations, soucieuses de servir l'économie générale du pays, font périodiquement récupérer des tonnes de vieux papiers d'archives qu'elles expédient aux fabriques de papier aux fins de réutilisation.

Récemment, les usines " Cenpa " à Schweighausen (Bas-Rhin), reçurent un wagon de ces vieux papiers. Les ouvriers procédaient au déchargement lorsque le directeur fut appelé au téléphone : un haut fonctionnaire des P. T. T.* l'avisait, de Paris, que parmi les vieux papiers livrés devaient se trouver un certain nombre de livrets de caisse d'Epargne.

Le directeur dut donc adjoindre de nombreux travailleurs à l'équipe de déchargement, qui s'employaient à trier méthodiquement toute cette paperasse. A la grandissime surprise de tous, on découvrit, en effet, *quatre cents* livrets de la Caisse d'Epargne Postale, tous récents et valables et dont la plupart semblaient avoir été déposés dans les bureaux de poste pour arrêté de compte ou inscription des intérêts.

Que penser de la légèreté des postiers jetant délibérément à la corbeille 400 livrets représentant les modestes économies de tant de braves gens ?

Qu'en un moment de surmenage ou de distraction, un employé égare un de ces livrets, passe encore, mais que le fait se reproduise quatre cents fois, voilà qui dépasse les bornes.

TRANSLATIONS:

Widespread Negligence

Administrations, anxious to serve the general economy of the country, periodically have (cause to be) collected tons of old papers of archives which they send to the paper factories with the object of re-using them.

Recently the factories " Cenpa " at Schweighausen (Lower Rhine) received a truck of those old papers. The workers proceeded with the unloading when the director was called to the telephone : a high official of the P.T.T. informed him from Paris that among those old papers must be (found) a certain number of savings books.

* P.T.T., the equivalent of the United States Post Office Department, and in full *Postes, Télégraphes et Téléphones.*

The manager had then to add numerous workers to the unloading gang, who set about sorting methodically all this scrap paper. To the very great surprise of all, they discovered, in fact, 400 Postal savings books, all recent and valid, and of which the greater number seemed to have been deposited in the post offices for closing of account or the entering of interest.

What can be thought of the slackness of postal officials deliberately throwing in the (wastepaper)basket 400 books representing the modest economies (savings) of so many worthy people?

That in a moment of overwork or of distraction, an employee should mislay one of those books can be understood, but that the fact should recur 400 times, that passes the limits.

Reading Vocabulary—17–18

CRAINTE, *fear*
créer, *to create*
creuser, *to dig*
cri, *cry, shout*
CRIER, *to cry, call out*
CRIME, *crime*
crise, *crisis*
CROIRE, *to believe*
croiser, *to cross*
croître, *to grow*

croix, *cross*
cueillir, *to gather*
CUIRE, *to cook*
CUISINE, *kitchen, cookery*
cuivre, *copper*
curiosité, *curiosity*
DAME, *lady*
DANGER, *danger*
danser, *to dance*
date, *date*

DÉBUT, *beginning*
déchirer, *to tear*
décider, *to decide*
décision, *decision*
déclarer, *to declare*
découvrir, *to discover*
décrire, *to describe*
DEDANS, *inside*
défaire, *to undo*
défaut, *failing*

DÉFENDRE, *to defend*
la défense, *defense*
dégager, *to free*
degré, *step, degree*
le DÉJEUNER, *lunch*
DÉJEUNER, *to lunch*
DEMAIN, *tomorrow*
DEMANDER, *to ask for*
demeure, *dwelling*
DEMEURER, *to dwell, live*

§ 3. Travel—At the Customs

la douane, customs (house)
le douanier, customs officer
le droit de douane, customs duty

la valise, suitcase
la malle, trunk
les effets personnels, personal effects

les échantillons de commerce, commercial samples

visiter les bagages, to examine the luggage

les articles passibles de droits, dutiable articles

exempt de droits de douane, free of duty

Do not forget what we told you in Lesson 1, § 5, about the use of **Monsieur.** When you speak to the French customs officer, address him as " **Monsieur,** " and do not be afraid to be a little more formal and polite than you might be if you were speaking to his American counterpart. Having found your officer, approach him gently and say :

> **Voici mes bagages, Monsieur. Voulez-vous les visiter, s'il vous plaît ?**

He may then say to you :

> **Est-ce que vous avez encore d'autres bagages ?** (*Is that all you have in the way of luggage?*) and your having reassured him, he will say: **Avez-vous quelque chose à déclarer?**

Or, in the terrifying way of contemporary life and travel, he may produce a long, elaborate list pasted on a board, show it to you and say :

> **Voyez-vous cette liste ? Avez-vous des articles qui se trouvent ici ?**

To which you may naturally reply:

> **Non, Monsieur. Rien. Rien à déclarer. Rien du tout.**

On the other hand, you may say :

> **Oui, Monsieur. J'ai du tabac, des cigares, des cigarettes, des allumettes, et une bouteille de whisky—mais tous pour mon usage personnel !**
> **Combien faut-il payer de droits ?**

Do not rush the gentleman, and before closing your luggage, you might say to him : **Est-ce que je puis fermer mes bagages maintenant ?** If he has found something dutiable, he will be easy enough—unless it is something considerable—and will merely make out a slip with the amount payable, saying : **Payez cela au bureau, s'il vous plaît.**

It is not very formidable.   But do not forget those words at the beginning of this section.   They help to get you through the customs.

¶ 8. CANDIDE

"Point du tout," dit-il, "car je ne l'ai jamais vu."   "Comment ? c'est le plus charmant des rois, et il faut boire à sa santé."   "Oh! très volontiers, messieurs"; et il boit.   "C'en est assez," lui dit-on, "vous voilà l'appui, le soutien, le défenseur, le héros des Bulgares; votre fortune est faite, et votre gloire est assurée."   On lui met sur-le-champ les fers aux pieds, et on le mène au régiment.   On le fait tourner à droite, à gauche, hausser la baguette, remettre la baguette, coucher en joue, tirer, doubler le pas, et on lui donne trente coups de bâton; le lendemain il fait l'exercice un peu moins mal, et il ne reçoit que vingt coups; le surlendemain on ne lui en donne que dix, et il est regardé par ses camarades comme un prodige.

Candide, tout stupéfait, ne démêlait pas encore trop bien comment il était un héros.   Il s'avisa un beau jour de printemps de s'aller promener, marchant tout droit devant lui, croyant que c'était un privilège de l'espèce humaine, comme de l'espèce animale, de se servir de ses jambes à son plaisir.

TRANSLATION : *"Not at all," said he, "for I have never seen him."   "What?   He is the most charming of kings, and we must drink his health."   "Oh!   Very willingly, gentlemen";   and he drinks.   "That's enough," they say to him, "you are now the support, the stay, the defender, the hero of the Bulgarians ;   your fortune is made, and your glory is assured."   They immediately put irons on his feet and take him to the regiment.   They make him turn right, turn left, draw the ramrod, return the ramrod, take aim, fire, double (the step), and they give him thirty blows with a stick ;   on the morrow he does the exercise (drills) a little less badly, and receives only twenty blows ;   the day after, they give him only ten, and he is looked upon by his comrades as a prodigy.*

Candide, quite stupefied, did not yet make out too well how he was a hero.   He bethought himself one fine day in spring to go for a walk, going straight ahead, believing that it was a privilege of the human species as of the animal species to make use of his legs at his (own) pleasure.

Reading Vocabulary—19

demoiselle, *young lady*

démontrer, *to prove, demonstrate*

une DENT, *tooth*

DÉPART, *departure*

dépasser, *to go beyond*

dépendre, *to depend*

dépense, *expense*

DÉPENSER, *to spend*

déplaire, *to displease*

déposer, *to set down, to lodge*

député, *deputy*

DÉRANGER, *to inconvenience*

DERNIER, *last*

dérober, *to hide, to steal*

DESCENDRE, *to go down*

désert, *desert*

désespérer, *to despair*

désigner, *to point out*

désir, *desire*

DÉSIRER, *to desire, to want*

§ 4. *Travel—By Air*

l'avion, airplane

la cabine, passengers' cabin

l'aérodrome, airport

l'aéroport, airport

voler, to fly

décoller, to take off

atterrir, to land

le transport par avion, air transport

les réseaux aériens, airways

les bagages en excédant, excess luggage

You will see that very little in the way of special vocabulary is required for air travel, and we have not repeated words used in rail travel which can also be used here. A little ingenuity will enable you to make up all the phrases you are likely to require. The following should help :

> **Je voudrais réserver une couchette dans l'avion partant le 3 mars à destination de Londres.**
>
> **Combien de bagages peut-on prendre ?**
>
> **Combien coûtent les bagages en excédant ?**
>
> **Est-ce qu'on sert des rafraîchissements** (refreshments) **pendant le voyage ?**
>
> **A quelle heure part l'avion ?**
>
> **A quelle heure arrive-t-il à l'aéroport ?**
>
> **Où faut-il aller pour se faire peser ?**
>
> **Ayez la bonté de me donner un peu de coton pour les oreilles.**

In a train, one usually speaks of *the seats* as **les places,** but in an airplane they are **les sièges,** and *reclining chairs* are **les chaises-longues.** Then, the French talk of *a single-engined plane as* **un avion à un moteur.** *Two-engined,* **bi-moteur.** *Three-engined,* **tri-moteur.** *Four-engined,* **quadri-moteur.** *Jet plane,* **un avion à réaction.** *A long-distance flight,* **un vol à longue distance.** *A nonstop flight,* **un vol direct.** And *a landing* is **un atterrissage.**

You may wish to know of some preventive of airsickness, in which case you could ask somebody: **Pardon, Monsieur, mais est-ce que vous pouvez me recommander quelque chose contre le mal de l'air ?**

The *starting runway* is **la piste d'envoi** . *Overseas flying service* is **le service transocéanique.**

It should be noted that these terms and phrases are given for those students who may be interested in flying. Those who are not particularly interested in it may be content with a knowledge of the words at the head of the section. After all, it is a very specialized subject, and what is given here is merely a starting point for those who may wish to extend their knowledge.

TEXT :

LE CINÉMA

Nous reprochons au cinéma américain de ne pas se renouveler mais quand il s'y essaie, il faut bien dire qu'il nous déçoit presque toujours. Cette impossibilité où il se trouve de sortir de certaines formes stéréotypées tient aux conditions même du travail dans les studios de Californie.

A l'exception des films réalisés par quelque John Ford, William Wyler, Orson Welles ou René Clair, qui savent imposer leur volonté, la production américaine est organisée de telle sorte que scénaristes et metteurs en scène sont aujourd'hui interchangeables. Quand un producteur s'est mis un sujet en tête, il changera dix fois d'auteurs, s'il le faut, jusqu'à ce qu'ils lui apportent exactement ce qu'il attend.

Il est certain que " l'art vit de contraintes et meurt de liberté," mais à la condition qu'il soit pratiqué par des artistes. Quand il l'est par des tâcherons qui n'acceptent une besogne fastidieuse qu'en raison du chèque hebdomadaire qui la sanctionne, les circonstances sont peu favorables à la création d'œuvres originales.

TRANSLATION:

THE CINEMA

We reproach the American cinema for not renewing itself, but when it tries to do so, one must frankly say that it disappoints us nearly always. This impossibility in which it finds itself of getting away from certain stereotyped forms is due to the very conditions of work in the California studios.

With the exception of the films made by a John Ford, William Wyler, Orson Welles, or René Clair, who know how to impose their will, American production is organized in such a way that script-writers and directors are today interchangeable. When a producer gets a subject into his head, he will change authors ten times if necessary until they bring him exactly what he expects.

It is certain that "art lives by restrictions and dies of liberty," but on condition that it be practiced by artists. When it is practiced by pieceworkers who only accept a fastidious task because of the weekly check which sanctions it, the circumstances are little favorable to the creation of original works.

Reading Vocabulary—20

dessin, *drawing*	développement, *development, unfolding*
destinée, *destiny*	
destiner, *to set apart*	développer, *to develop, unfold*
détacher, *to undo*	DEVENIR, *to become*
détail, *detail*	deviner, *to divine, predict, guess*
déterminer, *to determine*	le devoir, *duty*
détester, *to detest*	devoir, *to owe, must, ought*
détour, *turn, way round*	diable, *devil*
détourner, *to turn away* or *aside*	Dieu, *God*
DÉTRUIRE, *to destroy*	différence, *difference*
dette, *debt*	

§ 5. *Travel—By Sea and by Car or Bus*

le port, port	**le fumoir,** smoking room
le paquebot, mail steamer	**le pont,** deck
le bateau, boat	**la cabine,** cabin
la traversée, crossing	**le fauteuil,** deck chair
la salle à manger, dining room	**embarquer,** go on board
	débarquer, to land

à bord, on board
la cabine de 1ère classe, de 2ème classe
la côte, coast
le commissaire, purser

la passerelle, bridge (also gangway, for which a better word is **le passavant**)
le débarcadère, wharf

Again, you will find that most of the phrases used for rail travel are equally useful for sea-travel—we refer, of course, only to essentials. However, **un passage sur le bateau** is your *fare* or *seapassage.* And **le mal de mer** is *seasickness!* You may have to send a *radiotelegram,* in which case you will ask for **le poste de T.S.F. (télégraphie sans fils),** and in French it is **un radiotélégramme.** You may require **une carte de débarquement,** *a landing card*; and you will probably be glad to *arrive alongside the quay* (**aborder** or **accoster**)!

TRAVEL BY CAR OR BUS:

une automobile, car
un autobus, bus, coach
le garage, garage
un automobiliste, motorist
le taxi, taxi
le tourisme, touring
l'essence, gasoline
le distributeur d'essence, filling station
le conducteur-propriétaire, owner-driver
une voiture à deux places, two-seater car, coupe
les virages, curves

les feux de signalisation, traffic lights
garer, stationner, to park
un agent de la circulation, traffic policeman
une route à sens unique, one-way road
le croisement, crossroads
le passage à niveau, level crossing
ralentir, to slow down
la vitesse maxima, speed limit
un ticket d'appel, a numbered call-slip at bus stages

Combien de kilomètres y a-t-il jusqu'à Paris ?
Veuillez me montrer sur cette carte (map) la route à suivre. . . .
Connaissez-vous la route de Rouen ? (the road *to* Rouen)
Où peut-on garer la voiture ?
Pouvez-vous nous indiquer une station d'essence ?
Conduisez-nous à Versailles.

It is clearly impossible to give more than a few indications of what is required. These are merely " first aid " for the motorist, who, like the air enthusiast, must be prepared to build up the special vocabulary for his requirements. What we are concerned with here is to provide a mere framework, leaving the student interested in this subject to proceed independently in such studies when the course is completed.

¶ 9. CANDIDE

Il n'eut pas fait deux lieues que voilà quatre autres héros de six pieds qui l'atteignent, qui le lient, qui le mènent dans un cachot. On lui demanda juridiquement ce qu'il aimait le mieux d'être fustigé trente-six fois par tout le régiment, ou de recevoir à la fois douze balles de plomb dans la cervelle. Il eut beau dire que les volontés sont libres, et qu'il ne voulait ni l'un ni l'autre, il fallut faire un choix : il se détermina, en vertu du don de Dieu qu'on nomme *liberté*, à passer trente-six fois par les baguettes ; il essuya deux promenades. Le régiment était composé de deux mille hommes ; cela lui composa quatre mille coups de baguettes, qui, depuis la nuque du cou jusqu'au cul, lui découvrirent les muscles et les nerfs. Comme on allait procéder à la troisième course, Candide, n'en pouvant plus, demanda en grâce qu'on voulût bien avoir la bonté de lui casser la tête. Il obtint cette faveur ; on lui bande les yeux ; on le fait mettre à genoux. Le roi des Bulgares passe dans ce moment, s'informe du crime du patient ; et comme ce roi avait un grand génie, il comprit, par tout ce qu'il apprit de Candide, que c'était un jeune métaphysicien fort ignorant des choses de ce monde, et il lui accorda sa grâce avec une clémence qui sera louée dans tous les journaux et dans tous les siècles. Un brave chirurgien guérit Candide en trois semaines, avec les émollients enseignés par Dioscoride. Il avait déjà un peu de peau et pouvait marcher, quand le roi des Bulgares livra bataille au roi des Abares.

TRANSLATION : *He had not made two leagues when (there were) four other heroes six feet tall who overtook him, tied him, and took him to a cell. He was asked juridically (by judges) whether he would like best to be flogged thirty-six times by all the regiment or to receive all at once twelve leaden bullets in the brain. He said in vain that wills are free and that he wished neither the one nor the other, he had to make a choice : he determined by virtue of God's gift which is called* liberty, *to run the gauntlet thirty-six times and he suffered it twice. The regiment was composed of 2,000 men, that made for him 4,000 strokes which, from neck to seat, laid bare his muscles and nerves. Candide, unable to bear more, asked as a favor that they should be good enough to smash his head. He (obtained) was granted this favor ; they bound his eyes and made him go on his knees. The King of the Bulgarians passed at that moment and inquired about the condemned's crime ; and as the King had a great genius, he understood, from all he learned about Candide, that he was a young metaphysician who was very ignorant of the things of this world, and he granted him his pardon with a clemency which will be praised in all the newspapers and in all ages (centuries). A worthy surgeon cured Candide in three weeks with emollients taught by Dioscorides. He had already a little skin and could walk, when the King of the Bulgarians opened battle against the King of the Abares. (In this satire, the Bulgarians are the Prussians, and the Abares the French. —*ED.)

Reading Vocabulary—21

DIFFICULTÉ, *difficulty*

DIMANCHE, *Sunday*

diminuer, *diminish*

le dîner, *dinner*

dîner, *to dine*

DIRE, *to say*

directeur, *director*, *manager*

direction, *direction* (also *management*)

diriger, *to direct*

discours, *discourse*, *speech*

discussion, *discussion*

DISCUTER, *to discuss*, *argue*

DISPARAÎTRE, *to disappear*

disposer, *to dispose*, *prepare*

disposition, *disposition*, *inclination*

disputer, *to dispute*

dissimuler, *to conceal*, *to hide*

distance, *distance*

distinguer, *to distinguish*

diviser, *to divide*

§ 1. *Bicycling and Hiking*

FRANCE is a good country for cycling and hiking, especially in the Northwest, West, South, and East—in other words, excepting the Northeast, though that also has its attractions. For cycling, you require some special vocabulary, but in hiking you can probably get along with your general knowledge. For both you will require **une carte,** *a map.* The cyclist may have to deal with repairs, and the following words should help him in this and in general :

la bicyclette, bicycle (*also called* **la roue,** the wheel)

la selle, saddle

la pompe, pump

la roue, the wheel

la roue avant, front wheel

la roue arrière, back wheel

une enveloppe, un pneu, tire

la chambre à air, inner tube

le porte-bagages, luggage carrier

crever, to burst

la crevaison, puncture

le cycliste, cyclist

l'équipement de cycliste, cycling outfit

la sonnette, bell

la lanterne, lamp

la lampe de poche, flashlight

les lunettes noires, sunglasses

la boussole, compass

la pédale, pedal

la sacoche, toolbag

les outils, tools

la clef anglaise, adjustable spanner, wrench

le tournevis, screwdriver

l'eau potable, drinking water

le frein, brake

une panne, a breakdown

Always ask for **de l'eau potable,** and not just for **de l'eau.** For the rest, here are some general phrases :

Le frein ne fonctionne pas, the brake does not work.

NOTE : **fonctionner,** to *function, work,* can be used for most things.

Le pneu a crevé, the tire is punctured.

Il faut le réparer, it must be repaired.

Est-il possible d'avoir quelque chose à manger? Is it possible to have something to eat ? **à boire,** to drink.

Est-il possible d'être logé pour la nuit? Can one get a night's lodging ?

Où puis-je acheter . . . ? Where can I buy . . . ? Or: **Est-il possible d'acheter . . . ?** Is it possible to buy . . . ?

Est-il possible de louer une bicyclette pour la journée? Is it possible to hire a bicycle for the day ?

Peut-on mettre la bicyclette dans . . . ? Can one put the bicycle in . . . ? **Sera-t-elle en sécurité?** Will it be safe ?

Je voudrais bien trouver, I should like to find. . . .

Veuillez m'indiquer, Kindly direct me, show me.

Veuillez m'indiquer une auberge de la jeunesse, Kindly direct me to a youth hostel.

Où peut-on acheter un porte-cartes? Where can one buy a map case ?

¶ 10. CANDIDE

CHAPITRE III

Comment Candide se sauva d'entre les Bulgares, et ce qu'il devint

Rien n'était si beau, si leste, si brillant, si bien ordonné que les deux armées ; les trompettes, les fifres, les hautbois, les tambours, les canons, formaient une harmonie telle qu'il n'y en eut jamais en enfer. Les canons renversèrent d'abord à peu près six mille hommes de chaque côté ; ensuite la mousqueterie ôta du meilleur des mondes environ neuf à dix mille coquins qui en infectaient la surface ; la baïonnette fut aussi la raison suffisante de la mort de quelques milliers d'hommes. Le tout pouvait bien se monter à une trentaine de mille âmes. Candide, qui tremblait comme un philosophe, se cacha du mieux qu'il put pendant cette boucherie héroïque.

Enfin, tandis que les deux rois faisaient chanter des *Te Deum* chacun dans son camp, il prit le parti d'aller raisonner ailleurs des effets et des causes. Il passa par-dessus des tas de morts et de mourants, et gagna d'abord un village voisin ; il était en cendres ; c'était un village abare que les Bulgares avaient brûlé selon les lois du droit public : ici, des vieillards criblés de coups regardaient mourir leurs femmes égorgées, qui tenaient leurs enfants à leurs mamelles sanglantes ; là, des filles éventrées, après avoir assouvi les besoins naturels de quelques héros, rendaient les derniers soupirs ; d'autres à demi brûlées criaient qu'on achevât de leur donner la mort ; des cervelles étaient répandues sur la terre à côté de bras et de jambes coupés.

NOTES and WORDS : We now wish you to try hard by yourself to make the sense of Voltaire's book, and you should be able to do so with some help.

se sauva, saved himself, escaped

leste, agile, smart

le tambour, drum

renversèrent, overthrew, laid flat

ensuite, then

ôta (*from* **ôter**), took away

coquins, rascals, blackguards

se cacha (*from* **se cacher**), hid himself

prit le parti (*from* **prendre**), took the decision

pardessus, over, across

mourants, dying

gagna, *from* **gagner,** to win; *here means* reach

d'abord, first

abare, of the Abares (*see note p.* 200)

vieillards, old men

criblés, riddled

égorgées, murdered, throats cut

mamelles sanglantes, bleeding breasts

éventrées, disembowelled

assouvi, satisfied, satiated

à demi brûlées, half-burned

criaient . . ., etc., cried *or* shouted that one might finish (it by) giving them their death

cervelles, brains

Reading Vocabulary—22

docteur, *doctor*

doigt, *finger*

domaine, *domain, estate*

domestique, *domestic servant*

dominer, *to dominate*

don, *gift*

dorer, *to gild*

DORMIR, *to sleep*

DOS, *back*

DOUBLE, *double*

douceur, *gentleness*

douleur, *grief, pain*

DOUTE, *doubt*   DURER, *to last*
DOUTER, *to doubt*   eau, *water*
dresser, *to raise*, set (*up*)   écarter, *to put apart*
droit, *right*   ÉCHANGER, *to exchange*

§ 2. *Camping*

In all these activities—cycling, hiking, camping, etc.—the
official **Bureau de Tourisme** (*Tourist Office*) or **le Syndicat
d'Initiative** (*Association for the Encouragement of Touring*) will
help you with information and recommendations.   Do not be
afraid to go into one of these offices and ask for their help.   The
French use the English word **camping,** and you will hear it
pronounced the French way more often than the English.
Camper la nuit, *to camp for the night*.   A tent is **une tente de
camping.**   *A haversack* is **un sac de montagne ;** and *a
sleeping bag* is **un sac de couchage.**   *A can opener* is **un ouvre-
boîtes.**   If you go to certain parts of France, especially in the
South, you will require **une moustiquaire** (*mosquito net*)
against **les moustiques,** *the mosquitoes*; and everywhere you
will require **un seau de toile,** *a canvas pail*, and likewise
des ustensiles de cuisine, *cooking utensils*, and **la vaisselle de
camping,** *the culinary outfit for camping* (knives, forks, etc.,
which will be given in some detail later under the heading of
" Eating and Drinking ").

By this time you are becoming well equipped for moving
around, and, having decided for yourself which branch of travel-
ing and recreation you intend to pursue, you should start a
special notebook in which to jot down for memorizing all the
words required for that special activity.   Once again we emphasize
the importance of *words*.   The phrases which we give are merely
to provide examples, for you ought by this time to be able to
make up on your own initiative most of the phrases required.
Without the words, you are more often than not lost.   Whenever
you are lost for a word, try to describe the article required, and
it is surprising how a little miming will help.   The French are
extraordinarily quick on the uptake, and you will generally find,
especially in the country places, a great willingness to help.

For camping, this is a useful phrase :

Ayez la bonté de m'indiquer où l'on peut dresser une tente pour camper la nuit.
Be so good as (have the goodness) to tell me where one can (we can) put up a tent to camp for the night.

Finally, it is as well to be prepared for an accident, in which case you would ask for **De l'aide immédiatement—il y a un accident,** *Help immediately—there's an accident.*

TEXT :

MONSIEUR VERDOUX

MAINTENANT que le vrai M. Henri Verdoux a été débouté de l'action qu'il avait intentée aux distributeurs du film de Charlie Chaplin, sous prétexte que le personnage du film portait le même nom que lui, était comme lui employé de banque, etc., nous sera-t-il permis de raconter une petite histoire purement imaginaire ?

Il était une fois, en Amérique, un grand acteur-producteur qui avait eu l'idée de tourner un film où il jouerait le rôle d'un jardinier français.

" Très bien," dirent les distributeurs de son futur film, " attendez huit jours pour choisir le nom de votre personnage."

Ils prièrent un de leurs représentants en France de leur communiquer les nom et prénom d'un jardinier français, et le transmirent alors au grand acteur-producteur qui tourna le film.

*

Quand le film arriva en France, le représentant des distributeurs alla trouver le vrai jardinier et lui dit :

" Vous allez nous faire un procès pour usurpation de nom, de prénom, de fonctions et tout. . . ."

" Moi ? " répondit l'autre. " Mais ça me coûtera très cher, cette plainte, et tout ce qui s'ensuit. Et je suis sûr de perdre ! "

" C'est bien parce que vous êtes sûr de perdre et que, par conséquent, nous ne risquons rien, que nous vous demandons de nous faire ce procès. Pour les frais, ne vous faites pas de souci, nous payons tout.   Et on saura même, par ailleurs, reconnaître votre gentillesse."

*

Le vrai jardinier porta donc plainte en bonne et dûe forme. Pendant des jours et des jours, la presse, alertée, exposa l'affaire à la " une," en lettres grosses comme ça ; et remit ça lors du procès . . .

. . . Ce qui assura au film une publicité monstre, comme jamais aucun film n'en a connu, et qui avait en outre le mérite d'être *rigoureusement gratuite*. . . . Et c'est ainsi qu'on ferait les bonnes maisons si cette histoire n'était pas imaginaire.

TRANSLATION :

MONSIEUR VERDOUX

Now that the real M. Henri Verdoux has been dismissed from the action which he had brought against the distributors of the Charlie Chaplin film, under the pretext that the personage (principal character) in the film had the same name as he, was—like him—a bank employee, etc., would it be permitted to us to relate a purely imaginary little story ?

There was once in America a great actor-producer who had had the idea of shooting a film in which he should play the part of a French gardener.

" Very well," said the distributors of his future film, " wait eight days (a week) to choose the name of your principal character."

They asked one of their representatives in France to let them know the name and Christian name of a French gardener, and then transmitted it to the great actor-producer who made the film.

*

When the film arrived in France, the representative of the distributors went to find the real gardener and said to him :

" You're going to take proceedings against us for usurpation of name, Christian name, position and everything. . . ."

" I ? " replied the other.   " But that will cost me very dear, that lawsuit, and all that results from it.   And I am sure to lose ! "

" It is just because you are sure to lose and that consequently we risk nothing that we ask you to take the case against us.   As for the costs, don't worry yourself, we'll pay everything.   And besides your kindness will not be overlooked (one will even know how to recognize your niceness)."

*

The real gardener then took proceedings in good and due form. For days and days the press, put on the alert (warned), publicized (exhibited) the matter " full blast " in great big letters and did so again during the lawsuit . . .

. . . Which assured the film a (monster) vast publicity, such as no film has known, and which had furthermore the merit of being strictly free of cost. . . . And it is thus that one would make good houses, if this story was not imaginary.   (*From* Le Canard Enchaîné.)

Reading Vocabulary—23

ÉCHAPPER, *to escape*
écho, *echo*
éclairer, *to light*
éclat, *outburst, explosion*
éclater, *to burst out*
école, *school*
économie, *economy, saving*
ÉCOUTER, *to listen*
écraser, *to crush, run over*
ÉCRIER(S'), *to exclaim*

ÉCRIRE, *to write*
éducation, *education*
effacer, *to remove, efface*
effet, *effect*
efforcer(s'), *to strive*
effort, *effort*
effrayer, *to frighten*
égard, *respect*
ÉGLISE, *church*
élan, *bound, spring, dash*

§ 3. *Photography*

un appareil photographique, a camera
un appareil de cinéma, a movie camera
une pellicule, roll-film
le développement, development
l'agrandissement, enlarging
un négatif, negative (*also* **le cliché**)
la photographie, photography

développer, to develop
la pose, time exposure
l'instantané, snapshot
une épreuve, print
exposer, to expose
surexposer, to overexpose
le papier au citrate, sensitized paper
le film pack, film pack
mat, matte
brillant, glossy

J'ai besoin de pellicules, s'il vous plaît.
Pour cet appareil, for this camera.
Est-ce qu'on peut prendre des photographies ici ?
Je voudrais savoir le prix du développement et du tirage (printing), s'il vous plaît.
Quand peut-on les avoir ?
Tirez une épreuve de chaque négatif.
Quand sera-t-il prêt ?   Quel est le prix ?
Quand seront-t-elles prêtes ?

At this point, we may take advantage of photography to explain some differences in meaning of a few common French verbs :

Vouloir, to wish, desire, have need of
Pouvoir, to be able—physically
Savoir, to know how to, to know for a fact
Connaître, to be acquainted with

You have met all these words before, and you know their simple meanings. Nevertheless, in using them foreigners are apt to make little mistakes which can easily be avoided by getting a clear conception of the differences in meaning as set out above.

For instance, when you go into the druggist's and want some films developed, in English you might say **Can you develop these films for me ?** and you might be tempted to turn this literally into French (**Pouvez-vous,** etc.), not realizing that you are asking the person whether he can *physically* develop them ! The right turn of phrase is **Voudriez-vous développer ces pellicules ?** In other words, *Would you wish to, or care, to develop these films?* On the other hand, if you really mean in a physical sense—supposing, for example, you arrived just as the shop was shutting—you might then say **pouvez-vous** or better **pourriez-vous développer ces films ?**

> **SAVOIR** always means knowledge from *mental application.*
> **CONNAÎTRE** represents knowledge *acquired through the senses* or *by experience.*
> **Savez-vous prendre des photographies ?** *Can you (do you know how to) take photographs?*
> **Connaissez-vous ce monsieur ?** *Do you know that gentleman?*
> **Cet enfant sait écrire.** *This child knows how to write.*

But : **cet enfant peut écrire** means that he is *able to* write in a physical sense (now that his cut finger is better).

¶ 11. CANDIDE

Candide s'enfuit au plus vite dans un autre village : il appartenait à des Bulgares, et les héros abares l'avaient traité de même. Candide, toujours marchant sur des membres palpitants, ou à travers des ruines, arriva enfin hors du théâtre de la guerre, portant quelques petites provisions dans son bissac, et n'oubliant jamais mademoiselle Cunégonde.   Ses provisions lui manquèrent quand il fut en Hollande ; mais ayant entendu dire que tout le monde était riche dans ce pays-là, et qu'on y était chrétien, il ne douta pas qu'on ne le traitât aussi bien qu'il l'avait été dans le château de M. le baron, avant qu'il en eût été chassé pour les beaux yeux de mademoiselle Cunégonde.

Il demanda l'aumône à plusieurs graves personnages, qui lui répondirent tous que, s'il continuait à faire ce métier, on l'enfermerait dans une maison de correction pour lui apprendre à vivre.

Il s'adressa ensuite à un homme qui venait de parler tout seul une heure de suite sur la charité dans une grande assemblée. Cet orateur, le regardant de travers, lui dit : Que venez-vous faire ici ? y êtes-vous pour la bonne cause ?   Il n'y a point d'effet sans cause, répondit modestement Candide ;   tout est enchaîné nécessairement et arrangé pour le mieux : il a fallu que je fusse chassé d'auprès de mademoiselle Cunégonde, que j'aie passé par les baguettes, et il faut que je demande mon pain jusqu'à ce que je puisse en gagner ;   tout cela ne pouvait être autrement.   Mon ami, lui dit l'orateur, croyez-vous que le pape soit l'antechrist ?   Je ne l'avais pas encore entendu dire, répondit Candide ;   mais qu'il le soit ou qu'il ne le soit pas, je manque le pain.   Tu ne mérites pas d'en manger, dit l'autre ; va, coquin, va, misérable, ne m'approche de ta vie.   La femme de l'orateur ayant mis la tête à la fenêtre, et avisant un homme qui doutait que le pape fût antéchrist, lui répandit sur le chef un plein. . . . O ciel ! à quel excès se porte le zèle de la religion dans les dames !

Notes and Words :

s'enfuit, fled	**métier,** trade
appartenait, belonged to	**pour lui apprendre à vivre,** to teach him how to live
des membres palpitants, quivering limbs	**le regardant de travers,** looking at him askance
à travers, across	**enchaîné,** chained, linked up
hors, outside	**il a fallu que,** it has been necessary that
bissac, knapsack	
l'aumône, alms	

fusse, should be (in the subjunctive after **falloir**)

passé par les baguettes, passed through the rods, run the gauntlet

lui répandit sur le chef un plein . . ., emptied on his headpiece a full . . .

O ciel! Heavens!

Reading Vocabulary—24

élancer(s'), *throw oneself*
élément, *element*
élève, *pupil*
élever, *to elevate, to raise*
éloigner, *to remove*
embarras, *embarrassment*
embarrasser, *to embarrass*
EMBRASSER, *to embrace, kiss*
emmener, *to lead*
émotion, *emotion*

émouvoir, *to move*
EMPÊCHER, *to prevent*
EMPLOYER, *to employ*
EMPORTER, *to carry off*
empresser(s'), *to hasten*
enchanter, *to enchant*
endormir(s'), *to fall asleep*
ENDROIT, *spot, place*
énergie, *energy*
enfance, *childhood*

§ 4. *The Post Office*

le bureau de poste, post office

le bureau de poste central, the General Post Office

la boîte aux lettres, letter-box

un employé (une employée) des postes, P.O. official

la lettre, letter

la lettre express, special delivery letter

la lettre recommandée, registered letter

l'imprimé, printed matter

la carte postale, post card

par avion, by air mail

le télégramme, telegram

le port, postage

le timbre-poste, postage stamp

le colis, le paquet, parcel

le service des colis postaux, parcel post

la surtaxe postale, additional postage

une adresse, address

la distribution, delivery

la taxe de recommandation, registration fee

Faire suivre *written on an envelope means* Please forward

le mandat postal, postal order

imprimés, printed matter (to be marked on the packet)
affranchi, prepaid
recommander, to register
le règlement, regulation(s)
retourner, to return
téléphoner, to telephone
un expéditeur, sender
la signature, signature
le récépissé, receipt
le facteur, postman

le contrôleur, le receveur (-euse) des postes, postmaster, -mistress
le contenu, contents
le destinataire, addressee
fixer, coller, affix, stick on
une étiquette, label
aux bons soins de, c/o
la déclaration de douane, customs declaration
poste restante, c/o the P.O.

If you intend to travel in France you must learn these words sooner or later, though you need not do so now. Few people can avoid having to go to the post office at some time or other, and most people go there fairly often. You must therefore be your own judge of the expediency of learning these words now or postponing them until some time when you may have a visit to France in mind.

If you are having your letters addressed **poste restante** and wish to call for them, be sure to bring your passport : otherwise you are unlikely to be given your letters. You approach **le guichet,** have your passport handy, and say :

J'attends des lettres poste restante. Voici mon nom (showing the passport). **Est-ce qu'il y en a pour moi ?** Or : **Y a-t-il quelque chose pour moi ?** **J'attends une lettre recommandée.** Or you may wish to send something, in which case you say : **Je voudrais des timbres. Ceci doit être envoyé par avion, comme lettre recommandée** (or **paquet recommandé**), **comme express, comme imprimé, comme lettre ordinaire (paquet ordinaire).** The official may say to you : **Remplissez ce formulaire,** *Fill up this form,* and you may be presented with one of those complicated governmental forms in which the French specially rejoice. Be patient and polite. Let " **Toujours la politesse** " be your motto.

TEXT:
Si nous parlions du

sport...

GRAND ÉCART

Des finales du championnat suisse de boxe qui eurent lieu l'autre jour à Berne, deux choses peuvent être retenues.   D'abord, un incident assez comique.   La finale des poids " mouche " devait opposer Jolivet de Genève à Baertsch de Coire.   Mais, au pesage, l'après-midi, il s'avéra que Jolivet n'avait pas pris une purge suffisante pour se délester : il pesait encore cent grammes de trop pour sa catégorie.   Il fut donc disqualifié.   Par le fait même, Baertsch devenait champion suisse sans combattre. Seulement on décida qu'ils se battraient quand même le soir, pour que le programme fût complet.   Or, il arriva ceci, que Baertsch, proclamé champion suisse et acclamé comme tel, était knock out trois minutes plus tard !   On vit ainsi un champion tout frais, tomber évanoui sur une corde, comme du linge sale, puis étendu " mort " par terre, et, enfin, transporté par des aides comme pour une mise au tombeau.   De la gloire, le brave petit Grison s'effondrait dans la dernière humiliation.   Il allait rentrer à Coire à la fois avec son titre et le souvenir cuisant de sa débâcle. Image de la vie !   Toujours une joie est empoisonnée par un ennui.   Décidément la Roche tarpéïenne reste près du Capitole. Leçon : dans la boxe on devait épargner à un champion frais émoulu le risque de voir son diplôme traîner tout de suite dans le ridicule.

La deuxième observation est celle-ci : Les boxeurs amateurs se dépensent en général beaucoup trop.   L'autre soir, à Berne, ils se sont battus à en perdre le souffle, constamment accrochés l'un à l'autre.   Ils sé sont abandonnés à une vraie débauche de coups de poing, dont beaucoup allèrent se perdre dans le vide alors que d'autres étaient absolument sans efficacité, si bien que, au bout des trois rounds—neuf minutes—les boxeurs étaient " vidés " complètement, et erraient sur le ring comme des loques.

Quelle différence avec les professionnels hautains, distants, avares de gestes, calculateurs, économisant merveilleusement leurs poings et ne frappant qu'une ou deux fois par round, mais alors concentrant au bout du bras le maximum de leur puissance, de quoi assommer un bœuf. Tandis que des centaines de coups de petits amateurs pourraient à peine presser une éponge.

La boxe est un art, c'est-à-dire qu'il est fait d'économie et de sacrifice. Le boxeur est grand dans la mesure où il sait attendre le moment favorable pour frapper le coup dur. C'est bien pourquoi, si les amateurs sont usés en trois rounds, les professionnels, eux, peuvent tenir quinze rounds.

E. BIRBAUM.

NOTES and WORDS: We should like you to have a shot at making out the sense of this piece about boxing. Apart from the boxing terms, it is not very difficult. However, in these we shall help you.

grand écart, a big " side-step," error

championnat, championship

retenues, *past participle of* **retenir** (to retain), *here means* remembered

poids "mouche," flyweight

pesage, weighing

se délester, to lighten himself

par le même fait, by the very fact

quand même, all the same

or, now

il arriva ceci, this happened

évanoui, in a swoon, faint, unconscious

linge sale, dirty linen, washing

une mise à tombeau, a putting in a tomb, burial

s'effondrer, break down, slump

cuisant, boiling, cooking, *meaning* very hot; poignant

image de la vie, reflexion of life

la Roche tarpéïenne, the Tarpeian rock

épargner, to spare

frais émoulu, newly ground, made

traîner, drag

se dépenser, spend, exhaust

à en perdre le souffle, to the point of losing their wind, being winded

accrochés, hooked, " in clinches "

coups de poing, blows of the fist, punches

" vidés ", " emptied," exhausted

errer, wander

loques, worn out (*men*), literally " rags "

avares de gestes, miserly in gestures, sparing their energy

frapper, to strike

assommer un bœuf, to fell an ox

tandis que, while

à peine, hardly

dans le mesure où, in proportion as

attendre, to wait (for)

user, to wear out

tenir, to hold, to continue

il s'avéra, it turned out

Reading Vocabulary—25

enfermer, *to enclose, shut up*

enfoncer, *to sink, bury*

enfuir (s'), *to flee*

engager, *to enlist, engage in*

ENLEVER, *to carry off*

ENNEMI, *enemy*

ENNUI, *boredom*

ENSEIGNEMENT, *teaching*

ENSEIGNER, *to teach*

ENTENDRE, *to hear, listen*

enthousiasme, *enthusiasm*

entourer, *to surround*

entraîner, *to drag, draw, lead*

ENTRÉE, *entry*

entreprise, *undertaking*

ENTRER, *to enter*

entretien, *conversation*

entrevoir, *to see partly, glimpse*

envahir, *to invade*

envelopper, *to wrap up*

§ 5. *Money—Exchange—Banking*

l'argent, money

la petite monnaie, small change

la monnaie, change

la livre sterling, the pound sterling

le centime

le franc

le billet de banque, note

le billet de cinquante francs, fifty-franc note

le billet de cent francs, 100-franc note

la pièce de cent sous, five-franc piece

le comptant, ready cash

le chèque, check

les chèques de tourisme, travelers' checks

toucher, to cash

le caissier, cashier

le bureau de change, money exchange

changer, to change, exchange

la fête légale, bank holiday

le taux du change, rate of exchange (also **le cours du change**)

la lettre de crédit, letter of credit

négocier, to negotiate

Words you can hardly do without! Money generally talks, but you will save yourself time, trouble, and irritation if you can yourself say exactly what you want. Review the numerals in Lesson II if you think it necessary. The following phrases are useful :

Je veux changer de l'argent américain.

Où peut-on changer de l'argent étranger ?

Quel est le taux (le cours) du change ?

Pourriez-vous m'indiquer un bureau de change ?

Je voudrais négocier un chèque de tourisme.

Je voudrais changer cinq dollars.

Combien donnez-vous le dollar?

Je voudrais toucher un chèque de tourisme.

Voulez-vous accepter ce chèque ?

Voulez-vous me payer ce chèque ?

Veuillez me donner cinq billets de cent francs, s'il vous plaît.

Je voudrais savoir si vous avez reçu une remise télégraphique pour moi, I should like to know whether you have received a remittance by telegraph for me.

Je veux sortir de l'argent, I wish to draw out some money.

Je voudrais acheter des chèques de tourisme.

Est-ce que je peux tirer mille francs sur cette lettre de crédit ? Can I draw 1,000 francs on this letter of credit?

On the whole, you will not have any great difficulty so long as you have money in some form!

¶ 12. CANDIDE

Un homme qui n'avait point été baptisé, un bon anabaptiste, nommé Jacques, vit la manière cruelle et ignominieuse dont on traitait ainsi un des ses frères, un être à deux pieds sans plumes, qui avait une âme ; il l'amena chez lui, le nettoya, lui donna du pain et de la bière, lui fit présent de deux florins, et voulut même lui apprendre à travailler dans ses manufactures aux étoffes de Perse qu'on fabrique en Hollande. Candide, se prosternant presque devant lui, s'écriait : Maître Pangloss l'avait bien dit, que tout était au mieux dans ce monde ; car je suis infiniment plus touché de votre extrême générosité que de la dureté de ce monsieur à manteau noir et de madame son épouse.

Le lendemain, en se promenant, il rencontra un gueux tout couvert de pustules, les yeux morts, le bout du nez rongé, la bouche de travers, les dents noires, et parlant de la gorge, tourmenté d'une toux violente, et crachant une dent à chaque effort.

CHAPITRE IV

Comment Candide rencontra son ancien maître de philosophie, le docteur Pangloss, et ce qui en advint

Candide, plus ému encore de compassion que d'horreur, donna à cet épouvantable gueux les deux florins qu'il avait reçus de son honnête anabaptiste Jacques. Le fantôme le regarda fixement, versa des larmes, et sauta à son cou. Candide effrayé recule. Hélas! dit le misérable à l'autre misérable, ne reconnaissez-vous plus votre cher Pangloss? Qu'entends-je? vous, mon cher maître! vous, dans cet état horrible! quel malheur vous est-il donc arrivé? pourquoi n'êtes-vous plus dans le plus beau des châteaux? qu'est devenue mademoiselle Cunégonde, la perle des filles, le chef-d'œuvre de la nature? Je n'en peux plus, dit Pangloss.

NOTES AND WORDS:

un être, a being

amener, to lead, take with

nettoyer, to clean

étoffes de Perse, Persian stuffs

fabriquer, to manufacture

se prosterner, prostrate oneself

à manteau noir, with a black cloak

un gueux, a beggar

tout couvert de pustules, all covered with sores

la bouche de travers, the mouth awry

une toux violente, a violent cough

cracher, spit, spit out

ancien, old, former

ému, moved

épouvantable, horrible, terrible

le fantôme, phantom, ghost

verser des larmes, shed tears

sauter au cou de, throw arms round the neck of

effrayé, frightened

reculer, to withdraw, recoil

reconnaître, to recognize

Qu'entends-je? What do I hear?

malheur, misfortune

qu'est devenu . . . ., what has become of . . .

Je n'en peux plus, I'm finished, I can't do any more

Reading Vocabulary—26

ENVIE, *wish, fancy*

envisager, *to face*

envoyer, *to send*

ÉPAULE, *shoulder*

ÉPOQUE, *time, period, date*

épouser, *to marry*

épreuve, *proof, trial*

ÉPROUVER, *to experience*

épuiser, *to exhaust*

ERREUR, *mistake*

ESCALIER, *staircase*

espace, *space*

espèce, *kind, sort*

espérance, *hope*

ESPÉRER, *to hope*

ESPOIR, *hope*

ESPRIT, *spirit*

ESSAYER, *to try*

essuyer, *to wipe away*

estimer, *to esteem*

LESSON XV

§ 1. *Review—Laundry*

You will have noticed that in the last two lessons we have given you little in the way of grammar to learn. You have already been provided with the essentials of French grammar, and we have no desire to burden you with more. Furthermore, we fully realize that you will not have been able to absorb all we have given, so you need not be surprised if you find yourself continually having to worry out items here and there. That is precisely what we wish you to do! The chances are that, having worried out the sense of something which has puzzled you, you are unlikely to forget it. At this stage in the course, we are providing you with the everyday practical material you are certain to require, and it will always be useful. At the same time the reading continues to be your main *exercise*. Here a word of advice is necessary. From now on, review the grammar *systematically*. Go over every doubtful item, and not only that—start at the beginning and *every day read over at least one section of a past lesson*. **We hope that you continue to listen to French.** These are important matters, if you are to reap full benefit from the course. We may now continue with the everyday affairs of life.

LAUNDRY: You need not learn a whole laundry list. But you should know certain words:

la liste de blanchissage, laundry list
faire laver, to get washed
repasser, to iron
le mouchoir, handkerchief
la chemise, shirt
les caleçons, drawers, pants
les chaussettes, socks
les bas, stockings
les sous-vêtements, underwear

les robes, ladies' dresses
les shorts, shorts
la chemise de nuit, nightdress (ladies')
la blouse, blouse
les pyjamas, pajamas
repriser, to mend (socks, stockings, etc.)
le col, collar
une paire de, a pair of
le gilet, vest

Je voudrais faire laver des vêtements, I should like to have some clothes laundered.

Voulez-vous faire laver tout ce qui est inscrit sur la liste ? Would you get everything on this list washed ?

Il me les faut aussitôt que possible, I want them as soon as possible

Pouvez-vous faire repriser les bas ? Could you have the stockings mended ?

Il manque des choses, Things are missing

Ceci n'est pas à moi, This is not mine

Faites bien attention aux cols, Take care with the collars

¶ 13. CANDIDE

Aussitôt Candide le mena dans l'étable de l'anabaptiste, où il lui fit manger un peu de pain ; et quand Pangloss fut refait : Eh bien ! lui dit-il, Cunégonde ? Elle est morte, reprit l'autre. Candide s'évanouit à ce mot : son ami rappela ses sens avec un peu de mauvais vinaigre qui se trouva par hasard dans l'étable. Candide rouvre les yeux. Cunégonde est morte ! Ah ! meilleur des mondes, où êtes-vous ? Mais de quelle maladie est-elle morte ? ne serait-ce point de m'avoir vu chasser du beau château de monsieur son père à grands coups de pied ? Non, dit Pangloss, elle a été éventrée par des soldats bulgares, après avoir été violée autant qu'on peut l'être ; ils ont cassé la tête à monsieur le baron, qui voulait la défendre ; madame la baronne a été coupée en morceaux ; mon pauvre pupille traité précisément comme sa soeur ; et quant au château, il n'est pas resté pierre sur pierre, pas une grange, pas un mouton, pas un canard, pas un arbre : mais nous avons été bien vengés, car les Abares en ont fait autant dans une baronnie voisine qui appartenait à un seigneur bulgare.

A ce discours, Candide s'évanouit encore ; mais revenu à soi, et ayant dit tout ce qu'il devait dire, il s'enquit de la cause et de l'effet, et de la raison suffisante qui avait mis Pangloss dans un si piteux état. Hélas ! dit l'autre, c'est l'amour ; l'amour, le consolateur du genre humain, le conservateur de l'univers, l'âme de tous les êtres sensibles, le tendre amour. Hélas ! dit Candide, je l'ai connu cet amour, ce souverain des coeurs, cette âme de notre âme ; il ne m'a jamais valu qu'un baiser et vingt coups de pied au cul.

NOTES AND WORDS:

mener, to lead, conduct
étable, stable
rappeler, recall, bring back
par hasard, by chance
rouvrir, to reopen
couper en morceaux, to cut in pieces
une grange, a barn
un mouton, a sheep

un canard, a duck
vengés, avenged
enquérir, s'enquérir, *an irregular verb which makes* **s'enquit** *in the third person singular of the past definite means* to inquire, to make inquiries. *It is not much used.*
piteux, piteous

Reading Vocabulary—27

ÉTABLIR, *to establish, to fix*
étage, *story (of a building)*
ÉTAT, *state*
ÉTÉ, *summer*
éteindre, *to extinguish*
étendre, *to stretch*
étendue, *extent, scope*
ÉTOILE, *star*
étonnement, *astonishment*
ÉTONNER, *to astonish*
étouffer, *to stifle*

ÉTRANGER, *stranger, foreigner*
un ÊTRE, *person, human being*
étude, *study*
ÉTUDIER, *to study*
éveiller, *to wake up*
événement, *event*
éviter, *to avoid*
exagérer, *to exaggerate*
examen, *examination*

§ 2. *The Hairdresser*

chez le coiffeur, at the hairdresser's
court, short
la coupe de cheveux, haircut
moyen, medium
le shampooing, shampoo
le brûlage des pointes, singe
la nuque, neck (nape of)
les oreilles, ears
couper, to cut

rafraîchir, to trim
la lotion capillaire, hair lotion
raser, to shave
le rasoir, razor
une ondulation, a wave
les cheveux ondulés, wavy hair
une ondulation permanente, permanent wave
la friction, massage

We cannot attempt here to provide you with more than the simplest "outfit" of words and phrases, but what we give is first aid and, with the general knowledge of the language already made available, even ladies need not fear to enter a hairdresser's establishment for a trim, shampoo, and a wave. Gentlemen should be warned that it is not advisable to go into a French barber's shop when in a hurry : the old-fashioned French barber will *not* be hurried, though you can generally rely on him to do a good job. You may have to make an appointment (**prendre rendez-vous**). When a gentleman enters the establishment of **un coiffeur pour messieurs** and his turn comes, he says : **Les cheveux s'il vous plaît.** Then he gives his instructions :

> **Pas trop court,** not too short
> **Court sur la nuque et autour des oreilles seulement,** Short at the back and sides
> **Je voudrais aussi un brûlage des pointes et un shampooing,** I'd like also a singe and shampoo

And a lady :

> **Un shampooing et une mise en plis,** a shampoo and set

When a Frenchman sits down in the barber's chair, he usually says **Cheveux et barbe,** *a haircut and shave.* Many insist on **une coupe aux ciseaux,** *a " scissors cut,"* and will not have **la tondeuse,** *the clippers.* And will also insist : **Ne coupez-pas trop court,** *Don't cut it too short.* **La raie** is *the parting.* Ladies may require much more than this. We can give only a few of the commonest terms :

en boucles, in curls	**un filet à cheveux,** hairnet
blondir, décolorer, to bleach	**mettre les cheveux en plis,**
teindre, to dye	to set the hair
une épingle à cheveux, hairpin	**la manicure,** manicure

Let us hope that neither lady nor gentleman will require **un régénérateur des cheveux,** *a hair restorer.* And that neither is becoming bald (**devenir chauve**) !

UNE PIÈCE DE CARACTÈRE DE JEAN BARD : " LE DESPOTE "

La compagnie Jean Bard a donné récemment au Grand-Théâtre de Genève une création de Jean Bard lui-même dont il

assumait le premier rôle. " Le despote," pièce en trois actes,
nous place face à face avec un de ces êtres qui ne se contente pas
de ronger son existence, mais qui peu à peu réduit en poudre
celle de sa famille. En réalité, on ne devrait pas employer le
terme " famille," car le foyer du despote est bien plutôt un
lieu où l'on mange, où l'on boit, où l'on dort et où les mots
jaillissent comme des traits empoisonnés.

Qui ne connaît, nous dit Jean Bard, un de ces êtres auquel
l'orgueil tient lieu de souffle ? Le plus souvent c'est un faible
qui s'insurge contre lui-même. Et à tel point qu'il perd le
contact avec ses semblables. Définitivement, il a supprimé
en lui tout sentiment d'indulgence, de compassion, de charité.
Il n'écoute que ses propres conseils ; il ne voit que son propre
chemin. Et cela sans songer un instant qu'il pourrait s'égarer.
Il reste immuable.

Sabine, la fille du despote, est une jeune pianiste dévouée à
son art. Elle ne comprend rien à l'ambition de son père qui
voudrait qu'elle atteigne une certaine célébrité et qui désirerait
la placer sous l'aile—un peu crasseuse—d'un impresario-
industriel dont la tête est reproduite à quelques mille exemplaires
sur les boîtes de cigarettes Zabouloff.

NOTES AND WORDS :

une pièce de caractère, a
character piece
(**une pièce,** a play, for the
theatre)
le premier rôle, the leading
part, the lead
ronger, to fret away, to con-
sume, gnaw
le foyer, the hearth, home
jaillir, to shoot out
des traits empoisonnés,
poisoned missiles
(**trait,** dart, shaft, *also* a flash;
and many other meanings)
l'orgueil, pride

souffle, breath
un faible, a weak one
s'insurger, to rise against
ses semblables, his equals,
those like him
écouter, to listen to, hear
ses propres conseils, his own
counsels, advice
chemin, road
atteindre, to reach
qu'elle atteigne, that she
may reach, attain
placer sous l'aile, to place
under the wing
crasseux, squalid, dirty

Reading Vocabulary—28

examiner, *to examine*
excès, *excess*
exciter, *to encourage*
excuse, *excuse*
EXCUSER, *to excuse*
exécuter, *to carry out*
exemple, *example*
exercer, *to exercise*
exercice, *exercise*
exiger, *to demand*

existence, *life, existence*
exister, *to exist*
expérience, *experiment*
EXPLIQUER, *to explain*
exposer, *to expose*
expression, *expression*
exprimer, *to express*
extérieur, *exterior*
extrémité, *extremity*
FACE, *face, front*

§ 3. *Theater—Movies*

le théâtre
le cinéma
l'opéra
le ballet
la soirée, evening performance
la matinée, matinee

un fauteuil d'orchestre, orchestra seat
le balcon, dress circle
la seconde galerie, second balcony
la galerie, balcony

(What we call "peanut heaven" in a theater, the French call le poulailler, the "hen roost." French is rich in slang, but you must learn standard French first. Le poulailler indicates how picturesque slang can be.)

le bureau de location, box office
le vestiaire, cloakroom
la sortie, exit
bis! Means "twice" and is used when we would cry "encore"
salle comble, full house
le rôle, part
la pièce, play
faire la queue, to queue up
la place, seat
le spectacle, show (theater)
la scène, stage

le film parlant, talking film
la séance, show (movies)
l'écran, screen
le film, film
le film documentaire, documentary
le film muet, silent film
le film d'actualités, newsreel
filmer, to film
le billet, ticket
le billet d'avance, ticket in advance
tourner, to "put on" a film
louer, to book

A quelle heure commence la séance ? At what time does the (movie) show begin?

A quelle heure commence le spectacle ? At what time does the (theater) show begin?

Quand est-ce qu'on tourne le film d'actualités ? When do they put on the news reel ?

Combien coûtent les places du balcon ? How much do seats in the mezzanine cost?

Veuillez me donner deux places à . . . francs, Please give me two seats at . . . francs.

These few phrases and the words given above are about all that you require in the way of special linguistic material to get you into a theater or movie—which is what you will wish to do. You will, of course, watch the newspapers for theater and movie advertisements and, if you are really interested, you will buy one of the weeklies devoted to the subject. Here is an example of the sort of announcement you will see :

Sortie Parisienne de "Danger de Mort"
un film français original

Cette semaine, dans trois salles parisiennes : Cinécran Caumartin, Impérial, Portiques, sort le très curieux et original film de Gilles Grangier : " Danger de mort," adapté d'une idée de Ch. Exbrayat par René Wheeler. On y verra Fernand Ledoux se débattre dans une aventure tragicomique où les incidents pathétiques ou pleins d'humour ne manquent pas. (Distr. Pathé Consortium.)

Notes and Words :

sortir here means "*release*" (of a film)   **se débattre,** to flounder

¶ 14. CANDIDE

. . . Mais il faut vous faire guérir. Et comment le puis-je ? dit Pangloss ; je n'ai pas le sou, mon ami ; et dans toute l'étendue de ce globe on ne peut ni se faire saigner ni prendre un lavement sans payer, ou sans qu'il y ait quelqu'un qui paye pour nous.

Ce dernier discours détermina Candide; il alla se jeter aux pieds de son charitable anabaptiste Jacques, et lui fit une peinture si touchante de l'état où son ami était réduit, que le bonhomme n'hésita pas à recueillir le docteur Pangloss; il le fit guérir à ses dépens. Pangloss dans la cure ne perdit qu'un œil et une oreille. Il écrivait bien, et savait parfaitement l'arithmétique. L'anabaptiste Jacques en fit son teneur de livres. Au bout de deux mois, étant obligé d'aller à Lisbonne pour les affaires de son commerce, il mena dans son vaisseau ses deux philosophes. Pangloss lui expliqua comment tout était on ne peut mieux.

NOTES AND WORDS:

guérir, to cure

Et comment le puis-je? And how can I?

Je n'ai pas le sou . . . I haven't the cash

étendue, extent

saigner, to bleed

se faire saigner, to have oneself bled

une peinture, a picture, painting

recueillir, to succor, shelter

à ses dépens, at his expense

teneur de livres, bookkeeper

au bout de, at the end of

les affaires de son commerce, the affairs, matters of his business

un vaisseau, vessel

comment tout était on ne peut mieux, how all was, it could not be better; how all was for the best

Reading Vocabulary—29

FAÇON, *fashion, manner*

faculté, *faculty*

faiblesse, *weakness*

le fait, *fact, deed*

FALLOIR, *to be necessary*

FAMILLE, *family*

fantaisie, *whim, fancy*

FATIGUÉ, *tired*

fatiguer, *to fatigue*

FAUTE, *fault*

fauteuil, *armchair, seat (theater)*

faveur, *favor*

FEMME, *woman, wife*

FENÊTRE, *window*

FER, *iron*

ferme, *farm*

fermer, *to shut*

fête, *holiday, festival*

FEU, *fire*

feuille, *leaf*

Reading Vocabulary—30

fièvre, *fever*	FLAMME, *flame*
FIGURE, *face*	FLEUR, *flower*
figurer, *to imagine*	flotter, *to float*
fil, *thread, wire*	foi, *faith*
filer, *to spin*	FOIS, *time*
FILLE, *daughter*	folie, *madness*
FILS, *son*	fonction, *function*
FIN, *end*	FOND, *bottom*
FINIR, *to finish*	fonder, *to base*
fixer, *to fix*	fondre, *to melt*

§ 4. *Shopping*

It is not possible to provide the vocabulary you would require for all shopping, as each kind of shop demands a specialized vocabulary to itself. By the time you wish to shop in France, you will be able to use a dictionary * ; and the best thing you can do before going on a shopping expedition is to make a list of words. For example, if you think of buying *a bathing suit*, look it up and list it : **costume de bain ;** *a raincoat*, **imperméable ;** And so on. You must be your own vocabulary-maker for this purpose. However, you may be helped by these phrases :

Je désire . . . I want . . .

Avez-vous de . . . Have you any . . .

Je voudrais . . . I should like . . .

Pourriez-vous me montrer . . . Could you show me . . .

Je n'en veux aucun(e) . . . I don't want any of them . . .

Ça ne me va pas . . . That does not fit me . . .

Je désire quelque chose de mieux, I'd like something better

Quel est le prix de ceci ? What is the price of this ?

Je prends ceci, I will have this

Envoyez-le à cette adresse, Send it to this address

Je veux avoir ceci avant six heures aujourd'hui, I should like to have this before six o'clock today

* The FRENCH DICTIONARY for the Pocket by John Bellows (English–French and French–English) published by Longmans Green & Co., Ltd., can be recommended.

Voulez-vous me permettre de payer avec de l'argent étranger (américain)? Will you allow me to pay in foreign (American) money?

Voulez-vous me faire une note, s'il vous plaît? Will you please make out a bill for me?

Combien coûtera . . . ? How much will it cost . . . ?

Quand sera-t-il prêt? When will it be ready?

You will want to know the various shops, and here are the words :

le magasin, shop	**la pâtisserie,** pastry shop
le grand magasin, store (big)	**l'épicerie,** grocer's
le client, customer	**la boucherie,** butcher's
acheter, to buy	**la boulangerie,** baker's
vendre, to sell	**envelopper,** wrap up
choisir, to choose	**annuler,** to cancel
un(e) employé(e), assistant	**commander,** to order
le libraire, bookseller	**chez le boulanger,** at the
la papeterie, stationery	baker's
le débit de tabac, tobacconist	**chez l'épicier,** etc.
la confiserie, candy store	**le vendeur,** salesman
la fruiterie, fruit shop	**la vendeuse,** saleswoman

LE THÉÂTRE

Il y a cinquante-six ans, un poète de vingt-quatre ans achevait une pièce par laquelle il essayait de renouer, sous une forme moderne, avec le théâtre religieux du moyen âge. C'était une œuvre pleine de promesses, de maladresses, et traversée de quelques fulgurants éclairs de beauté, " L'Annonce faite à Marie " n'a pas vieilli, ce qui montre qu'une maladresse sincère vaut mieux qu'une trop intelligente adresse.

M. Claudel n'a pas vieilli non plus, malgré ses quatre-vingts ans. Il est toujours un jeune poète plein d'avenir. Pour peu que Dieu lui prête vie, il apprendra sans doute, l'expérience aidant, à se corriger de ses défauts qui sont très gros et très visibles, et par conséquent faciles à détacher. Alors il sera mûr pour commencer une œuvre impérissable, car ses qualités sont aussi grosses et aussi visibles que ses défauts.

M. Claudel a vu mourir un siècle, traversé trois guerres, et senti le souffle proche de la quatrième sans rien perdre de sa naïveté ni de sa sérénité.   Il le doit à une foi d'une merveilleuse abondance, plantée dans sa chair autant que dans son esprit et dans son cœur.   Il est semblable à cette terre dont il sait si bien parler, qui ne s'use point, qui ne saigne pas, qui se renouvelle de ses propres fruits, et sur laquelle les chars d'assaut peuvent déferler sans l'empêcher, à la saison suivante, de tendre vers le ciel ses mains de fleurs et d'épines.

NOTES AND WORDS:

il y a cinquante-six ans, fifty-six years ago
essayer, to try, attempt
renouer, to reknot, connect up again
la maladresse, clumsiness
et traversée, etc., and interspersed with some lightning flashes of beauty
vieillir, to grow old
vieilli, grown old
plein d'avenir, full of future, with a great future
pour peu que, if only
prêter, to lend
apprendre, to learn

corriger, to correct
mûr, ripe
impérissable, imperishable
le souffle proche, the near breath
la naïveté, simplicity, artlessness
(naïf, naïve, guileless, naïve)
la chair, flesh
semblable à, similar to
les chars d'assaut, assault chariots, *that is,* tanks
déferler, unfurl
empêcher, to prevent
tendre, to stretch
une épine, thorn

Reading Vocabulary—31–32

FORCE, *strength, power, force*
forcer, *to force*
forêt, *forest*
forme, *form*
former, *to form*
fortune, *fortune*
fouiller, *to search*
FOULE, *crowd*
fournir, *to furnish, provide*
foyer, *hearth, fire*

les frais, *expenses*
franc, *franc (a coin)*
franchir, *to go across*
frapper, *to strike, knock*
frère, *brother*
FROID, *cold*
FRONT, *forehead, front*
FRUIT, *fruit*
fuir, *flee, fly*
fuite, *flight*

FUMÉE, *smoke*
fusil, *rifle*
futur, *future*
gagner, *to gain*
gaieté, *gaiety*
galerie, *gallery*
gamin, *young boy*
garde, *care, guard*
garder, *to guard, keep*
GARE, *station*

gâter, *to spoil*
gêner, *to inconvenience*
général, *general*
génie, *genius*
genou, *knee*
genre, *kind, sort*
les GENS, *people*
gentilhomme, *nobleman*
geste, *gesture*
glace, *ice, (plate) glass*

§ 5. *Hotel—Boardinghouse*

l'hôtel, hotel
la pension, boardinghouse
une auberge, inn
la note, bill
la chambre, room
la chambre à deux lits,
   room with two beds
la salle à manger, dining-
   room
le bain, bath
la clef, key
le numéro, number
le prix, terms, price
le portier, porter, doorman

le propriétaire, proprietor
la pension complète, full
   board
**les chambres communi-
   cantes,** rooms with com-
   municating doors, adjoining
   rooms
chambre seule, room without
   meals
le service, service
le registre, hotel register
un commissionnaire, mes-
   senger
tout compris, inclusive

Je voudrais une chambre (à un lit, deux lits), I want a
   room with (single bed, two beds)
**Pourriez-vous me montrer une chambre (plus petite,
   plus grande)?** Could you show me a smaller, bigger
   room?
Quel est le numéro de ma chambre? What is the
   number of my room?
Je sors maintenant et je rentrerai à 7 heures, I'm going
   out now and shall return at 7 o'clock
Quel est le prix d'une chambre par nuit, par semaine?
   What is the price of a room per night, per week?
Je désire la pension complète, I want full board

Je désire la chambre seulement, I want a room only

Je voudrais être réveillé à 7 heures du matin, I want to be called at 7 o'clock in the morning

Est-ce que ma chambre est prête ?   Is my room ready ?

Je vais partir demain matin à 10 heures, I'm leaving to-morrow at 10 o'clock

Veuillez préparer la note, s'il vous plaît, Please make out my bill

Est-ce que vous pouvez envoyer mes bagages à la gare ?   Can you send my luggage to the station ?

Quel est le montant de la note ?   How much is the bill ?

Vous m'avez compté trop pour . . . You have charged too much for . . .

Voulez-vous accepter des chèques de tourisme ? Will you accept travelers' checks?

Je suis bien content de mon séjour, I am very pleased with my stay

Faites suivre mon courrier à . . . Send my mail on to . . .

If you have been satisfied, do not hesitate to say so; and vice versa. And if you wish to ingratiate yourself for another occasion, thank the proprietor or manager and assure him : **Je vais revenir un jour, peut-être bientôt.**

¶ 15. CANDIDE

Jacques n'était pas de cet avis. Il faut bien, disait-il, que les hommes aient un peu corrompu la nature, car ils ne sont point nés loups, et ils sont devenus loups. Dieu ne leur a donné ni canons de vingt-quatre, ni baïonnettes, et ils se sont fait des baïonnettes et des canons pour se détruire. Je pourrais mettre en ligne de compte les banqueroutes, et la justice qui s'empare des biens des banqueroutiers pour en frustrer les créanciers. Tout cela était indispensable, répliquait le docteur borgne, et les malheurs particuliers font le bien général ; de sorte que plus il y a de malheurs particuliers, et plus tout est bien. Tandis qu'il raisonnait, l'air s'obscurcit, les vents soufflèrent des quatre coins du monde, et le vaisseau fut assailli de la plus horrible tempête, à la vue du port de Lisbonne.

FIN DU CHAPITRE IV

NOTES AND WORDS: This is the end of the excerpts from Voltaire's **Candide,** sufficient, we believe, to make you decide to read it all one day. There are several translations in English, perhaps the most accurate being that of Richard Aldington. It would be a good exercise to have the French text before you, and to compare it with one of these translations. You may be surprised to find how inaccurate some of them are!

avis, opinion

il faut bien, etc., men must have corrupted nature a little

nés loups, born wolves

devenu(s), become

se détruire, to destroy oneself

en ligne de compte, in the line of account (*i.e.,* include)

s'emparer de, to seize

frustrer, to frustrate, to deprive of

les créanciers, creditors

borgne, one-eyed

les malheurs particuliers font le bien general, private misfortunes make the public good (interest)

de sorte que, so that

s'obscurcir, grow dark

souffler, to blow, whistle

Reading Vocabulary—33

glisser, *to slide, glide*

gloire, *glory*

gorge, *throat*

GOÛT, *taste*

goûter, *to taste*

goutte, *drop*

gouvernement, *government*

grâce. *mercy*

grain, *seed*

grandeur, *greatness*

GRANDIR, *to grow*

gré, *will*

gronder, *to growl, scold*

groupe, *group*

GUERRE, *war*

s'habiller, *to dress oneself*

habit, *clothes*

habitant, *inhabitant*

habiter, *to inhabit*

habitude, *habit*

LESSON XVI

§ 1. *Eating and Drinking*

We now come to what some students may regard as the most important lesson of the whole course : eating and drinking! We shall take drinking first, as it is—linguistically—less complicated. You will require the following words :

une tasse, a cup
un verre, glass
le thé, le café, tea, coffee
du café au lait, café crème, coffee with milk
le sucre, sugar
la crème, cream
le chocolat, chocolate
chaud, hot
tiède, lukewarm
froid, cold
glacé, iced
café noir, black coffee
faible, weak
fort, strong
la citronnade, lemonade
orangeade, orangeade
l'eau minérale, mineral water
l'eau gazeuse, aerated water
l'eau de seltz, soda water
le cidre, cider
une bouteille, bottle
la bière, beer
la bière blonde, light beer
un bock, means either a beer-glass *or* a glass of beer
la bière noire, dark beer (*or* stout, *also called* **le stout**)

le vin, wine
un whisky and soda
rouge, red
blanc, white
vin rosé, a light, pink wine
un apéritif, appetizer
l'eau de vie, brandy
le cognac, cognac
une liqueur, liqueur
un vin doux, a sweet wine
un vin sec, a dry wine
chambrer, to take the chill off (claret)
le vin nouveau, new season's wine
tiré du tonneau, drawn from cask
vin de Bordeaux, claret
un cocktail
la serveuse, waitress (call her " Mademoiselle ")
un cocktail de jus de fruits, fruit cocktail
le garçon, waiter
le vin ordinaire, " ordinary " cheap wine
la bière brune, dark beer

You will probably not go thirsty in France if you know these words. But, there is more to it than that! France produces a greater variety of wines than any country in the world; a knowledge of them can be a lifetime's study. What wine to drink with what food?—this is a question over which French people dining out confer with the deepest gravity. French wines take their names from the place of origin or the vineyard. **Le vin de Bordeaux,** for example, covers the whole range of clarets, of which the most esteemed come from Médoc, Graves, and St. Emilion districts. **Le vin de Bourgogne** covers all the wines from the old province of Burgundy, white and red, not just red wines as is generally thought in America. **Cognac** is brandy from the Cognac district—and *no other*. **Champagne** is the name given to the most famous of sparkling wines—white and red. They come from the former province of Champagne. **Grande Champagne** is the name given to some of the finest brandy produced in a small part of the **Charente.** The word **fine** conveys the idea of good-quality brandy. **A votre santé,** *to your health!*

Note on Flaubert's *Salammbô*

You are now about to begin reading Gustave Flaubert's *Salammbô*. Flaubert is notable for his choice of **le mot juste,** the exact word; and for the perfection of his style. He is not an easy author for the foreigner, and in *Salammbô* he uses many words which you might not meet elsewhere in a lifetime. You need not attempt to learn more of these words than your common sense tells you are likely to be useful. It will suffice if you *read and understand* the excerpts which follow. The principal object in introducing you to Flaubert is to accustom you to the work of a master of style.

As in the case of *Tartarin de Tarascon* and *Candide*, THE TRANSLATION GIVEN HERE IS LITERAL AND NOT LITERARY. It is intended merely as a key or legitimate " crib " to assist you in understanding the French text—and nothing more. One day, after you have finished the whole course, you may find it interesting to see what an expert translator has made of *Salammbô*— say, the translation by Powys Mathers.

At this point, it would be advisable to reread the note on "Translations of Reading Matter" in Lesson V, § 2, page 81.

¶ 1. SALAMMBÔ

Par Gustave Flaubert

I

LE FESTIN

C'était à Mégara, faubourg de Carthage, dans les jardins d'Hamilcar.

Les soldats qu'il avait commandés en Sicile se donnaient un grand festin pour célébrer le jour anniversaire de la bataille d'Éryx, et comme le maître était absent et qu'ils se trouvaient nombreux, ils mangeaient et ils buvaient en pleine liberté.

Les capitaines, portant des cothurnes de bronze, s'étaient placés dans le chemin du milieu, sous un voile de pourpre à franges d'or, qui s'étendait depuis le mur des écuries jusqu'à la première terrasse du palais; le commun des soldats était répandu sous les arbres, où l'on distinguait quantité de bâtiments à toit plat, pressoirs, celliers, magasins, boulangeries et arsenaux, avec une cour pour les éléphants, des fosses pour les bêtes féroces, une prison pour les esclaves.

TRANSLATION:

THE FEAST

It was at Megara, (a) suburb of Carthage, in the gardens of Hamilcar.

The soldiers whom he had commanded in Sicily were giving themselves (holding) a great festival (feast) to celebrate the anniversary (day) of the battle of Eryx, and as the master was absent and they found themselves (were) numerous, they ate and drank in full liberty (freedom).

The captains, wearing buskins of bronze, had placed themselves in the central road (alley), under an awning of purple with gold fringes which extended from the wall of the stables as far as the first terrace of the palace; the commonalty (rank and file) of the soldiers was spread out (scattered) under the trees, where one could see (a) number of buildings with flat roofs, wine presses, cellars, stores, bakeries and arsenals, with a courtyard for the elephants, pits for fierce beasts (wild animals), a prison for slaves.

Reading Vocabulary—34

haie, *hedge*

haine, *hatred*

hasard, *chance*

hâte, *haste*

hausser, *to shrug*

HAUT, *top*

HAUTEUR, *height*

HERBE, *grass*

hésitation, *hesitation*

hésiter, *to hesitate*

HEURE, *hour*

heurter, *to stumble against*

HIER, *yesterday*

HISTOIRE, *story*, *history*

HIVER, *winter*

HOMME, *man*

HONNEUR, *honor*

HONTE, *shame*

horizon, *horizon*

horreur, *horror*

§ 2. *Eating—The Principal Meals, etc.*

La cuisine est l'art français par excellence, le seul art dans lequel, depuis quatre cents ans, nos compatriotes n'eurent jamais de rivaux.—*Le carnet d'Epicure.*

Cookery is preeminently the French art, the only art in which, for four hundred years, our compatriots have never had rivals.—*Epicurus's Notebook.*

With little or no knowledge of the language, you can get a meal or some sort of food in France. But with the normal abundance and varieties of food *and* a knowledge of **Le répertoire de la Cuisine**—*the " repertory " of the kitchen (or cookery)*—you can do better than that. Furthermore, as French cookery and the French of **le menu** (" *Bill of Fare* ") are to be found all over the world, we shall, in this and the next three sections of this lesson, provide you with vocabulary and phrases to meet most situations.

le petit déjeuner : usually coffee (**du café au lait**) and rolls or **croissants** (crescents of bread), or **brioches.**

le déjeuner : from about midday until 2.30 p.m. This corresponds to lunch, but is more elaborate.

le dîner : from about 6.30 onward.

Tea is becoming popular, and afternoon tea is called **le thé anglais.** There may also be **un souper,** before going to bed. Most of the following words are essential :

le couteau, knife
la fourchette, fork
la cuillère, spoon
le plat, dish
une assiette, plate
le verre, glass
la tasse, cup
le pot au lait, milk pitcher
le sel, salt
le poivre, pepper
la moutarde, mustard
le pain, bread
le vinaigre, vinegar
l'huile, salad oil
le petit pain, roll
la brioche, brioche
le beurre, butter

un œuf, an egg
les œufs (pr. *lèzeu*), eggs
un œuf à la coque, boiled egg
un œuf sur le plat, fried egg
les œufs pochés, brouillés, poached, scrambled eggs
le jambon, ham
le lard, bacon
les œufs au lard, eggs and bacon
la confiture, jam
la marmelade, compote (of fruit)
le biscuit, biscuit
une serviette, a napkin
le bacon, bacon

In this list, you have the " tools " and vocabulary to get you even an American breakfast should you insist on one.

You will often come across the term **à la** in French menus, especially those compiled abroad. In France **à la** has a definite meaning, which is *in the manner of, after the style of* and nothing else. Thus **un œuf à la coque** means *an egg, shell-style.* **Une omelette à la Portugaise,** *an omelet in the manner of the Portuguese,* which means an omelet seasoned with tomatoes. **à la Portugaise** generally indicates tomatoes.

Text :

A Nos Lecteurs

Deux jours après sa mise en vente, de nombreux acheteurs se plaignent de ne plus trouver *Les Lettres Françaises.* C'est qu'un hebdomadaire ne peut être distribué comme un quotidien à très grand tirage. Nous voulons éviter les retours d'invendus, qui vont peser très lourd sur le budget des administrations imprévoyantes, les messageries demandant plus d'un franc par exemplaire retourné, somme qui s'ajoute encore au prix de revient.

Aussi invitons-nous nos lecteurs à acheter leur numéro chez le même dépositaire. S'ils ne le trouvent plus dans de petites bourgades ou dans certains kiosques où la vente est irrégulière, mieux vaut pour eux souscrire un abonnement. Dans l'un et l'autre cas, ils auront la certitude d'être servis.

TRANSLATION :

To Our Readers

Two days after it was put on sale, numerous buyers complain(ed) of no more finding Les Lettres Françaises. It is that (because) a weekly cannot be distributed like a daily with a great circulation. We wish to avoid the return of unsold (copies), which are going to weigh very heavily on the budget of unforeseeing administration(s), the carriers asking more than one franc per returned copy, a sum which is further added to the price of the production.

So we invite our readers to buy their issue at the same newsagent's. If they cannot find it any more in the small towns or in certain newsstands where the sale is irregular, better (it would be) for them to take out a subscription. In either case, they will have the certainty (be certain) to be served.

Reading Vocabulary—35

HÔTEL, *hotel*
humanité, *humanity*
humeur, *humor*
idéal, *ideal*
IDÉE, *idea*
ignorer, *to be unaware of*
île, *island*
illusion, *illusion*
image, *image, reflection*
imagination, *imagination*
imaginer, *to imagine*

imbécile, *imbecile, fool*
imiter, *to imitate*
impatience, *impatience*
importance, *importance*
importer, *to be important, to matter*
imposer, *to impose*
impression, *impression*
imprimer, *to print*
incident, *incident*

§ 3. *The French Menu*—**Déjeuner** *et* **Dîner**

A French poet has written :

**Un menu! C'est le plus adorable poème ;
C'est le plus délicat chef-d'œuvre . . .**

*A bill of fare! 'Tis the most adorable poem :
It is the most delicate masterpiece . . .*

Certainly, **le menu** of a good French restaurant can be a
" most delicate masterpiece "; and it is worth understanding.
The dishes (**les plats**) come under different headings, in the order
in which they should be eaten.   Thus :

HORS D'ŒUVRES : Side dishes or appetizers

POTAGES : Soups, either thick (**purée** or **crème**),
or thin (**le consommé**)

ŒUFS : Eggs, usually a great variety, including
omelettes

POISSONS : Fish, including shellfish

ENTRÉES : In categories : (1) **les entrées d'abats,**
which we would call " offal "—liver,
kidneys, etc.; (2) **les entrées volantes**
—poultry in various forms, including
game; (3) **les entrées relevées**—
meat prepared in various ways; (4)
les entrées rôties—various roast
meats

SALADES : Simple and complex

LÉGUMES : Vegetables

PÂTES : " Farinaceous pastes "—such are maca-
roni, spaghetti, ravioli, etc.

ENTREMETS : Sweets, fruits, ices, etc.

This is the framework of a full **menu** for **déjeuner** or **dîner**.
The French add "savories" for the benefit of English and
American diners.   They rarely use them themselves, and the
finer palates say they " spoil a good meal."   Cheese (**le
fromage**) is often omitted from the **menu** or put as a footnote.
There are many kinds of it in France.

The **menu** is arranged according to season and the foodstuffs available. The great authority on French culinary art, Brillat Savarin, says : " The order of eatables is from the substantial to the lighter ones ."

Let not the student get the idea that French people in general eat with a **menu** like this to choose from. Not at all. This represents the luxury hotel or luxury restaurant standard. But even in the little restaurants the main principles are the same, and in them and in les bistros (pubs) the standard of cooking is high—often superb—and there is variety. In the next section you order a meal, and in § 5 we shall give you a food vocabulary for reference.

¶ 2. SALAMMBÔ

TEXT :

Des figuiers entouraient les cuisines ; un bois de sycomores se prolongeait jusqu'à des masses de verdure, où des grenades resplendissaient parmi les touffes blanches des cotonniers, des vignes, chargées de grappes, montaient dans le branchage des pins ; un champ de roses s'épanouissait sous des platanes ; de place en place sur des gazons se balançaient des lis ; un sable noir, mêlé à de la poudre de corail, parsemait les sentiers, et, au milieu, l'avenue des cyprès faisait d'un bout à l'autre comme une double colonnade d'obélisques verts.

Le palais, bâti en marbre numidique tacheté de jaune, superposait tout au fond, sur de larges assises, ses quatre étages en terrasses. Avec son grand escalier droit en bois d'ébène, portant aux angles de chaque marche la proue d'une galère vaincue, avec ses portes rouges écartelées d'une croix noire, ses grillages d'airain qui le défendaient en bas de scorpions, et ses treillis de baguettes dorées qui bouchaient en haut ses ouvertures, il semblait aux soldats, dans son opulence farouche, aussi solennel et impénétrable que le visage d'Hamilcar.

TRANSLATION : *Fig trees surrounded the kitchens; a sycamore wood stretched as far as masses of verdure, where pomegranates shone brightly among white tufts of cotton plants; vines loaded with grapes were climbing among the branches of the pine trees; a field of roses bloomed under some plane trees; from place to place (here and there) on the lawns lilies balanced themselves; a black sand mixed with coral dust was scattered over the footpaths and, in the middle, the avenue of cypresses made from one end to the other as (it were) a double colonnade of green obelisks.*

The palace built of Numidian marble spotted (mottled) with yellow superimposed (raised) well in the background, on broad foundations, its four storeys in terraces. With its great, straight staircase in wood of ebony, bearing at the angles of each step the prow of a vanquished galley, with its red doors quartered by a black cross, its brass lattice-work which defended it below from scorpions, and its trellises of gilded bars which closed its openings above, it seemed to the soldiers, in its fierce opulence, as solemn and impenetrable as Hamilcar's face.

Reading Vocabulary—36

INCONNU, *unknown*
indépendance, *independence*
indiquer, *to indicate*
individu, *individual*
industrie, *industry*
influence, *influence*
INFORMER, *to inform*
s'inquiéter, *to be uneasy, anxious*
inquiétude, *anxiety, uneasiness*
inscrire, *to enroll*

INSISTER, *to insist*
inspirer, *to inspire*
installer, *to install*
instant, *moment*
instinct, *instinct*
institution, *institution*
instruction, *instruction*
instruire, *to instruct*
intelligence, *intelligence*
intention, *intention*

§ 4. *Ordering a Lunch or Dinner*

You have probably had **le petit déjeuner** in your hotel or **pension**. And you may wish to have luncheon or dinner out. First you find or ask for a table. **Je voudrais une place**—if you are alone. **Nous voudrions une table pour . . . deux, trois, quatre**—*We want a table for . . . two, three, four.* Or : **Cette table est-elle retenue ?** *Is this table taken (reserved)?* Then you ask for **la carte du jour,** *today's bill of fare.* You may lunch or dine in one of two ways : **à la carte,** choosing your dishes; or **table d'hôte** (which is **à prix fixe,** *at a fixed price*), accepting dishes as offered by the " host " or proprietor. (You will rarely be dissatisfied if you elect for **table d'hôte** and, if you are not sure of yourself, you should do so.) You may require **la liste des vins** from which to choose a bottle; or you may elect for **une bouteille de vin ordinaire** (familiarly called **le pinard**); or **une bouteille de Vichy,** *a bottle of Vichy water.*

" *Avoid ordinary water* " is the general rule observed by experienced travelers in France. Then:

Garçon, qu'est-ce que vous pouvez recommander ?
Waiter, what can you recommend ?

Nous voudrions, we should like . . .

Donnez-moi une portion de . . . Give me a portion of . . .

Qu'est-ce que vous avez comme rôti ? What have you in the way of a roast (meat) ?

Pourrais-je avoir, Could I have . . .

Pour suivre je voudrais, To follow I should like . . .

Garçon, je n'aime pas ce plat, Waiter, I don't like this dish

Passez-moi la moutarde, s'il vous plaît, Pass the mustard, please

Je mangerai à la bonne franquette (*or* **à la fortune du pot**), I'm willing to take pot luck

Garçon, la note (or **l'addition**) **s'il vous plaît,** Waiter, the bill please

Combien est-ce que ça fait en tout, How much is that altogether ?

Chacun paiera pour soi, Each one will pay for himself

Le service est-il compris ? Is service included ?

If the service is not included, you will give the waiter **un pourboire** (*a tip*), which ought not to exceed 8 per cent of the bill; nor should it be less, if you wish to return to the same restaurant!

TEXT:

LES PROMOTIONS DANS LA LÉGION D'HONNEUR

Une importante promotion dans la Légion d'Honneur va sortir incessamment au " Journal officiel." La place faite aux artistes y est sensiblement plus importante que dans les promotions précédentes et nous ne saurions trop nous réjouir de cette amélioration due à l'activité de la Direction des Arts et Lettres et à la compréhension du grand Chancelier.

Il y a quelques jours a paru le texte élevant M. Robert Rey à la dignité de commandeur. Tous les artistes à qui il a porté depuis des années tant de preuves de dévouement applaudissent à cette élévation et voudront s'associer au juste hommage qui lui est ainsi rendu.

TRANSLATION :

PROMOTIONS IN THE LEGION OF HONOR

An important promotion in the Legion of Honor is going to come out immediately (appear) in the " Official Journal." The place made (given) to artists is perceptibly more important than in the preceding promotions, and we cannot too much rejoice over this improvement due to the activity of the Governing Body of Arts and Letters and to the understanding of the great Chancellor.

A few days ago appeared the text raising (promoting) M. Robert Rey to the dignity of commander. All the artists to whom he has brought for (so many) years proofs of devotion applaud this promotion and will wish to associate themselves with the just homage which is thus rendered to him.

Reading Vocabulary—37–38

interdire, *to forbid*
INTÉRESSER, *to interest*
intérêt, *interest*
intérieur, *interior*
interroger, *to question*
interrompre, *to interrupt*
intervention, *interruption, intervention*
introduire, *to introduce*
inventer, *to invent*
invention, *invention*

JOUER, *to play*
jouir, *to enjoy*
JOUR, *day*
JOURNAL, *newspaper*
JOURNÉE, *day (duration)*
juge, *judge*
jugement, *judgment*
JUGER, *to judge*
jurer, *to swear*
justice, *justice*

INVITER, *to invite*
JAMBE, *leg*
JARDIN, *garden*
JETER, *to throw*
JEU, *game*
JEUDI, *Thursday*
JEUNESSE, *youth*
JOIE, *joy*
JOINDRE, *to join*
JOUE, *cheek*

lâcher, *to let go*
laine, *wool*
LAISSER, *to let, allow*
lampe, *lamp*
lancer, *to throw, to fling*
langage, *language*
LANGUE, *tongue*
LARME, *tear*
LEÇON, *lesson*
LECTURE, *reading*

§ 5. *Food Vocabulary—For Reference*

hors-d'œuvres (variés), hors d'œuvres (mixed)

la soupe, soup

le potage, soup—usually vegetable

le consommé, thin soup

crème de, purée de, thick soup (of)

la soupe au poisson, fish soup

bouillon de poulet, chicken soup (clear)

le saumon, salmon

la truite, trout

la sole, sole

la morue, cod

une anguille, eel

le turbot, turbot

le flétan, halibut

le carrelet, plaice

les sardines, sardines

les huîtres, oysters

le homard, lobster

l'écrevisse, crayfish

le crabe, crab

les moules, mussels

une omelette aux fines herbes, herb omelet

une omelette bonne femme, made with bacon, mushrooms and onion

omelette espagnole, made with tomatoes and onions

omelette au jambon, ham omelette

la dinde, turkey

le faisan, pheasant

le canard, duck

le caneton, duckling

le poulet, chicken

rôti, roast

le lapin, rabbit

le lièvre, hare

le bœuf, beef

le bifteck, beefsteak

le bœuf bouilli, boiled beef

le bœuf braisé, braised beef

le filet de bœuf, fillet

la queue de bœuf, oxtail

le mouton, mutton

l'agneau, lamb

le ragoût de mouton, 'Irish' *or* mutton stew

le rôti de mouton, roast mutton

le rôti d'agneau, roast lamb

la selle de mouton, saddle of mutton

la côtelette de mouton, lamb or mutton cutlet *or* chop

le lard, bacon (also **le bacon**)

le porc, pork

la côtelette de porc, pork chop

le porc rôti, roast pork

le jambon, ham

la saucisse, sausage

la saucisse de porc, pork sausage

grillé, grilled

frit, fried

fumé, smoked

mariné, pickled

en ragoût, stewed

bien cuit, well cooked

saignant, rare

cru, raw

à l'anglaise, English style (of cooking)

à la française, French style

le jus, la sauce, gravy, sauce

la sauce tomate, tomato sauce

le beurre fondu, melted butter

l'huile d'olive, olive oil

la sauce mayonnaise, mayonnaise

la salade, salad

la salade de laitue, lettuce salad

s. de pomme de terres, potato salad

la salade aux œufs, egg salad

la salade de tomates, tomato salad

s. de légumes crus, raw vegetable salad

les légumes, vegetables

les pommes de terre frites or sautées, fried potatoes

les tomates, tomatoes

le céleri, celery

les pois, peas

les fèves, broad beans

les haricots verts, French beans

les aspèrges, asparagus

le chou-fleur, cauliflower

les champignons, mushrooms

les poireaux, leeks

les oignons, onions

les carottes, carrots

les navets, turnips

le chou, cabbage

les épinards, spinach

la salade de fruits, fruit salad

le pouding, pudding

le gâteau, cake *and also various kinds of* puddings, *such as* le gâteau de riz, rice pudding, le gâteau de pommes, apple pudding

The above list is far from being exhaustive, but it contains the general run of dishes.

¶ 3. SALAMMBÔ

Le Conseil leur avait désigné sa maison pour y tenir ce festin : les convalescents qui couchaient dans le temple d'Eschmoûn, se mettant en marche dès l'aurore, s'y étaient traînés sur leurs béquilles. A chaque minute, d'autres arrivaient. Par tous les sentiers, il en débouchait incessamment, comme des torrents qui se précipitent dans un lac. On voyait entre les arbres courir les esclaves des cuisines, effarés et à demi nus ; les gazelles sur les pelouses s'enfuyaient en bêlant ; le soleil se couchait et le parfum des citronniers rendait encore plus lourde l'exhalaison de cette foule en sueur.

Il y avait là des hommes de toutes les nations, des Ligures, des Lusitaniens, des Baléares, des Nègres et des fugitifs de Rome. On entendait, à côté du lourd patois dorien, retentir les syllabes celtiques bruissantes comme des chars de bataille, et les terminaisons ioniennes se heurtaient aux consonnes du désert, âpres comme des cris de chacal. Le Grec se reconnaissait à sa taille mince, l'Égyptien à ses épaules remontées, le Cantabre à ses larges mollets.

TRANSLATION : *The Council had allocated to them its house to hold this feast there : the convalescents who lay in the temple of Eschmoûn setting off to walk at dawn, had dragged themselves there on their crutches. Every minute others arrived. By all the footpaths they debouched (streamed in) incessantly, like torrents which flung themselves into a lake. One saw among the trees slaves running from the kitchens, bewildered and half-naked; the gazelles on the lawns fled bleating; the sun set and the perfume of citron trees rendered still heavier the exhalation of that crowd in perspiration (that perspiring crowd).*

There were there men of all nations, Ligurians, Lusitanians, Balearic Islanders, Negroes, and fugitives from Rome. One heard by the side of the heavy Doric patois resound Celtic syllables rattling like battle chariots, and Ionian endings clashed with desert consonants harsh as jackal's cries. The Greek was recognized by his slim figure, the Egyptian by his high shoulders, the Cantabarian by his stout calves.

Reading Vocabulary—39

LENDEMAIN, *next day*
LETTRE, *letter*
lever, *to lift*, (se-) *to get up*
lèvre, *lip*
liberté, *liberty*
lien, *bond, chain*
lier, *to bind, to attach*
LIEU, *place*
lieutenant, *lieutenant*
LIGNE, *line*

limite, *limit*
LIRE, *to read*
LIT, *bed*
LIVRE (f), *pound*; (m), *book*
livrer, *to deliver, to surrender*
LOI, *law*
le long de, *alongside*
louer, *to rent*
lumière, *light*
LUNDI, *Monday*

LESSON XVII

§ 1. *Getting around Paris—Asking the Way*

LET us assume that you are visiting Paris and wish to see something of the city. First equip yourself with the *words* you are almost certain to require. Below is an essential list : You should buy immediately on arrival **Un Guide-Indicateur des Rues de Paris,** for preference one which gives **les stations du Métropolitain (le métro),** which you will find at any **kiosk** or newsagents. If you know your essential words, that is half the battle :

la rue, street
le trottoir, sidewalk
un agent de police, policeman
l'agent de la circulation, traffic policeman (Don't worry him!)
la chaussée, roadway
un arrêt, a stop
un arrêt facultatif, request stop
un arrêt obligatoire, compulsory stop
un autobus, bus
le billet, ticket
le refuge, refuge
une grande voie, main road, street
le bâtiment, building
un monument, monument
un immeuble de rapport, tenement, apartment house, or **immeuble**

une visite des curiosités, " sightseeing "
la galerie d'art, art gallery
le jardin botanique, botanical garden(s)
la cathédrale, cathedral
une église, church
une exposition, exhibition
Le Musée des Beaux Arts, Museum of Fine Arts
le musée, museum
L'Hôtel de Ville, Town Hall
une université, university
le jardin zoologique, zoo
le renseignement, information
renseigner, to inform
l'entrée, admission
gratuit(e), free
Ouvert de . . . à, open from . . . to
Défense d'entrer, " No Admittance "

Accès interdit, "Trespassing forbidden"
les bateaux, boats (on the Seine)
à gauche, to the left
à droite, to the right, **tout droit,** straight on
la salle d'attente, waiting room

> **Je voudrais un guide-indicateur de Paris, avec les stations du métro et des renseignements utiles sur la ville,** I want a street guide to Paris, with useful information about the city.
>
> **Qu-est-ce qu'il y a d'intéressant à voir par ici ?** What is there interesting to see hereabouts ?
>
> **Pardon, monsieur, où est la rue Pasquier,** I beg your pardon (Sir), where is the rue Pasquier ?
>
> **Je désire aller à . . .** I want to go to . . .
>
> **Est-ce que je descends ici ?** Do I get down here ?
>
> **Est-ce que c'est loin d'ici à . . .** Is it far from here to . . .
>
> **Ce train va-t-il à . . . ?** Does this train go to . . . ?
>
> **Où est l'arrêt pour l'autobus qui va à . . .** Where is the stop for the bus to . . .

And never forget to say " **Merci, Monsieur** " whether you get the information or not!

¶ 4. SALAMMBÔ

TEXT:

Des Cariens balançaient orgueilleusement les plumes de leur casque, des archers de Cappadoce s'étaient peints avec des jus d'herbes de larges fleurs sur le corps, et quelques Lydiens portant des robes de femmes dînaient en pantoufles et avec des boucles d'oreilles. D'autres, qui s'étaient par pompe barbouillés de vermillon, ressemblaient à des statues de corail.

Ils s'allongeaient sur les coussins, ils mangeaient accroupis autour de grands plateaux, ou bien, couchés sur le ventre, ils tiraient à eux les morceaux de viande, et se rassasiaient appuyés sur les coudes, dans la pose pacifique des lions lorsqu'ils dépècent leur proie. Les derniers venus, debout contre les arbres, regardaient les tables basses disparaissant à moitié sous des tapis d'écarlate, et attendaient leur tour.

Les cuisines d'Hamilcar n'étant pas suffisantes, le Conseil leur avait envoyé des esclaves, de la vaisselle, des lits ; et l'on voyait au milieu du jardin, comme sur un champ de bataille quand on brûle les morts, de grands feux clairs où rôtissaient des boeufs.

TRANSLATION : _Carians proudly waved the feathers (plumes) of their helmets, archers from Cappadocia had painted themselves with juices of herbs large flowers on the body, and some Lydians wearing women's robes (garb) were dining in slippers and with ear rings. Others, who had ostentatiously daubed themselves with vermilion, resembled coral statues._

They were stretched out on cushions, they ate squatting around great dishes, or else, lying on their stomach(s), they drew towards them pieces of meat and glutted themselves resting on elbows in the peaceful pose of lions when they dismember their prey. The last comers, standing upright against the trees, looked at the low tables half concealed under scarlet coverings, and were waiting their turn.

Hamilcar's kitchens not being sufficient, the Council had sent them slaves, table service, beds; and one saw in the middle of the garden, as on a field of battle when the dead are burned, great clear (blazing) fires where oxen were roasting.

Reading Vocabulary—40

LUNE, _moon_	mal, _harm, injury_
lutte, _struggle_	MALADIE, _illness_
lutter, _to fight_	malheur, _misfortune_
luxe, _luxury_	MANGER, _to eat_
MACHINE, _machine_	manière, _manner_
MAIN, _hand_	manifester, _manifest_
maintenir, _to maintain_	MANQUER, _to lack, to fail_
MAISON, _house_	manteau, _mantle_
MAÎTRE, _master_	marchand, _trader, merchant_
maîtresse, _mistress_	marche, _march_

§ 2. _Getting around Paris_—contd.

le marché, the market

les Halles (centrales), the central market of Paris

le langage des Halles, " billingsgate "

le commissariat _or_ **le poste de police,** police station

le consulat, consulate

Consulat américain, American Consulate

le consul, consul

le bureau de poste, post office

le bureau de poste central, General Post Office

continuer, to continue

descendre, to get down (from a bus or train)

traverser, to cross (a street)

le carrefour, crossroads

arriver à, to reach, arrive at

la route la plus courte, the shortest way

arrêter, to stop

prendre, to take

le tramway, streetcar

le coin, corner

la Bourse, Stock Exchange

le chemin, the way

de nouveau, again

If you can afford it, one of the quickest and best ways of getting a general glimpse of Paris is to take a taxi, though there's nothing like going about on foot if you wish to have a " close up " of the city and its people. And, of course, there are organized trips to places of interest. The following phrases should help :

Chauffeur, je veux aller à . . . Driver, I want to go to . . .

Quel est le prix par heure ? How much does it cost per hour ?

Je voudrais voir les endroits les plus intéressants, I want to see the most interesting places.

Menez-moi d'abord à . . . First take me to . . .

Est-ce qu'il y a des excursions pour . . . Are there trips to . . . ?

Veuillez me (nous) réserver une place (. . . places) pour le circuit de 10 heures, Kindly reserve me (us) a seat (. . . seats) for the 10 o'clock trip.

A quelle heure est le départ pour . . .? At what time do they start for . . .

A quelle heure revient-on ? What time do we get back ?

Y a-t-il des promenades à pied intéressantes à faire par ici ? Are there any interesting walks about here ?

C'est assez. Ramenez-nous aussi vite que possible, That's enough. Take us back as quickly as possible.

Attendez-moi ici, Wait for me here.

Arrêtez un instant, je veux . . . Stop a moment, I wish to . . .

Paris is divided into **arrondissements** or wards, each one numbered: **le premier arrondissement, le deuxième arrondissement,** etc. (1ᵉʳ, 2ᵉᵐᵉ, etc.).   Numbers 1–8, beginning in the center near the Louvre and going clockwise, represent the center of the city. The next band of **arrondissements,** Nos. 9–20, represent the outer parts and suburbs.

TEXT :

Pour ceux qui ne partent pas

Nous parlions, la semaine dernière, des cinq mille jeunes Normands des deux sexes qui veulent s'expatrier au Canada, n'ayant plus, en France, ni travail, ni logement, ni pain.

Et pourtant, malgré les difficultés présentes, malgré l'avenir qui paraît sans espérance, combien veulent tenter leur chance en France même ?   Encore faudrait-il qu'ils soient aidés.

Un jeune père de six enfants, ingénieur d'agriculture, connaissant particulièrement le machinisme agricole moderne, possédant trois permis, ayant une longue pratique de la culture, et dont la femme est elle-même diplômée de l'Ecole d'Agriculture de Coëtlogon, cherche en vain, depuis la Libération, une situation équivalente à celle que la guerre et sa mobilisation lui avaient fait perdre, et qui lui permettrait, tout en restant attaché au sol, d'élever sa nombreuse famille.

TRANSLATION :

For those who do not go

We spoke last week of the five thousand young Normans of both sexes who wish to expatriate themselves to Canada, having no longer in France either work or lodging or bread.

And, however, in spite of present difficulties, in spite of the future which seems without hope, how many wish to take their chance in France itself? It would still be necessary to help them.

A young father of six children, an agricultural engineer, knowing particularly (well) the machinery of modern agriculture, in possession of three permits, having a long practice of cultivation, and whose wife herself has a diploma from the Coëtlogon School of Agriculture, seeks in vain since the Liberation a situation equivalent to that which the war and his mobilization had caused him to lose (and) which would permit him, while remaining attached to the soil, to bring up his numerous family.

ANNONCE—ADVERTISEMENT

Reading Vocabulary—41-42

MARCHÉ, *market*
MARCHER, *to march*
MARDI, *Tuesday*
MARI, *husband*
MARIAGE, *marriage*
marier(se), *to get married*
marque, *mark*
marquer, *to mark*
masse, *mass*
matériel, *material*

mener, *to lead*
mensonge, *untruth*
mépris, *disdain*
MER, *sea*
MERCREDI, *Wednesday*
MÈRE, *mother*
mériter, *to merit*
mérite, *merit*
messe, *Mass*
mesure, *measure*

matière, *matter*
MATIN, *morning*
MÉDECIN, *doctor*
mélancolie, *melancholy*
mêler, *to mingle*
membre, *limb*
MÉMOIRE, *memory*
menacer, *to threaten*
ménage, *housekeeping, -hold*
ménager, *to take care of*

mesurer, *to measure*
méthode, *method*
métier, *business, work*
METTRE, *to put*
MEUBLE, *furniture*
MIDI, *south, midday*
MILIEU, *middle*
millier, *thousand*
million, *million*
mine, *expression (facial)*

§ 3. *Getting around Paris*—contd.

la rive, bank (of a river)
la rive droite, right bank
la rive gauche, left bank
le pont, bridge

le quai, quay
vers, toward
la Cité universitaire, university city

la cimetière, cemetery
le parc, park
l'avenue, avenue
le champ, field
le bois, wood
le sentier, path, pathway
le boulevard, boulevard (also rampart)
le boulevardier, man about town
les événéments du boulevard, life about town
le quartier commerçant, business quarter
le (la) concièrge, caretaker, house porter (-ess)
le Palais de Justice, Law Courts
la fontaine, fountain
le fleuve, river

la flèche, spire of a church (*also* arrow)
manger en plein air, to eat in the open air
le tombeau, tomb
le rond-point, traffic circle, rotary
aboutir, to end at
écarter, to seclude
au bout de, at the end of
les pompiers, firemen
la place, square (in a town)
la caserne, barracks
le faubourg, suburb
le stationnement des taxis, cabstand
la rue commerçante, shopping street
le château, castle

Qu'est-ce que nous ferons aujourd'hui ? What shall we do today?

Faisons une promenade à pied (un tour à pied), Let us take a walk around.

Allons voir la ville, Let us go and see the city.

Allons à pied jusqu'à . . . et alors nous pourrons prendre un autobus, Let us go on foot to . . . and then we can take a bus.

Allons au Bois de Boulogne, Let us go to the Bois de Boulogne.

Je suis fatigué. Asseyons-nous sur une des chaises du parc. I'm tired. Let us sit on one of the park chairs.

Allons voir les ponts sur la Seine, Let us go and see the bridges on the Seine.

Promenons-nous en taxi, Let us take a ride in a taxi.

Très bien ! C'est ça ! Right you are. That's the idea !

Savez-vous qu'il faut payer pour passer certains ponts ? Do you know that one must pay to cross some of the bridges ?

J'ai la bouche sèche. Allons boire un verre de vin. I'm thirsty (My mouth is dry). Let's go and have a glass of wine.

Où peut-on se baigner ? Where can one bathe ?

¶ 5. SALAMMBÔ

Les pains saupoudrés d'anis alternaient avec les gros fromages plus lourds que des disques, et les cratères pleins de vin, et les canthares pleins d'eau auprès des corbeilles en filigrane d'or qui contenaient des fleurs. La joie de pouvoir enfin se gorger à l'aise dilatait tous les yeux ; ça et là, les chansons commençaient.

D'abord on leur servit des oiseaux à la sauce verte, dans des assiettes d'argile rouge rehaussée de dessins noirs, puis toutes les espèces de coquillages que l'on ramasse sur les côtes puniques, des bouillies de froment, de fève et d'orge, et des escargots au cumin, sur des plats d'ambre jaune.

Ensuite les tables furent couvertes de viandes ; antilopes avec leurs cornes, paons avec leurs plumes, moutons entiers cuits au vin doux, gigots de chamelles et de buffles, hérissons au garum, cigales frites et loirs confits. Dans des gamelles en bois de Tamrapanni flottaient, au milieu du safran, de grands morceaux de graisse. Tout débordait de saumure, de truffes et d'assa foetida.

TRANSLATION : *Loaves of bread sprinkled with aniseed alternated with great cheeses heavier than discuses, and bowls full of wine and flagons full of water near baskets in gold filigree which contained flowers. The joy of being able at last to gorge oneself at ease dilated all eyes; here and there songs began.*

First they were served with birds in green sauce, in plates of red clay embossed with designs in black, then every kind of shellfish that is gathered on the Punic coasts, gruel (made) of wheat, beans and barley, and snails (seasoned) in cumin on dishes of yellow amber.

Next the tables were covered with meats; antelopes with their horns, peacocks with their feathers, whole sheep cooked in sweet wine, haunches of she-camels and buffaloes, hedgehogs with garum, fried grasshoppers and preserved dormice. In bowls (made) of wood of Tamrapanni there floated in the midst of saffron great pieces of fat. Everything overran with pickle, truffles and asafetida.

Reading Vocabulary—43

ministère, *ministry*
ministre, *minister*
MINUTE, *minute*
misère, *misery*
mission, *mission*
MODE, *fashion*
modifier, *to modify*
les mœurs, *customs, habits*
MOINS, *less*
MOIS, *month*
MOITIÉ, *half*

MOMENT, *moment*
MONDE, *world*
MONSIEUR, *sir, gentleman*
MONTAGNE, *mountain*
MONTER, *to go up, to mount,*
     to amount
MONTRER, *to show*
moquer(se), *to make fun of*
MORCEAU, *piece*
MORT, *death*

§ 4. *Getting around Paris*—contd.

The French **Café** bears little resemblance to any American establishment of that name. It is, however, uniquely important in French social life. In it there are tables, newspapers, and writing materials. Here you can sit down, order coffee, ask for the day's newspapers, a weekly or a magazine; and remain as long as you please. Ask for writing materials (**de quoi écrire**) and you will nearly always get them: the penpoint may be old, the ink purple, and the paper thin. But they will do for an emergency, and no doubt the waiter can also provide you with a stamp (**un timbre**). In summer the tables are put outside **en plein air** or under an awning—and that is called **la terrasse**. In many **Cafés** you can enjoy **le petit déjeuner** with **petits pains** or **brioches**. The selection of **apéritifs** and other drinks will astound the newcomer to France.. You will hear people asking for drinks by their proprietary names : **un Pernod** (substitute for absinthe, now forbidden); **un Amer Picon ; un Dubonnet.** There is also a variety of cordials and syrups, and Frenchmen go in for drinks that are all but unknown in America or indeed anywhere but France. For example: **un Picon-Citron à l'eau de Seltz,** which is a dark bitters with lemon syrup and soda water; or **un Vermouth-Cassis à l'eau de Seltz.** In summer a good light drink is **un vin blanc Citron à l'eau de Seltz ;** in winter **un café Cognac** or **rhum.** You see people playing cards, dominoes, checkers, chess and other games which you may not recognize; and, although the games are played with keenness, the conversation never ceases. The **Café** is the Frenchman's club, and he brings his wife and children there. **Café** life is an important part of French life, for which there is no equivalent with us. If you go to France and do not visit a **Café**, you are missing an institution.

Most beer drinking is done in bars, not in the cafés. You order **un bock**. It is a light, lager-type of drink, and you may find it too watery for your taste.

In Lesson XVI, § 1, you will find most of the essential words, and in § 4 of that Lesson you will find useful phrases.

The rest you must learn by experience, and very pleasant it can be.

TEXT:

LA RADIO

En offrant aux auditeurs de la radiodiffusion l'adaptation de " Madame Bovary," d'après Gustave Flaubert, réalisée par Roger Breuil—le jeune écrivain dont nous annoncions la mort la semaine dernière—l'actif et intelligent metteur en ondes Maurice Cazeneuve avait pris de redoutables responsabilités, car la transposition d'un tel chef-d'œuvre présente des difficultés presque insurmontables. Réduire à quatre-vingt-dix minutes d'écoute le grand et gros roman supposait un choix, un aménagement et, pour tout dire, un " condensé " : redoutable épreuve. D'autre part, les épisodes ramenés à l'état de séquences devaient pouvoir se relier entre eux par l'artifice d'une unité musicale de transition. D'où la composition, par Mme Elsa Barraine, d'une partition originale.

Cette adaptation de " Madame Bovary " à la radio constitue une tentative du plus vif intérêt, mais pas absolument convaincante. En dépit des très louables efforts de tous les animateurs de cette émission, l'auditeur aura eu peine à reconnaître dans une adaptation, heurtée en son découpage, alourdie par de trop fréquentes interventions de l'orchestre (impeccablement stylé, d'ailleurs, de Marc Vaubourgoin) le visage romantique et romanesque d'Emma Rouault, femme Bovary.

TRANSLATION :

THE RADIO

*In offering to listeners of broadcasting the adaptation of " Madame
Bovary " from Gustave Flaubert, made by Roger Breuil—the young
writer whose death we announced last week—the active and intelligent
radio producer Maurice Cazeneuve had taken redoubtable responsi-
bilities, for the transposition of such a masterpiece presents almost
insurmountable difficulties.   To reduce to ninety minutes listening
the great and fat (thick) novel presupposed (demanded) a selection, an
arrangement and, to say everything (in a word) a ". condensation " :
a redoubtable test.   On the other hand, the episodes brought (reduced) to the state of sequences must be able to connect among themselves by the artifice of a musical unity of transition.   Hence, the
composition by Mme Elsa Barraine of an original score.*

*This adaptation of " Madame Bovary " for radio constitutes
an attempt of the greatest (sharpest) interest, but (is) not entirely
convincing.   In spite of very praiseworthy efforts on the part of
all those actively engaged in this transmission, the listener will have
had difficulty in recognizing in an adaptation, abrupt (impaired) in the
cutting, made heavy by too frequent orchestral interventions (impeccably
arranged, incidentally, by Marc Vaubourgoin), the romantic face and
the romanticism of Emma Rouault, Bovary's wife.*

[*Newspaper Excerpt*]

Reading Vocabulary—44

MOT, *word*

mouchoir, *handkerchief*

mouiller, *to wet*

MOURIR, *to die*

MOUVEMENT, *movement*

MOYEN, *means*

MUR, *wall*

muraille, *wall, rampart*

musique, *music*

mystère, *mystery*

naissance, *birth*

NAÎTRE, *to be born*

nation, *nation*

nature, *nature*

nécessité, *necessity*

négliger, *to neglect*

neige, *snow*

nez, *nose*

NOM, *name*

nombre, *number*

§ 5. Getting around Paris—Public Notices

It is not only in getting about Paris that you will see public
notices.   You will find them everywhere and, if you should be
motoring or cycling, you will ignore some of them at your peril.
First, there are those common notices which everybody should
understand :

ENTRÉE, Entrance
SORTIE, Exit
MESSIEURS, Gentlemen
DAMES, Ladies
Cabinet, toilet, water closet
HOMMES, Men
RÉSERVÉ, Reserved

ARRÊT, stopping place
Attention à la peinture, WET PAINT
SALLE D'ATTENTE, Waiting room
FERMÉ, Closed

DÉFENSE DE or **IL EST INTERDIT DE** or **INTERDIT DE** followed by the verb indicates that something is FORBIDDEN : **Défense de fumer. Interdit de marcher sur la pelouse :** *Walking on the grass is forbidden.* **Il est interdit de donner de la nourriture aux animaux :** *Do not give food to the animals.* **INTERDIT AUX CYCLISTES :** *Cycling forbidden.* **DÉFENSE D'ENTRER :** No admittance. You may see :

On peut téléphoner, You may telephone from here
Réservé aux employés, Employees only
Porte de secours, Emergency exit
à louer, to let

à vendre, for sale
Piétons, Pedestrians.
TIREZ, Pull
POUSSEZ, Push
Éteignez la lumière, Turn off the light

ROAD SIGNS

ROUTE BARRÉE, No thoroughfare
TRAVAUX, Work going on
ÉCOLE, School
PASSAGE À NIVEAU, Railway crossing
DANGER, Danger
CROISEMENT, Cross-roads
LENTEMENT, Slowly
sens unique, One way
HALTE ! or **ARRÊTEZ-VOUS !** Stop !
VITESSE MAXIMA, Speed Limit . . .

Défense de stationner, Do not stop (i.e. park)
Défense de parquer, Parking forbidden
Parc, Parking place
Poste de Secours, First-aid station
Route principale, Main road
Route privée, Private road
Déviation, Traffic diverted
Allure modérée, Drive slowly, *or, more often,* **RALENTIR !**
ATTENTION ! Warning !
AVIS, Notice

Tenez à droite, Keep right   **Virage,** Turn, curve
Tenez à gauche, Keep left   **Tournant brusque,** Dangerous
CASSIS, Obstruction, excava-   curve
tion

In the trains, you will see the **signal d'alarme,** and in many places **Attention aux voleurs,** *Beware of pickpockets.*

Finally, our old friend : **Prenez garde au chien,** *Beware of the dog.*

¶ 6. SALAMMBÔ

Les pyramides de fruits s'éboulaient sur les gâteaux de miel, et l'on n'avait pas oublié quelques-uns de ces petits chiens à gros ventre et à soies roses que l'on engraissait avec du marc d'olives, mets carthaginois en abomination aux autres peuples. La surprise des nourritures nouvelles excitait la cupidité des estomacs. Les Gaulois aux longs cheveux retroussés sur le sommet de la tête, s'arrachaient les pastèques et les limons qu'ils croquaient avec l'écorce. Des Nègres n'ayant jamais vu de langoustes se déchiraient le visage à leurs piquants rouges. Mais les Grecs rasés, plus blancs que des marbres, jetaient derrière eux les épluchures de leur assiette, tandis que des pâtres du Brutium, vêtus de peaux de loups, dévoraient silenciuese- ment, le visage dans leur portion.

La nuit tombait. On retira le velarium étalé sur l'avenue de cyprès et l'on apporta des flambeaux.

Les lueurs vacillantes du pétrole qui brûlait dans des vases de porphyre effrayèrent, au haut des cèdres, les singes consacrés à la lune. Ils poussèrent des cris, ce qui mit les soldats en gaieté.

TRANSLATION : *Pyramids of fruits fell over on honeycombs, and they had not forgotten some of those little dogs with plump bellies and pink, silky (hair) which were made fat with olive marc (lees from pressings), a Carthaginian dish abominable to other peoples. The surprise of the new (novel) foods excited the cupidity of stomachs. The Gauls with long hair turned on the top of the head snatched watermelons and lemons which they crunched including the rind. Negroes (who) having never seen lobsters tore their faces with their red spines. But the shaven Greeks, whiter than marble, threw behind them the refuse from their plate(s) while shepherds from Brutium, clothed in skins of wolves, devoured silently, their faces (buried) in their portion(s).*

Night fell. The awning spread over the cypress avenue was withdrawn and torches were brought.

The wavering flashes of the paraffin which burned in porphyry vases frightened in the top of the cedars the monkeys sacred to the moon. They uttered cries, which put the soldiers in gaiety (gave mirth to the soldiers).

Reading Vocabulary—45

nommer, *to name*

NORD, *north*

note, *note*

noter, *to note*

nourrir, *to nourish*

NOUVELLES, *news*

noyer, *to drown*

nuage, *cloud*

nuance, *shade*

NUIT, *night*

OBÉIR, *to obey*

OBJET, *object*

obligation, *obligation*

obliger, *to force*

observation, *observation*

observer, *to observe*

obtenir, *to obtain*

occasion, *opportunity*

occupation, *occupation*

occuper, *to occupy, to concern*

LESSON XVIII

§ 1. *At the Seaside*

au bord de la mer, at the seaside

la plage, the beach, sands

la plage de galets, pebble-strewn beach

le canot, rowboat

le canot de sauvetage, lifeboat

la vague, wave

les brisants, breakers, surf

la jetée, jetty

une esplanade, promenade

le phare, lighthouse

la pêche, fishing

le pêcheur, fisherman

pêcher, to fish

nager, to swim

se baigner, to bathe

se basaner, brunir, to get tanned

le bain de soleil, sunbath

une promenade en mer, sea-trip

un abri, shelter

une cabine, (individual) bathhouse, cabana

le costume de bain, bathing suit (*also* **le maillot**)

le bonnet de bain, bathing cap

une pension de famille, boardinghouse

un appartement meublé, furnished apartment

une tente, tent

la serviette de bain, towel

le casino, casino

le bassin de natation, swimming-pool

le tremplin, diving-board

le nageur, la nageuse, swimmer

plonger, dive, plunge

louer une cabine, rent a cabana

les espadrilles, playshoes

se réhabiller, get dressed again

se sécher, to dry oneself

se frotter, to rub oneself

les lunettes de plage, sunglasses

la marée, tide

se noyer, to get drowned

Défense de se baigner, No swimming

One thing you must remember if you go to a French seaside. Do not confuse the word **pêcher**, *to fish*, with **pécher**, *to sin*! Or **la pêche**, *fishing*, with **le péché**, *the sin*. Incidentally, **la**

pêche also means *peach*; and **le pêcher**, *the peachtree*. It is as well to know these things. **Le pêcher** must not be confused with **le pécheur.**

Apart from vocabulary—always important—there are no special phrases necessary. After all, life at the seaside does not differ greatly from life in an inland town, except for the beach and its recreations, most of which are included in the vocabulary given above.

Every French seaside resort or spa has its **casino,** and the visitor is often tempted to visit it and **risquer quelques francs,** *risk a few francs.* If you should do so, it would be as well to remember that an *odd number* is called **impair** and an *even* is **pair.** You can put your stake *on one number*, and then it is **en plein.** Or, you can divide it *between two numbers*, and then it is **à cheval** (*on horseback*). The gaming room of the **casino** is called **la salle de jeu** but there is usually more than one, and they are **les salles de jeu.** **Le croupier** is the *banker* for the **casino.** He calls : " **Faites vos jeux,**" and at a given moment " **Rien ne va plus !** " You then await your luck.

¶ 7. SALAMMBÔ

Des flammes oblongues tremblaient sur les cuirasses d'airain. Toutes sortes de scintillements jaillissaient des plats incrustés de pierres précieuses. Les cratères, à bordure de miroirs convexes, multipliaient l'image élargie des choses ; les soldats se pressant autour s'y regardaient avec ébahissement et grimaçaient pour se faire rire. Ils se lançaient, par-dessus les tables, les escabeaux d'ivoire et les spatules d'or. Ils avalaient à pleine gorge tous les vins grecs qui sont dans des outres, les vins de Campanie enfermés dans des amphores, les vins des Cantabres que l'on apporte dans des tonneaux, et les vins de jujubier, de cinnamome et de lotus. Il y en avait des flaques par terre où l'on glissait. La fumée des viandes montait dans les feuillages avec la vapeur des haleines. On entendait à la fois le claquement des mâchoires, le bruit des paroles, des chansons, des coupes, le fracas des vases campaniens qui s'écroulaient en mille morceaux, ou le son limpide d'un grand plat d'argent.

TRANSLATION : *Oblong flames flickered on brass breastplates. All sorts of scintillations flashed from dishes encrusted with precious stones. Bowls with convex mirror borders multiplied the enlarged reflection of things; soldiers pressed (crowded) around and looked in them with astonishment and made faces to make themselves laugh. They threw to each other , over the tables, the ivory stools and golden spatulas. They swallowed with full throat (in deep draughts) all the Greek wines which are in skins, wines of Campania in jars, wines of Cantabria brought in casks, and wines of the jujube tree, cinnamon and lotus. There were pools of it on the ground where one slipped. The smoke of the meats went up into the foliage with the vapor of their breathing (steam of breaths). One heard at the same time the clacking of jaws, the noise of words, songs, cups, the crash of Campanian vases which shivered into a thousand pieces, or the limpid sound (note) of a great silver dish.*

Reading Vocabulary—46

odeur, *odor, smell*
ŒIL, *eye*
œuvre, *work*
office, *office functions*
OFFICIER, *officer*
OFFRIR, *to offer*
OISEAU, *bird*
ombre, *shadow*
ONCLE, *uncle*
opération, *operation*

opinion, *opinion*
opposer, *to oppose*
or, *gold*
orage, *storm*
ordonner, *to command*
ordre, *order*
oreille, *ear*
organiser, *to organize*
orgueil, *pride*
origine, *origin*

§ 2. *In the Provinces—The Countryside*

You have visited Paris and you have been to the seaside. There remain the provincial centers and the countryside. What a choice you have ! There is not **une province** (*a province*), not **une cité, une ville, un hameau** (*city, town, hamlet*) in France which cannot offer something of interest to the stranger, and **la campagne, les fleuves, les rivières, les ruisseaux**— *the countryside, the big rivers, the streams, the brooks*—all contribute. **Les petits ruisseaux font les grandes rivières** is a proverb. *Little brooks make big streams* or, as we say, "Mighty oaks from little acorns grow." A French *county* is called **un departement.** **Une commune** is a *civil parish.* **Un arrondissement** (*a word you learned in Paris) is a *ward* or administrative district, being a subdivision of **un département**. **La paroisse** is a *parish*. The district is generally called **la région,** and the chief town of **la région** is called **le chef-lieu**. **Le comté** (*county*) still exists as a word, but the county is no longer an administrative unit. The capital of a province is **la capitale d'une province**. **La Provence** is the name of a province, not to be confused with **la province,** *the province*. **Le conseil municipal** is *the town council,* and **le maire** is *the mayor,* a most important gentleman. Then there is **le préfet** or *prefect,* an omnipotent official of the central government and peculiar to France. If there is trouble, **le préfet** becomes a powerful local governor. There is one thing you must not forget if you should decide to go into the highways and byways of the countryside: you are unlikely to meet many people with any knowledge of English. Hence, you should be fairly sure of your French. On the other hand, the small towns and the country will teach you more French and more about France than you can learn on the beaten track of foreign visitors. This is the great advantage in getting off the beaten track. The vocabularies in the next sections will be of great help in getting about, and, as much of French literature deals with the small towns and countryside, they will always be useful.

But, take them gently. Strictly, many of the words given hardly come within the definition of " basic " vocabulary. They will help you to clothe the framework and be useful as " background " vocabulary.

Un Général Astucieux

Dans la guerre, comme d'ailleurs dans toutes leurs activités, les Chinois recourent volontiers à la ruse. Et la chose ne date pas d'hier, ainsi qu'en témoigne cette histoire que rapporte Carl Crow, sans en garantir, et pour cause, l'authenticité.

L'exploit se situe à l'époque où l'armement des guerriers consistait en un arc et des flèches. Une armée assiégeait une ville située au bord du Fleuve Bleu, de son nom chinois : Yang-Tsé-Kiang, qui traverse la Chine centrale sur une longueur de près de cinq mille kilomètres. Le général qui la commandait avait tenté maints assauts, mais tous avaient échoué. Et, ce qui était plus grave, il avait épuisé ses munitions ; les arcs de ses soldats manquaient de flèches. Allait-il devoir se résigner à lever le siège ? Non pas, car une idée géniale lui vint soudain à l'esprit.

Il fit construire en grand secret des embarcations ressemblant comme des sœurs à celles que ses troupes avaient utilisées pour approcher des murs de l'impénétrable citadelle. Mais leurs coques étaient en paille recouverte d'une toile peinte et, au lieu de soldats, il les garnit de mannequins également bourrés de paille, qui s'y tenaient bien en évidence, tandis que dans le fond des bateaux se dissimulaient quelques guerriers en chair et en os.

Et un jour, où un épais brouillard enveloppait le fleuve, il lança l'étrange flottille vers la ville. Quand les embarcations furent au pied des murailles, les soldats sans quitter leur abri, firent entendre des clameurs qui alertèrent les assiégés. Ceux-ci lancèrent sur les bateaux qu'ils distinguaient mal, une nuée de flèches qui se fichèrent dans la paille des mannequins et des coques. Alors, le général fit revenir à lui les embarcations tirées par des cordes. Et il approvisionna ses soldats avec les flèches ennemies.

Sa ruse lui avait fourni à bon compte les munitions qui lui faisaient défaut. Grâce à elles, il put entreprendre un nouvel assaut, cette fois, avec de vraies embarcations et de vrais soldats. Et il réussit enfin à se rendre maître de la ville !

A. H.

NOTES AND WORDS: In the excerpts from *Salammbô* you will have noticed the rich vocabulary. There are in them many words which are seldom met : for example, all that description of the various components of the feast may be passed over quickly, as you need only follow the original with the aid of the translation in order to *understand* it, not to memorize all the words. The object of these extracts is to get you accustomed to reading good French. In time you will find that much of it remains in your memory without special effort—providing always you have made a genuine attempt to understand, and go over it a few times.

For the above piece, we give you little help. This time, you will try to work it out yourself ! However, here are some words which will not yet be familiar to you.

astucieux, astute, artful
d'ailleurs, furthermore
recourir, have recourse to
un arc, bow
flèches, arrows
épuisé, exhausted, used up
embarcations, boats
coques, shells, hulls
paille, straw
une toile, cloth, fabric
peint(e), painted
mannequins, dummies

bourré(s), stuffed
se dissimuler, to hide oneself
un épais brouillard, a thick fog
le fleuve, big river
murailles, walls
abri, shelter
une nuée, cloud
se ficher, to stick
faire défaut, to be short of
grâce à, thanks to

Reading Vocabulary—47

orner, *to ornament*
OSER, *to dare*
ôter, *to take off*
OUBLIER, *to forget*
ouverture, *opening*
ouvrage, *work*
ouvrier, *workman*
OUVRIR, *to open*
PAGE, *page*
paille, *straw*

PAIN, *bread*
PAIX, *peace*
PALAIS, *palace*
PAPIER, *paper*
paquet, *packet, parcel*
PARAÎTRE, *to appear*
parc, *park*
parcourir, *to pass through*
PARDON, *pardon*
PARDONNER, *to pardon*

§ 3. *Provinces and Countryside*—contd.

l'agriculture, agriculture
un pays agricole, an agricultural country
la moisson, harvest
un cultivateur, farmer, grower
un vigneron, vine grower
la viniculture, vine-growing
un vignoble, vineyard

la vendange or **les vendanges,** grape-gathering, wine harvest
vendanger, to gather the grapes
le fermier, farmer (**la fermière,** farmer's wife)
la ferme, farm

le paysage, landscape

le paysan, laborer, country-man

une écurie, stable

une étable, cow shed

le villageois, villager

le bétail (*pl.* **les bestiaux**), cattle

le grenier, hayloft

le propriétaire, landlord

la grange, barn

le chariot, cart

le troupeau, flock (" troop ")

la cour, courtyard, farmyard

une chèvre, nanny goat

le berger, la bergère, shepherd-ess

la charette, light cart

une poule, hen

un dindon, une dinde, turkey (cock, hen)

un poussin, chick

un poulet, chicken

un laboureur, ploughman

le tracteur, tractor

une chaumière, thatched cottage

la saison, season

labourer, to plough

moissonner, récolter, to harvest, to reap

semer, to sow

bêcher, to dig

Each district in France is notable for some specialties in the way of food, depending, of course, upon local production. **La gastronomie,** which might be called the " science of good eating," is taken seriously by all French people, from the rich down to the peasants, and the latter have their own excellent **cuisine.** Food is not just nourishment in France : it is something to be enjoyed, and even something to be studied. Local specialities are usually inexpensive. The visitor who bears this in mind can add to the pleasures of his trip.

In Normandy, for example, local cookery is based upon butter, milk, cream, cheese, fowl, eggs, and sea fish. The local drink is **le cidre,** *cider,* as there is little local wine; the local liqueur is **le calvados,** a strong one made from apples. Specialized Norman dishes are **le canneton à la rouennaise** (*duckling Rouen style*), **les tripes à la mode de Caen** (*tripe in the fashion of Caen*), **la sole normande** (*Normandy sole*), and **l'andouille** (*chitterlings*). Each town is notable for one or more dishes : Dieppe for **le maquereau au vin blanc** (*mackerel cooked in white wine*); Cherbourg for **les demoiselles** or *lobsters*; and Arques for its **truites** (*trout*). There are about twenty kinds of cheese in Normandy. Honfleur's shellfish are famous. The province is rich in apples, which accounts for its delicious cider and great variety of apple dishes and sweets.

¶ 8. SALAMMBÔ

A mesure qu'augmentait leur ivresse, ils se rappelaient de plus en plus l'injustice de Carthage. En effet, la République, épuisée par la guerre, avait laissé s'accumuler dans la ville toutes les bandes qui revenaient. Giscon, leur général, avait eu cependant la prudence de les renvoyer les uns après les autres pour faciliter l'acquittement de leur solde, et le Conseil avait cru qu'ils finiraient par consentir à quelque diminution. Mais on leur en voulait aujourd'hui de ne pouvoir les payer. Cette dette se confondait dans l'esprit du peuple avec les trois mille deux cents talents exigés par Lutatius, et ils étaient, comme Rome, un ennemi pour Carthage. Les Mercenaires le comprenaient ; aussi leur indignation éclatait en menaces et en débordements. Enfin, ils demandèrent à se réunir pour célébrer une de leurs victoires, et le parti de la paix céda, en se vengeant d'Hamilcar qui avait tant soutenu la guerre. Elle s'était terminée contre tous ses efforts, si bien que, désespérant de Carthage, il avait remis à Giscon le gouvernement des Mercenaires. Désigner son palais pour les recevoir, c'était attirer sur lui quelque chose de la haine qu'on leur portait. D'ailleurs la dépense devait être excessive ; il la subirait presque toute.

Fiers d'avoir fait plier la République, les Mercenaires croyaient qu'ils allaient enfin s'en retourner chez eux, avec la solde de leur sang dans le capuchon de leur manteau. Mais leurs fatigues, revues à travers les vapeurs de l'ivresse, leur semblaient prodigieuses et trop peu récompensées.

NOTES AND WORDS :

à mesure que, in proportion as
ivresse, drunkenness
rappeler, remember, recall
épuiser, to exhaust

renvoyer, send away, back
acquittement, payment
cru, believed
en vouloir, to bear a grudge (against)

éclater, break out, burst

débordement, outbreak

céder, to yield

se venger de, to take revenge on

désespérer, to have no hope

remettre, remis, to hand over, handed over

désigner, to allocate

attirer, to attract

la haine, hatred

subir, to sustain, suffer

fier, proud

faire plier, to cause to bend, yield

s'en retourner, to return from it

la solde, the wages, pay

manteau, cloak

récompenser, to reward

Reading Vocabulary—48

parent, *relative*

parer, *to adorn, to deck*

parfum, *perfume*

PARLER, *to speak*

parole, *word*

PART, *share, side, part*

partager, *to share, divide*

parti, *party, decision*

partie, *part* (also *game*)

PARTIR, *to set out*

parvenir, *to arrive, to succeed*

PAS, *step*

passage, *passage*

passé, *past*

passer, *to pass*

passion, *passion*

patience, *patience*

patrie, *fatherland*

patron, *master, boss*

PAYER, *to pay*

§ 4. *Provinces and Countryside*—contd.

le sol, soil

la terre, ground, earth

bêcher le sol, dig the ground

préparer le sol, prepare the ground

atteler à, to harness to

paître, to graze

planter, to plant

croître, to grow

abreuver, to water (animals)

mûrir, to ripen

l'herbe, grass

le blé, corn

tirer, to draw, pull

faucher, to mow

sécher, to dry

le grain, grain

traire, to milk

charger, to load

la farine, flour

décharger, to unload

moudre, to grind corn

conduire, to drive a horse, cow, etc.

le moulin, mill
cueillir, pick, gather (fruit, etc.)
aiguiser, to sharpen, grind
élever, to raise, breed
le verger, orchard
la forêt, forest
la bêche, spade
la fourche, fork (for hay-making)
le bois, wood
à l'ombre, in the shade
couper, to cut
peindre, to paint
un pique-nique, picnic
pique-niquer, to picnic
la tondeuse, mowing machine

la pelle, shovel
le pâturage, pasture land
un étang, pond
la houe, hoe
la pioche, pickaxe
la pompe à l'eau, water-pump
le cheval, horse
la faux, scythe
la faucille, sickle
la vache, cow
le veau, calf (also veal)
les ciseaux, scissors, shears
le marteau, hammer
le seau, bucket, pail
le moulin à vent, windmill

The first time you go through this course, you need not learn all these words about the provinces and countryside. But make it a point to learn about twenty from each list, the remainder to be mastered on a second perusal.

In the last section we dwelt for a moment on the gastronomic joys of Normandy, but that province is not the only **paradis du gastronome**, *gastronome's paradise*. Bordeaux and the west, in addition to a fair range of special dishes, have their unparalleled wines, though they are curiously lacking in cheeses. **La cuisine bordelaise** is notable for its subtlety rather than for a great number of regional dishes. In Bordeaux and the whole of the province of La Gironde, the traditional soup called **le tourin** (made from pork, onions, and yolk of eggs) is much favored. The vineyard workers make wonderful vegetable soup, to which they add white wine and tomato juice. Fruits and vegetables abound hereabouts, and the rivers give fresh-water fish, which the people know how to prepare and cook to perfection. Once again it may be necessary to emphasize that one need not be rich to enjoy these bounties. It is always a matter of finding the right little restaurant.

Text :

Parade chez le libraire

Deux clowns au visage enfariné et un monsieur Loyal, en habit bleu de roi à boutons d'or, font le boniment à la porte de cette librairie du boulevard.

A l'intérieur, devant une petite table s'est installé Grock, tout à fait méconnaissable, en tenue de ville et sans son maquillage habituel, qui signe et dédicace son livre de souvenirs intitulé *Sans blague* et orné de sa caricature. A ses côtés, son fidèle partenaire l'aide, une fois de plus, en passant les volumes. Ainsi donc ce monsieur d'aspect gourmé, au visage assez neutre, au nez chevauché de lunettes, c'est l'illustre clown qui a plutôt l'air d'un chef de bureau retraité quand il se penche avec application pour écrire ses dédicaces.

Et le petit cérémonial de la signature se déroule selon le rite prévu. Le partenaire interroge les acheteurs munis du volume.

" Votre nom ? "

Une fiche placée dans le bouquin est transmise à Grock, qui, inlassablement, sur la page de garde, dessine lui-même son portrait-charge avec cette invariable dédicace : " A Madame ou à Monsieur X . . ., bons souvenirs de Grock."

Translation :

Parade at the Bookseller's

Two clowns with floured face(s) and a gentleman (named) Loyal, in a royal (blue) coat with gold buttons are coaxing (inviting) at the door of that boulevard bookshop.

Inside, in front of a little table, Grock is installed, completely unrecognizable, in morning clothes and without his usual make-up, signing and dedicating his book of memories entitled Sans blague *(" Without Joke ," " No Joke ") and adorned with his caricature. At his side, his faithful partner helps him once again in passing the volumes. So then that gentleman of stiff appearance, with face quite neutral, with spectacles straddling his nose, is the illustrious clown who looks more like a retired office chief (clerk) when he bends with application to write his dedications.*

And the little ceremonial of the signature goes on in accordance with the agreed rite. The partner interrogates the buyers furnished with the volume.

" Your name? "

A note placed in the book is transmitted to Grock, who, untiring, on the fly leaf himself draws his caricature portrait with this invariable dedication: " To Madame or Mr. . . . good remembrances (wishes) from (of) Grock."

Reading Vocabulary—49

PAYS, *country*
paysage, *landscape*
paysan, *peasant*
PEAU, *skin*
peindre, *to paint*
peine, *trouble, difficulty*
pencher, *to lean, to bend*
pendre, *to hang*
pénétrer, *to penetrate*
PENSÉE, *thought*

PENSER, *to think*
PENSION, *boardinghouse*
pente, *slope*
percer, *to pierce*
PERDRE, *to lose*
PÈRE, *father*
péril, *peril*
PERMETTRE, *to permit*
personnage, *personage*
PERSONNE, *person, nobody*

§ 5. *Provinces and Countryside*—contd.

le pot-au-feu, stockpot, *also* beef broth *or* stew
du pays, of the country, as le vin du pays, le fromage du pays, local wine, cheese
la mouche, fly
une abeille, bee
une guêpe, wasp
le moustique, mosquito
une fourmis, ant
la sauterelle, grasshopper
le grillon, cricket
la grenouille, frog
le crapaud, toad
la piqûre, sting
le ver, worm
la plante, plant
la fleur, flower
la racine, root
la feuille, leaf
un oiseau, bird
chanter, to sing (*also* to crow)
un arbre, tree

-IER, *the ending for trees, as* la poire, pear, le poirier, pear tree; la pomme, le pommier
la vigne, vine
un orme, elm
le chêne, oak tree
grimper sur, to climb on
le fruit, fruit
la pomme, apple
la poire, pear
la prune, plum
la cerise, cherry
la pêche, peach
l'olive, olive
le noyer, walnut tree
la noix, nut (walnut)
le tilleul, lime tree
le platane, plane tree
le buisson, bush
un arbuste, shrub
le rameau, la branche, branch

One piece of advice may be given to the visitor to France who may be at a loss to know where he can be sure of getting a fairly good meal. **Le buffet de la gare** is generally reliable. Food in the railroad stations can usually be relied on to be pretty good. You are less likely to be disappointed with it than with what you may get in an American station. Actually, the restaurant in France which does not provide good food and—excepting in **les restaurants de luxe**—at a reasonable current price cannot long survive. It would not be patronized. The French know what shortage of food is, and they can bear it; but they will *not* suffer *bad* cookery. That is a national characteristic.

If it should be your luck to go as far as the Mediterranean coast—**la côte d'azur,** with its almost certain blue sky most of the year—you will experience cookery which has elements of the French in general combined with those of **La Provence** and Italy. You will find a great variety of omelets, some which may seem quite exotic: for example, **l'omelette aux fleurs d'acacia, flambée au rhum,** *omelet with acacia flowers "flaming with rum."* The **Département du Var** is an important wine region—the sixth in France. Along this coast, as elsewhere, each town has its specialties. You must discover them.

¶ 9. SALAMMBÔ

Ils se montraient leurs blessures, ils racontaient leurs combats, leurs voyages et les chasses de leur pays. Ils imitaient le cri des bêtes féroces, leurs bonds. Puis vinrent les immondes gageures; ils s'enfonçaient la tête dans les amphores, et restaient à boire sans s'interrompre comme des dromadaires altérés. Un Lusitanien, de taille gigantesque, portant un homme au bout de chaque bras, parcourait les tables tout en crachant du feu par les narines. Des Lacédémoniens qui n'avaient point ôté leurs cuirasses, sautaient d'un pas lourd. Quelques-uns s'avançaient comme des femmes en faisant des gestes obscènes; d'autres se mettaient nus pour combattre, au milieu des coupes, à la façon des gladiateurs, et une compagnie de Grecs dansait autour d'un vase où l'on voyait des nymphes, pendant qu'un nègre tapait avec un os de bœuf sur un bouclier d'airain.

Tout à coup, ils entendirent un chant plaintif, un chant fort et doux, qui s'abaissait et remontait dans les airs comme le battement d'ailes d'un oiseau blessé.

C'était la voix des esclaves dans l'ergastule. Des soldats, pour les délivrer, se levèrent d'un bond et disparurent.

Ils revinrent, chassant au milieu des cris, dans la poussière, une vingtaine d'hommes que l'on distinguait à leur visage plus pâle. Un petit bonnet de forme conique, en feutre noir, couvrait leur tête rasée ; ils portaient tous des sandales de bois et faisaient un bruit de ferrailles comme des chariots en marche.

NOTES and WORDS :

montrer, to show
une blessure, wound
raconter, relate, tell of
vinrent, came (past definite of **venir**)
immonde, disgusting, foul
gageures, wagers
s'enfoncer, plunge
amphores, amphoras, two-handled jar *or* vase
altéré, thirsty
cracher, spit
les narines, nostrils
ôter, to take off, away
sauter, to leap, jump

nu, naked
combattre, to fight
taper, to tap, beat
un bouclier d'airain, a brazen shield
entendre, to hear
s'abaisser, fall, to get lower
remonter, rise, get higher
ailes, wings
ergastule, ergastulum, work-place, *or* prison
feutre, felt
raser, to shave
un bruit de ferrailles, a noise, clatter of old iron

Reading Vocabulary—50

persuader, *to persuade*
perte, *loss*
PESER, *to weigh*
PEU, *little*
PEUPLE, *people, nation*
PEUR, *fear*
phénomène, *phenomenon*
phrase, *sentence*
PIÈCE, *piece*
PIED, *foot*

PIERRE, *stone*
pipe, *pipe*
piquer, *to sting, to prick*
pitié, *pity*
place, *place, square*
placer, *to place*
plaindre, *to pity*
plaine, *plain*
plainte, *complaint, moan*
plaire, *to please*

§ 1. *Sports and Games*

le **football,** football
le **golf,** golf
le **tennis,** tennis
le **hockey,** hockey
le **jeu, la partie,** game
le **match,** match
le **match nul,** drawn game
jouer (au football, golf, etc.), to play
le **rugby,** rugby
l'**association,** association
le **ballon,** ball
le **concours,** competition
un **arbitre,** referee, umpire
une **équipe,** team
le **but,** goal
le **zéro,** nil
5 **buts à zéro,** 5 goals to nil
la **raquette,** racket
gagner, to win (*also* **vaincre,** to conquer, **battre,** to beat)
perdre, to lose
le **set,** set (at tennis)
le **simple,** single (at tennis)
le **double,** double
le **filet,** net
la **ligne de service,** service line
servir, to serve
prendre, to take
renvoyer, to return, send back

un **amateur,** amateur
le **compétiteur,** competitor
un **adversaire,** opponent
le **joueur,** player
le **nombre de points,** score
un **entraîneur,** trainer
la **victoire,** the win
la **finale,** final
le **handicap,** handicap
l'**entraînement,** training, practice
le **champion,** champion
la **boxe,** boxing
la **natation,** swimming
la **lutte,** wrestling
le **patinage,** skating
le **patinage à roulettes,** roller skating
patiner (sur roulettes), to skate (to roller skate)
le **links, le parcours,** links
le **trou,** hole
la **pelouse,** green
la **banquette,** bunker
les **clubs,** clubs de golf
driver, brassie, spoon, same as English
les **chaussures de football,** football boots
les **patins,** skates

If you are keen on sports, this list provides sufficient word-material for a start, though no doubt you will have to supplement it by making a specialized vocabulary to deal with the particular sport in which you are most interested. **Quel est le score?** *What is the score?* **L'équipe française a gagné par cinq contre deux,** *The French team won by 5 to 2.* The French call a foul **un coup déloyal ;** and *a shot,* they often call **un shoot!** **La mi-temps** is *half-time,* and a sporting event is **un évenement sportif.** *The membership fee* to a tennis or golf club is **la cotisation,** and, if you are not staying permanently, you may ask for one for a week, a fortnight, or a month. **Le coup** is a most useful word. **Le coup de pied** is *the kick*; it is also *stroke* in tennis or golf; and **le coup de tête** is the *butt.* **Coup** can be used for all sorts of things. A few examples: **un coup de froid,** *a cold snap*; **un coup de crayon,** *a pencil stroke*; **un coup de cloche,** *peal of a bell*; **le coup de bâton,** *whack with a stick*; and **un coup de dents** is *a bite!*

¶ 10. SALAMMBÔ

Ils arrivèrent dans l'avenue des cyprès, où ils se perdirent parmi la foule, qui les interrogeait. L'un d'eux était resté à l'écart, debout. A travers les déchirures de sa tunique on apercevait ses épaules rayées par de longues balafres. Baissant le menton, il regardait autour de lui avec méfiance et fermait un peu ses paupières dans l'éblouissement des flambeaux ; mais quand il vit que personne de ces gens armés ne lui en voulait, un grand soupir s'échappa de sa poitrine : il balbutiait, il ricanait sous les larmes claires qui lavaient sa figure : puis il saisit par les anneaux un canthare tout plein, le leva droit en l'air au bout de ses bras d'où pendaient des chaines, et alors regardant le ciel et toujours tenant la coupe, il dit :

" Salut d'abord à toi, Baal-Eschmoûn libérateur, que les gens de ma patrie appellent Esculape ! et à vous, Génies des fontaines, de la lumière et des bois ! et à vous, Dieux cachés sous les montagnes et dans les cavernes de la terre ! et à vous, hommes forts aux armures reluisantes, qui m'avez délivré ! "

Puis il laissa tomber la coupe et conta son histoire. **On le**

nommait Spendius. Les Carthaginois l'avaient pris à la bataille
des Égineuses, et parlant grec, ligure et punique, il remercia
encore une fois les Mercenaires ; il leur baisait les mains ; enfin,
il les félicita du banquet, tout en s'étonnant de n'y pas apercevoir
les coupes de la Légion sacrée.

Notes and Words :

parmi la foule, among the crowd
à l'écart, aside
à travers de, through
les déchirures, tears, rents
rayer, to be marked in lines
balafres, scars
baisser, to lower
le menton, chin
avec méfiance, with mistrust
les paupières, eyelids
l'éblouissement, glare
le flambeau, torch
en vouloir, to bear a grudge, ill will
un soupir, sigh
échapper, to escape
la poitrine, chest

balbutier, to stammer
ricaner, laugh derisively
une larme, tear
laver, to wash
un anneau, ring
canthère, cantharus, goblet
Salut ! Hail !
cacher, to hide
armures reluisantes, glittering armour
laisser tomber, to let fall
conter, to relate
une histoire, history, story
pris, taken (*from the verb* **prendre**)
encore une fois, once again
baiser, to kiss
féliciter, to congratulate
apercevoir, to perceive

Reading Vocabulary—51

PLAISIR, *pleasure*
plan, *plan*
plante, *plant*
planter, *to plant*
PLEURER, *to cry, weep*
plier, *to bend*
plonger, *to plunge*
PLUIE, *rain*
PLUME, *feather, pen*
PLUPART, *greater part*

POCHE, *pocket*
poésie, *poetry*
poète, *poet*
POIDS, *weight*
poing, *fist*
point, *dot, full stop*
pointe, *tip, point*
POISSON, *fish*
poitrine, *chest*
POLICE, *police*

§ 2. *Newspapers—Reviews—Books*

la librairie, the bookshop

le journal, daily newspaper

un hebdomadaire, weekly paper

le mensuel, monthly

le périodique, periodical

la revue, review

la revue mensuelle, monthly review

le kiosque, street stall where newspapers are sold

illustré, illustrated

la revue de commerce, trade journal

le journal, la revue de modes, the fashion paper, review

le journaliste, journalist

le correspondant, correspondent

le rédacteur, editor

un éditeur, publisher

une édition, edition

le livre, book

le livre illustré, illustrated book

lire, to read

imprimer, to print

une annonce, advertisement

un article, article

un article de fond, leading article

un exemplaire, copy (of a book)

le volume, le tome, volume

un auteur, author

le dramaturge, dramatist

le roman, novel

la biographie, biography

les belles lettres, purely literary studies, humanities

un homme de lettres, man of letters

être lettré, to be a scholar

la typographie, the print, typography

la reliure, binding

le fascicule, installment

le feuilleton, serial (in a newspaper)

la poésie, poetry

le journal du matin, morning paper

le journal du soir, evening paper

les nouvelles, news

un journal comique, satirique, comic paper

une édition en deux volumes, an edition in two volumes

la bibliothèque, library

le libraire, bookseller

la bibliothèque de prêt, lending library

épuisé, out of print

relié, bound

un livre broché, paper-bound book

commander, to order

recommander, to recommend

We assume that it will not be your intention when you have finished this course to rest on your laurels and be satisfied with what you have been taught here. While this course provides fundamentals, it does not pretend to exhaust the French language. That cannot be done ! Hence, this is a most important list of words and, as it is not a difficult list, you should learn all of them now or on some future occasion. You must not forget. **un plan de Paris** or **un guide-plan,** and you may require **un dictionnaire de poche,** which should be **Français-Anglais** as well as **Anglais-Français.*** After what we have told you about French food, you may even wish to inquire about **un guide gastronomique de la région,** *a gastronomic guide to the district.* You will generally find the French bookseller to be a man of intelligence and good taste, and if you ask for **un roman policier** (*a detective novel*), he will not *look down his nose* (**faire le nez**) at you, though he may well say of an author : **" Je l'ai dans le nez,"** " *I can't stand him !* "

MUSIQUES POUR L'ŒIL

Impression gratuite, ou réalité toute simple ? Je ne sais pas.

Toujours est-il qu'en sortant du concert où nous conviait samedi M. André Cluytens et la Société des Concerts, j'avais le sentiment persistant d'avoir assisté à la projection de trois films de court métrage. Je serais désolé que les auteurs de ces trois partitions le prissent en mauvaise part : dans mon esprit, il n'y a rien là de péjoratif ; et le seul fait qu'elles m'aient si impérieusement suggéré des images précises dit assez la vertu évocatrice que je reconnais à ces trois musiques. Le drame, le drôle de drame, serait que les dits auteurs ne l'aient pas voulu ainsi—ce qui est fort probable—ou encore que ce que j'ai vu ne corresponde nullement à ce qu'ils ont voulu montrer.

De ces trois partitions, c'est celle de M. Yves Baudrier, intitulée *Le Musicien dans la cité* qui me paraît se suffire le moins à elle-

---

* The Bellows FRENCH DICTIONARY (Longmans Green) or the Pocket Dictionary by Kettridge are better than the bi-lingual dictionaries published in France.

même, et qui me semble demander avec le plus d'exigence de commenter des images. Une certaine facilité de conception, je ne sais quoi d'un peu lâché, dans la forme comme dans la trame instrumentale, une absence de concision et de densité font paraître l'œuvre un peu longuette. Tous défauts qui s'effaceraient si passaient réellement devant nos yeux des images surgies de quelque scénario d'après Eugène Dabit, avec des personnages très pâles, très pauvres, très malheureux et très fatalistes évoluant, par une nuit pluvieuse, quelque part entre le canal Saint-Martin et la fête foraine de la place Jean-Jaurès.

NOTES AND WORDS:

convier, to invite
assister à, to be present at
court métrage, short length in meters
être désolé, to be distressed
une partition, musical score
prendre en mauvaise part, to take in bad part
suggérer, to suggest
le drôle de drame, the funny, odd drama
fort probable =très probable
nullement, in no way
suffire, to suffice

sembler, to seem
un peu lâché, somewhat slovenly
la trame instrumentale, instrumental texture
faire paraître, cause to appear
longuette, on the long side
effacer, to efface
s'effacer, to fade away
surgir, to spring from, rise, loom up
évoluer, to evolve
par une nuit pluvieuse, on a rainy night

Reading Vocabulary—52

politesse, *politeness*
politique, *politics*
PONT, *bridge*
PORT, *port*
PORTE, *door*
portée, *reach*
PORTER, *to carry, to take, to wear*
portrait, *portrait*
poser, *to place*
position, *position*

posséder, *to possess*
possession, *possession*
poste, *post*
poursuite, *pursuit*
poursuivre, *to pursue*
POUSSER, *to utter, to push, to grow*
POUSSIÈRE, *dust*
le POUVOIR, *power*
POUVOIR, *to be able, can*
PRATIQUE, *practice*

§ 3. *War—Peace—International Affairs*

La Société des Nations, League of Nations

L'Organisation des Nations Unies, l'ONU, UN, United Nations

la démocratie, democracy

le fascisme, fascism

le communisme, communism

un état, state

un état totalitaire, totalitarian state

la guerre mondiale, world war

l'armée de l'air, air force

l'armée de terre, army

l'armée de mer, navy

la propagande, propaganda

la diplomatie, diplomacy

le diplomate, diplomat

diplomatique, diplomatic

en temps de guerre, in time of war

la paix, peace

éclater, to break out (war)

la zone, zone

faire la guerre (à), to make war (against)

le service des renseignements, intelligence service

le service des nouvelles, news service

le blocus, blockade

violer la neutralité, to violate neutrality

souhaiter la paix, to wish for peace

la force prime le droit, " Might is right "

le mensonge, lie, untruth

les possédants, the " haves "

les non-possédants, " have-nots "

la Charte Atlantique, Atlantic Charter

le traité, treaty

le Pacte Atlantique, the Atlantic Pact

la trêve, truce

A list for controversy or discussions ! To be used with discretion and tact in speaking to strangers, that is, unless you wish to get into what nearly always ends in heated argument or **un argument pour manière d'argument,** *an argument for argument's sake.* **Discuter tout,** *to argue about everything,* is a French weakness—or strength. If you are that way inclined, you will not lack opportunities.

Furthermore, this list is useful for listening to news on the radio and for reading newspapers, which are the values we have immediately in mind. With the list given in the preceding section, it should be very useful. **Le bloc,** *the block*, is a word much used in French : **le bloc oriental, le bloc occidental,** *the Eastern, Western block*. **Les intérêts des puissances se heurtent,** *The interests of the powers conflict*, is a constantly recurring phrase, as is **Les négociations entre les puissances aboutissent à une impasse,** *Negotiations between* (*among*) *the powers reach a deadlock*. **Une impasse,** *a blind alley, a dead end, deadlock*. **Se trouver dans une impasse,** *to find oneself in a dilemma*, in a position from which there is no retreat. **Les droits imprescriptibles,** *the inalienable rights* is another phrase beloved by diplomatic correspondents and leader writers.

¶ 11. SALAMMBÔ

Ces coupes, portant une vigne en emeraude sur chacune de leurs six faces en or, appartenaient à une milice exclusivement composée des jeunes patriciens, les plus hauts de taille. C'était un privilège, presque un honneur sacerdotal ; aussi rien dans les tresors de la République n'était plus convoité des Mercenaires. Ils détestaient la Légion à cause de cela, et on en avait vu qui risquaient leur vie pour l'inconcevable plaisir d'y boire.

Donc ils commandèrent d'aller chercher les coupes. Elles étaient en dépôt chez les Syssites, compagnies de commerçants qui mangeaient en commun. Les esclaves revinrent. A cette heure, tous les membres des Syssites dormaient.

" Qu'on les réveille ! " répondirent les Mercenaires.

Après une seconde démarche, on leur expliqua qu'elles étaient enfermées dans un temple.

" Qu'on l'ouvre ! " répliquèrent-ils.

Et quand les esclaves, en tremblant, eurent avoué qu'elles étaient entre les mains du général Giscon, ils s'écrièrent :

" Qu'il les apporte ! "

Giscon, bientôt, apparut au fond du jardin dans une escorte de la Légion sacrée. Son ample manteau noir, retenu sur sa tête à une mitre d'or constellée de pierres précieuses, et qui pendait tout à l'entour jusqu'aux sabots de son cheval, se confondait, de loin, avec la couleur de la nuit. On n'apercevait que sa

barbe blanche, les rayonnements de sa coiffure et son triple collier
à larges plaques bleues qui lui battait sur la poitrine.

NOTES AND WORDS:

une vigne, vine
emeraude, emerald
milice, militia
les plus hauts de taille, highest stature
convoité, coveted
à cause de, because of
y boire, to drink (from it)
donc, then
commander, to give orders
aller chercher, to go and look for
une coupe, cup (*large, like a goblet*)
en dépôt, deposited
réveiller, to awaken
une seconde démarche, a second effort
expliquer, to explain

"Qu'on ouvre! ", " Let it be opened! "
répliquer, to reply
avouer, to admit
apporter, to bring
constellé(e), starred
pendre, to hang
tout à l'entour, all around
sabots de cheval, horse's hoofs
se confondre, to become confused
les rayonnements de sa coiffure, the (shining) rays from his headdress
une plaque, plaque, plate
battre, to beat, *but here* beat against, dance

Reading Vocabulary—53

précaution, *precaution*
précéder, *to proceed*
précipiter, *to rush, to hurl*
préciser, *to state precisely*
précision, *precision*
préférer, *to prefer*
PRENDRE, *to take*
préparer, *to prepare*
présence, *presence*
présent, *present*

PRÉSENTER, *to present, introduce*
président, *president*
presser, *to press, to hurry*
prétendre, *to claim*
prétention, *pretension*
PRÊTER, *to lend*
prétexte, *pretext*
prêtre, *priest*
PREUVE, *proof*
PRÉVENIR, *to warn*

§ 4. *Countries and Nationalities—Places*

l'Amérique, les États-Unis, America, United States	un américain, une américaine, an American
l'Autriche, Austria	un autrichien, an Austrian
la Belgique, Belgium	un belge, a Belgian
la Grande Bretagne, Great Britain	un britannique
l'Angleterre, England	un anglais
l'Écosse, Scotland	un écossais
le Pays de Galles, Wales	un gallois, Welshman
l'Irlande, Ireland	un irlandais, Irishman
le Canada, Canada	un canadien
la Chine, China	un chinois
la Tchécoslovaquie, Czechoslovakia	un tchécoslovaque
la Grèce, Greece	un grec, une grecque
la Hollande ⎫ Holland, The les Pays-Bas ⎭ Netherlands	un hollandais
la Yougoslavie, Yugoslavia	un yougoslave
la Norvège, Norway	un norvégien
la Pologne, Poland	un polonais
La Russie l'Union des Républiques Socialistes Soviétiques, U.R.S.S. l'Union Soviétique ⎱ Russia, U.S.S.R., Soviet Union	un russe, a Russian
la Suisse, Switzerland	un suisse, Swiss
la Suède, Sweden	un suédois, a Swede
la Turquie, Turkey	un turc, une turque

l'Afrique l'Asie	l'Australie l'Europe
l'Océan Atlantique	la Mer Méditerranée
la Mer du Nord	la Manche, the English Channel

You will remember that *in* is **EN** for countries when fem. : **en France, en Amérique.** Masc. : **au Japon, aux États-Unis ; aux Indes** (fem.), *in India.* For towns and cities, **à** : **à Londres, à Paris.**

Le Havre (the haven, harbor) **Au Havre,** in Le Havre
La Haye, The Hague **à la Haye,** at The Hague
en Angleterre, in England **dans le midi,** in the south

N.B.—**dans** is more definite than **en.**

The above list needs no comment : **Voilà qui se passe de commentaire,** *It " does without " comment.* **Se passer de,** *to do without.*

Reading Vocabulary—54

prévoir, *to foresee*
prier, *to pray*
prière, *prayer*
prince(sse), *prince, princess*
principal, *principal*
principe, *principle*
PRINTEMPS, *springtime*
prise, *capture*
prison, *prison*
PRISONNIER, *prisoner*

priver, *to deprive*
PRIX, *prize, price*
problème, *problem*
procédé, *process, method*
PRODUIRE, *to produce*
profit, *profit*
profiter, *to take advantage of*
profondeur, *depth*
progrès, *progress*
projet, *project*

MESSAGE CÉLESTE

Ces jours derniers, un Lausannois se trouvait harcelé de questions par son fils âgé de neuf ans. La poste n'avait-elle pas apporté au domicile paternel une lettre à l'adresse du garçonnet ? A quelle heure le facteur faisait-il sa tournée ? Est-ce que . . . est-ce que ? . . .

Le père, un peu surpris, s'enquit des raisons de cette anxiété :
" Enfin, Alfred, qu'est-ce que c'est que cette correspondance ? Avec qui entretiens-tu des relations épistolaires aussi pressantes ? "

Le garçon rougit jusqu'aux oreilles mais garda le silence.

" Alfred, je t'ai posé une question ou plutôt deux. Cela mérite une réponse que j'exige d'ailleurs."

Fort embarrassé, le garçonnet entra dans la voie des aveux. Il avait, à l'approche de Pâques, écrit une lettre à . . . saint Pierre, portier du ciel, pour s'enquérir de l'heure à laquelle les cloches de la région partiraient pour Rome afin de s'y faire bénir ! Rien que cela !

" Vous me croirez, si vous voulez, nous a déclaré le père, mais j'avoue n'avoir pas trouvé cela si ridicule. Il ne me déplaît pas de penser qu'en ces tristes temps sans fantaisie, mon fils entretient dans son esprit un peu de poésie, même chimérique et que sous son impulsion, il écrit à des destinataires qu'on pourrait redouter beaucoup pires, en somme."

Mais le bouquet, c'est qu'Alfred, ce samedi, a reçu une réponse. Un plaisantin qui doit être un fonctionnaire postal au cœur bien placé, a répondu non sans déférence à l'enfant, de " la part de saint Pierre empêché," que l'incertitude de la situation politique dissuadait les cloches de faire le voyage transalpin et que les messagères de bronze se contenteraient de la bénédiction de l'an passé.

Il paraît qu'Alfred considère depuis lors, avec quelque condescendance, l'auteur de ses jours, et que celui-ci, bon prince, joue à merveille les pères confus.

NOTES AND WORDS :

un Lausannois, person from Lausanne

harceler, to harass, torment

garçonnet, little boy

le facteur, postman

s'entretenir, to engage in

pressant, urgent, pressing

rougir, to blush

exiger, to insist upon

la voie des aveux, the way of confession

portier, gate, doorkeeper

s'enquérir, to inquire

les cloches, bells (church)

s'y faire bénir, to have oneself blessed there

avouer, admit

déplaire, to displease

redouter, to dread

en somme, in short

le bouquet, bouquet, *here* the best of it, to crown it

un plaisantin, joker

au cœur bien placé, with heart in the right place

empêché, who was prevented

se contenter de, to be satisfied with

l'an passé, last year

depuis lors, from then

condescendance, condescension

jouer, to play

confus, confused, puzzled

à merveille, marvellously

bon prince, *here* good fellow

Reading Vocabulary—55

prolonger, *to prolong*
PROMENADE, *walk*
PROMENER, *to walk*
promettre, *to promise*
prononcer, *to pronounce*
proposer, *to propose*
proposition, *proposition*
propriétaire, *proprietor*
propriété, *property*
protection, *protection*

protéger, *to protect*
protester, *to protest*
prouver, *to prove*
province, *province*
provoquer, *to provoke*
PUBLIC, *public*
publier, *to publish*
puissance, *power, strength*
qualité, *quality*
quantité, *quantity*

§ 5. *Weights and Measures*

le kilogramme, 2 lb. 3 oz. (*is called* **le kilo**)
le mètre, 1·09 yards
le kilomètre, ⅝ of 1 mile app.
le litre, 1¾ pint (about)
le centimètre, 0·393 inch (⅖)
l'hectare, 2·47 acres (about 2½)
un pouce, an inch
la livre, pound (sterling and weight)
la demi-livre, half a pound
le poids, weight
la hauteur, height
la longueur, length
la largeur, breadth
la distance, distance

le volume, volume
le mille, mile (little used)
l'épaisseur, thickness
la balance (à ressort), spring balance
la bascule automatique, automatic weigher
la superficie, area
de longueur, de largeur, in length, breadth
peser, to weigh
mesurer, to measure
évaluer, to estimate
calculer, to calculate
faire sur mesure, to make to measure

And note : **être long de cinq mètres,** to be 5 m. long
être large de 5 m., to be 5 m. wide

and the same with **épais,** *thick* ; **haut,** *high* ; and **profond,** *deep*

vendre au poids, to sell by weight

faire bon poids, to give good weight

You can also say : **avoir 5 mètres de long, de large.**

You must learn the simple weights and measures, as the metric system, universal in France, differs from ours. The housekeeper cannot do without them. **Prendre les mesures pour** is *to take the measurements for* anything—for a suit (**un costume, un complet**). Do not forget that **le livre** is *book* and **la livre** is *pound*. And note well the French ways of expressing length and breadth, that given last above being the easiest to remember and the one to be memorized for speaking. You should be able to recognize the others.

¶ 12. SALAMMBÔ

Les soldats, quand il entra, le saluèrent d'une grande acclamation, tous criant :

" Les coupes !   Les coupes ! "

Il commença par déclarer que, si l'on considérait leur courage, ils en étaient dignes.   La foule hurla de joie, en applaudissant.

Il le savait bien, lui qui les avait commandés là-bas et qui était revenu avec la dernière cohorte sur la dernière galère !

" C'est vrai !   c'est vrai ! " disaient-ils.

Cependant, continua Giscon, la République avait respecté leurs divisions par peuples, leurs coutumes, leurs cultes ; ils étaient libres dans Carthage !   Quant aux vases de la Légion sacrée, c'était une propriété particulière.   Tout à coup, près de Spendius, un Gaulois s'élança par-dessus les tables et courut droit à Giscon, qu'il menaçait en gesticulant avec deux épées nues.

Le général, sans s'interrompre, le frappa sur la tête de son lourd bâton d'ivoire : le Barbare tomba.   Les Gaulois hurlaient, et leur fureur, se communiquant aux autres, allait emporter les légionnaires.   Giscon haussa les épaules en les voyant pâlir. Il songeait que son courage serait inutile contre ces bêtes brutes, exaspérées.   Il valait mieux plus tard s'en venger dans quelque ruse ;   donc il fit signe à ses soldats et s'éloigna lentement. Puis, sous la porte, se tournant vers les Mercenaires, il leur cria qu'ils s'en repentiraient.

NOTES AND WORDS:

digne, worthy
là-bas, yonder
cependant, however
culte, religion
une propriété particulière, a private property
tout à coup, all of a sudden
s'élancer par-dessus, leaped over
courir, to run
épée, sword
hurler, to howl, yell
emporter, to carry away

hausser les épaules, to shrug the shoulders
pâlir, to grow pale
songer, to dream, imagine, think
bête, stupid
il valait mieux, it would be better
s'en venger, to take revenge
faire signe à, to make a sign to
s'éloigner, to go away
lentement, slowly
se repentir, to repent of, regret

Reading Vocabulary—56

QUART, *quarter*
quartier, *district*
QUESTION, *question*
queue, *tail*
quitter, *to leave*
race, *race*
RACONTER, *to relate*
rage, *rage*
RAISON, *reason*
ramasser, *to pick up*

ramener, *to bring back*
rang, *rank*
ranger, *to arrange*
RAPPELER, *to remember*
rapport, *report*
rapporter, *to bring back, to refer*
rapprocher, *bring nearer*
rassembler, *to collect*
rassurer, *to reassure*
ravir, *to delight*

PART III
THE SPIRIT OF THE LANGUAGE

LESSON XX

§ 1. *The Importance of Pronunciation*

FROM now until the end of the course you must take upon yourself responsibility for *review*. In your spare moments go over the grammar again, especially Lessons V, VI, and VII, dealing with the verb. Next, you must reread *Tartarin de Tarascon* and all the other literary pieces—reread them again and again until you are familiar with every word and turn of phrase. Finally, never forget oral practice. And you must do all these things, even though you have the advantage of a teacher and class work. A foreign language *cannot* be mastered without this personal effort. In Lessons I to XIX you have been provided with an excellent framework of structural fundamentals and vocabulary for speaking and reading. From now onwards you will be initiated into the wider aspects of the French language and culture: so that, when you have completed the course, you will not be satisfied to rest content with the knowledge given here, but will wish to extend it by further practice, reading, and experience. The importance of pronunciation has already been emphasized, and this can again be usefully brought to mind.

SPOKEN FRENCH: To speak French well, two primary conditions must be fulfilled : first, you must *know* certain material, which includes grammar, words, and some idioms; second, you must be able to *pronounce* at least passably well (which means that you must be understood). But you should aim at something better than a merely passable pronunciation; and there is no reason why you should not learn to pronounce well. The whole secret of learning to pronounce well lies in *careful listening* to good speakers and *accurate imitation* of good French speech. Practice, practice, practice ! You will notice that the speech of good French speakers has a certain rhythm : that they tend to raise the voice slightly at the end of most sentences. Try to catch that rhythm, and to imitate it. A slip in grammar will always be pardoned; a bad pronunciation is often misunderstood or not understood at all.

BIEN PARLER, C'EST D'ABORD BIEN PRONONCER

¶ 13. SALAMMBÔ

Le festin recommença. Mais Giscon pouvait revenir, et, cernant le faubourg qui touchait aux derniers remparts, les écraser contre les murs. Alors ils se sentirent seuls malgré leur foule; et la grande ville qui dormait sous eux, dans l'ombre, leur fit peur, tout à coup, avec ses entassements d'escaliers, ses hautes maisons noires et ses vagues dieux encore plus féroces que son peuple. Au loin, quelques fanaux glissaient sur le port, et il y avait des lumières dans le temple de Khamon. Ils se souvinrent d'Hamilcar. Où était-il? pourquoi les avoir abandonnés, la paix conclue? Ses dissensions avec le Conseil n'étaient sans doute qu'un jeu pour les perdre. Leur haine inassouvie retombait sur lui; et ils le maudissaient, s'exaspérant les uns les autres par leur propre colère. A ce moment-là, il se fit un rassemblement sous les platanes. C'était pour voir un nègre qui se roulait en battant le sol avec ses membres, la prunelle fixe, le cou tordu, l'écume aux lèvres. Quelqu'un cria qu'il était empoisonné. Tous se crurent empoisonnés. Ils tombèrent sur les esclaves; une clameur épouvantable s'éleva, et un vertige de destruction tourbillonna sur l'armée ivre. Ils frappaient au hasard, autour d'eux, ils brisaient, ils tuaient: quelques-uns lancèrent des flambeaux dans les feuillages; d'autres s'accoudant sur la balustrade des lions, les massacrèrent à coups de flèches; les plus hardis coururent aux éléphants, ils voulaient leur abattre la trompe et manger de l'ivoire.

NOTES AND WORDS:

cerner, to encircle, surround
les derniers remparts, the outermost ramparts
écraser, to crush
se sentir, to feel (themselves)
malgré, in spite of
entassement, heap, mass, accumulation
escaliers, stairways
fanal, lantern

glisser, slide, glide

un jeu pour les perdre, a game (trick) to lose (undo) them

assouvir, to appease, hence—

inassouvie, unappeased

maudire, to curse

un rassemblement, a gathering, rally

platane, plane tree

la prunelle, eyeball

le cou, neck

tordre, to twist

tordu, twisted

une écume, foam

se crurent, past definite of— croire, to believe

un vertige, frenzy, madness

tourbillonner, to whirl (le tourbillon, the whirlwind)

frapper, to strike

briser, to break

tuer, to kill

accouder, to lean

abattre, to knock, pull down, *here* to cut off

manger de l'ivoire, *not* to eat the ivory, *but* to destroy it

Reading Vocabulary—57

rayon, *ray*

réaliser, *to realize*

réalité, *reality*

RECEVOIR, *to receive*

recherche, *pursuit, search*

rechercher, *to look for*

récit, *story, account*

réclamer, *to entreat*

recommander, *to command, to entrust*

recommencer, *to commence again*

reconnaissance, *gratitude*

RECONNAÎTRE, *to recognize*

recouvrir, *to cover over*

recueillir, *to gather*

reculer, *to retreat*

redevenir, *to become again*

redouter, *to fear, to dread*

RÉDUIRE, *to reduce*

réfléchir, *to reflect*

reflet, *reflection*

§ 2. *A Further Note on Vocabulary*

In his authoritative and inspiring book *Le Génie de la Langue Française* (1947), Albert Dauzat says :

> Une langue se compose de mots, qui s'agencent en phrases. Le vocabulaire, c'est le matériel du langage, dont la grammaire est l'architecture. On peut pousser plus loin la comparaison : si les noms sont les pierres de l'édifice, les particules n'en forment-elles pas le ciment qui les agrège ? et n'a-t-on pas dit à juste titre que le verbe est la charpente de la phrase ?

> *A language is composed of words which are arranged in*
> *sentences. Vocabulary is the material of the language, of*
> *which grammar is the architecture. The comparison can be*
> *extended (pushed further): if nouns are the stones of the*
> *edifice, do not particles* form the cement which unites them?*
> *And have we not said with good reason that the verb is the*
> *frame(work) of the sentence?*

In those few lines you have a perfect description of the composition of a language and the relative values of vocabulary,
grammar, nouns, particles, and the verb. As for the verb,
the famous **Grammaire de l'Académie Française** says : **Le**
verbe est le mot essentiel de la langue. In other words,
Dauzat says that the verb is the " frame " of the sentence (holding together the other words) and the French Academy calls it
the " essential " word of the language.

Here, we are concerned with vocabulary. French is a rich
language in vocabulary, though there are richer. Where French
scores over other languages is in the sharpness, the exactness in
meaning of its words. You will have noticed this in the reading
matter. We should like to emphasize that the French do not
like vagueness, ambiguity, or mystification; they like what is
clear, direct, unmistakable, and precise. In the extract given
above there are two words for *language* : **langue** and **langage**.
La langue is the language *in general* of a whole people—as used
by *everybody*; **le langage** is the *language of the individual*.
La langue is *speech*. **Le langage des fleurs,** *the language of*
flowers; **le langage des signes,** *sign language*. **Quelle langue** !
What a chatterbox ! It is this quality in the vocabulary, combined
with a delicate and extensive though fairly rigid grammar, which
makes French one of the *clearest* languages in the world. In this
sense, English cannot equal it.

Un Congrès d'Histoire Littéraire

Le 30 mars s'ouvrira à Paris, à la Sorbonne, le quatrième
Congrès international d'Histoire littéraire. Ce congrès aura

---

* Particles are those short, indeclinable words such as conjunctions
and prepositions : **et, à, de, dans,** etc.

pour thème " la littérature moderne et les mouvements politiques et sociaux." Le troisième congrès avait eu lieu à Lyon en 1938.

Vingt nations seront représentées. Parmi les congressistes étrangers citons : le sénateur Benedetto Croce, le grand philosophe italien ; Son Excellence Jean Wu, ambassadeur de Chine au Vatican, qui est l'un des plus grands écrivains chinois contemporains ; M. Julian Huxley, directeur général de l'U.N.E.S.C.O. ; le professeur Charlier, de l'Académie belge de langue française ; le sénateur Franck, du Sénat belge, et M. Wesniewski, de l'Académie polonaise.

Parmi les congressistes français signalons : MM. André Maurois et Robert d'Harcourt, de l'Académie française ; André Billy, de l'académie Goncourt ; Frédéric Lefèvre, rédacteur en chef des " Nouvelles Littéraires."

Nous serons heureux d'accueillir en France des écrivains que nous n'avions pas vus depuis la guerre, et en particulier Benedetto Croce, philosophe de l'esthétique et historien de l'Italie. Son attitude à l'époque du fascisme fut constamment des plus courageuses. Sa venue en France, qu'il n'a pas vue depuis une vingtaine d'années, n'en est que plus significative.

On parlera particulièrement à ce congrès de la Révolution de 48 et des lettres européennes. La question ne saurait manquer d'intéresser le public lettré, qui est invité à ces séances.

La séance solennelle de clôture aura lieu à l'amphithéâtre Richelieu, vendredi 2 avril, à 10 h. 20. Les discours de clôture seront prononcés par MM. André Maurois et Robert d'Harcourt.

NOTES AND WORDS :

congressistes, congressmen
signaler, to note
accueillir, to welcome
la venue, coming, visit
une vingtaine, score
significatif(-ve), significant

les lettres, letters, literature
ne saurait manquer, can hardly fail
la séance, session
le discours, speech
la clôture, closing, winding up

Reading Vocabulary—58–59

réflexion, *reflection*
REFUSER, *to refuse*
regard, *look*
REGARDER, *to look at*
régime, *system, rule*
régiment, *regiment*
région, *region*
règle, *rule*
régler, *to regulate*
régner, *to reign*
regret, *regret*

remonter, *to remount*
remords, *remorse*
remplacer, *to replace*
REMPLIR, *to fulfill, to fill*
remuer, *to move*
rencontre, *meeting*
RECONTRER, *to meet*
RENDRE, *to render*
renfermer, *to enclose*
renoncer, *to renounce*
renseignement, *information*

regretter, *to regret*
rejeter, *to throw away*
rejoindre, *to rejoin*
réjouir, *to rejoice*
relever, *to gather up, to lift up,*
    to get up
RELIGION, *religion*
remarquer, *to notice, to remark*
REMERCIER, *to thank*
remettre, *to hand back, to*
    restore
rente, *income*
RENTRER, *to return*
renverser, *to overturn*
RENVOYER, *to send away,*
    back
répandre, *to spread, to scatter*
repartir, *to set out again*
repas, *meal*
RÉPÉTER, *to repeat*
répliquer, *to answer*

§ 3. *The Function of Grammar*

To quote Albert Dauzat again :

> **L'architecture grammaticale, autant et plus que le système de la prononciation, caractérise la langue. Reprenons notre comparaison, si les mots pleins, noms et verbes, constituent les pierres de l'édifice, les particules sont le ciment qui les agrège; et le verbe est la charpente de la phrase. Le langage des enfants ou des primitifs n'a pas de charpente centrale. . . . Charpentées par le verbe, les langues construites sont plus ou moins cimentées.**

> *The grammatical architecture, as much as and more than the system of pronunciation, characterizes the language. Let*

us make (take) our comparison again, if the full words, nouns and verbs, constitute the stones of the edifice, the particles are the cement which unites them; and the verb is the frame of the sentence. The language of children and primitives has no central framework. . . . Framed by the verb, the constructed languages are more or less cemented.

French is an excellent example of **une langue construite,** a constructed or " built-up " language. You cannot have failed to observe this in the previous lessons, especially those dealing with the verb. French grammar is logical on the whole, notwithstanding exceptions. You can " get along " in English with very little grammar; you cannot do so in French. Have you ever asked yourself : What *is* grammar ? And what are its functions ? Grammar may be said to be the rules to be observed when putting words together to form sentences in accordance with the best usage. Hence, when you make a mistake in French grammar, you are going counter to what French people regard as the best usage, or at least " correct " usage. But, you may be doing something much worse than that : you may be making a sentence which will *not be understood!* In reading French, if you do not know your grammar fairly well, you will not make sense of a text, as one might in English. Thus, there is *no avoiding* grammar in French. Any " system " which claims to do so is falsely based.

Your first aim is to understand and to make yourself understood. You can make yourself understood perfectly by using simple sentences, and for this you must be able to *use* grammar, which means that you must know the essentials *thoroughly.* If you do not know them all by now, review again and again until you do. There is nothing like plenty of reading for driving home grammar; and this also applies to vocabulary. Later you may forget about grammar, rules, etc., when practice has made you at home with the language.

¶ 14. SALAMMBÔ

Cependant des frondeurs baléares qui, pour piller plus commodément, avaient tourné l'angle du palais, furent arrêtés par une haute barrière faite en jonc des Indes. Ils coupèrent avec

leurs poignards les courroies de la serrure et se trouvèrent alors
sous la façade qui regardait Carthage, dans un autre jardin
rempli de végétations taillées.   Des lignes de fleurs blanches,
toutes se suivant une à une, décrivaient sur la terre couleur
d'azur de longues paraboles, comme des fusées d'étoiles.   Les
buissons, pleins de ténèbres, exhalaient des odeurs chaudes,
mielleuses.   Il y avait des troncs d'arbre barbouillés de cinabre,
qui ressemblaient à des colonnes sanglantes.   Au milieu, douze
piédestaux de cuivre portaient chacun une grosse boule de verre,
et des lueurs rougeâtres emplissaient confusément ces globes
creux, comme d'énormes prunelles qui palpiteraient encore.
Les soldats s'éclairaient avec des torches, tout en trébuchant
sur la pente du terrain, profondément labouré.

Mais ils aperçurent un petit lac, divisé en plusieurs bassins
par des murailles de pierres bleues.   L'onde était si limpide
que les flammes des torches tremblaient jusqu'au fond, sur un
lit de cailloux blancs et de poussière d'or.   Elle se mit à
bouillonner, des paillettes lumineuses glissèrent, et de gros
poissons, qui portaient des pierreries à la gueule, apparurent
vers la surface.

Les soldats, en riant beaucoup, leur passèrent les doigts dans
les ouïes et les apportèrent sur les tables.

C'étaient les poissons de la famille Barca.   Tous descendaient
de ces lottes primordiales qui avaient fait éclore l'œuf mystique
où se cachait la Déesse.   L'idée de commettre un sacrilège
ranima la gourmandise des Mercenaires; ils placèrent vite du
feu sous des vases d'airain et s'amusèrent à regarder les beaux
poissons se débattre dans l'eau bouillante.

NOTES AND WORDS:

des frondeurs baléares, some
 Balearic slingers
piller, to pillage
commodément,   conveniently
jonc, rattan
courroie, thong, strap

la serrure, lock
se suivant une à une, following one another
décrire, describe
les fusées d'étoiles, star-
 rockets
le buisson, bush, shrub

mielleux, honeyed
barbouiller, to daub, smear
le piédestal, pedestal
une boule, ball, sphere
rougeâtre, reddish (the French ending -âtre to adjectives, corresponds to our -ish)
emplir, to fill
creux, empty, hollow
trébucher, to stumble
la pente, slope
le bassin, basin, pool
l'onde, wave, *here means* "water"

le caillou, pebble
bouillonner, to bubble
des paillettes lumineuses, bright spangles
pierreries, stones, precious stones
apparurent, appeared (*from* **apparaître,** to appear)
les ouïes, gills
les lottes, lotes (species of fish)
éclore, to hatch
se débattre, struggle
l'eau bouillante, boiling water

*Reading Vocabulary—*60

RÉPONDRE, *to reply*
RÉPONSE, *reply*
REPOS, *peace, rest*
reposer(se), *to rest oneself*
repousser, *to reject*
REPRENDRE, *to resume*
représenter, *to represent*
reproche, *reproach*
reprocher, *to reproach*
RÉPUBLIQUE, *republic*

réputation, *reputation*
réserve, *reserve*
RÉSERVER, *to reserve*
résigner, *to resign*
résister, *to resist*
résolution, *resolution*
résoudre, *to resolve*
respecter, *to respect*
respect, *respect*
respirer, *to breathe*

§ 4. *Written French and Spoken French*

There is, fundamentally, no difference between written and spoken French, though there is **le langage populaire de Paris** —a racy, slangy speech used by the ordinary people of Paris *among themselves*, which the foreigner learns only by living there for a considerable time. The French you have been learning is that which is spoken and written by contemporary French people; the reading matter consists of both classical literature and extracts from newspapers and reviews of the late 1940s. From the eighteenth century on, French has changed only in the development and expansion of its vocabulary, and what you have been taught here should enable you, with little more than dictionary aid, to read French literature from about 1600 on. What a field this opens!

But in French, as in nearly all languages, the written sentence is not always quite the same thing as that which is spoken. The French author is a careful, conscientious, and precise writer who is highly conscious of his beautiful language. Gustave Flaubert, whose SALAMMBÔ you have been reading, would spend days in quest of **le mot juste,** *the exact word*, the right word to express exactly his meaning. That is one reason why he is difficult to translate. This sort of thing is rare in English, in which, generally speaking, style is somewhat freer and the writer is granted or takes far more license than the French **homme de lettres.** The classical tradition of **clarté** and precision still dominates French literature, and this tradition is maintained by many of the reviews and even in some of the daily newspapers. There is much more " discipline " as regards language in French journalism than in ours, which makes it a pleasure to read what often might otherwise be considered a rag.

All this is eased in speaking. If you have listened attentively to French, you will have noticed how freely the speakers express themselves. If you know your grammar and vocabulary, if you read with some ease, and if you can understand even the gist of what is spoken, all you require is intercourse with French people —that is *practice in the spoken language*—and you will very quickly find yourself speaking French with surprising fluency.

LES ARTS

Il se fait actuellement à l'étranger une campagne contre l'art français. N'y pas donner prise nous semble devoir être notre premier objectif. Chaque geste maladroit renforce la position de nos adversaires. L'incident dont nous allons parler nous semble à ce sujet un parfait exemple de ce qu'il convient de ne pas faire.

Dans son dernier numéro, la revue américaine *The Architectural Forum* donne le compte rendu de la conférence récente d'un jeune architecte français actuellement aux Etats-Unis.

Cet architecte, ancient élève de l'Ecole des Beaux-Arts, a voulu faire du zèle. Mal inspiré, notre compatriote n'a su que faire voir le petit côté de l'enseignement de l'Ecole des Beaux-Arts. Les réflexions de la revue américaine le lui ont prouvé.

Voici les faits :

Ancien Grand Massier, Robert Louard arrivait en Amérique en octobre, avec une bourse d'étudiant de l'Ecole. Il avait emporté une exposition de travaux d'élèves déjà présentée l'année dernière à Milan lors d'un congrès d'étudiants architectes, comptant faire quelque propagande à son école et ainsi lui prouver sans doute sa gratitude. C'est à la suite d'une conférence qu'il fit à des professionnels à la *N.-Y. Architectural League*, au cours de laquelle il présenta cette exposition et tenta d'expliquer comment se pratiquaient les études d'architecture en France, que parut l'article auquel nous faisons allusion plus haut.

NOTES AND WORDS :

actuellement, at the present time

une campagne, campaign

donner prise à, to give aid to

maladroit, clumsy

il convient, it is necessary, suitable

massier, student-treasurer

le compte rendu, report, considered report

faire du zèle, make a show

une bourse d'étudiant, scholarship

emporter une exposition, to take an exhibition, *that is*, take it with him

tenter, to attempt

*Reading Vocabulary—*61

ressembler, *to resemble*

ressource, *resource*

RESTE, *remainder*

RESTER, *to remain*

résulter, *to result*

RETARD, *lateness*

retenir, *to detain, retain*

retentir, *to resound*

RETIRER, *to withdraw*

retomber, *to fall down*

RETOUR, *return*

RETOURNER, *to return*

retraite, *retreat*

retrouver, *to find again*

réunion, *reunion, meeting*

réunir, *to reunite*

RÉUSSIR, *to succeed*

revanche, *revenge*

rêve, *dream*

réveiller, *to awaken*

Reading Vocabulary—62

révéler, *to reveal*	rivière, *river*
REVENIR, *to return*	robe, *dress*
rêver, *to dream*	roi, *king*
revêtir, *to put on, reclothe*	rôle, *part*
revoir, *to see again*	ROMPRE, *to break*
révolution, *revolution*	ronde, *round*
richesse, *riches*	rougir, *to blush, turn red*
rideau, *curtain*	rouler, *to roll*
RIRE, *to laugh*	ROUTE, *road*
risquer, *to risk*	RUE, *street*

§ 5. *French Poetry*

French poetry differs profoundly from English poetry—so much so that our first impulse is to advise the student to avoid it altogether for a year or so, until he or she feels very confident of ability to read almost anything in prose without difficulty. And yet, we feel on second thoughts that this is not the best advice that can be given. We may perhaps compromise by saying that, for at least a year or eighteen months, even those students who love poetry should be content with reading only the simplest French poems, of which there are many. It is not that words and grammar in poetry are much more difficult than in prose, but that the *spirit* of French poetry differs greatly from the spirit of our poetry. The reason is not far to seek: poetry represents an elevation of the human spirit, and the best poets possess great powers of the imagination and of expression. We feel therefore that it is absolutely essential for the learner of French—or any language—to master *first* the *normal* mode of expression—which is prose. Once this has been achieved, the field of poetry offers joys of a nature that are peculiar to itself.

However, there is one piece of French verse with which you can hardly fail to make acquaintance : **La Marseillaise,** written by Rouget de Lisle on April 26th, 1792, to express the patriotic upsurge of the nation arming itself to fight for independence against a European coalition. This inspiring song is the French national anthem. You should know at least the first verse :

Allons, enfants de la patrie,
Le jour de gloire est arrivé !
Contre nous de la tyrannie
L'étendard sanglant est levé ! (*bis*)
Entendez-vous, dans les campagnes,
Mugir ces féroces soldats ?
Ils viennent jusque dans nos bras
Égorger vos fils, vos compagnes.

Aux armes citoyens ! formez vos bataillons !
Marchons ! (*bis*) Qu'un sang impur abreuve nos sillons !

étendard, standard
sanglant, blood-stained
les campagnes, countryside
mugir, to roar
égorger, to massacre, cut the throat

compagne, female companion
compagnes, womenfolk
abreuver, to water, *but here it means* to drench
le sillon, furrow, *but here it can mean* " our fields "

It is worth learning by heart, especially if you know the tune.

¶ 15. SALAMMBÔ

La houle des soldats se poussait. Ils n'avaient plus peur.
Ils recommençaient à boire. Les parfums qui leur coulaient
du front mouillaient de gouttes larges leurs tuniques en lambeaux, et s'appuyant des deux poings sur les tables qui leur
semblaient osciller comme des navires, ils promenaient à l'entour
leurs gros yeux ivres, pour dévorer par la vue ce qu'ils ne pouvaient
prendre. D'autres, marchant tout au milieu des plats sur les
nappes de pourpre, cassaient à coups de pied les escabeaux
d'ivoire et les fioles tyriennes en verre. Les chansons se mêlaient
au râle des esclaves agonisant parmi les coupes brisées. Ils
demandaient du vin, des viandes, de l'or. Ils criaient pour
avoir des femmes. Ils déliraient en cent langages. Quelques-
uns se croyaient aux étuves, à cause de la buée qui flottait autour
d'eux, ou bien, apercevant des feuillages, ils s'imaginaient être à

la chasse et couraient sur leurs compagnons comme sur des
bêtes sauvages. L'incendie de l'un à l'autre gagnait tous les
arbres, et les hautes masses de verdure, d'où s'échappaient de
longues spirales blanches, semblaient des volcans qui commencent
à fumer. La clameur redoublait; les lions blessés rugissaient
dans l'ombre.

Le palais s'éclaira d'un seul coup à sa plus haute terrasse, la
porte du milieu s'ouvrit, et une femme, la fille d'Hamilcar elle-
même, couverte de vêtements noirs, apparut sur le seuil. Elle
descendit le premier escalier qui longeait obliquement le premier
étage, puis le second, le troisième, et elle s'arrêta sur la dernière
terrasse, au haut de l'escalier des galères. Immobile et la tête
basse, elle regardait les soldats.

Derrière elle, de chaque côté, se tenaient deux longues
théories d'hommes pâles, vêtus de robes blanches à franges
rouges qui tombaient droit sur leurs pieds. Ils n'avaient
pas de barbe, pas de cheveux, pas de sourcils. Dans leurs
mains étincelantes d'anneaux ils portaient d'énormes lyres et
chantaient tous, d'une voie aiguë, un hymne à la divinité de
Carthage. C'étaient les prêtres eunuques du temple de Tanit,
que Salammbô appelait souvent dans sa maison.

NOTES AND WORDS:

la houle, surge
se pousser, to push forward
une goutte, drop
en lambeaux, ragged, in rags
s'appuyer, to lean, press upon
à l'entour, round about
une nappe, cloth (table)
casser, to break
à coups de pied, with kicks
les escabeaux, stools
les fioles, phials
le râle, rattle (in the throat)
étuves, steam baths
la buée, mist

l'incendie, fire
rugir, to roar
le seuil, doorstep, threshold
longer, to go, run along
le premier étage, the first
  storey
au haut de, at the height of,
  on a level with
théories, *here means* proces-
  sions
sourcils, eyebrows
étincelant, sparkling
aigu (aiguë), sharp, shrill,
  (*lit.* acute)

Reading Vocabulary—63

ruine, *ruin*

ruiner, *to ruin*

SABLE, *sand*

sac, *sack, knapsack*

sacrifice, *sacrifice*

SAISIR, *to seize*

saison, *season*

SALLE, *hall*

SALON, *drawing room*

SALUER, *to salute*

salut, *salvation*

SANG, *blood*

SANTÉ, *health*

satisfaction, *satisfaction*

satisfaire, *to satisfy*

SAUTER, *to jump*

SAUVER, *to save*

savant, *savant*

SAVOIR, *to know*

scène, *scene*

LESSON XXI

§ 1. *Parisian French*—Le **langage populaire**

IN the preceding lesson (§ 4) we informed you that written French is more " disciplined " than spoken French, and we also referred to **le langage populaire.** The French spoken by the educated Parisian is considered to be the " best " French; and it is the standard, in pronunciation, grammar, and modes of expression to be aimed at. That is what you have been learning throughout this course. But, we should hardly do justice to the course if we omitted mention of **le langage populaire,** the speech of ordinary people and of the working class in general. This is not to be confused with **l'argot,** *slang,* the speech of the **Apaches,** of the roughs and toughs, which you will avoid. The French do not disregard **le langage populaire.** Some years ago a learned professor published a magnificent book on the subject, a work which was crowned by the Academy. This fact, and the fact that **le langage populaire** is very much alive —you will hear it all around you in Paris—justifies introducing the subject here, although it is one almost invariably avoided in such courses as this. Its avoidance largely explains why students who have worked hard at French find themselves baffled or often completely at a loss to understand the simplest conversation around them. We do not propose to offer more than a sketch of **le langage populaire,** but that should be sufficient to make you aware of its existence and help you to deal with it.

First, there are certain differences in pronunciation between **le langage populaire** and " standard French," only one of which you need note. This is the stress on a word. In standard French, the stress is always on the *last* syllable; in popular French, especially in Paris, the syllables of a word are either stressed equally or on the syllable *before* the last. This may seem a very small matter, but it can make a considerable difference to sound. The word **Paris,** for example, is correctly pro-

nounced with the stress on the **-is ;** the Parisian will often pronounce it **PAris,** with the stress on the **Pa.** When you hear
this in all sorts of words—**adMISSion, PARler, PENsée**—you
can be fairly sure that a Parisian speaks. Furthermore, the
voice is raised slightly with the stress, which gives it a musical
intonation characteristic of **le français de la capitale.**

¶ 16. SALAMMBÔ—Fin

Enfin elle descendit l'escalier des galères. Les prêtres la
suivirent. Elle s'avança dans l'avenue des cyprès, et elle
marchait lentement entre les tables des capitaines, qui se reculaient
un peu en la regardant passer.

Sa chevelure, poudrée d'un sable violet, et réunie en forme de
tour selon la mode des vièrges chananéennes, la faisait paraître
plus grande. Des tresses de perles attachées à ses tempes
descendaient jusqu'aux coins de sa bouche, rose comme une
grenade entr'ouverte. Il y avait sur sa poitrine un assemblage
de pierres lumineuses, imitant par leur bigarrure les écailles
d'une murène. Ses bras, garnis de diamants, sortaient nus de sa
tunique sans manches, étoilée de fleurs rouges sur un fond tout
noir. Elle portait entre les chevilles une chaînette d'or pour
régler sa marche, et son grand manteau de pourpre sombre,
taillé dans une étoffe inconnue, traînait derrière elle, faisant à
chacun de ses pas comme une large vague qui la suivait.

Les prêtres, de temps à autre, pinçaient sur leurs lyres des
accords presque étouffés, et dans les intervalles de la musique,
on entendait le petit bruit de la chaînette d'or avec le claquement
régulier de ses sandales en papyrus.

Personne encore ne la connaissait. On savait seulement
qu'elle vivait retirée dans des pratiques pieuses. Des soldats
l'avaient aperçue la nuit, sur le haut de son palais, à genoux
devant les étoiles, entre les tourbillons des cassolettes allumées.
C'était la lune qui l'avait rendue si pâle, et quelque chose des
Dieux l'enveloppait comme une vapeur subtile. Ses prunelles
semblaient regarder tout au loin au delà des espaces terrestres.
Elle marchait en inclinant la tête, et tenait à sa main droite une
petite lyre d'ébène.

Ils l'entendaient murmurer : " Morts ! Tous morts ! "

NOTES AND WORDS:

le prêtre, priest	**les écailles d'une murène,**
suivre, to follow	the scales of a muraena
se reculer, to withdraw	(lamprey)
la chevelure, hair	**les chevilles,** ankles
le sable, sand	**une chaînette,** a little chain
réunir, to join	**une vague,** wave
chananéennes, Canaanite	**pincer,** to pluck, play a stringed
la tempe, temple	instrument
le coin, corner	**étouffé,** stifled, muffled
entr'ouvert, half-open	**cassolettes,** perfume pans, in-
bigarrure, medley	cense burners

This completes the excerpts from **Salammbô**, and they should give you a very good idea of the verve and power of Flaubert. Although the subject is historical, and therefore many of the words deal with somewhat unfamiliar subjects, we decided that the advantages of reading such magnificent passages of French far outnumber the disadvantages. You have made the acquaintance of the language, if not at its best then certainly on a high level. A second reading—which is necessary—should increase your appreciation. Flaubert can be read again and again, always with benefit.

Reading Vocabulary—64

science, *knowledge*	semblables, *fellow men*
scrupule, *scruple*	SEMBLER, *to seem*
séance, *meeting*	semer, *to sow*
seconde, *second*	sens, *direction*
secouer, *to shake*	sensation, *feeling*
SECOURS, *help*	sentier, *path*
secret, *secret*	sentiment, *sentiment*
secrétaire, *secretary*	SENTIR, *to smell of ; to feel*
seigneur, *lord*	SÉPARER, *to separate*
SEMAINE, *week*	SÉRIE, *series*

§ 2. Le langage populaire—*suite*

In French popular speech, words are often modified or abbreviated, and such words are not difficult to recognize.   Here are some examples :

un apéritif, aperitive, becomes **un apéro**
une photographie   „   **une photo**
un mécanicien, mechanic, becomes **un mécano**
le pharmacien, druggist   „   **le pharmaco**
le Métropolitain, the Paris Underground subway   }**le Métro**

The names of streets and places are abridged in all sorts of ways which even the foreigner can recognize :

le boulevard Sébastopol   **le Sébasto**
les Fortifications   **les Fortifs**

A very common word is **rigoler,** which has two meanings :
(1) *to laugh* and (2) *to have fun, enjoy oneself*.   If one person says something silly or stupid, another will reply : **Ça me fait rigoler.**   Une **rigolade** is *a lark*; and **un rigoleur, un rigolot,** is *a funny chap, a joker* or, it may be, a person not to be taken seriously.   Ordinary people tend to consider counting in **centimes** as rather " elegant," and instead they count in **sous.** **Un sou = 5 centimes.**   Thus, **deux sous = 10 centimes. Cent sous = 5 francs.   Vingt sous = 1 franc.**   Until you get accustomed to it, this can be disconcerting.*

Sufficient has been said already to give some idea of the difference between **le langage populaire** and academic French, and in the next sections of this lesson you will be given a selection of nouns, adjectives, verbs, as well as some phrases which you are likely to hear any day in Paris.

We have warned you against **l'argot** and against confusing it with **le langage populaire. L'argot des malfaiteurs,** the slang of the " tough guys," is used by them, but it is also used for " swank " by a rather unpleasant type of **boulevardier** whom it is better not to know.   The foreigner who attempts to use this **argot** among decent French people is liable to be looked at

* With inflation the **sou** becomes useless and tends to disappear.

askance, the inference being that he has been frequenting the
company of very bad people.   At the same time, a slang word
creeps here and there into **le langage populaire** and becomes
hallowed by usage.   It is sometimes difficult to draw the line
between the two.

Those students who are not likely to visit France for some
time need not learn the lists which follow.   Such students
should concentrate on reading, shortwave broadcasts, and records, and attendance at French films.

Le Cinéma

Il arrive trop souvent, dans l'une des premières phases de la
création d'un film : l'établissement du " découpage ," qu'on
ne tient pas suffisamment compte du rôle *actif* que pourrait
avoir la musique dans certains passages du film.   En général,
dans la plupart des " découpages ," la dernière colonne mentionne
les apparitions de la musique d'une façon plus ou moins vague.
Il y a des exceptions, comme par exemple les découpages de
J. Grémillon, où la fonction de la musique désirée est soigneuse-
ment désignée, minutieusement expliquée.   Mais le plus souvent
le découpage ne fait qu'indiquer assez sommairement les
interventions musicales.

Dans presque tous ces cas, la musique ne semble, dans l'esprit
de l'auteur du film, jouer qu'un rôle, à l'arrière-plan, de toile de
fond : elle devra, bien sûr, agir sur le spectateur, mais sans
qu'il en soit vraiment conscient.   La musique n'est-elle pas, de
tous les arts, celle qui agit sur l'inconscient avec le plus de
subtilité et de profondeur ?   " On ne doit jamais écouter une
musique de film, mais la subir " semble d'ailleurs l'adage favori
à cet égard de beaucoup de techniciens de la mise en scène,
particulièrement à Hollywood.   Cet adage peut et doit certes
être vrai en beaucoup d'occasions.   Pourtant on néglige par
trop d'autres possibilités que la musique offre parmi les facteurs
d'expression décisifs du film, et le rôle de tout premier plan
qu'elle pourrait parfois jouer.   On ne sait pas assez prévoir les
passages où toute une scène peut être axée sur sa propre musique,
et il est étrange que seule une exception soit de mise à cet égard :
celle du dessin animé.   Là, des gags—idées ou mouvements—

reposent exclusivement sur une intime subordination de l'image à la musique, mariage—on l'a souvent remarqué—analogue, quoique plus intime encore, à celui du ballet. Mais, là encore, ce principe n'a donné naissance chez les Américains qu'à une pauvre série de poncifs (le poulailler jouant une ouverture d'opéra, le jazz d'animaux sauvages) qui nous ravissaient au début—mais, à force de répétitions, nous lassent maintenant, jusqu'à déterminer la crise des ateliers américains. Pourtant quelles richesses inouïes n'existe-t-il pas dans ce pays féerique dont on n'a fait qu'entrouvrir une des portes. Et pourquoi limiter cet emploi impérieux de la musique au seul dessin animé ?

NOTES AND WORDS :

Il arrive, it happens

le découpage, the cutting (editing of a film)

tenir compte de, to take account of

sommairement, summarily

à l'arrière plan, background

l'inconscient, the unconscious

subir, to submit to

la mise en scène, production (of a film, play)

prévoir, to foresee

le dessin animé, animated drawing

le poncif, conventional pattern, conventionalism

le poulailler, hen roost, "peanut heaven"

ce pays féerique, fairyland

entrouvrir, to half-open

*Reading Vocabulary—*65

serrer, *to squeeze, to put away, to lock*

servante, *servant* (f.)

service, *service*

SERVIR, *to serve*

serviteur, *servant* (m.)

seuil, *threshold*

SIÈCLE, *century*

siège, *siege*

signe, *sign*

signer, *to sign*

signifier, *to signify, to indicate*

silence, *silence*

simplicité, *simplicity*

situation, *situation*

situer, *to be situated*

société, *society*

SŒUR, *sister*

SOIF, *thirst*

soigner, *to take care of*

SOIN, *care, attention*

§ 3. **Le langage populaire**—*Some Common Nouns*

LANGAGE POPULAIRE	LANGUE ÉCRITE	ENGLISH
Acrais !	Attention !	*Look out ! Danger !*
un aristo	aristocrate	*aristocrat, a " somebody "*
un as	aviateur celèbre	*famous aviator,* or *any " first-class man "*
une bâfre	coup, gifle	*blow, smack*
une balade	promenade	*walk, stroll*
le ballon, la tôle	la prison	*jail, " clink "*
une balle	un franc	*franc. Cinq balles, etc.*
une bande (de)	réunion, groupe	*gang of, etc. (a term of insult)*
la barbe. La barbe !	ennui, Assez !	*A bore. Enough ! Shut up !*
une bécane	bicyclette	*" bike "*
le beuglon	café-concert	*a café with music, dancing and concert*
la bidoche	la viande	*meat, " grub "*
un bisteck	un bifteck	*beefsteak*
un bistro	marchand de vin	*wine shop*
la blague. Sans blague !	plaisanterie, mensonge	*joke, tall story. Impossible !*
le bloc	poste de police	*police station*
la bombe	la noce, fête	*" celebration," spree*
la boniche	la bonne	*maid, servant*
le boulot	le travail	*work, occupation*
le bourre	agent en bourgeois	*plain-clothes policeman*
le cafard	la tristesse	*sadness, blues*
le canard	histoire fausse	*lie, false story, low newspaper*
un canon	litre, bouteille de vin	*a liter or bottle of wine*
un chameau	femme ou personne, désagréable	*unpleasant person, usually female*
le chichi	minauderie	*simper, smirk*
la chose (also le machin)	chose	*the " what's its name," thingumajig*
Monsieur Chose	Monsieur un tel	*Mr. "What's-his-name"*
le copain	ami, camarade	*friend, pal*
la croûte	croûte, nourriture	*food, grub*
la dèche	pauvreté	*hardupness*
le dodo	le sommeil	*sleep. faire dodo*
une engueulade	insulte, injure	*abuse, wordy attack*
un fafiot	billet de banque	*banknote*
un flic	agent de police	*policeman, " cop "*
les frites	pommes de terre frites	*fried potatoes*

HISTOIRE VÉRIDIQUE DE "L'AIR" DE MAILLOL

Nous avons reçu de M. Paul Mesplé, conservateur du Musée des Augustins, une intéressante communication touchant la véridique histoire de la statue de Maillol L'Air qui vient d'être placée dans le jardin royal de Toulouse.

En attendant son érection, elle avait été déposée au terrain Maury, terrain municipal qui est à la fois dépôt des marbres, dépôt de bois, magasin de décors et d'une manière générale réserve des encombrements que la ville ne sait où caser. La statue y passa quelques mois, puis lorsque les menaces de bombardement se précisèrent, l'adjoint aux Beaux-Arts de l'époque, le regretté M. André Igon, et moi-même, jugeâmes que le terrain Maury, situé près de la gare, était un lieu trop exposé pour conserver un chef-d'œuvre et nous la fîmes transporter au Musée des Augustins, hors de la zone dangereuse. *L'Air* n'y fut nullement caché, mais fut au contraire le " clou " des nombreuses expositions que le musée organisa pendant la guerre en faveur des artistes réfugiés. Quand les Allemands occupèrent Toulouse, ils purent voir la statue autant qu'ils le voulurent. Ils ne tentèrent jamais de l'enlever. Peut-être que s'ils avaient gagné la guerre . . . mais ils ne l'ont pas gagnée.

NOTES AND WORDS:

véridique, true
conservateur du musée, curator of the museum
le terrain, ground, site
magasin de décors, store for (house) decorations.
un encombrement, encumbrance

caser, to house
l'adjoint, assistant
cacher, to hide
le clou, nail, *but here* " chief attraction "
enlever, to carry off

Reading Vocabulary—66

SOIR, *evening*
soirée, *evening* (*duration*)
SOL, *earth, soil*
SOLDAT, *soldier*
SOLEIL, *sun*
solitude, *solitude*
somme, *sum*
SOMMEIL, *sleep*
SON, *sound*
songer, *to think, dream*

SONNER, *to sound, ring a bell*
sort, *fate*
sorte, *kind*
sortie, *exit, sally*
SORTIR, *to go out, to come out*
sou, *copper* (20 sous = 1 franc)
souci, *care*
souffle, *puff*
souffler, *to blow*
souffrance, *suffering*

*Reading Vocabulary—*67

SOUFFRIR, *to suffer*
SOUHAITER, *to wish*
soulever, *to lift up*
SOULIER, *shoe*
soumettre, *to subdue, submit*
soupçonner, *to suspect*
soupir, *sigh*
source, *spring*
sourire, *to smile*
le sourire, *smile*

soutenir, *to sustain, to support*
le souvenir, *keepsake, recollection*
souvenir(se), *to remember*
spectacle, *spectacle*
station, *station*
statue, *statue*
style, *style*
subir, *to suffer, to undergo*
succéder, *to follow*
SUCCÈS, *success*

§ 4. **Le langage populaire**—*Nouns and Adjectives*

Langage populaire	Langue écrite	English
une gaffe	erreur, bêtise	*mistake, "boner"*
un gaga	imbécile	*fool, idiot*
la gare. A la gare !	le diable	*the devil, " Get out ! ", " Let me have peace ! "*
un gonze, une gonzesse	homme, femme	*man, woman*
un, une gosse	enfant	*child*
la gueule	la bouche	*mouth, face*
un, une mioche	enfant	*child, " kid "*
le monde	les gens	*people*
le noir	tristesse, dégout	*sadness, " fedupness "*
un numéro	individu	*strange, odd person*
la panade	misère, gêne	*hardupness, brokenness*
le piston	recommendation	*(use of) influence*
le Parigot	le Parisien	*Parisien*
le pinard	vin (ordinaire)	*wine*
le poilu	homme fort, soldat	*soldier, French " Tommy "*
la popote	cuisine	*food, meal*
un raseur (-euse)	importun	*persistent bore*
le rond	sou, argent	*copper, cash,* **dix ronds** *= 10 sous*
le salaud	méchant	*unpleasant man, " pig "*
le sergot	sergent de ville	*policeman, copper*
le singe	conserve de bœuf	*canned beef*
le soûlot, soûlard	ivrogne	*drunkard*
le tuyau	renseignement	*information, " tip off "*
la veine	chance, bonne chance	*good luck*
Voui	oui	*often pronounced like this in Paris*
Zut ! Zut alors !		*A rather vulgar expression for which there is no equivalent. Perhaps "What the hell!" comes nearest.*

Some common Adjectives, etc.

allume	excité, ivre	*excited, " lit up "*
baba	étonné	*surprised*
ben	bien	*Eh ben ! And so . . .*
blèche	laid	*ugly*
bon sang !	Mon Dieu !	*Heavens !*
bu	ivre	*drunk, " tight "*
chenu	riche, bon, beau	*good, nice, fine*
crapule	mauvais, faux	*bad, evil*
cruche	stupide	*stupid*
épatant	merveilleux	*wonderful, grand, fine*
fichu	perdu, fini	*finished, " all in "*
gaga	imbécile	*silly, idiotic, "dumb"*

And there are many more !

MARCEL PROUST

Dans les lettres à lui adressées par Marcel Proust au temps de leur jeunesse et publiées sous le titre *A un ami*, par leur destinataire : M. Georges de Lauris, lui-même romancier délicat et parfait mémorialiste, il y a, comme toujours en pareil cas, tellement de choses qui font penser ou qui font rêver qu'on en est parfois ému comme si l'auteur même était là devant vous, et vous parlait.

Et l'on ne peut s'empêcher d'évoquer, avec mélancolie, ce temps, ce " temps perdu," si proche de nous en chronologie, si lointain à tous les autres points de vue, si *détaché* du nôtre, si coupé d'avec le nôtre, où les gens avaient le loisir de s'écrire, de se confesser les uns aux autres, de se confier leurs inquiétudes, leurs joies, tous leurs secrets.

On appelle ça " se regarder vivre," et l'on prétend que cela empêche de vivre. Je ne le crois guère. Entre l'introspection mécanique, acharnée, continuelle d'un Maine de Biran ou même d'un Amiel et ces épanchements ingénus, au jour le jour, sans arrière-pensée pédagogique ou philosophique, il y a une différence fondamentale.

Dans le cas (si caractéristique) de Marcel Proust, non seulement sa correspondance n'a pas nui à son œuvre proprement dite, mais elle lui a servi, et il est visible qu'elle lui sert, qu'il l'emploie un

peu à cet usage. Que de fois il revient sur les problèmes de
la création littéraire! que de fois il interroge ses amis, leur
demande conseil, les met au courant de ce qui le tracasse (même
dans le domaine de la publication proprement dite)! Mais
ce qui frappe avec le plus d'évidence, c'est justement ce lien
vivant qui existe ici entre l'homme et l'œuvre.

NOTES AND WORDS:

le destinataire, addressee
le romancier, novelist
en pareil cas, in such a case
rêver, to dream
s'empêcher de, to prevent
  oneself from
si coupé d'avec, so cut off
  from
le loisir, leisure
se confier, to confide in
se regarder vivre, to look at
  oneself living, alive
acharné, eager, keen, in-
  veterate

épanchements ingénus, in-
  nocent outpourings
au jour le jour, from day to
  day
arrière pensée, mental re-
  servation, *also* "ulterior
  motive"
nuire, to injure
Que de fois . . .! how often
  . . . !
au courant de, up to date
  with
tracasser, to worry
le lien, link, bond

Reading Vocabulary—68

SUFFIRE, *to suffice*
SUITE, *result, what follows*
SUIVRE, *to follow*
sujet, *cause, subject*
supplier, *to pray, to entreat*
supporter, *to endure*
supposer, *to suppose*
SUPPRIMER, *to suppress, to
  abolish*
surface, *surface*
SURPRENDRE, *to surprise*

surprise, *surprise*
SURTOUT, *overcoat*
surveiller, *to watch over*
suspendre, *to suspend, hang*
sympathie, *sympathy*
système, *system*
TABLE, *table*
tableau, *picture*
TÂCHE, *task*
TÂCHER, *to try*

§ 5. Le langage populaire—*Some Verbs and Phrases*

LANGAGE POPULAIRE	LANGUE ÉCRITE	ENGLISH
avoir	vaincre, attraper	*beat, catch out*, **on les** **aura,** *we'll beat them*
balader	se promener	*to walk*
barber	importuner	*annoy*
blaguer	plaisanter, mentir	*to joke, tell lies*
se boler	s'amuser beaucoup, rire	*to enjoy oneself greatly*
bouffer	manger	*to eat*
bourrer le crâne à quelqu'un	conter des mensonges	*to " tell the tale " to somebody*
casser la croûte	manger un morceau	*break one's hunger*
causer	parler	*much used in Paris for " to chat," " talk "*
chiner	se moquer de	*to make fun of*
crâner	être fier de, se vanter	*boast of, brag*
crever, crever de faim	mourir, mourir de faim	*to die, of hunger*
s'emballer	s'emporter	*to be carried away, excited*
engueuler	insulter, injurier	*to insult, go for*
épater	surprendre, étonner	*surprise, cause admiration*
la fermer	se taire	*to shut up*
ficher, se ficher de, ficher à la porte, ficher le camp	mettre, faire, aller, se moquer de, jetter à la porte, s'en aller	*a much-used verb*, **and** applied to most **things.** **Fichez-moi le camp!** *Clear off !*
gueuler	crier, parler haut	*to bawl, squall, yell*
marcher	marcher, travailler	*to go, function*
ça ne marche pas		*It won't work*
je ne marche pas		*I don't want to*
pieuter (se)	} coucher, se mettre au lit	*to go to bed, " hit the hay "*
plumer (se)		
rogner	grogner, être en colère	*to be angry, in a huff*
taper	emprunter à	*to borrow, touch for money*
se tordre	rire beaucoup	*to double with laughter*
zigouiller	tuer	*to kill*

Le langage populaire is rich in words of such a nature that we should not wish to reproduce them here. The French do not take " low " expressions as seriously as we do ! Many of them in everyday use become impossible when translated into English. The French think nothing of them.

Au temps ou la Seine possédait trois bras Paris était inondé chaque année

Les inondations sont devenues rares à Paris. On se souvient de l'hiver 1910 où l'on allait en barque à la gare St Lazare. Depuis les crues de la Seine n'ont jamais dépassé la menace d'inondation. Il n'en était pas de même aux temps anciens, où le fleuve débordait presque tous les ans. Car la Seine, comme le remarque M. Robert Christophe dans *Le Monde*, au lieu de traverser Paris par les deux bras actuels qui forment les îles Saint-Louis et de la Cité, en possédait autrefois trois.

Cet ancien bras de la Seine, moins large que les deux autres, traversait l'actuelle rive droite, entourant une grande île de 3 Km. de long sur 1.500 mètres de largeur. Si on prend une carte du Paris moderne on peut dire que ce bras quittait le lit principal aux environs de Bercy, passait par la Bastille, la République, la rue de Provence, le quartier Saint-Lazare pour rejoindre enfin le fleuve vers la place dé l'Alma.

C'était donc deux fleuves que l'on devait endiguer en temps de crue. Grégoire de Tours raconte qu'en 583 les eaux montèrent jusqu'à Saint-Laurent, c'est-à-dire près de l'actuelle gare de l'Est. En 1415, l'inondation devait durer jusqu'à la mi-avril. Quelques années plus tard, au mois de juin, une inondation subite venait éteindre les feux de joie de la nuit de la Saint-Jean.

On ignore à quelle date disparut ce troisième bras de la Seine. Il est remarquable que lors de la crue de 1910 l'inondation fit reprendre à la Seine l'ancien parcours du troisième bras : des traces de vin prélevées dans l'eau recouvrant la rue St Lazare montrèrent que le flot venait de Bercy.

[From: *La France* (published in London).]

Notes and Words :

en barque, in a boat
la crue, rising (of a river)
déborder, to overflow
au lieu de, instead of
autrefois, formerly
quitter, to quit, leave
endiguer, to dam up

la mi-avril, mid-April
éteindre, to extinguish
ignorer, not to know, be ignorant of
le parcours, course (of river)
prélever, taken from
flot, flood

Reading Vocabulary—69

taille, *stature*

taire (se), *to remain silent*

talent, *ability*

tapis, *carpet*

tarder, *to delay*

TÉMOIN, *witness*

TEMPS, *time, weather*

tendre, *to hold out*

tendresse, *tenderness*

TENIR, *to hold*

tenter, *to attempt*

tenue, *dress*

terme, *rent*

TERMINER, *to finish*

terrain, *land*

TERRE, *earth*

terreur, *terror*

TÊTE, *head*

théâtre, *theater*

théorie, *theory*

LESSON XXII

§ 1. *Pitfalls for the Unwary*

We have earlier in the course drawn your attention to the thousands of similar words in French and English, and told you that you should take advantage of this fact to enlarge your French vocabulary. But we should be failing in our duty if we did not also draw your attention to the fact that sometimes a word which is the same or almost the same in both languages can mean quite different things in each. Take, for example, the English word *control* and the French **contrôler** and **le contrôle**. *Control* is defined in *Webster's New Collegiate Dictionary* as *power or authority to control; reserve or restraint.* *To control* is *to check or regulate, to exercise directing, guiding,* or *restraining power over.* On looking up **le contrôle** in a good French-English dictionary, you will find that it means, among other things, *the checking or verification of information; the auditing* or *checking of accounts.* It also means the checking point in a race or test (or pilot) run. **Contrôle des présences** means *checking attendance* or *timekeeping.* The French verb **contrôler** means to *check, supervise, verify a fact,* and *to examine* passports or tickets. **Le contrôle des passeports** means *the examination* or *checking of passports.* **Le contrôleur** is the *inspector, supervisor, examiner, ticket collector* (on a train). The adjective *contrôlable* means that which *can be checked or verified.*

This one example should suffice to put you on your guard for pitfalls. From what we have said, you will realize that **contrôle des prix** would mean *checking* or *examination of prices* and not *control of prices*—this would be **la surveillance des prix.** For a person to *control himself* is **se dominer,** and for a teacher to control his pupils is **tenir ses elèves**—**contrôler ses elèves** would mean *to check* or *count them over.*

Another example of a common French word which requires care in translation : **actuel (-le)** means *of the present day, existing, current.* Thus **à l'heure actuelle** means *at the present*

320

hour—that is, day. **Le gouvernement actuel** is *the present government*. **L'actualité** means *reality* and **les actualités** are *current events*. If you go to the movies you may see **Vues d'actualité**, which we would call *news reels*.

LE PROPHÈTE PÉGUY

Devant ces deux gros volumes blancs où le critique littéraire de *France-Illustration* vient de donner à son œuvre la forme définitive, je songe à la publication première en plusieurs fascicules qui, l'un après l'autre, nous arrivaient naguère. Nous étions dans les ténèbres de l'occupation. *Le Prophète Péguy* (La Baconnière, Neuchâtel, et Albin Michel, Paris) paraissait à Genève, aux nobles " Cahiers du Rhône," dont Albert Béguin avait su faire " le plus bel organe de la pensée libre et de l'art courageux dans le monde asservi," comme le dit très bien André Rousseaux lui-même à la fin de sa préface. Ces élégants livrets bleu clair—la couleur angélique—étaient bien en vérité de précieux messagers ailés et qui nous apportaient l'air pur de la Suisse. André Rousseaux m'avait remis la première partie de son grand livre—celle qui s'appelle *le Poète de l'Incarnation*—au cours d'un voyage furtif à Paris, et j'ai sous les yeux sa dédicace : " En souvenir d'une soirée d'amitié et d'espérance, 26 août 1943." Ce soir-là, en effet, il avait évoqué ce *Péguy*, tout ce qu'il y mettait déjà, tout ce qu'il y devait mettre, tout ce que l'entreprise signifiait, enfin, pour lui, pour nous, pour la France. Qu'on m'excuse de rappeler ainsi un sentiment personnel ! Mais si j'ai voulu l'exprimer, et dès l'abord, c'est que le livre de Rousseaux apparaît essentiellement comme un témoignage et un témoignage historique. Combien elles sont éloquentes, dans leur simplicité lapidaire, les deux dates où s'encadre la composition du livre : *Lyon, 6 décembre 1940*; *Dieulefit, 14 août 1944* ! Dans cette œuvre des années tragiques, ce n'est point hasard si le choix de l'auteur s'est invinciblement fixé sur ce modèle. On sait qu'il y a des temps où, si les hommes se taisent, ce sont les pierres mêmes qui crient. Mais, lorsque les hommes sont contraints de se taire, les plus fiers d'entre eux inventent quelque moyen détourné de parler quand même. Cette voix, de surcroît, pour les uns ce fut la poésie, pour d'autres quelque ouvrage sur un héros du passé dont la stature prenait alors sa vrai hauteur.

NOTES AND WORDS: Charles Péguy (1872-1914), a writer whose fame increases with the passage of time. " Truth at any cost " was his dominating principle. He wrote: **" Qui ne gueule pas la vérité, quand il sait la vérité, se fait le complice des menteurs et des faussaires "**—" *He who does not shout the truth when he knows the truth becomes the accomplice of the liars and fakers.*"

en fascicules, in installments
naguère, only lately
asservi, enslaved
ailé, winged
remettre, to send, deliver
la dédicace, dedication
dès l'abord, from the outset
encadrer, to frame, enclose

se taisent, *from* **se taire,** to keep silent
crier, to shout
un moyen détourné, a roundabout way
quand même, just the same, even so
surcroît, in addition

Reading Vocabulary—70

TIRER, *to fire ; to take* or *draw out*
titre, *title*
toile, *cloth, material*
toilette, *toilet*
TOIT, *roof*
TOMBER, *to fall*
ton, *tone*
torrent, *torrent, stream*
TORT, *wrong, harm*
total, *total*

TOUCHER, *to touch*
le tour, *turn, round*
la tour, *tower*
TOURNER, *to turn*
trace, *track, impression*
tradition, *tradition*
traduire, *to translate*
trahir, *to betray*
train, *train*
traîner, *to drag*

§ 2. *Further Examples of Pitfalls*

There is another kind of pitfall for the unwary. As you know, we use many French words and phrases in English. For example, we shout *Encore!* at the theatre, and we often talk of a writer having a *nom de plume*. You may be a little surprised to learn that the French do not use these expressions. When we would say *Encore!* the French would say **Bis!** which literally means *twice*; and they use either **pseudonyme** or **nom de guerre** for *pen name*. In English we use the French word **massage** outside its significance for the French, which tends to be strictly medical in reference to human beings, though it also means rubbing down a horse! At the French hairdresser's " a massage " is **une friction**—and a shampoo becomes **un shampoo-ing**. Ladies should be extremely wary about using in France those French words relating to fashions and clothes which have become somewhat hallowed in the English-speaking world. **Un modèle**, for example, in France means simply a *pattern;* a sample of cloth is **un échantillon**. **Une brassière** is the old-fashioned corset cover, and for what is called in America a **brassière**, the French say **un soutien-gorge**. The chances are about ten to one that the French use quite a different term to express those "French" expressions which our **modistes** and **couturières** use as their jargon in the fond belief that they are being very "smart" and up to date. Ladies must be on guard about this sort of thing.

Let us take still another example of the pitfall : **opportunité** and the English *opportunity*. **L'opportunité** is seldom used at all in French, but when used it means *timeliness, opportuneness* or *expediency*. The ordinary French word for *opportunity* is **occasion**. **Saisir** or **prendre l'occasion de** is *to seize* or *take the opportunity to* (*do something.*) **Je prends l'occasion de vous parler,** *I take the opportunity to speak to you.* **A la première occasion,** *on the first opportunity*. **A l'occasion,** *in case of need*. And note the term **d'occasion,** which means *secondhand:* **des livres d'occasion,** *secondhand books*. **Une vente d'occasion** can mean a " *bargain sale* " as well as a *sale of secondhand goods*. And for a *job lot* the term is **des marchandises d'occasion**.

We can often afford to be a little slipshod in English; but the French prefer accuracy. Experience will teach you this.

La Comédie Parisienne
Par J.-L. Forain

"Ma pauvre enfant, tous mes regrets, mais je n'ai pas de monnaie, je n'ai qu'un louis."

"Mais, monsieur, ça ne fait rien, papa va vous rendra."

NOTES AND WORDS: **un louis,** *a gold piece of* 20 *francs,* long disappeared. It was called **un Louis d'or. Ça ne fait rien,** *That does not matter.* **rendre,** *to give back, return;* here " to give change."

Reading Vocabulary—71

trait, *feature (of one's face)*

traité, *treaty*

traiter, *to treat*

transformer, *to transform*

transport, *transport*

transporter, *to transport*

TRAVAIL, *work*

TRAVAILLER, *to work*

traverser, *to traverse, to pierce*

trembler, *to tremble*

tremper, *to soak*

trésor, *treasure*

triomphe, *triumph*

tristesse, *sadness*

TROMPER, *to deceive*

TROU, *hole*

trouble, *trouble, agitation*

troubler, *to disturb*

troupe, *company*

TROUVER, *to find*

§ 3. *Some uses of the Verb* FAIRE

The verb **FAIRE,** *to do, to make, to cause to,* requires special attention not only because it is used in so many ways but because it is one of the most frequently recurring verbs in the language. Yet, if one always remembers its " basic " meaning, there is no great difficulty about grasping its various usages. **Que faire ?** *What to do?* obviously means *What is to be done?* with the further implication *What is to be done about it?* **J'aurai de quoi faire,** *I shall have something to do,* can be appreciated in its extended meaning : *I shall have my work cut out.* **Un homme à tout faire,** *a man to do everything,* is clearly what we call a *factotum.* **Cela fait mon affaire,** *That makes my business*—in other words, *That suits me.* **Qu'est-ce que ça fait ?** *What does that make = What does it matter?* **Ça ne fait rien !** *That does not matter !*

You will remember that **FAIRE** is used for the weather. **Il fait beau,** *it is fine.* **Il fait mauvais temps,** *The weather is bad.* **Il fait chaud, froid,** *It is hot, cold,* and so on.

Faire faire, *to cause to be made.* **J'ai fait faire un costume,** *I have had a suit (costume) made.*

Ne faire que, *only to, to do nothing but* . . . Thus : **Ma sœur ne fait que coudre toute la journée,** *My sister does nothing but sew all day.*

Se faire, with an infinitive, *to have oneself;* **je me fais photographier,** *I have myself photographed.* **Se faire** also means *to become, to develop.* Thus : **Voilà un jeune homme qui se**

fait, *There's a young man who is developing.*   **Le fromage s'est
fait,** *The cheese has become (ripe).*   **Se faire protestant, catho-
lique,** *to become a protestant, catholic.*   **Il se fait tard,** *It is
growing late.*

All these are logical and straightforward enough.   But there
are other uses of **faire** of which the same cannot be said with
such confidence.   **Y FAIRE** means *to avail.*   Thus : **Rien n'y
fait,** *Nothing avails, There is nothing to be done about it,* and
Qu'y faire ? *What's to be done about it?*   **EN FAIRE** means
to do about something.   Thus : **Ce qu'il en fait, c'est pour
nous tous,** *What he is doing (about it) is for all of us.*   Finally,
our slang expression *to pull a fast one,* meaning to deceive or
bamboozle somebody, is **LA FAIRE. Je la lui ai fait à la
vertu,** *I have done it to him in the virtuous way = I pulled a fast
one on him with a virtuous attitude.*   And : **On ne me la fait
pas !** *Nothing doing ! I'm not to be swindled !*

Emile Zola et " J'Accuse "

Le 13 janvier 1898, le numéro 83 de *L'Aurore,* édition spéciale
tirée à plus de 300,000 exemplaires, répandait dans Paris, dans
la France et dans le monde entier, une lettre ouverte d'Emile
Zola à Félix Faure, président de la République.

Elle portait sur toute la largeur de la page ce titre de feu :
" *J'accuse !* ", dont on a su par la suite qu'il était dû au génie
journalistique de Georges Clemenceau.

" *J'accuse !* " . . . Les mémoires de nombreux contemporains
enregistrent le choc qu'ils ont subi en lisant d'une traite ce docu-
ment qui, sous la forme d'un réquisitoire provocant, était avant
tout un plaidoyer révolutionnaire pour la vérité.   Personne ne
demeurait indifférent.   Léon Blum, dans " Souvenirs sur
l'Affaire," raconte : " *Un matin d'hiver, le père Granet (son
concierge), frappant du dehors à mon volet, me réveilla en
s'écriant: " Vite, monsieur, lisez ça. . . . C'est un article de
Zola dans* L'Aurore."   Et Octave Mirbeau, dans une lettre à
Zola : " *Jamais je n'ai été aussi ému, jamais je n'ai été pris aux
entrailles d'une façon aussi violente qu'en lisant, tout à l'heure, votre
lettre dans* L'Aurore. *C'est un jaillissement infini de lumière, et il
est douloureux de penser qu'il puisse se trouver quelque part
quelqu'un qui n'en soit pas baigné tout entier . . .*"

J'ai feuilleté les trente-neuf pages manuscrites que Zola a portées lui-même, le 12 janvier au soir, aux bureaux de *L'Aurore*. L'écriture y est large, ouverte, comme appliquée, achevée sans nervosité ; elle se déroule presque sans rature. Les pages sont numérotées de la main même de Zola de 1 à 39 parce que deux pages portent le numéro 23. Comme par respect pour ce texte, ni la rédaction ni l'imprimerie ne l'ont surchargé des multiples et usuelles indications typographiques.

NOTES AND WORDS: Émile Zola (1840–1902), famous " Naturalist " writer, whose **J'accuse** in defense of Dreyfus caused a sensation. **tirer,** literally *to draw*, is also used for *to publish, to circulate.*

le tirage, printing, circulation	**un jaillissement,** a gush
répandre, to pour out	**appliqué,** studious, careful
la largeur, the breadth, width	**se dérouler,** to unfold
titre de feu, fiery title	**rater,** to misfire, spoil
subi, sustained, *from* **subir**	**raturer,** to scratch out
une traite, stretch, sitting	**sans rature,** without an
un plaidoyer, pleading	erasure
le volet, shutter	**surcharger,** to surcharge,
les entrailles, bowels (of mercy)	write over, overload

Reading Vocabulary—72

TUER, *to kill*	vanité, *vanity*
type, *type*	varier, *to vary*
union, *union*	veille, *day before, eve*
unir, *to unite*	veiller, *to watch over*
usage, *use*	VENDRE, *to sell*
USER, *to wear out*	VENIR, *to come*
utiliser, *to utilize*	VENT, *wind*
VAINCRE, *to conquer, to beat*	VENTE, *sale*
VALEUR, *value*	VÉRITÉ, *truth*
VALOIR, *to be worth*	VERRE, *glass*

§ 4. *French Proverbs*

The French language has its proverbs, though it is perhaps not so rich in them as some other languages. Moreover, they are not greatly used in ordinary conversation as they are, for example, in Spanish—this being possibly due to the fact that the

French outlook is a little cynical, and hence there is a tendency to regard the person who uses proverbs in conversation as sententious. But they are not uncommon in literature. In all languages, but especially in French, proverbs are short, pithy sayings representing the wisdom or outlook of the race. They should not be confused with those trite or platitudinous sayings to which recourse is had by the dull speaker or writer.

As regards grammar, there is one point to note in French proverbial sayings : the article is often omitted where it would otherwise be necessary. Thus : **à bon chat, bon rat,** literally *To a good cat, a good rat* or as we might say *A thief to catch a thief*. And : **Contentement passe richesse,** *Contentment is better than riches*. Otherwise the proverb follows the general rules and usage of the language.

Here are some examples of proverbs which are said to be essentially French :

> **A la chandelle la chèvre semble demoiselle,** By light of the candle, the she-goat seems a young lady. (All cats are grey in the dark.)
>
> **Autant vaut être mordu d'un chien que d'une chienne,** It is the same whether one is bitten by a dog or by a bitch.
>
> **Bouche serrée, mouche n'y entre,** A shut mouth no fly enters.
>
> **Brebis qui bêle perd sa goulée,** A sheep which bleats loses a mouthful.
>
> **C'est le double plaisir de tromper le trompeur,** It is a double pleasure to deceive the deceiver.
>
> **L'habit ne fait pas le moine,** The habit does not make the monk.
>
> **Chacun pour soi et Dieu pour tous,** Each for himself and God for all.
>
> **Contre fortune bon cœur,** Against (ill-) fortune set a stout heart.
>
> **Donner un œuf pour avoir un bœuf,** To give an egg to have an ox.
>
> **D'un sac à charbon ne sort de blanche farine,** From a coal sack, white flour does not come.

NOTES AND WORDS:

rédiger, to draw up, edit, prepare
une équipe, team, group, gang of workmen
aider, to help
un ouvrage, work

signaler, to indicate
un compte rendu, report (carefully made)
abonner, subscribe
tarder, to delay

Reading Vocabulary—73–74

vers, *verse*
verser, *to pour out*
vertu, *virtue*
VÊTEMENT, *garment*
VÊTIR, *to dress*
vice, *vice*
victime, *victim*
VICTOIRE, *victory*
VIE, *life*
village, *village*

VILLE, *town*
VIN, *wine*
violence, *violence*
VISAGE, *face*
viser, *to aim*
VISITE, *visit*
visiter, *to visit*
VITESSE, *speed*
vitre, *pane of glass*
VIVRE, *to live*

vocabulaire, *vocabulary*
vœu, *vow*
voie, *way*
VOIR, *to see*
VOISIN, *neighbor*
VOISINAGE, *neighborhood*
VOITURE, *carriage*
VOIX, *voice*
LA VOLAILLE, *fowl*
le vol, *theft*

le volant, *(steering) wheel*
VOLER, *to fly ; to steal*
VOLONTÉ, *will*
voter, *to vote*
VOULOIR, *to wish*
vouloir dire, *to mean*
VOYAGEUR, *traveler*
vrai, *true*
VUE, *view, sight*

§ 5. *Maxims and Writers of Maxims*

The writing of "maxims" seems to have attracted French thinkers and writers from early times, so much so that the **maxime** is a literary form for which the French have been famous since the great La Rochefoucauld published his immortal **Réflexions ou Sentences et Maximes morales** in 1665 and established a fashion. There are many collections of **Maximes,** with which may be included the **Pensées** ("Thoughts") of such authors as Pascal. We mention the maxims here, first, because of their popularity and, second, because no modern language is by its nature better suited to their composition. The essence of the French maxim is its conciseness and clarity, to which is added wit or wisdom. There can be no disguising one thing : the **Maximes** or the **Pensées** of the great writers are not always easy reading for the foreigner. They are often the despair of translators precisely because of the immense pains taken by their writers to make them perfect as regards precision and form. To understand a French **maxime** or **pensée,** you must know the *exact* meaning of every word and its connotation in the particular example. While we do not recommend the student to devote much time to this branch of literature until he is confident of his knowledge, this is not to say that he need ignore it entirely. There can be no better exercise than to tackle a few maxims from time to time, and work at them until their wisdom has been extracted and their literary beauty appreciated.

Take, for example, the one that is said to be the basis of La Rochefoucauld's philosophy : **Nos vertus ne sont le plus souvent que des vices déguisés.** This is not difficult to understand : *Our virtues more often (than not) are only disguised vices.* The term **amour-propre,** much used by this writer, has no exact equivalent in English, into which it can be rendered by any of the following : *egoism, self-esteem, vanity, conceit, self-respect, legitimate pride.* Now consider La Rochefoucauld's maxims : **L'amour-propre est le plus grand des flatteurs** and **L'amour-propre est plus habile que le plus habile homme du monde.** *Self-esteem is the greatest of flatterers* and *Self-esteem is cleverer than the cleverest man in the world.* No English equivalent is ever entirely satisfactory. But you can appreciate the meaning, and enjoy the perfect style. One day you will revel in these *Maximes!*

DIAGNOSTIC A LA MODE INDIENNE

Les sorciers-guérisseurs d'une tribu indienne de Chili ont, depuis des temps immémoriaux, fait une juste remarque, à savoir que, pour être bien renseigné sur la maladie, rien ne vaut l'examen direct des organes du malade. Ce n'est pas à dire, d'ailleurs, qu'ils font précéder leur diagnostic de l'autopsie de leur client. Ils procèdent par un détour, qui révèle, sinon des connaissances médicales indiscutables, du moins une grande ingéniosité.

Le sorcier, après un rapide examen du malade, se fait apporter soit un agneau, soit un porcelet bien vivant. Ayant étudié minutieusement l'animal, s'il le juge apte à ce qu'il attend de lui, il le confie à deux hommes présents, qui le saisissent, l'un par les pattes de devant, l'autre par les pattes de derrière, et l'étendent sur la couche du malade, tout contre celui-ci, de façon que le poitrail de la bête touche la poitrine du patient, que son museau (ou son groin) colle à sa bouche. Cette exigence n'a rien à voir avec les embrassades dont certaines femmes civilisées sont prodigues à l'égard d'animaux domestiques qu'elles élèvent avec amour; elle s'inspire de préoccupations strictement médicales. En effet, l'un des hommes ouvre de force la gueule de l'animal et le malade crache dedans, cependant qu'à genoux, le sorcier supplie Nguénéchen, le " Dominateur des hommes " de permettre la transfusion du mal du corps de son client dans celui de son voisin de lit, qui est ensuite relâché.

Le lendemain, on recommence l'opération, pour le cas où la transfusion désirée n'aurait pas été réalisée. Puis on tue l'agneau ou le porcelet, et le sorcier procède à un examen détaillé et appesanti de ses organes. Ayant décelé " de visu " la lésion qui affecte l'un ou l'autre, il sait dès lors le mal dont souffre son client. Il ne lui reste plus qu'à passer au traitement.

Quant à la bête autopsiée, il l'emporte dans sa hutte et, indifférent à la contagion, il la met à la casserole !

(D'après E. Housse.)

NOTES AND WORDS :

les   sorciers-guérisseurs: sorcier, magician, guérisseur, healer; witch doctors, medicine men

une tribu, tribe

les temps immémoriaux, immemorial time(s)

renseigné, informed

la maladie, illness

le malade, sick man

le diagnostic, diagnosis

l'autopsie, autopsy
le client, client, patient
un agneau, lamb
un porcelet, young pig
attendre, to expect
confier, to trust, entrust
la patte, paw, foot
étendre, to spread out
le poitrail, breast
la poitrine, chest
le museau, muzzle
le groin, snout (of a pig)

coller, to stick
cracher, to spit
la gueule, mouth (of an animal)
à genoux, on the knees
relâcher, to release
tuer, to kill
appesanti, weighty
déceler, to disclose
" de visu," by having seen
la hutte, hut
la casserole, pot

LESSON XXIII

§ 1. *Literature: the Key to Culture*

IN this course our chief concern has been and is to present you with the essentials of the language so that you may be able to read and understand it and, of course, make yourself understood in it. The ability to read is of great importance in that it enables you to make the acquaintance of French literature. And French literature is the repository of French culture. You have been helped to sample the work of Alphonse Daudet, a charming and simple writer; of Voltaire, a classical writer famous for his sparkle and lucidity; of Flaubert, a master of style and **le mot juste.** Now we introduce Maupassant, whose short story **Clair de Lune** exemplifies his vivid, vigorous style and his realistic outlook on life. We hope that what you have read will whet your appetite for French literature generally, about which in this and the next lesson we propose to give you a brief account which will at the same time provide a general guide to your further reading.

What you have already read should tell you why French literature is so famous and influential. You find in it a conscious effort to achieve truth, beauty, and absolute honesty of thought. In this sense there is no literature to equal it since that of Greece in the age of Plato. Then, there is its **clarté.** It is rightly said **" Ce qui n'est pas clair, n'est pas français "**—What is not clear is not French : a saying which you must make your motto. This clarity is partly due to the sharp, logical nature of the language, and partly due to deliberate and consistent effort on the part of the best writers. With it goes a conscious effort to get to the root of things and draw conclusions of great generalizing power. Finally, the French can justly claim for their literature another, and a most engaging quality : its recognition and toleration of human frailty.

Toleration of human frailty, a humanist approach—how very necessary these are, especially in the age in which we live! If there is one thing which can be guaranteed to the student, it is that, having once well started to enjoy this great literature, he will wish to continue.   One is also willing to guarantee that he will never regret doing so.   That is why we now propose to tell him something more about it.

¶ 1. CLAIR DE LUNE
Par Guy de Maupassant

Il portait bien son nom de bataille, l'abbé Marignan.   C'était un grand prêtre maigre, fanatique, d'âme toujours exaltée, mais droite.   Toutes ses croyances étaient fixes, sans jamais d'oscillations.   Il s'imaginait sincèrement connaître son Dieu, pénétrer ses desseins, ses volontés, ses intentions.

Quand il se promenait à grands pas dans l'allée de son petit presbytère de campagne, quelquefois une interrogation se dressait dans son esprit : " Pourquoi Dieu a-t-il fait cela ? " Et il cherchait obstinément, prenant en sa pensée la place de Dieu, et il trouvait presque toujours.   Ce n'est pas lui qui eût murmuré dans un élan de pieuse humilité : " Seigneur, vos desseins sont impénétrables ! "   Il se disait : " Je suis le serviteur de Dieu, je dois connaître ses raisons d'agir, et les deviner si je ne les connais pas."

Tout lui paraissait créé dans la nature avec une logique absolue et admirable.   Les " Pourquoi " et les " Parce que " se balançaient toujours.   Les aurores étaient faites pour rendre joyeux les réveils, les jours pour mûrir les moissons, les pluies pour les arroser, les soirs pour préparer au sommeil et les nuits sombres pour dormir.

Les quatre saisons correspondaient parfaitement à tous les besoins de l'agriculture ; et jamais le soupçon n'aurait pu venir au prêtre que la nature n'a point d'intentions et que tout ce qui vit s'est plié, au contraire, aux dures nécessités des époques, des climats et de la matière.

NOTES AND WORDS : **Clair de Lune,** *Moonlight.* Marignan is the name of a battle, hence the abbé *rightly bore the name of a battle.*

desseins, designs
à grands pas, with great steps
l'allée, garden path
se dresser, to form itself
agir, to act
créer, to create

mûrir, to ripen
la moisson, harvest
arroser, to water, sprinkle
se plier, to conform with, to
  be adapted to
la matière, matter

§ 2. *Early Literature to Malherbe*

It will be some time before you are able to read early French literature, which, like early English literature, demands specialized knowledge. It is chiefly of interest to specialists; and few foreigners study it. Nevertheless, it is the root of the nation's literature, and that root may be said to be unchanging throughout the centuries and very much alive today. Therefore, we cannot afford to avoid mention of the early writers.

The early literature of France, beginning in the eleventh and twelfth centuries, consists of **chansons de geste,** songs which glorified heroic figures and were sung by wandering troubadors. From them sprang heroic romances, mostly poetical, and cycles like the Arthurian romances. Next came the **fabliaux,** tales of everyday life such as we have in the works of Chaucer. There was also much lyrical poetry, some drama and " chronicles "—of the latter, those of Froissart (1337–1400) can be read in Lord Berners' admirable version in English. A very great early poet was François Villon, whose period was the middle of the fifteenth century. His **Grand Testament** and **Petit Testament** contain poems which live today as vigorously as when they were written. But it was the Renaissance of the sixteenth century which marks the beginning of French literature for your purpose. Then appeared the great François Rabelais (*c.* 1490), whose *Works,* by their nature and difficulty, are not for everybody, though in parts they reach very high peaks of the human spirit. Do not try to read them in French until you have read them in translation. Montaigne is another great humanist of the period. His **Essais,** like the works of Rabelais, are universally read. They cover almost the whole range of human thought, are written in a faultless style, and may be said to have been the first real " essays " in European literature. These you can read in Florio's admirable translation—again, the French would be somewhat strange to you. You need not be afraid to read these or any other early works in translation. It is even advisable to do so until you feel very sure of your French. Everything from the seventeenth century on, you may try to read in French; and there is no reason why you should not be able to do so. By that period, the language had become the French we know today; the seventeenth century was a sort of " Golden Age " or Classical Period of French literature. The Academy was founded in 1635 with the object of standing guard over the language and encouraging the best in literature. It has published a dictionary and a grammar which are final authorities.

¶ 2. CLAIR DE LUNE—*Suite*

Mais il haïssait la femme, il la haïssait inconsciemment, et la méprisait par instinct. Il répétait souvent la parole du Christ : " Femme, qu'y a-t-il de commun entre vous et moi ? " et il ajoutait : " On dirait que Dieu lui-même se sentait mécontent de cette œuvre-là." La femme était bien pour lui l'enfant douze fois impur dont parle le poète. Elle était le tentateur qui avait entraîné le premier homme et qui continuait toujours son œuvre de damnation, l'être faible, dangereux, mystérieusement troublant. Et plus encore que leur corps de perdition, il haïssait leur âme aimante.

Souvent il avait senti leur tendresse attachée à lui et, bien qu'il se sût inattaquable, il s'exaspérait de ce besoin d'aimer qui frémissait toujours en elles.

Dieu, à son avis, n'avait créé la femme que pour tenter l'homme et l'éprouver. Il ne fallait approcher d'elles qu'avec des précautions défensives, et les craintes qu'on a des pièges. Elle était, en effet, toute pareille à un piège avec ses bras tendus et ses lèvres ouvertes vers l'homme.

Il n'avait d'indulgence que pour les religieuses que leur vœu rendait inoffensives ; mais il les traitait durement quand même, parce qu'il la sentait toujours vivante au fond de leur cœur enchaîné, de leur cœur humilié, cette éternelle tendresse qui venair encore à lui, bien qu'il fût un prêtre.

Il la sentait dans leurs regards plus mouillés de piété que les regards des moines, dans leurs extases où leur sexe se mêlait, dans leurs élans d'amour vers le Christ, qui l'indignaient parce que c'était de l'amour de femme, de l'amour charnel ; il la sentait, cette tendresse maudite, dans leur docilité même, dans la douceur de leur voix en lui parlant, dans leurs yeux baissés, et dans leurs larmes résignées quand il les reprenait avec rudesse.

NOTES AND WORDS :

haïr, to hate

inconsciemment, instinctively, unconsciously

mépriser, to despise, scorn

mécontent, discontented

tentateur, tempter

âme aimante, loving soul

frémir, to quiver, tremble

éprouver, to test

une crainte, fear

le piège, trap

toute pareille à, all equal to, similar to

la religieuse, nun

le vœu, vow

sentir, to feel

le regard, look

mouillé, moistened, wet

le moine, monk

maudit, accursed

baissé, lowered

résigner, to resign

reprendre, reprove

la rudesse, harshness

ARE YOU LISTENING REGULARLY
TO
SPOKEN FRENCH

§ 3. *The Classical Period*

The establishment of the Academy took place in a period in which literature flourished and in which there was not only pride in the language but a desire to discipline writers in its use. From then until now, the French author comes under the invisible influence of this august body—and a very good thing this is for the foreign student, in that it has helped to keep the language free from impurities and absurdities, while never acting as a restraint on originality. It is largely due to its influence that the French language maintained and maintains its high standards

§ 4. *The Age of Enlightenment*

Montesquieu, Voltaire, and Rousseau are the three literary giants of eighteenth-century France. Montesquieu stands in a class by himself not only for his delightful style but because of his supreme intellectual honesty. However unpalatable the conclusions might be to his analyses of ideas, he never hesitated to set them out in their full force. His **L'Esprit des Lois** is a treatise on political science, his aim being to show men how they can best order their public affairs. His outlook was progressive and humanist, and his great book—from which we shall give you samples in Lesson XXIV—created a method of dialectic which has been a model for advanced thinkers since then. Naturally, such a book did not please everybody, for **L'Esprit des Lois** helped to crystallize ideas which culminated in the French Revolution. He it was who defined the theory and practice of **Liberté, Egalité, Fraternité,** the slogan of that Revolution.

Voltaire was not only the greatest literary figure in Europe during the century, but is one of the prodigies of all literature. He is, above all other writers, the exponent of clarity in style—which means that he is an *easy* author to read. He wrote some fifty plays, a great number of poems, essays, histories, short stories, prose tales (of which you have had a sample in **Candide**), the famous **Dictionnaire Philosophique,** and some of his innumerable letters have been published in a collection which runs to 10,000. From the point of view of the foreigner who is studying French, there could hardly be a better author than Voltaire. His prose is always lucid and impeccable, and you can hardly fail to improve your knowledge of the language by reading any work from his pen.

Rousseau is a less important writer than either of the above, but his **Contrat Social** has had a vast influence on subsequent history because of the ideas it propounds. If Voltaire was the apostle of Liberty, Rousseau was the apostle of Equality and Fraternity, and Montesquieu the analyst and dialectician who sifted grain from chaff. Rousseau's autobiography, which he calls **Confessions,** is now his most widely read book; in it we see him as the progenitor of the " Romantic Movement " which spread all over Europe and influenced all its literatures, including our own.   Just as the Age of Enlightenment sprang from criticism of classicism, so the Romantic Movement sprang from Rousseau.

¶ 4. CLAIR DE LUNE—*Suite*

Quand il se retrouva en état de réfléchir et de parler, il s'écria : " Ce n'est pas vrai, vous mentez, Mélanie ! "

Mais la paysanne posa la main sur son cœur : " Que Notre-Seigneur me juge si je mens, monsieur le curé. J'vous dis qu'elle y va tous les soirs sitôt qu'votre sœur est couchée. Ils se r'trouvent le long de la rivière.   Vous n'avez qu'à y aller voir entre dix heures et minuit."

Il cessa de se gratter le menton, et il se mit à marcher violemment, comme il faisait toujours en ses heures de grave méditation. Quand il voulut recommencer à se barbifier, il se coupa trois fois depuis le nez jusqu'à l'oreille.

Tout le jour il demeura muet, gonflé d'indignation et de colère. A sa fureur de prêtre devant l'invincible amour, s'ajoutait une exaspération de père moral, de tuteur, de chargé d'âme, trompé, volé, joué par une enfant ; cette suffocation égoïste des parents à qui leur fille annonce qu'elle a fait, sans eux et malgré eux, choix d'un époux.

Après son dîner, il essaya de lire un peu, mais il ne put y parvenir ; et il s'exaspérait de plus en plus.   Quand dix heures sonnèrent, il prit sa canne, un formidable bâton de chêne dont il se servait toujours en ses courses nocturnes, quand il allait voir quelque malade.   Et il regarda en souriant l'énorme gourdin qu'il faisait tourner, dans sa poigne solide de campagnard, en des moulinets menaçants.   Puis, soudain, il le leva et grinçant les dents, l'abattit sur une chaise dont le dossier fendu tomba sur le plancher.

Il ouvrit sa porte pour sortir ; mais il s'arrêta sur le seuil, surpris par une splendeur de clair de lune telle qu'on n'en voyait presque jamais.

Et comme il était doué d'un esprit exalté, un de ces esprits que devaient avoir les pères de l'Église, ces poètes rêveurs, il se sentit soudain distrait, ému par la grandiose et sereine beauté de la nuit pale.

Notes and Words:

retrouver, to find again
mentir, to tell lies, to lie
le paysan, -nne, peasant
poser, to place
sitôt que, as soon as
gratter, to scratch
le menton, chin
se barbifier, to shave (*little used*)
muet, dumb, silent
gonfler, inflated, distended, *here* full of
colère, anger
ajouter, to add
tuteur, guardian, protector
chargé d'âme, entrusted with a soul
voler, *has two meanings*: to fly, to rob. *Here* **volé** *means* cheated

un époux, husband
parvenir, to succeed
chêne, oak
courses nocturnes, nightly sallies
le gourdin, cudgel
le campagnard, countryman
des moulinets menaçants, threatening twirls
grincer, grind
abattre, bring down
le dossier, back (of a seat)
fendu (*from* **fendre**), shattered, split
le plancher, the floor
doué, gifted
rêveur, dreamer, dreaming
distrait, distracted, diverted
ému, moved

§ 5. *The Nineteenth Century*

The student of French literature will find the nineteenth century one of absorbing interest. Rousseau had shown what could be achieved by presenting personal and subjective feelings and observation, by offering the picturesque, the passionate, and the spontaneous, all with beauty as an aim, rather than the strictly formal. The whole of a work of literature became more important than its parts. This was the driving impulse of the Romantic Movement of the nineteenth century, beginning with Madame de Staël and Chateaubriand and followed by poets and prose writers of such stature as Alfred de Vigny, Victor Hugo, and the prodigal Alexander Dumas. It was a period of great exuberance. Stendhal wrote the forerunners of the modern "psychological" novel in **Le Rouge et le Noir** and **La Chartreuse de Parme.** Honoré de Balzac conceived a grandiose plan to describe every activity and aspect of humanity and, in a series of novels which were a blend of the romantic and the realistic, with emphasis on the latter, presented us with his great **Comédie Humaine.** This realism was in turn a reaction against an overdose of Romanticism. So many writers were affected by it that they became another important influence, incorporating the doctrine of " Art for art's sake," by which they meant the absolute independence of art from morality, and perfection of form independent of content. Gautier, Flaubert, and Maupassant are representative of this school.

Flaubert is the outstanding novelist of the later part of the century. **Madame Bovary** is his masterpiece, but his colorful and powerful **Salammbô**—of which you have had a generous sample—shows the perfection of his style and his scrupulous regard for accuracy and detail. Years of research and personal inspection of the territory preceded the actual work of writing. Maupassant was his disciple, and the sample which we give of his work in **Clair de Lune** shows the influence of the master. Maupassant wrote some 300 of these **Contes,** beginning with **Boule de Suif,** a masterpiece in its own right. After the realists came the " Naturalists," who carried realism a stage farther. The names of the authors caught up in these tendencies or " movements " are too numerous to mention. It was a period of great prose writers and of many poets. The end of the century marks the beginning of the modern period.

¶ 5. CLAIR DE LUNE—*Suite*

Dans son petit jardin, tout baigné de douce lumière, ses arbres fruitiers, rangés en ligne, dessinaient en l'ombre sur l'allée leurs grêles membres de bois à peine vêtus de verdure ; tandis que le chèvrefeuille géant grimpé sur le mur de sa maison, exhalait des souffles délicieux et comme sucrés, faisait flotter dans le soir tiède et clair une espèce d'âme parfumée.

Il se mit à respirer longuement, buvant de l'air comme les ivrognes boivent du vin, et il allait à pas lents, ravi, émerveillé, oubliant presque sa nièce.

Dès qu'il fut dans la campagne, il s'arrêta pour contempler toute la plaine inondée de cette lueur caressante, noyée dans ce charme tendre et languissant des nuits sereines. Les crapauds à tout instant jetaient par l'espace leur note courte et métallique, et des rossignols lointains mêlaient leur musique égrenée qui fait rêver sans faire penser, leur musique légère et vibrante, faite pour les baisers, à la seduction du clair de lune.

L'abbé se remit à marcher, le cœur défaillant, sans qu'il sût pourquoi. Il se sentait comme affaibli, épuisé tout à coup, il avait envie de s'asseoir, de rester là, de contempler, d'admirer Dieu dans son œuvre.

Là-bas, suivant les ondulations de la petite rivière, une grande ligne de peupliers serpentait. Une buée fine, une vapeur blanche que les rayons de lune traversaient, argentait, rendaient luisante, restait suspendue autour et au-dessus des berges, enveloppait tout le cours tortueux de l'eau d'une sorte de ouate légère et transparente.

Notes and Words:

baigner, to bathe
dessiner, to draw, make a design
grêle, slender
le chèvrefeuille, honeysuckle
grimper sur, climb upon
tiède, warmish, lukewarm
respirer, to breathe
un ivrogne, drunkard
à pas lents, with slow steps
ravi, entranced
émerveillé, in wonder
oublier, to forget
la nièce, niece
noyer, to drown
le crapaud, toad

le rossignol, nightingale
lointain, distant
mêler, to mix
égrenée, sweet, choice
défaillir, to fail, become feeble
affaibli, weakened
épuisé, exhausted
avoir envie de, to wish to
rester, to remain
le peuplier, poplar
serpenter, to wind
une buée, mist
argenter, to make silver color
la berge, steep bank (of a river)
la ouate, raw cotton

LESSON XXIV

§ 1. *Symbolism and the Moderns*

EVERY literary movement or trend seems to bring its own reaction. The reaction against the Realists and Naturalists was started by Baudelaire long before their influence had begun to wane. He and others revolted against the building of literary edifices by piling up detail upon detail with scientific accuracy, and said that art should be " suggestive " rather than " explicit ." From that sprang the " Symbolists," mostly poets to begin with : Mallarmé, Verlaine, and Rimbaud. Their influence quickly reached the novel and even the drama, and soon a considerable Symbolist Movement showed itself. This restlessness and desire for change and improvement upon old methods is characteristic of modern French literature. The intention is always fundamentally progressive—an attempt to produce something *fresh*. And it accounts for the vast *variety* of reading matter in French at our disposal. Of the Symbolists, the poets are the most interesting; the novels are not striking. Yet, even in prose the influence was beneficial, as it helped to make storytelling a little less harsh and more graceful than it had been in the works of Zola, though certainly not more powerful.

Anatole France struck a sort of balance in all this by writing from a well-stocked mind works in which a spirit of tolerant irony dominates the whole. In style, he returns to the classical tradition. He always writes with consummate artistry, grace, and wit, and at times shows that he is capable of a Rabelaisian robustness of expression. He died in 1924 and, for a time, the new generation denigrated his work. But not for long. His place as one of the greatest of modern writers is assured. Because of the clarity and simplicity of much of his work, he is a writer to be cultivated by the foreign student. When you have finished this course, you could hardly do better than start to read his very amusing **La Rôtisserie de la Reine Pédauque** (the *"roasting house"* or restaurant with the sign " *web-footed queen* "). We mention his work chiefly because of its easy, straightforward style, and not because it is superior in merit to that of some other writers of the modern period. There is Romain Rolland, the novelist of morals, whose vast **Jean-Christophe,** one continuous work represented in a shelf of books, has given him a place in world literature. Although modern in period, these authors are not " modernist " in method. They stand in the established tradition.

¶ 6. CLAIR DE LUNE—*Suite*

Le prêtre encore une fois s'arrêta, pénétré jusqu'au fond de l'âme par un attendrissement grandissant, irrésistible.

Et un doute, une inquiétude vague l'envahissait ; il sentait naître en lui une de ces interrogations qu'il se posait parfois.

Pourquoi Dieu avait-il fait cela ? Puisque la nuit est destinée au sommeil, à l'inconscience, au repos, à l'oubli de tout, pourquoi la rendre plus charmante que le jour, plus douce que les aurores et que les soirs, et pourquoi cet astre lent et séduisant, plus poétique que le soleil et qui semble destiné, tant il est discret, à éclairer des choses trop délicates et mystérieuses pour la grande lumière, s'en venait-il faire si transparentes les ténèbres ?

Pourquoi le plus habile des oiseaux chanteurs ne se reposait-il pas comme les autres et se mettait-il à vocaliser dans l'ombre troublante ?

Pourquoi ce demi-voile jeté sur le monde ? Pourquoi ces frissons de cœur, cette emotion de l'âme, cet alanguissement de la chair ?

Pourquoi ce déploiement de séductions que les hommes ne voyaient point, puisqu'ils étaient couchés en leurs lits ? A qui étaient destinés ce spectacle sublime ; cette abondance de poésie jetée du ciel sur la terre ?

Et l'abbé ne comprenait point.

Mais voilà que là-bas, sur le bord de la prairie, sous la voûte des arbres trempés de brume luisante, deux ombres apparurent qui marchaient côte à côte.

L'homme était plus grand et tenait par le cou son amie, et, de temps en temps, l'embrassait sur le front. Ils animèrent tout d'un coup ce paysage immobile qui les enveloppait comme un cadre divin fait pour eux. Ils semblaient, tous deux, un seul être, l'être à qui était destinée cette nuit calme et silencieuse.

NOTES AND WORDS :

s'arrêter, to stop
grandir, to increase, grow
un attendrissement, feeling of pity
envahir, to invade
naître, to give birth, to be born
astre, star
éclairer, to light
s'en venait-il . . . did it come out
un oiseau chanteur, singing bird

vocaliser, to give voice
demi-voile, half veil
frissons de cœur, thrills, heart thrills
alanguissement, languor
déploiement, deployment, display
la prairie, grass land, meadow
tremper, to soak
côte à côte, side by side
le front, forehead
un cadre, frame

§ 2. *Marcel Proust and the Long Novel*

Balzac in his **Comédie Humaine,** Zola in his **Rougon-Macquart** novels and Romain Rolland in his **Jean-Christophe** gave the world something for which we have no exact parallel in English : the great work of fiction in many volumes containing a picture of life as conceived by the novelist. In Marcel Proust (1871–1922) came a writer who set himself such a task and completed it superbly. His **À la Recherche du Temps Perdu** in seven volumes under this general title and various subtitles provides a complete analysis and synthesis of his own life and its spiritual background. This is one of the great works of all modern literature : grandiose in conception and marvelously finished. Proust must be mentioned here, although we should hesitate to recommend him as an author to be read just yet. His style, though perfect for its purpose, is a little too involved for any but an experienced reader, and what we recommend in his case is what we would recommend in all similar cases : read him first in translation, and then read the original. You may feel that this is not necessary and, if so, so much the better.   But Proust is an author you must sooner or later read.   Furthermore, there is no better way of becoming familiar and intimate with the language and French psychology than the perusal of a long, absorbing work such as this.

Proust was an invalid who wrote most of his work in bed and at night.   He attempted to recapture the whole past, and believed that memory worked best in these circumstances.   Time meant little in the turning over of his memory to clarify an event or an episode; or to reconstruct an atmosphere.   This restful and endlessly painstaking method resulted in the masterpiece we know.   It showed him as a man of great originality, as a great innovator in literature, although always essentially French. His influence on writers in and outside France has been great, for it has been said of him that he turned the general conception of the French novel upside down and inside out, thereby providing a sort of blueprint for those who came after him.   In the version of Scott Montcrief we have in English a perfect translation of this literary monument, and the student who reads it is liberally rewarded.   Proust's work marks the beginnings of " Modernism " in French literature.

¶ 7. CLAIR DE LUNE—*Fin*

Et ils s'en venaient vers le prêtre comme une réponse vivante, la réponse que son Maître jetait à son interrogation.

Il restait debout, le cœur battant, bouleversé, et il croyait voir quelque chose de biblique, comme les amours de Ruth et de Boaz, l'accomplissement d'une volonté du Seigneur dans un de ces grands décors dont parlent les livres saints.   En sa tête se mirent à bourdonner les versets du Cantique des Cantiques, les cris d'ardeur, les appels des corps, toute la chaude poésie de ce poème brûlant de tendresse.

Et il se dit : " Dieu peut-être a fait ces nuits-là pour voiler d'idéal les amours des hommes."

Il reculait devant ce couple embrassé qui marchait toujours. C'était sa nièce pourtant ; mais il se demandait maintenant s'il n'allait pas désobéir à Dieu.   Et Dieu ne permet-il point l'amour, puisqu'il l'entoure visiblement d'une splendeur pareille ?

Et il s'enfuit, éperdu, presque honteux, comme s'il eût pénétré dans un temple où il n'avait pas le droit d'entrer.

NOTES AND WORDS :

bouleversé, upset, " bowled over "

biblique, biblical

accomplissement, fulfillment

décors, *here* " setting," " scene " (*as in a theatre*)

bourdonner, buzz, hum, *here* " run through "

versets, verses (*biblical*)

Le Cantique des Cantiques, Song of Songs

brûler, to burn

voiler, to veil (to veil ideally *here*)

désobéir, to disobey

entourer, surround

s'enfuir, to flee

honteux, ashamed, in shame

(End of the Story)

§ 3. *André Gide and the Critics*

Although André Gide was born in 1869 (and died in 1951), literary critics in France after the Second World War were still describing him as a " modernist " writer, and with good reason. For half a century this writer in his critical articles and essays had shown himself to be, in a country notable for literary critic- ism, one of the greatest of critics.   And, because of this, his influence on at least two generations of writers has been profound. But he wrote other things besides criticism, among them several notable novels in which his outlook seems to have been based on a maxim of La Rouchefoucauld, which is :

> **Les vices entrent dans la composition des vertus, comme les poisons entrent dans la composition des remèdes.**
>
> Vices enter into the composition of virtues, as poisons in the compounding of (medical) remedies.

His novels **Les Faux-Monnayeurs, L'Immoraliste,** and **Les Caves du Vatican** deal largely with this theme, and he shows us in his sharp prose the good in the worst and the bad in the best characters, the combination in either case often representing his norm for human nature.   It has been said of him that he carries this so far that he embarrasses everybody, himself included! But, whatever the critics may say about his themes, they are all agreed on one thing : that he is one of the greatest of French writers. Gide has written of himself :

" Dire ce que je suis ? C'est simple : à peu près le contraire de ce qu'on me croit. Mais si je venais à le dire, qui me croirait? Mieux vaut laisser aux lecteurs futurs le plaisir de cette découverte."

Gide is perhaps the most important of a considerable group of great men of letters, among whom may be mentioned Julien Benda, Paul Valéry, and Valery Larbaud. Paul Valéry has written much poetry; his art criticism stands in a class by itself. French literature, especially modern and contemporary literature, excels in criticism. We have nothing to equal it in English literature, in which the best critics for the most part follow in the footsteps of the French and often are not ashamed to acknowledge their debt. Criticism has achieved the status of an art in France, with a tradition to which the best authors have contributed. One day you will enjoy reading this criticism, but it is best first to be sure of the language and to have read the authors criticized.

TEXT :
DE L'ESCLAVAGE DES NÈGRES

Si j'avais à soutenir le droit que nous avons eu de rendre les nègres esclaves, voici ce que je dirais :

Les peuples d'Europe ayant exterminé ceux de l'Amérique, ils ont dû mettre en esclavage ceux de l'Afrique, pour s'en servir à défricher tant de terres.

Le sucre serait trop cher, si l'on ne faisait travailler la plante qui le produit par des esclaves.

Ceux dont il s'agit sont noirs depuis les pieds jusqu'à la tête; et ils ont le nez si écrasé, qu'il est presque impossible de les plaindre.

On ne peut se mettre dans l'esprit que Dieu, qui est un être très sage, ait mis une âme, surtout une âme bonne, dans un corps tout noir.

Il est si naturel de penser que c'est la couleur qui constitue l'essence de l'humanité, que les peuples d'Asie qui font des eunuques privent toujours les noirs du rapport qu'ils ont avec nous, d'une façon plus marquée.

On peut juger de la couleur de la peau par celle des cheveux, qui chez les Egyptiens, les meilleurs philosophes du monde, étaient d'une si grande conséquence, qu'ils faisaient mourir tous les hommes roux qui leur tombaient entre les mains.

Une preuve que les nègres n'ont pas le sens commun, c'est qu'ils font plus de cas d'un collier de verre que de l'or, qui, chez des nations policées, est d'une si grande conséquence.

Il est impossible que nous supposions que ces gens-là soient des hommes ; parce que, si nous les supposions des hommes, on commencerait à croire que nous ne sommes pas nous-mêmes chrétiens.

De petits esprits exagèrent trop l'injustice que l'on fait aux Africains ; car, si elle était telle qu'ils le disent, ne serait-il pas venu dans la tête des princes d'Europe, qui font entre eux tant de conventions inutiles, d'en faire une générale en faveur de la miséricorde et de la pitié ?

TRANSLATION :

ON NEGRO SLAVERY

[From Montesquieu's *Esprit des Lois*. Here, the author uses irony as his weapon against slavery.]

If I had to sustain (defend) the right we have had to make negroes slaves, here is what I should say:

The peoples of Europe having exterminated those of America, they had to put into slavery those of Africa to use them to bring under cultivation (to clear) so many lands.

Sugar would be too dear if one did not with slaves cultivate the plant which produces it.

Those referred to are black from feet to head; and their noses are so flat (squashed) that it is almost impossible to pity them.

One cannot admit in the mind that God, who is a very wise being, should have put a soul, above all a good soul, in a body all black.

It is so natural to think that it is color which constitutes the essence of humanity, that the peoples of Asia who make eunuchs always deprive the blacks of the relationship they have with us in a more marked fashion.

One can judge the color of the skin by that of the hair which, among the Egyptians, the best philosophers in the world, was of so great consequence (importance) that they put to death all red (haired) men who fell into their hands.

A proof that the negroes have not common sense is that they make more fuss of a glass necklace than (one) of gold, which among the policed (organized) nations is of such great importance.

It is impossible for us to suppose that those people are men; because. if we supposed them (to be) men, one would begin to believe that we are not ourselves Christians.

Small minds exaggerate too much the injustice done to the Africans; for, if it were such as they say, would it not have come into the heads of princes of Europe, who make among themselves so many useless agreements, to make a general one in favor of mercy and pity?

§ 4. *Popular Authors: Georges Simenon*

Hitherto, we have kept to a somewhat high plane of French literature, the object being to inform you briefly of the great store of good things which a knowledge of the language opens to you. We have mentioned by name only authors who have achieved an important place in the national heritage. But there is in France as elsewhere the "popular writer," the author who may not be considered by the best critics as in the top flight but who nevertheless provides entertainment for a vast public. France is rich in such authors and, on the whole, they write better than their counterparts in Britain or America.

The detective novel, which has its origins in the work of Edgar Allan Poe and was popularized by Conan Doyle—two writers of Irish origin—has become widely popular in France. In recent years France has produced some remarkable " mystery " and detective novels as well as " thrillers," but they are not quite the same as ours. The French writers are more realistic than ours, and work closer within the bounds of probability : because the average French reader is somewhat skeptical by nature and will never accept what is not strictly reasonable. Furthermore, the careless or slipshod writer's works are cast aside with indignation. All this raises the general standard of these novels above ours. One writer of such works has achieved an international reputation : Georges Simenon. His output is prodigious, and it is said that he can turn out a novel in about half the time taken by the late Edgar Wallace. In a few years he has written nearly one hundred novels, and the remarkable thing

about them is that, although varying in interest, they are never
dull.   If you like detective novels, mysteries, and thrillers, you
must not miss Georges Simenon!   You will also be able to say
to yourself in complete confidence that in reading any of his
works you are reading excellent French, French of today.   We
have singled him out for special mention as a popular writer,
because he is in a class by himself.   But that is not to say that
there are not others too numerous to mention here.   It is better
that you should not be confused at this stage by long lists of
names which would mean nothing.   Much better to concentrate
attention within definite limits to begin with, and many of
Simenon's books are available in English to help you.

La Liberté

Il est vrai que, dans les démocraties, le peuple paraît faire ce
qu'il veut ; mais la liberté politique ne consiste point à faire
ce que l'on veut.   Dans un état, c'est-à-dire, dans une société
où il y a des lois, la liberté ne peut consister qu'à pouvoir faire
ce que l'on doit vouloir, et à n'être point contraint de faire ce
que l'on ne doit pas vouloir.

Il faut se mettre dans l'esprit ce que c'est que l'indépendance,
et ce que c'est que la liberté.   La liberté est le droit de faire tout
ce que les lois permettent ; et, si un citoyen pouvait faire ce qu'elles
défendent, il n'aurait plus de liberté, parce que les autres auraient
tout de même ce pouvoir.

La démocratie et l'aristocratie ne sont point des états libres par
leur nature.   La liberté politique ne se trouve que dans les
gouvernements modérés.   Mais elle n'est pas toujours dans les
états modérés ; elle n'y est que lorsqu'on n'abuse pas du pouvoir :
mais c'est une expérience éternelle, que tout homme qui a du
pouvoir est porté à en abuser ; il va jusqu'à ce qu'il trouve des
limites.   Qui le dirait ?   la vertu même a besoin de limites.

Pour qu'on ne puisse abuser du pouvoir, il faut que, par
la disposition des choses, le pouvoir arrête le pouvoir.   Une
constitution peut être telle, que personne ne sera contraint de
faire les choses auxquelles la loi ne l'oblige pas, et à ne point faire
celles que la loi lui permet.   (XI–III & IV.)

De la liberté du citoyen

La liberté philosophique consiste dans l'exercice de sa volonté, ou du moins (s'il faut parler dans tous les systèmes) dans l'opinion où l'on est que l'on exerce sa volonté. La liberté politique consiste dans la sûreté, ou du moins dans l'opinion que l'on a de sa sûreté.

Cette sûreté n'est jamais plus attaquée que dans les accusations publiques ou privées. C'est donc de la bonté des lois criminelles que dépend principalement la liberté du citoyen. (XII–II.)

TRANSLATION :

MONTESQUIEU ON LIBERTY
[From *L'Esprit des Lois*.]

It is true that, in the democracies, the people seem to do what they wish; but political liberty does not consist in doing what one wishes. In a State, that is to say, in a society in which there are laws, liberty can consist only in being able to do that which one ought to wish, and not to be constrained to do what one ought not to wish.

It is necessary to get into one's mind what independence is and what liberty is. Liberty is the right to do all that which the laws permit; and if a citizen could do that which they forbid, he would have no more liberty, because the others would have equally this power.

Democracy and aristocracy are not free states by their nature. Political liberty is only found in (under) moderate governments. But it is not always (to be found) in moderate States; it is there only when power is not misused: but it is an eternal experience that any man who has power is inclined to misuse it; he goes on until he finds the limits. Who would say it? Virtue itself (even virtue) has need of limits.

In order that power cannot be misused, it is necessary that, by arrangement of things, power should arrest (stop) power. A constitution can be such that nobody will be constrained to do the things which law does not oblige him (to do), and not to do those which the law permits him.

Of the Liberty of the Citizen

Philosophic liberty consists in the exercise of one's will, or at least (if it is necessary to speak in all systems) in the opinion one has that one exercises one's will. Political liberty consists in security, or at least in the opinion (belief) that one has security.

This security is never more attacked than in public or private accusations. It is then on the goodness of the criminal laws that the liberty of the citizen chiefly depends.

§ 5. Conclusions on Literature

In these two lessons we have given you a bird's-eye view not of French literature so much as of those parts of French literature toward which the student who has worked through this course might with best advantage turn his attention. In Lesson XXVI we shall provide you with more definite suggestions for a program of reading which will carry you forward for at least a couple of years—after which you will become your own guide. Little attention is given here to poetry, not because it is unimportant but because you should be well accustomed to French prose before you begin to read poetry. If you do not accept this, then you may turn to some good anthology. The *Oxford Book of French Verse* can be recommended as a good beginning.

There are one or two points which we should like to emphasize by way of conclusion. First, if there is any subject in which you are particularly interested, you should try to obtain books on it in French. This is not meant to apply only to literature but to *anything*. If you are a student of engineering, find books in French on the branch of engineering you are studying. When you read them, you will be killing two birds with one stone, for you will be improving your knowledge of both engineering and French. If you are interested in photography, read about it in French. There is no subject you can mention that is likely to be entirely neglected by the French, and there are many in which they excel. You may be sure that *anything* to do with the arts —sculpture, painting, architecture, not to mention literature, drama, and even movies—has been seriously dealt with, and often much better than in the books available in English.

Finally, although you are given many pointers based on wide experience, you will probably benefit most if you strike out on your own lines and follow your own inclinations. Read books about France in English by all means; but be sure that they are written by recognized authorities. If you cannot find a work in the original, read it in translation rather than miss it altogether. If you like reading novels or plays, read them; similarly, biography or history. Your knowledge of French should become a source of pleasure and entertainment as well as of instruction;

and it will depend entirely upon yourself to make it so. But, above all things, it must *not* be a source of boredom through being made an onerous task. Whenever you find yourself bored, change to something else.

TEXT :

UN NOBLE HOMMAGE DU PAPE À LA LANGUE FRANÇAISE

L'Académie Française, qui a décerné sa grande médaille d'or de la langue française au Pape Pie XII, vient de recevoir de ce dernier une lettre de remerciements. C'est la première fois depuis sa fondation, il y a trois siècles, que l'illustre compagnie reçoit un message du souverain pontife.

Adressée au secrétaire perpétuel, cette lettre est ainsi conçue:

" A M. Georges Lecomte, secrétaire perpétuel de l'Académie Française.

" L'estime singulière que, depuis Nos jeunes années, Nous avons sans cesse nourrie pour la langue française, dans laquelle Notre goût personnel autant que Nos fonctions Nous ont de jour en jour confirmé, ne pouvait que Nous faire apprécier davantage le très noble geste par lequel l'Académie décidait à l'unanimité, dans sa séance solennelle du 18 décembre 1947, de Nous offrir une exceptionnelle Médaille d'Or, à l'effigie du Cardinal de Richelieu, son immortel fondateur.

" Nous l'avons reçue avec une réelle émotion, que faisait revivre devant Nos yeux, comme en un panorama splendide, les fastes tricentenaires du célèbre Institut, spécialement créé pour la défense et l'illustration d'un des plus riches idiomes que Dieu ait donné aux hommes de parler. En effet, on ne louera jamais assez la langue française pour sa clarté, sa précision, sa distinction, qui en ont fait par excellence le langage de la diplomatie et des sciences spéculatives. Et cela non par le fait d'une élection arbitraire, car elle est également, par sa finesse, la langue de l'art, de la littérature, de la poésie, la langue de l'esprit et du cœur. C'est surtout à travers vos auteurs classiques que Nous l'avons connue, admirée, aimée et parmi eux comment ne manifesterions-nous pas, en cette heureuse conjoncture, une secrète préférence pour votre grand Bossuet. Nôtre aussi pour-

rions-Nous dire, en raison du profit personnel que Nous avons
tiré de sa fréquentation assidue et fervente ?   Sans compter que
Nous trouvons chez lui, à un rare degré, cet accent de profonde
charité, que l'on sent vibrer dans la parole de tant d'orateurs
sacrés, qui ont honorés la chaire française et chrétienne."

TRANSLATION :

NOBLE TRIBUTE BY THE POPE TO THE FRENCH LANGUAGE
(1948)

*The French Academy, which has awarded its large gold medal for
the French language to Pope Pius XII, has just received from the
latter a letter of thanks.   It is the first time since its foundation three
centuries ago that the illustrious company receives a message from the
sovereign pontiff.   Addressed to the perpetual secretary, this letter
is worded thus:*

" *To M. Georges Lecomte, Perpetual Secretary of the French
Academy.*

" *The singular esteem which, since Our early years, We have cease-
lessly cultivated for the French language, in which Our personal taste
as much as Our office have confirmed Us from day to day, could only
make Us appreciate still more the very noble gesture by which the
Academy decided unanimously, in the solemn session of December 18th,
1947, to offer Us an exceptional Gold Medal with the head (effigy) of
Cardinal Richelieu, its immortal founder.*

" *We have received it with a real emotion, which caused to relive
before Our eyes, as in a splendid panorama, the tercentenary celebra-
tions of the celebrated Institute, specially created to protect and to
shed luster upon one of the richest languages which God has given men
to speak.   In fact, the French language will never be sufficiently
praised for its clarity, its precision, its distinction, which have made of
it pre-eminently the language of diplomacy and of the speculative
sciences.   And that not by the fact of an arbitrary choice, for it is
equally by its subtlety the language of art, of literature, of poetry, the
language of the spirit and of the heart.   It is above all through your
classical authors that We have known, admired, loved it, and among
them why should we not evince, in this happy conjuncture, a secret preference for your great Bossuet.*   Ours also can We say, by reason of
the personal profit which we have drawn from (his) constant and fervent
association?   Without counting that We find in him to a rare degree
that accent of profound charity, which one feels vibrating in the
word(s) of so many sacred orators who* ¹ *have honored the French and
Christian pulpit.*

* Jacques Bénigne Bossuet (1627–1704), famous for his eloquence,
especially in his **Oraisons Funèbres**.

LESSON XXV

§ 1. *Synopsis of Grammar : Articles, Nouns, Adjectives*

See Lesson I, § 4, and Lesson II, § 5, for elements.

An article is used before nouns in French : **l'homme a des pieds.**

In French the article is used when not used in English :

(1) Before names of seasons and countries : **l'Angleterre, l'été.** But not after **en. En France.**

(2) Before parts of the body when we should use a possessive adjective in English. *Where are her eyes?* **Ou a-t-elle les yeux ?**

The article is omitted in French :

(1) With nouns of profession or trade : **Il est boulanger, Elle est chanteuse.**

(2) Before **cent** and **mille** : **cent francs, mille francs,** *a hundred, a thousand francs.*

DU, DE LA, DES : These are used when *some* or *any* are implied before a noun : **Il a du courage.**

DE is used alone *before* an adjective and *after* a negative : **Elle a de beaux yeux. Il n'a pas de tabac.**

Nouns : See Lesson I, §§ 4–5, for elements.

Nouns form the plural by adding **-s.** Exceptions are nouns in **-s, -x, -z,** which do not change; nouns in **-au, eu,** which add **-x ;** nouns in **-al,** which change it to **-aux.**

Note : **le ciel, les cieux—le genou, les genoux—le bijou, les bijoux—le travail, les travaux.**

Gender of Nouns : See Lesson I, § 4, and Lesson IX, § 2, for elements.

Note the double genders :

un aide, helper	**le mort,** dead man
une aide, help	**la mort,** death

359

This is a typical page of advertising matter, chosen at random from the *Almanach Hachette* (1948), that hardy annual which provides France with the sort of information we find in *The World Almanac*—and much more. Browse over these advertisements—there is little in them that you will not understand. We give you little help from now on, as we wish all the effort to be on your side.

le livre, book	**la vapeur,** steam
la livre, pound	**le tour,** turn
le vapeur, steamer	**la tour,** tower

ADJECTIVES : For elements, see Lesson II, § 2.

Feminine of adjectives, note the following irregularities :

blanc, blanche	**franc, franche**
doux, douce	**long, longue**
faux, fausse	**public, publique**
frais, fraîche	**sec, sèche**

Agreement : Articles agree in gender and number with their nouns, but when used to qualify more than one noun the adjective is in the plural : **Il a la main et le pied sales.**

Position : The article is placed *after* the noun.

The following come *before* : **beau ; bon ; cher ; court ; grand ; gros ; jeune ; joli ; long ; mauvais ; méchant ; meilleur ; moindre ; petit ; sot ; vieux ; vilain.**

And note :

un brave homme, a worthy man	**un grand homme,** a great man
un homme brave, a brave man	**un homme grand,** tall, big man

§ 2. *Synopsis of Grammar : Pronouns*

For elements, see Lessons III and IV.

Position : The general rule is that the object pronoun immediately *precedes* the verb except in the imperative affirmative.

Thus : **Je le donne.   Donnez-le.**

When there are two pronouns, the direct object precedes the indirect.

Thus : **je le lui donne.   Je les leur donne.**

When the persons are mixed, **me, te, nous, vous** are placed *before* **le, la, les.**

Thus : **Je vous le donne.**

When the pronouns come after the verb—that is, in the imperative affirmative—the direct object precedes the indirect :

Thus : **Donnez-les-leur.**

**EN = de + *noun*. Je donne du pain. En donnez-vous ?
J'ai du beurre. En avez-vous ?**

EN must be used to represent a noun to supplement a number.
J'ai cinq doigts. Combien en avez-vous ?

EN is used for persons and things.

Y, use for things only ; it takes the place of a preposition
plus a noun. **Est-il sous la table ? Il y est,** *He is under it.*

The past participle agrees with the direct object which goes
before : **nous les avons donnés.**

Note that **MOI** is used instead of **je,** and **EUX** instead of **leur** :
(*a*) in answer to questions and (*b*) after **C'EST, CE SONT.**

Thus : **Qui a fait cela ? Moi. Qui est là ? Ce sont eux.**
Also after **à. Pensez à moi.** And with the word **même,** *self.*
Thus : **moi-même, eux-mêmes.**

Relative Pronouns : The relative pronoun is never omitted in
French. *What I said,* **Ce que j'ai dit.**

à qui, *whose,* when ownership is concerned. Otherwise **de
qui.**

And note : **À qui est la table ? Elle est à moi.**

In French, the article is used for parts of the body.
Thus :

Je vais me laver les mains, I'm going to wash my hands.

Il avait le chapeau à la main, He had his hat in his hand.

§ 3. *Synopsis of Grammar : Adverbs, Prepositions, Conjunctions*

For elements, see Lesson VII.

Note the following :

Adjectives ending in **-ANT, -ENT** change these to **-amment,
-emment** to form adverbs.

Thus : **prudent, prudemment.** But not **lent,** which makes
lentement.

Note the following irregularities :

  **gentil, gentiment   bref, brièvement
  traître, traîtreusement**

Adverbs are placed after the verb or auxiliary : **j'ai bien vu.
Il parle bien.**

Adverbs of quantity are followed by **de** : **j'ai très peu de pain.**
But not **plusieurs** : **plusieurs hommes.**

The **pas** of **ne . . . pas** can be omitted with the verbs
SAVOIR, POUVOIR, and **OSER. Je ne sais quoi,** *I don't
know what.* **Je ne puis voir. Je n'ose parler.**

TOUT as an adverb meaning *quite, altogether* varies in gender
and number before a feminine adjective beginning with a
consonant. **Il est tout pâle. Elle est toute pâle. Elles sont
toutes pâles.**

PREPOSITIONS : For elements, see Lesson VII, § 4.
Note the French equivalents for the following :

AT : At the same time, at my father's house. **En même
temps, chez mon père.**

BY : loved by all, **aimé de tous.** 3 o'clock by my watch,
3 heures à ma montre. Pas à pas, step by step.
Mot à mot, word by word.

FOR : For example, **par example.**

IN : **au printemps,** in spring. **à la campagne,** in the
country. **à Londres,** in London. **à mon avis,** in my
opinion. **à l'avenir,** in the future. **Par le passé,** in the
past. In France, **en France.** In the South of France,
dans le Midi de la France.

OF : to think of, **penser à.**

ON : on the 1st of January, **le 1ᵉʳ janvier.** On Monday,
lundi. On horseback, **à cheval. à bicyclette.** On
the contrary, **au contraire.**

FROM : to drink from a glass, **boire dans un verre.** To
look out of the window, **regarder par la fenêtre.** Out
of, through negligence, **par négligence.**

WITH : the girl with black hair, **la jeune fille aux cheveux
noirs.** Covered with snow, **couvert de neige.** Pleased
with, **content de.**

CONJUNCTIONS : See Lesson VII, § 5, for elements.
Note the following :

both . . . and, **et . . . et**
neither . . . nor, **ni . . . ni**
either . . . or, **ou . . . ou**

FERNANDEL

FERNAND, JOSEPH, DESIRÉ CONSTANTIN, dit Fernandel, né à Marseille le 8 mai 1903, mort — pour le cinéma — le même jour, par la faute d'une denture éclatante et chevaline, que découvre un sourire à nul autre pareil, et qui lui tiendra toute sa vie lieu de talent.

La fantaisie de Maurice Henry a monté, il y a quelques semaines, ci-dessus, face à face, le Minotaure et Fernandel, les cornes méditatives du premier et la mâchoire avantageuse du second. C'était l'image même de la perplexité où se trouve aujourd'hui le Minotaure, au moment de définir l'amuseur le plus populaire de ce temps. Car il lui semble bien, à ce signataire, que de Fernandel il n'y a rien à dire : il n'y a qu'à le regarder.

Des soixante-dix films et plus tournés par Fernandel, il ne surnage que deux ou trois titres : le Rosier de Mme Husson, puis Angèle et Regain. Il a été le chéri de sa concierge et le coq du régiment, le dégourdi de la 11e et le bleu de la marine, l'héritier des Mondésir et le gueux au paradis, et le voilà nouvellement doté d'un cœur de coq. Après s'être fait un nom, il s'est fait des prénoms : il a été Ignace, Ferdinand, Barnabé, Raphaël, Lidoire, Hercule, Ernest, Hector, Adrien, et il a été encore Simplet. Il est comme ces trésors ecclésiastiques, ces châsses miraculeuses que l'on sort de temps à autre pour les promener en procession : lui, Fernandel, on le met dans un film, il parle, les gens se tordent, et la farce est jouée. Pas le moindre travail, et un avenir assuré. Car il est de taille à nous enterrer tous.

L'œil suave, le cheveu pommadé, la lèvre riche : et cette fameuse mâchoire.

Il y en a deux comme ça, de mâchoires, qui valent leur pesant d'or : la sienne et celle de Michel Simon. Mais derrière celle de Michel Simon il y a un cerveau : le talent donnant le bras au génie. Derrière la mâchoire de Fernandel, néant, des courants d'air : son génie (car il en a, du moment qu'il est comme il est) se bat les flancs.

On le lui a dit, on le lui redit : ayez du talent, puisque vous avez déjà du génie. Fernandel répond : voire. A la manière de Panurge. Car il est, au demeurant, et à n'en pas douter, le meilleur fils du monde. Bon compagnon, bon père, bon administrateur. Il a multiplié les déclarations tendant à marquer qu'il fait ce qu'il peut, mais que, puisque le public veut le voir dans des vaudevilles militaires et des farces méridionales, il renonce à l'idée d'inscrire son nom à la suite de ceux de Sarah Bernhardt et de Greta Garbo dans l'histoire du spectacle.

Existence fortunée : avant de débuter, très jeune, sur les planches, Fernandel exerce plusieurs métiers, dont celui de garçon de banque. Est-ce qu'il conçoit le projet de devenir un capital incarné, qui n'aura qu'à se laisser fructifier, avec l'aide (scénaristique) de son beau-frère et (réalisatrice) de quelques compatriotes. Toujours est-il que depuis ses débuts à l'écran, il y est resté et s'y laisse vivre, ce qui lui permet d'élever gentiment ses enfants et de prendre son apéritif la conscience tranquille.

L'anecdote la plus typique (et sans doute apocryphe) de Fernandel est celle que l'on racontait pendant la drôle de guerre : notre homme, mobilisé, est commandé pour monter la garde à l'Ecole Militaire ; la foule s'attroupe et, quoi qu'il fasse, rit ; de fil en aiguille, on est amené à le démobiliser.

Typique, cette anecdote l'est surtout par rapport à la France de la drôle de guerre...

Le Minotaure

NOTES AND WORDS: **chevaline,** *like a horse,* equine. **la mâchoire,** *jaw.* **amuseur,** *comedian, entertainer.* **surnager,** *survive* (a shipwreck). **dégourdi,** *cunning one.* **le gueux,** *beggar.* **la drôle de guerre,** *the queer, odd, funny war;* the "*phony war*" of 1939–40, until the Germans attacked in the West in spring 1940.

§ 4. *Synopsis of Grammar: Verbs*

The French verb has been outlined in Lessons V, VI, and VII, but there remain certain idiomatic turns and peculiarities which constant reading and experience will teach. Here, we can deal only with a few of the commonest, of which **FAIRE** is the most important.

FAIRE is used for *to make* or *to cause* somebody to do something. Thus: **Faites-le venir,** *make him come.* **Je l'ai fait venir,** *I have made him come.* **Il fait venir sa femme,** *He is making his wife come.*

Note that the infinitive is used after **faire** in this sense. The infinitive is used also where we should use the past participle: **je l'ai fait bâtir,** *I had it built.*

Do not forget that in French the ordinary way of saying *Is . . . ?* is to put the subject first and follow it with the verb. Thus: *Is breakfast ready?* **Le déjeuner est-il prêt?** You can also say: **Est-ce que le déjeuner est prêt?**

Although it is necessary for you to be acquainted with the passive form of the verb—it follows a regular course—you should *avoid using it.* Thus, instead of saying *I have been told,* you use the active form with **on : on m'a dit.**

After verbs of fearing, the word **ne** is used:

J'ai peur qu'il ne parte, I fear that he will go.

After **de peur que, de crainte que, à moins que,** meaning *for fear that, unless,* the **ne** with the subjunctive is used: **à moins qu'il ne vienne, je m'en irai,** *unless he comes, I shall go away.* You should be able to recognize this.

You will not forget the following uses of **AVOIR :**

avoir chaud, froid, faim, soif, to be hot, cold, hungry, thirsty.

avoir raison, tort, to be right, wrong.

avoir peur, honte, to be afraid, ashamed.

avoir lieu, to take place.

avoir mal à, to have a pain in (**J'ai mal aux dents**).

avoir envie de, to wish, desire to. **J'ai envie de m'en aller,** I wish to go.

avoir besoin de, to have need of.

and :

Qu'est-ce qu'il y a, What is the matter ?

Qu'a-t-il ? What is the matter with him ?

L'EXISTENTIALISME

Les deux auteurs français les plus en vogue à l'étranger sont Jean de Létraz et Jean-Paul Sartre. Rien de commun entre eux, bien entendu. Le premier est très prisé en Hongrie et en Roumanie. Le second dynamite l'opinion au Danemark et en Amérique.

A Paris, une première de Jean de Létraz amuse un quart d'heure, tandis qu'une première de Sartre provoque un tel raz-de-marée que la salle ne désemplit pas pendant plusieurs semaines. Jean-Paul Sartre a remplacé Jean Cocteau dans le scandale théâtral, et sa *Machine à écrire*, aujourd'hui s'appelle *Morts sans sépulture*.

Le quartier le plus éprouvé par cet enfant terrible du siècle est le plus paisible, le plus snob, le plus entiché de sa tradition et de ses belles manières, le Boulevard Saint-Germain, chef-lieu des duchesses et des salonnards.

C'est là qu'on applaudit le plus le second acte de *Morts sans sépulture* et *la Putain respectueuse*, et ce sont les voix du Boulevard Saint-Germain qui ont donné la réplique aux violentes protestations de la répétition des couturières.

Le Boulevard Saint-Germain, contaminé par l'existentialisme dont Sartre est l'actuel Grand-Prêtre, ne pouvait pas se désintéresser de cette polémique. Il a pris parti, mais, pour la première fois, Sartre ne s'est pas senti suffisamment fort, malgré ses troupes fidèles ; il a baissé pavillon devant le bon sens. Accusé d'emprunter au Grand-Guignol, il a dû abréger la fameuse scène de tortures du second acte. Somme toute, ce n'est qu'un acte de

galanterie à l'égard des femmes par trop enclines à l'évanouisse-
ment.

L'existentialisme n'a donc pas perdu une plume dans cette
dernière bataille, et la philosophie désespérée de Sartre s'en tire
une fois encore avec tous les honneurs dus à son rang.   La crosse
du cardinal Suhard devra frapper encore très fort pour réussir à
ébranler cette nouvelle tendance du matérialisme qui, par son
caractère pessimiste et désabusé, bourbeux et affligeant, rappelle
curieusement par endroits—et révérence parler—l'amertume
janséniste.

La Bible de l'existentialisme, c'est l'*Etre et le Néant*, de
J.-P. Sartre.

NOTES AND WORDS: This and the newspaper extract in
the next section we leave you to work out yourself.   Make a
list of all the words you do not know, and see if you can find
them in the preceding lessons.   You will not find *L'existentialisme*, and you may not find it in a dictionary!   It is the philosophy which Jean-Paul Sartre has compounded from other
philosophers, to satisfy the French soul of the 1930's and
1940's. **entiché**, *infatuated*.

§ 5. *Synopsis of Grammar: Miscellaneous Items*

There are many odd little items which you will have noticed
in the course of the reading matter provided—we have not
thought it necessary to draw your attention to them until now,
because we did not wish to distract your attention from more
important matters.

In French, each syllable begins with a consonant: this applies
to both speech and writing.   When two consonants come
together, the division takes place between them: **tom-ber.**

The following syllables are *always mute*—that is, they are not
pronounced:

unaccented **e : il parle.**   Usually at the end of a word.
> **-es** as a verbal ending: **tu parles.**
> **-ent** as a verbal ending: **ils parlent.**
> **-es** as an ending of nouns or adjectives: **les
> mères.   Les misérables.**

DU 26 AOUT AU 1er SEPTEMBRE 1947

«Je suis vieux je n'écrirai plus»

nous assure Maurice Maeterlinck

qui, après sept ans d'exil revient avec sept pièces et intente sept procès

Cannes, ... août (*de notre corr. part. R. Chasseuil*)

LE crépuscule d'une belle journee d'été tombe lentement sur la baie de Cannes. Au loin, la Croisette brille de tous ses feux. C'est l'heure où les rapides hors-bord, voiliers et canots de course, rentrent au port. Au centre de la rade, comme pour compléter ce cadre féerique, un paquebot s'illumine. C'est le *Sobieski*, battant pavillon polonais, qui débarque ses passagers de New-York.

Accoudé au bastingage, indifferent à la foule brillante qui l'entoure, un robuste vieillard contemple avec émotion les côtes de France. C'est Maurice Maeterlinck — le comte Maurice Maeterlinck — l'un des plus grands écrivains de notre temps. Il porte un costume en tissu Prince de Galles un peu fatigué, et un vieux chapeau de paille jauni, au ruban bleu déteint, sur ses cheveux blancs maintenus par un léger filet. Après sept ans d'exil, l'auteur de La Vie des Termites, (œuvre pour laquelle il aurait pu emprunter à Duhamel le titre « Scènes de la vie future ») rentre enfin en France.

«*Ma carrière d'écrivain est terminée*»

Malgré ses 86 ans, Maeterlinck est très alerte et fait face vaillamment au feu roulant des questions qui lui sont posées par les reporters de la presse mondiale. Seuls les photographes, qui surgissent de toutes parts, l'inquiètent quelque peu :

— Ils semblent avoir un malin plaisir à publier les photos qui vous montrent sous le jour le plus défavorable, dit-il un peu agacé, sous prétexte qu'elles sont les plus originales et les plus inattendues.

You may have noticed that in such verbs as **LEVER, MENER,** when the **-er** ending (which is pronounced like **ai**) is changed in writing to one which is silent, the first syllable takes a grave accent (`). Thus : **il lève, il mène.** The reason for this is that the French do not like to see or hear two mute **e**'s following one another. By putting the accent on the first, this is avoided. Accents are not placed on capital letters, except in textbooks for foreign students, to impress the accentuation.

The names of days and months are always written with small letters (**minuscules**) and never capitals (**majuscules**) : **lundi, le 3 mars.**

Never write **Mons.** as an abbreviation for **Monsieur.** **Mons.** is very often used for **Monseigneur,** *Monsignor,* which is very different! The correct form is : **Mgr.**

Monsieur is written with a capital **M** when it comes before a proper noun : **Monsieur Dupont.** It is written with a small letter when it means *gentleman* : **Ce monsieur est assez laid,** *That gentleman is ugly enough,* " *pretty ugly.*"

Quotation marks are coming into fashion, though they have not been greatly used in the past. Instead, one finds « . . . » and very often speech is represented by a dash before the opening word :

   —**Venez me voir avant de partir, disait-il.**
   " Come and see me before you go," said he.

LESSON XXVI

§ 1. *How Best to Benefit from this Course*

You will reap most benefits from this course if, from this time onward for at least another six months, you go over the lessons and reading again and again until you are familiar with every line, every word. In this course you have all the fundamentals of French and a very practical vocabulary. Your problems now are : (1) to become so familiar with all that is given here that it becomes as much a part of yourself as your knowledge of your own language—a high ideal to set yourself; (2) to extend that knowledge by reading, by listening to French, and by practising *thinking in French*.

There are certain matters about which we can give you certain assurances. You are unlikely—unless you wish to become an expert in the language—ever to require more *grammar* than is provided in these pages; though you may wish to know more about the irregular verbs, which would be commendable. For ordinary, everyday purposes, the vocabulary given here is more than enough. You may wish to specialize, in which case you have an excellent all-purpose foundation of the language. On it you can build as you please.

In one direction you will find it necessary to extend your knowledge : *words*. Again, we repeat and would emphasize again what we have said before : *words are the raw material of the language*. It is unlikely that you will pick up a French book or newspaper without finding a word or words that you do not know. People who know French well and who have lived for years in France are accustomed to this experience. Do not be either surprised or dismayed by it ! For one thing, the language is continually developing, new words and new combinations of words are constantly cropping up. Keep a notebook and jot down every new word; and learn it. You ought not to have to do very much of this; but you will certainly have to do some of it, and for some time. Finally, do not confuse yourself by

attempting to do too much at a time.   Better a little every day
than big doses at irregular intervals.   *Get the habit* of reading a
piece of French *every day*—even if it is only a matter of a few
lines.   But make sure that you know exactly what it all means
before you put it down.   As it is a *foreign* language you are
learning, and not your mother tongue, and as you are an adult
and not a child, this constant application and concentration are
necessary.   While some learners absorb a foreign language more
quickly than others, it can be stated that, as a general rule, the
so-called " linguistic ability " or " facility " in learning foreign
languages nearly always comes back to two very old acquaint-
ances : PATIENCE AND PERSEVERANCE.

§ 2. *On Using the Dictionary*

From now on, a dictionary is indispensable.   The part
most required is the French–English and, as you will *always*
require a French–English Dictionary, it is worth your while to
provide yourself with a good one—say Mansion's Shorter work,
published by Henry Holt, or Kittredge's dictionary, put out
by David McKay.   We also recommend Bellow's little *Pocket
Dictionary*; but you will hardly need both.   A French–English
dictionary is indispensable for further study after this course has
been completed.   You may not need an English–French
dictionary, unless you are going to live in France.

Some people just hate looking up words in a dictionary.   You
must quickly get rid of that handicap, if you should happen to
suffer from it.   The dictionary must become your guide, philosopher, and friend, and you must accustom yourself to the
habit of looking up every word of which you are not absolutely
certain.   You have on several occasions been told of the clarity
and sharpness of French, a language which all the time insists
upon a much greater accuracy in the use of words than our
somewhat " free and easy " English.   As a general rule, a French
sentence is intended to mean *only one thing*.   IF IT IS AMBIGU-
OUS, IT IS BAD FRENCH.   **Ce qui n'est pas clair n'est pas
français.**   To get at the one meaning of a sentence in French,
you must know accurately what each word means.   It is essential,

therefore, if you wish to be competent in French, to get into the habit of scrutinizing closely as you read, and of never, *never* being satisfied with a vague or hazy comprehension of an author's text. The chances are that he has devoted great pains to framing his sentences; or he may be a genius and write them with ease. In either case you cannot afford to skim over quickly what he has written; and, the greater the author, the more care he is worth on your part. So, do not become impatient if he compels you to look up in a dictionary the exact meaning of his words. After a time you will find that looking up words can be extremely interesting, a sort of exciting game for which the prizes are often out of all proportion to the work involved. By knowing the meaning of his words, you can share in the joy of understanding the thoughts of a great philosopher, or have that other kind of pleasure which comes from appreciating the ironical humor of, say, Anatole France.

3. Building up a Library

You are probably aware by this time whether or not you like French as a language. The probability is that, having got so far, your interest in it will have been well aroused.

Let us assume that you have taken to French and intend to pursue your studies further. *Reading* French must be your principal stand-by, and reading comes under two general headings: first, newspapers and magazines; second, books. If you wish to read a newspaper, yet cannot buy French-language papers in your city, you might get a subscription to *France-Amérique,* 127 East 81 St., New York City 28. A French-language magazine that is put out expressly to inform Americans about events in France and French culture is *Revue de la Pensée Française,* 58 West 57 St., New York City 19. French magazines written and published in France, and all kinds of French books can be ordered by mail from French and European Publications, 610 Fifth Ave., New York City 20. Membership in the French Book Club, whose headquarters are at 119 West 57 St., New York City, is a good way to keep up with current French literature. This operates just like any other book club, except that it specializes in French-language books. Another service that this book club offers its members, is to sell them any current French book, whether or not it is one of their selections, at its Paris retail price (payable in dollars, of course). Since book prices are lower in Paris than in the United States, this can represent a saving. If you prefer to borrow French books instead of buying them, it is possible to do so from the Library of the French Institute, at 22 East 60 St., New York City 22. This Library will mail books to its members anywhere in the United States. They charge a fee of $10 a year, plus a deposit for postage.

To begin with, be prepared to read almost *anything* in French. After a while your mind will become more selective. If you can, read some popular modern fiction first—Colette and Simenon are authors we recommend, and then work through some nineteenth century authors. But there is one exception: Voltaire—because of his simple style. You can read Voltaire anytime. As you find your favorite authors, collect and study their works, you will build your personal library.

UN PROBLÈME DÉMOGRAPHIQUE:
STABILISER NOTRE POPULATION

Notre population est " vieille," au sens démographique du mot. Elle ne saurait passer d'un seul coup à l'état de jeunesse qui nous assurerait sans aucun doute une prospérité plus grande et surtout plus durable.

Limitant notre objectif, cherchons d'abord à déterminer l'apport qui la rendrait stationnaire, c'est-à-dire qui arrêterait sa décroissance et assurerait son renouvellement, par l'arrivée continue d'éléments jeunes à l'âge de la procréation.

Il faut pour cela modifier son volume et sa structure. Cette dernière est révélée par l'examen de la *pyramide des âges*. Si l'on compare la pyramide de 1944 avec celle de 1900 par exemple, on observe deux " trous " nettement marqués entre 0 et 10 ans et entre 20 et 30 ans, qui sont dus à la diminution des naissances pendant la guerre de 1914–18, conséquence de la séparation des ménages, ainsi qu'aux pertes résultant des deux guerres.

Dans une étude récente,[1] M. Paul Vincent exprime au moyen du tableau ci-dessous le redressement qui serait nécessaire pour rendre notre population stationnaire.

AGES	POPULATION française réelle (en milliers)	POPULATION française stationnaire	DIFFERENCES
de plus de 70 ans	2.672	2.971	— 299
de 50 à 69 ans	8.204	8.770	— 566
de 35 à 49 ans	8.854	8.470	+ 384
de 25 à 34 ans	4.803	6.111	— 1308
de 15 à 24 ans	6.624	6.381	+ 243
de 0 à 14 ans	8.534	9.885	— 1351
	39.691	42.588	— 2897

[1] Revue *Population* n° 2 de 1946.

Un Programme Minimum

Commentant ces résultats, M. Paul Vincent fait les observations suivantes :

1° *Nous avons besoin de 1.300.000 immigrants de 25 à 34 ans, soit accompagnés d'un nombre à peu près équivalent d'enfants de moins de 15 ans, soit suivis, un peu plus tard. Ou une immigration équivalente de sujets de 15 à 25 ans.* La première méthode, si elle est possible, est meilleure, car elle suppose l'immigration de familles constituées, qui manifesteront sans doute une plus grande stabilité.

2° Aucun immigrant de plus de 35 ans ne constitue un apport utile. Nous nous plaçons ici, bien entendu, sur un plan strictement démographique : il est naturellement possible qu'un savant ou un écrivain, même âgé, honore et serve grandement la France par sa présence.

3° Il n'y a pas avantage à encourager la venue d'un trop grand nombre de célibataires. En effet, les célibataires, surtout les hommes, peuvent apporter une solution passagère au problème de la main-d'œuvre. Mais, s'il y a un trop grand déséquilibre entre les sexes, ces hommes (ou des Français en nombre équivalent) ne se marieront pas, et l'avenir de la population en sera partiellement compromis. On peut admettre 200 à 300.000 hommes célibataires, et 600.000 familles de 4 personnes. La réalisation d'un tel plan, sur cinq ans environ, paraît compatible avec les possibilités d'accueil de la France.

4° L'immigration de familles est plus souhaitable que l'immigration d'adultes seuls à l'âge où ils deviennent actifs, en raison du puissant facteur d'assimilation que constitue l'école.

Si l'on tient compte des estimations plus sévères de certains auteurs, et des besoins considérables en main-d'œuvre, on conviendra que le programme suggéré est le plus modeste auquel on puisse songer.

La démographie; *démographique*. Demography, demographic. The science which represents a study of statistics of births, diseases, death-rates of a community or nation, with the object of drawing conclusions and illustrating conditions. Because of circumstances, it is a science of vital importance to France.

Cities where French-Language
Radio Programs Can be Heard

States and Cities	Stations	States and Cities	Stations
ALABAMA		**CALIFORNIA** (contd.)	
University	WUOA	San Mateo	KEAR
Montevallo	WRSD	Santa Clara	KSCU
ARIZONA		Sonora	KROG
Flagstaff	KGPH	Stockton	KCVN
Kingman	KGAN	**COLORADO**	
ARKANSAS		Alamosa	KGIW
Paragould	KDRS	Colorado	
CALIFORNIA		Springs	KRCC
Arcata	KHSC	**CONNECTICUT**	
Chico	KCSC	Danbury	WLAD
Claremont	KPCR	Hartford	WTIC
Hollywood	KFWB	**D. C.**	
Los Angeles	KFAC	Washington	WASH
	KSCS		WAMU
Modesto	KBEE	**FLORIDA**	
	KRJC	Clearwater	WTAN
Monterey	KXXL	Cocoa	WKKO
Napa	KVON	Coral	
Needles	KSFE	Gables	WVCG
Pasadena	KPPC	Fort	
Petaluma	KAFP	Walton	WFTW
Pomona	KMSA	Lakeland	WFSI
San Bernardino		Miami	WTHS
	KVCR	Miami	
San Francisco		Beach	WAHR
	KRON	New Smyrna	
	KXKX	Beach	WSBB

377

States and Cities	Stations	States and Cities	Stations
FLORIDA (contd.)		INDIANA (contd.)	
Plant City	WPLA	Muncie	WBST
Sanford	WTRR	New	
Tallahas-		Albany	WNAS
see	WFSU	New	
Tampa	WTUN	Castle	WCTW
Vero			WYSN
Beach	WNTM	Notre	
Winter		Dame	WNDU
Park	WPRK	Wabash	WSKS
GEORGIA		Warsaw	WKAM
Albany	WALB	West	
Atlanta	WABE	Lafayette	WCCR
Valdosta	WGAF	IOWA	
IDAHO		Ames	WOI
Boise	KGEM	Grinnell	KGRW
ILLINOIS		Iowa City	WSUI
Chicago	WBEZ		KSUI
	WFJL	Mason City	KGLO
	WUCB	Muscatine	KWPC
De Kalb	WNIC	KANSAS	
Evanston	WNUR	Hays	KAYS
Greenville	WGRN	Lawrence	KFKU
Jackson-			KANU
ville	WMMC	Wichita	KMUW
Urbana	WILL	KENTUCKY	
	WIUC	George-	
INDIANA		town	WGTC
Bloom-		Lexington	WBKY
ington	WFIU	Louisville	WFPL
Evansville	WIKY	Richmond	
Green-		Eastern Kentucky	
castle	WGRE	State College	
Hunting-		LOUISIANA	
ton	WVSH	New	
Michigan		Orleans	WDSU
City	WIMS		WTPS
		MAINE	
		Augusta	WFAU

States and Cities	Stations	States and Cities	Stations
MAINE (contd.)		**MICHIGAN** (contd.)	
Brunswick	WBOA	Highland	
Houlton	WABM	Park	WHPR
Lewiston	WCOU	Kalamazoo	WMCR
Presque		Midland	WMDN
Isle	WAGM	Traverse	
Rumford	WRUM	City	WTCM
MARYLAND		**MINNESOTA**	
Baltimore	WBJC	Minne-	
Takoma Pk.	WAFT	apolis	WMMR
			KUOM
MASSACHUSETTS		Northfield	KARL
Amherst	WMUA		WCAL
Boston	WBUR	Red Wing	KAAA
	WGBH	St. Paul	WBOM
	WMEX	**MISSISSIPPI**	
	WVOM	Biloxi	WLOX
Brockton	WBET	Hatties	
Fort		burg	WMSU
Devens	WFDH	**MISSOURI**	
New		Columbia	KWWC
Bedford	WBSM	Fort Leonard	
	WNBH	Wood	Hospital
	WFMR	Independ-	
North		ence	KIMO
Adams	WMNB	Joplin	KFSB
Pittsfield	WBEC	Rolla	KTTR
Spring-		St. Charles	KCLC
field	WSRB	St. Louis	KFUO
MICHIGAN			KSLH
Ann Arbor	WUOM	West Plains	KWPM
Benton		**MONTANA**	
Harbor	WHFB	Billings	KBMY
Detroit	WDET	Bozeman	KBMN
	WDTR	**NEBRASKA**	
East		Chadron	KCSR
Lansing	WKAR	**NEVADA**	
Flint	WFUM	Las Vegas	KENO
	WFBE	Reno	KNEV

States and Cities	Stations	States and Cities	Stations
NEW HAMPSHIRE		NEW YORK (contd.)	
Durham	WMDR		WKCR
Rochester	WWNH		WRCA
NEW JERSEY			WNYU
Bridgeton	WSNJ	Bronx High School	
Newark	WBGO	of Science	
New Bruns-		City College	
wick	WRSU	Niagara	
South		Falls	WHLD
Orange	WSOU	Olean	WHDL
NEW MEXICO		Rochester	WBBF
Albuquerque		Saratoga	
	KHFM	Springs	WSPN
Farmington	KVBC	Schenectady	
Portales	KENM		WRUC
NEW YORK		Springville	WSPE
Albany	WOKO	Syracuse	WAER
Amsterdam	WCSS	Troy	WRPI
Annandale	WXBC		WFLY
Bristol		Utica-Rome	
Center	WRRE		WRUN
Canton	KSLU	Watertown	
Cherry			WWNY
Valley	WRRC	Wethersfield-	
De Ruyter	WRRD	Bliss	WRRL
Floral Park	WSHS	NORTH CAROLINA	
Great Neck		Chapel	
Great Neck		Hill	WUNC
Public Schools		Charlotte	WGIV
Houghton	WJSL	Greensboro	WGPS
Ithaca	WRRA	Marion	WMIT
	WITJ	Raleigh	WVWP
	WVBR	Wake	
Liberty	WVOS	Forest	WFDD
Lynbrook		Washington	
High School			WHED
Massena	WMSA	NORTH DAKOTA	
New York	WABF	Dickinson	KDIX
	WFUV		

States and Cities	Stations	States and Cities	Stations

NORTH DAKOTA (contd.)

Grand
  Forks KFJM
Hettinger KNDC

OHIO
Alliance WFAH
Athens WOUI
Cleveland WBOE
  WDOK
Columbus WOSU
Dover WJER
Granville WDUB
Mt. Vernon
  WMVO
Oberlin WOBC
Oxford WMUB
Toledo WTDS
  Central Catholic
  High School
Washington Court
  House WCHO

OKLAHOMA
Norman WNAD
Shawnee KOBU
Stillwater KURO
Tulsa KWGS

OREGON
Eugene KRVM
La Grande KLBM
Lebanon KGAL
McMinnville
  KMCM
Portland KDUP
  KLAC
  KBPS
Redmond KSGA

PENNSYLVANIA
Barnesboro WNCC

PENNSYLVANIA (contd.)
Bethlehem WLRN
  WGPA
Carbondale WCDL
Clearfield WCPA
Easton WEEX
  WJRH
Gettysburg
  WWGC
Harrisburg WHP
Haverford WHRC
Homestead WHOD
Lewisburg WVBU
Loretto KSFC
Philadelphia WFIL
  WFLN
  WJMJ
  WPWT
  WRTI
Pittsburgh WDUQ
  WRCT
Pottsville WPPA
Scranton WUSV
State Coll. WDFM
Swarthmore WSRN
Williamsport
  WLYC

RHODE ISLAND
Newport WADK
Providence WPJB

SOUTH CAROLINA
Anderson WAIM
  WCAC
Columbia WUSC

SOUTH DAKOTA
Brookings KAGY
Rapid City KRSD
Sioux Falls KISD
Vermillion KUSD

States and Cities	Stations	States and Cities	Stations
TENNESSEE		**VIRGINIA** (contd.)	
Knoxville	WUOT	Hopewell	WHAP
TEXAS		Norfolk	WTAR
Abilene	KACC		WRVC
Austin	Universtiy of Texas	Richmond	WRVA
			WRVB
Corpus Christi	KSIX	**WASHINGTON**	
Dallas	KIXL	Cheney	KEWC
Denton	WCST	Pullman	KWSC
El Paso	KEPO	Seattle	KUOW
Galveston	KGBC	Tacoma	KTOY
Houston	KUHF	Yakima	KYAK
Levelland	KLVT	**WEST VIRGINIA**	
Lubbock	KTTC	Huntington	
Plainview	KHBL		WHTN
Nacogdoches	KSFA	Martinsburg	
UTAH			WEPM
Logan	KVSC	Oak Hill	WOAY
Provo	KBYU	**WISCONSIN**	
	KEYY	Auburndale	WLBL
St. George	KDIX	Brule (Superior)	
Salt Lake City	KSL		WHSA
		Chilton	WHKW
VERMONT		Colfax	WHWC
Burlington	WRUV	Delafield	WHAD
	WJOY	Highland	WHHI
Newport	WIKE	Ladysmith	WLDY
St. Johnsbury		Madison	WHA
	WTWN	Milwaukee	
VIRGINIA		U. of Wisconsin	
Bristol	WCYB	Wausau	WHRM
Crewe	WSVS	West Salem	
			WHLA

Nouns from the Reading Vocabulary
with the Article Given to Show Gender

un abbé, *abbot*
un abri, *shelter*
une absence, *absence*
un accent, *accent, tone*
un accident, *accident*
un accord, *agreement, understanding*
un acte, *act*
une action, *action*
un adieu, *farewell*
une administration, *administration*
une admiration, *admiration*
une adresse, *skill, adress*
un adversaire, *adversary*
les affaires (f.), *business, affairs*
une affection, *affection*
un âge, *age*
un agent, *agent*
un aide, *male assistant*
une aide, *aid, help*
une aile, *wing*
un air, *air*
une aise, *ease*
une allée *passage, path*
une allure, *pace, gait, bearing*
une ambition, *ambition*

une âme, *soul*
un ami, *friend*
une amitié, *friendship*
un amour, *love*
un an, *year*
une angoisse, *agony*
un animal, *animal*
une année, *year*
un août, *August*
un appareil, *apparatus*
une apparence, *appearance*
un appartement, *apartment, flat*
un appel, *roll call, call*
une après-midi, *afternoon*
un arbre, *tree*
une ardeur, *ardor, fervor*
un argent, *money*
une arme, *weapon, arm*
une armée, *army*
une arrivée, *arrival*
un art, *art*
un article, *article*
un ou une artiste, *artist*
un aspect, *aspect*
une attaque, *attack*
une attention, *attention, care*
une attitude, *attitude, position*

383

un auteur, *author*

une autorité, *authority*

une avance, *start, advance*

un avantage, *advantage*

un avenir, *future*

une aventure, *adventure*

un avis, *opinion*

un banc, *bench*

une bande, *band*

une barbe, *beard*

un bas, *bottom; stocking*

une bataille, *battle*

un bâtiment, *building*

un bâton, *stick*

une besogne, *task*

un besoin, *need*

une bête, *beast*

un billet, *note, ticket*

un blessé, *wounded man*

une blessure, *wound*

un bois, *wood*

une boîte, *box*

un bonheur, *good fortune*

un bonhomme, *good fellow*

une bonté, *goodness*

un bord, *edge, bank*

une bouche, *mouth*

une boule, *ball*

un bouquet, *bouquet*

un bout, *end, extremity*

une bouteille, *bottle*

une branche, *branch*

un bras, *arm*

un bruit, *noise*

un bureau, *office*

un but, *goal, aim, target*

un cabinet, *study, private room; water closet*

un café, *coffee*

une caisse, *chest, cashbox, till*

un camarade, *comrade*

un camp, *camp*

une campagne, *country*

un capitaine, *captain*

une capitale, *capital*

un caractère, *character, temper*

une carrière, *career*

une carte, *map, card*

un cas, *case*

une cause, *cause*

une centaine, *about a hundred*

un centre, *center*

un cercle, *circle, club*

une certitude, *certainty*

une cesse, *ceasing*

un chagrin, *grief, sorrow*

une chaise, *chair*

une chaleur, *heat*

une chambre, *room*

un champ, *field*

une chance, *luck*

un changement, *change*

un chant, *song, poem*

un chapeau, *hat*

une charge, *expense*

un charme, *charm*

une chasse, *hunting*

un château, *castle*

un chef, *chief*

un chemin, *road*

une chéminée, *chimney, fire-place*

un cheval, *horse*

les cheveux (m.), *hair*
un chien, *dog*
un chiffre, *figure*
un choix, *choice*
une chose, *thing*
un chrétien, *Christian*
une chute, *fall*
un ciel, *sky*
une circonstance, *circumstance*
une cité, *city*
une civilisation, *civilization*
une clarté, *brightness*
une clef, *key*
un coeur, *heart*
un coin, *corner*
une colère, *anger*
une colonie, *colony*
un combat, *combat*
un commencement, *beginning*
un commerce, *commerce*
une compagnie, *company*
un compagnon, *companion*
un compte, *account*
un comte, *count* (title)
une condition, *condition*
une conduite, *conduct*
une confiance, *confidence*
une connaissance, *conscious-ness, knowledge of*
une conscience, *conscience*
un conseil, *advice, council*
une conséquence, *consequence*
une considération, *considera-tion*
un contact, *contact*
une conversation, *conversation*
une conviction, *conviction*

un corps, *body*
un costume, *costume*
une côte, *coast*
un côté, *direction, side*
un cou, *neck*
un coucher, *going to bed*
une couleur, *color*
un coup, *blow, shot, stroke*
une couple, *couple*
une cour, *yard, court*
un courage, *courage*
un courant, *current*
un cours, *course*
une course, *journey, course, race*
un cousin, *cousin*
un couteau, *knife*
une coutume, *custom*
un couvert, *cover*
une couverture, *blanket*
une crainte, *fear*
un cri, *cry, shout*
un crime, *crime*
une crise, *crisis*
une croix, *cross*
une cuisine, *kitchen, cookery*
un cuivre, *copper*
une curiosité, *curiosity*
une dame, *lady*
un danger, *danger*
une date, *date*
un début, *beginning*
une décision, *decision*
un défaut, *failing*
une défense, *defense*
un degré, *step, degree*
un déjeuner, *lunch*

une demeure, *dwelling*

une demoiselle, *young lady*

une dent, *tooth*

un départ, *departure*

un dépense, *expense*

un député, *deputy*

un désert, *desert*

un désir, *desire*

un dessin, *drawing*

une destinée, *destiny*

un détail, *detail*

un détour, *turn, way round*

une dette, *debt*

un développement, *development, unfolding*

un devoir, *duty*

un diable, *devil*

le Dieu, *God*

une différence, *difference*

une difficulté, *difficulty*

le dimanche, *Sunday*

un dîner, *dinner*

un directeur, *director, manager*

une direction, *direction* (also *management*)

un discours, *discourse, speech*

une discussion, *discussion*

une disposition, *disposition, inclination*

une distance, *distance*

un docteur, *doctor*

un doigt, *finger*

un domaine, *domain, estate*

une domestique, *domestic servant*

un don, *gift*

un dos, *back*

une douleur, *grief, pain*

un doute, *doubt*

un droit, *right*

une eau, *water*

un écho, *echo*

un éclat, *outburst, explosion*

une école, *school*

une économie, *economy, saving*

une éducation, *education*

une effet, *effect*

une effort, *effort*

un égard, *respect*

une église, *church*

un élan, *bound, spring, dash*

un élément, *element*

un **ou** une élève, *pupil*

un embarras, *embarrassment*

une émotion, *emotion*

un endroit, *spot, place*

une énergie, *energy*

une enfance, *childhood*

un ennemi, *enemy*

un ennui, *boredom*

un enseignement, *teaching*

un enthousiasme, *enthusiasm*

une entrée, *entry*

une entreprise, *undertaking*

un entretien, *conversation*

une envie, *wish, fancy*

une épaule, *shoulder*

une époque, *time, period, date*

une épreuve, *proof, trial*

un escalier, *staircase*

un espace, *space*

une espèce, *kind, sort*

une espérance, *hope*

un espoir, *hope*

un esprit, *spirit*

un étage, *story* (of a building)

un état, *state*

un été, *summer*

une étendue, *extent, scope*

une étoile, *star*

un étonnement, *astonishment*

un étranger, *stranger, foreigner*

un être, *person, human being*

une étude, *study*

un événement, *event*

un examen, *examination*

un excès, *excess*

une excuse, *excuse*

un exemple, *example*

un exercice, *exercise*

une existence, *life, existence*

une expérience, *experiment*

une expression, *expression*

un extérieur, *exterior*

une extrémité, *extremity*

une face, *face, front*

une façon, *fashion, manner*

une faculté, *faculty*

une faiblesse, *weakness*

un fait, *fact, deed*

une famille, *family*

une fantaisie, *whim, fancy*

une faute, *fault*

un fauteuil, *armchair, seat* (theater)

une faveur, *favor*

une femme, *woman, wife*

une fenêtre, *window*

un fer, *iron*

une ferme, *farm*

une fête, *festival, holiday*

un feu, *fire*

une feuille, *leaf*

une fièvre, *fever*

une figure, *face*

un fil, *thread, wire*

une fille, *daughter*

un fils, *son*

une fin, *end*

une flamme, *flame*

une fleur, *flower*

une foi, *faith*

une fois, *time*

une folie, *madness*

une fonction, *function*

un fond, *bottom*

une force, *strength, power, force*

une forêt, *forest*

une forme, *form*

une fortune, *fortune*

une foule, *crowd*

un foyer, *hearth, fire*

les frais, (m.), *expenses*

un franc, *franc* (a coin)

un frère, *brother*

un froid, *cold*

un front, *forehead, front*

un fruit, *fruit*

une fuite, *flight*

une fumée, *smoke*

un fusil, *rifle*

un futur, *future*

une gaieté *gaiety*

une galerie, *gallery*

un gamin, *young boy*

une garde, *care, guard*

une gare, *station*
un général, *general*
un génie, *genius*
un genou, *knee*
un genre, *kind, sort*
les gens (f.), *people*
un gentilhomme, *nobleman*
un geste, *gesture*
une glace, *ice*, (plate) *glass*
une gloire, *glory*
une grâce, *mercy*
un grain, *seed*
une grandeur, *greatness*
un gré, *will*
un groupe, *group*
une guerre, *war*
un habit, *clothes*
un habitant, *inhabitant*
une habitude, *habit*
une haie, *hedge*
une haine, *hatred*
un hasard, *chance*
une hâte, *haste*
un haut, *top*
une hauteur, *height*
une herbe, *grass*
une hésitation, *hesitation*
une heure, *hour*
une histoire, *story, history*
un hiver, *winter*
un homme, *man*
un honneur, *honor*
une honte, *shame*
un horizon, *horizon*
une horreur, *horror*
un hôtel, *hotel*
une humanité *humanity*

une humeur, *humor*
un idéal, *ideal*
une idée, *idea*
une île, *island*
une illusion, *illusion*
une image, *image, reflection*
une imagination, *imagination*
un **ou** une imbecile, *imbecile, fool.*
une impatience, *impatience*
une importance, *importance*
une impression, *impression*
un incident, *incident*
une indépendence, *independence*
un individu, *individual*
une industrie, *industry*
une influence, *influence*
une inquiétude, *anxiety, uneasiness*
un instant, *moment*
un instinct, *instinct*
une institution, *institution*
une instruction, *instruction*
une intelligence, *intelligence*
une intention, *intention*
un intérêt, *interest*
un intérieur, *interior*
une intervention, *intervention, interruption*
une invention, *invention*
une jambe, *leg*
un jardin, *garden*
un jeu, *game*
le jeudi, *Thursday*
la jeunesse, *youth*
une joie, *joy*

une joue, *cheek*

un jour, *day*

un journal, *newspaper*

la journée, *day* (duration)

un juge, *judge*

un jugement, *judgment*

une justice, *justice*

une laine, *wool*

une lampe, *lamp*

un langage, *language*

la langue, *tongue*

une larme, *tear*

une leçon, *lesson*

une lecture, *reading*

une lettre, *letter*

une lèvre, *lip*

une liberté, *liberty*

un lien, *bond, chain*

un lieu, *place*

un lieutenant, *lieutenant*

une ligne, *line*

une limite, *limit*

un lit, *bed*

la livre, *pound*

le livre, *book*

une loi, *law*

une lumière, *light*

le lundi, *Monday*

une lune, *moon*

une lutte, *struggle*

un luxe, *luxury*

une machine, *machine*

une main, *hand*

une maison, *house*

un maître, *master*

une maîtresse, *mistress*

un mal, *harm, injury*

une maladie, *illness*

un malheur, *misfortune*

une manière, *manner*

un manteau, *mantle*

un marchand, *trader, merchant*

une marche, *march*

un marché, *market*

le mardi, *Tuesday*

un mari, *husband*

un mariage, *marriage*

une marque, *mark*

une masse, *mass*

une matière, *matter*

un matin, *morning*

un médecin, *doctor*

une mélancolie, *melancholy*

un membre, *limb*

une mémoire, *memory*

un ménage, *housekeeping,—hold*

un mensonge, *untruth*

un mépris, *disdain*

une mer, *sea*

le mercredi, *Wednesday*

une mère, *mother*

un mérite, *merit*

une messe, *Mass*

une mesure, *measure*

une méthode, *method*

un métier, *business, work*

un meuble, *furniture*

un midi, *south, midday*

un milieu, *middle*

une mine, *expression* (facial)

un ministère, *ministry*

un ministre, *minister*

une minute, *minute*

une misère, *misery*
une mission, *mission*
une mode, *fashion*
les moers (f.), *customs, habits*
un mois, *month*
une moitié, *half*
un. moment, *moment*
un monde, *world*
un monsieur, *sir, gentleman*
une montagne, *mountain*
un morceau, *piece*
une mort, *death*
un mot, *word*
un mouchoir, *handkerchief*
un mouvement, *movement*
un moyen, *means*
un mur, *wall*
une muraille, *wall, rampart*
une musique, *music*
un mystère, *mystery*
une naissance, *birth*
une nation, *nation*
une nature, *nature*
une nécessité, *necessity*
une neige, *snow*
un nez, *nose*
un nom, *name*
un nombre, *number*
un nord, *north*
une note, *note*
les nouvelles (f.), *news*
un nuage, *cloud*
une nuance, *shade*
une nuit, *night*
un objet, *object*
une obligation, *obligation*
une observation, *observation*

une occasion, *opportunity*
une occupation, *occupation*
une odeur, *odor, smell*
un oeil, *eye*
un oeuvre, *work*
un office, *office functions*
un officier, *officer*
un oiseau, *bird*
une ombre, *shadow*
un oncle, *uncle*
une opération, *operation*
une opinion, *opinion*
un or, *gold*
un orage, *storm*
un ordre, *order*
une oreille, *ear*
un orgueil, *pride*
une origine, *origin*
une ouverture, *opening*
un ouvrage, *work*
un ouvrier, *workman*
un page, *page*
une paille, *straw*
un pain, *bread*
une paix, *peace*
un palais, *palace*
un papier, *paper*
un paquet, *packet, parcel*
un parc, *park*
un pardon, *pardon*
un parent, *relative*
un parfum, *perfume*
une parole, *word*
une part, *share, side, part*
un parti, *party, decision*
une partie, *part* (also *game*)
un pas, *step*

un passage, *passage*

un passé, *past*

une passion, *passion*

une patience, *patience*

une patrie, *fatherland*

un patron, *master, boss*

un pays, *country*

un paysage, *landscape*

un paysan, *pleasant*

une peau, *skin*

une peine, *trouble, difficulty*

une pensée, *thought*

une pension, *boardinghouse*

une pente, *slope*

un père, *father*

un péril, *peril*

un personnage, *personage*

une personne, *person, nobody*

une perte, *loss*

un peuple, *people, nation*

une peur, *fear*

un phénomène, *phenomenon*

une phrase, *sentence*

une pièce, *piece*

un pied, *foot*

une pierre, *stone*

une pipe, *pipe*

une pitié, *pity*

une place, *place, square*

une plaine, *plain*

une plainte, *complaint, moan*

un plaisir, *pleasure*

un plan, *plan*

une plante, *plant*

une pluie, *rain*

une plume, *feather, pen*

une plupart, *greater part*

une poche, *pocket*

une poésie, *poetry*

un poète, *poet*

un poids, *weight*

un poing, *fist*

un point, *dot, full stop*

une pointe, *tip, point*

un poisson, *fish*

une poitrine, *chest*

une police, *police*

une politesse, *politeness*

une politique, *politics*

un pont, *bridge*

un port, *port*

une porte, *door*

une portée, *reach*

un portrait, *portrait*

une position, *position*

une possession, *possession*

une poste, *post*

une poursuite, *pursuit*

une poussière, *dust*

un pouvoir, *power*

une pratique, *practice*

une précaution, *precaution*

une précision, *precision*

une présence, *presence*

un présent, *present*

un président, *president*

une prétention, *pretension*

une prétexte, *pretext*

un prêtre, *priest*

une preuve, *proof*

une prière, *prayer*

un **ou** une prince (sse), *prince, princess*

un principal, *principal*

un principe, *principle*
un printemps, *springtime*
une prise, *capture*
une prison, *prison*
un prisonnier, *prisoner*
un prix, *prize, price*
un problème, *problem*
un procédé, *process, method*
un profit, *profit*
une profondeur, *depth*
un progrès, *progress*
un projet, *project*
une promenade, *walk*
une proposition, *proposition*
un **ou** une propriétaire, *proprietor*
une propriété, *property*
une protection, *protection*
une province, *province*
un public, *public*
une puissance, *power, strength*
une qualité, *quality*
une quantité, *quantity*
un quart, *quarter*
un quartier, *district*
une question, *question*
une queue, *tail*
une race, *race*
une rage, *rage*
une raison, *reason*
un rang, *rank*
un rapport, *report*
un rayon, *ray*
une réalité, *reality*
une recherche, *pursuit, search*
un récit, *story, account*
une reconnaissance, *gratitude*

un reflet, *reflection*
une réflexion, *reflection*
un regard, *look*
un régime, *system, rule*
un régiment, *regiment*
un région, *region*
une règle, *rule*
un regret, *regret*
une religion, *religion*
un remords, *remorse*
une rencontre, *meeting*
un renseignement, *information*
une rente, *income*
un repas, *meal*
une réponse, *reply*
un repos, *peace, rest*
un reproche, *reproach*
une république, *republic*
une réputation, *reputation*
une réserve, *reserve*
une résolution, *resolution*
un respect, *respect*
une ressource, *resource*
un reste, *remainder*
un retard, *lateness*
un retour, *return*
une retraite, *retreat*
une réunion, *reunion, meeting*
une revanche, *revenge*
un rêve, *dream*
une révolution, *revolution*
une richesse, *riches*
un rideau, *curtain*
une rivière, *river*
une robe, *dress*
un roi, *king*
un rôle, *part*

une route, *road*
une rue, *street*
une ruine, *ruin*
un sable, *sand*
un sac, *sack, knapsack*
un sacrifice, *sacrifice*
une saison, *season*
une salle, *hall*
un salon, *drawing room*
un salut, *salvation*
un sang, *blood*
une santé, *health*
une satisfaction, *satisfaction*
un savant, *savant*
une scène, *scene*
une science, *knowledge*
un scrupule, *scruple*
une séance, *meeting*
une seconde, *second*
un secours, *help*
un secret, *secret*
un secretaire, *secretary*
un seigneur, *lord*
une semaine, *week*
les semblables (m.), *fellow-men*
un sens, *direction*
une sensation, *feeling*
un sentier, *path*
un sentiment, *sentiment*
une série, *series*
une servante, *servant*
un service, *service*
un serviteur, *servant*
un seuil, *threshold*
un siècle, *century*
un siège, *siege*

un signe, *sign*
un silence, *silence*
une simplicité, *simplicity*
une situation, *situation*
une société, *society*
une soeur, *sister*
une soif, *thirst*
un soin, *care, attention*
un soir, *evening*
une soirée, *evening* (duration)
un sol, *earth, soil*
un soldat, *soldier*
un soleil, *sun*
une solitude, *solitude*
une somme, *sum*
un sommeil, *sleep*
un son, *sound*
un sort, *fate*
une sorte, *kind*
une sortie, *exit, sally*
un sou, *copper*
  (20 sous = 1 franc)
un souci, *care*
un souffle, *puff*
une souffrance, *suffering*
un soulier, *shoe*
un soupir, *sigh*
une source, *spring*
un sourire, *smile*
un souvenir, *keepsake, recollection*
un spectacle, *spectacle*
une station, *station*
une statue, *statue*
un style, *style*
un succès, *success*
une suite, *result, what follows*

un sujet, *cause, subject*

une surface, *surface*

une surprise, *surprise*

un surtout, *overcoat*

une sympathie, *sympathy*

un système, *system*

une table, *table*

un tableau, *picture*

une tâche, *task*

une taille, *stature*

un talent, *ability*

un tapis, *carpet*

un témoin, *witness*

un temps, *time, weather*

une tendresse, *tenderness*

une tenue, *dress*

un terme, *rent*

un terrain, *land*

une terre, *earth*

une terreur, *terror*

une tête, *head*

un théâtre, *theater*

une théorie, *theory*

un titre, *title*

une toile, *cloth, material*

une toilette, *toilet*

un toit, *roof*

un ton, *tone*

un torrent, *torrent, stream*

un tort, *wrong, harm*

un total, *total*

un tour, *turn, round*

une tour, *tower*

une trace, *track, impression*

une tradition, *tradition*

un train, *train*

un trait, *feature* (of one's face)

un traité, *treaty*

un transport, *transport*

un travail, *work*

un trésor, *treasure*

un triomphe, *triumph*

une tristesse, *sadness*

un trou, *hole*

un trouble, *trouble, agitation*

une troupe, *company*

un type, *type*

une union, *union*

un usage, *use*

une valeur, *value*

une vanité, *vanity*

une veille, *day before, eve*

un vent, *wind*

une vente, *sale*

une vérité, *truth*

une verre, *glass*

un vers, *verse*

une vertu, *virtue*

un vêtement, *garment*

un vice, *vice*

une victime, *victim*

une victoire, *victory*

une vie, *life*

un village, *village*

une ville, *town*

un vin, *wine*

une violence, *violence*

un visage, *face*

une visite, *visit*

une vitesse, *speed*

une vitre, *pane of glass*

un vocabulaire, *vocabulary*

un voeu, *vow*
une voie, *way*
un voisin, *neighbor*
un voisinage, *neighborhood*
une voiture, *carriage*
une voix, *voice*

une volaille, *fowl*
un vol, *theft*
un volant, (steering) *wheel*
une volonté, *will*
un voyageur, *traveler*
une vue, *view, sight*

Index

397

— COLLEGE OUTLINE SERIES —

Barnes & Noble, Inc., 105 Fifth Ave., New York 3, N. Y.

Books in the College Outline Series provide authoritative, economical handbooks for students and laymen who need to master a subject quickly and for adults interested in self-education as a process that never ceases. (Price ranges from $.50 to $2.00.)

ANTHROPOLOGY, SOCIOLOGY

ANTHROPOLOGY
SOCIOLOGY, Principles of
SOCIOLOGY, Readings in

ART, MUSIC

ART, HISTORY of
MUSIC, HISTORY of

EDUCATION, PHILOSOPHY, PSYCHOLOGY

EDUCATION, History of
PHILOSOPHY, An Introduction
PHILOSOPHY, Handbook in Hist. of
PHILOSOPHY, Readings in
PSYCHOLOGY, Child
PSYCHOLOGY, Educational
PSYCHOLOGY, General
PSYCHOLOGY, Readings in General

ECONOMICS, BUSINESS

ACCOUNTING, Elementary
ACCOUNTING PROBLEMS
BUSINESS AND GOVERNMENT
BUSINESS LAW
BUSINESS MANAGEMENT
CORPORATION FINANCE
ECONOMIC HISTORY of the U.S.
ECONOMICS, Dictionary of
ECONOMICS, Principles of
ECONOMICS, Readings in
LABOR PROBLEMS & Trade Unionism
MARKETING, An Introduction
MONEY AND BANKING
STATISTICAL METHODS
STATISTICIANS, Tables for

ENGLISH

AMERICAN LITERATURE
ENGLISH GRAMMAR
ENGLISH LITERATURE: Dictionary
ENGLISH LITERATURE to Dryden
ENGLISH LITERATURE since Milton
GERMAN LITERATURE
JOURNALISM, New Survey of
PLAY PRODUCTION
PRONUNCIATION, Manual of
SHAKESPEARE'S PLAYS: Outlines
SHAKESPEAREAN NAMES: Dictionary
SPEECH
TUDOR AND STUART PLAYS
WORLD LITERATURE, 2 Vols.

HISTORY, GOVERNMENT

AMERICAN Colonial & Rev. History
AMERICAN POLITICS: Dictionary
ANCIENT HISTORY
ANCIENT, Medieval, & Modern History
ENGLAND, History of
EUROPE, 1500-1848
EUROPE since 1815
GOVERNMENT, American
INTERNATIONAL RELATIONS
LATIN AMERICA, History of
LATIN AMERICA in Maps
LATIN AMERICAN Civilization: Rdgs.
MIDDLE AGES, History of
POLITICAL SCIENCE
RUSSIA, History of
UNITED STATES to 1865
UNITED STATES since 1865
WORLD since 1914, History of

MATHEMATICS, ENGINEERING

ALGEBRA, College
CALCULUS
ENGINEERING DRAWING
GEOMETRY, Analytic
GEOMETRY, PLANE: Problems
LOGARITHMIC and Trigonometric Tables
TRIGONOMETRY, Plane and Spherical

MODERN LANGUAGES

FRENCH GRAMMAR
GERMAN GRAMMAR
SPANISH GRAMMAR

SCIENCE

BACTERIOLOGY
BIOLOGY
BOTANY
CHEMISTRY, First Year College
CHEMISTRY, Organic
CHEMISTRY, Physical
CHEMISTRY PROBLEMS
GEOLOGY, Principles of
PHYSICS, First Year College
PHYSICS without Mathematics
ZOOLOGY

STUDY AIDS

DOCUMENTED PAPERS
EXAMINATIONS, How to Write Better
RESEARCH AND REPORT Writing
STUDY, Best Methods of

(For complete list of Everyday Handbooks, see front of this volume.)